Literary Theory and Criticism

Literary Theory and Criticism

AN INTRODUCTION

Anne H. Stevens

broadview press

Library and Archives Canada Cataloguing in Publication

Stevens, Anne H., 1971-, author
    Literary theory and criticism : an introduction / Anne H. Stevens.

Includes bibliographical references and index.
ISBN 978-1-55481-237-0 (paperback)

    1. Criticism. 2. Criticism—History. 3. Literature—History and criticism—Theory, etc. I. Title.

PN86.S74 2015   801.9509   C2015-903060-9

Broadview Press is an independent, international publishing house, incorporated in 1985.

We welcome comments and suggestions regarding any aspect of our publications—please feel free to contact us at the addresses below or at broadview@broadviewpress.com.

North America	PO Box 1243, Peterborough, Ontario K9J 7H5, Canada
	555 Riverwalk Parkway, Tonawanda, NY 14150, USA
	Tel: (705) 743-8990; Fax: (705) 743-8353
	email: customerservice@broadviewpress.com
UK, Europe, Central	Eurospan Group
Asia, Middle East,	3 Henrietta St., London WC2E 8LU, United Kingdom
Africa, India,	Tel: 44 (0) 1767 604972; Fax: 44 (0) 1767 601640
and Southeast Asia	email: eurospan@turpin-distribution.com
Australia and	Footprint Books
New Zealand	1/6a Prosperity Parade, Warriewood, NSW 2102, Australia
	Tel: 1300 260 090; Fax: 02 9997 3185
	email: info@footprint.com.au

www.broadviewpress.com
Edited by Michel Pharand and Martin R. Boyne

Broadview Press acknowledges the financial support of the Government of Canada through the Canada Book Fund for our publishing activities.

PRINTED IN CANADA

Contents

List of Tables and Illustrations ✦ 10

Acknowledgements ✦ 11

Chapter 1: Introduction ✦ 13
Theory vs. Criticism ✦ 16
Close Reading and Literary Studies ✦ 18
Criticism through the Ages ✦ 19
    Literary Studies Comes to the University ✦ 20
    The "Theory" Revolution ✦ 23
Theory and Criticism Today ✦ 26
Literary Form ✦ 28
Literary Characters ✦ 29
The Importance of Context ✦ 31
The Identity of the Author ✦ 32
The Role of the Reader ✦ 33
Reading as Education, Reading as Entertainment ✦ 34
Diversity ✦ 35
The Uses of Theory and Criticism ✦ 36
Getting Started ✦ 39

Chapter 2: The Ancient World ✦ 46
Plato: The First Literary Theorist ✦ 47
    Plato's *Republic* ✦ 48
        Plato's Theory of Forms ✦ 49
        The Allegory of the Cave ✦ 51
    Speech vs. Writing ✦ 53

Aristotle ◆ 54
    Classification ◆ 55
    Narrative Form ◆ 57
    Mimesis ◆ 59
    Rhetoric ◆ 60
Horace's Poetic Art ◆ 62
Quintilian's Figures of Speech ◆ 63
Longinus's Sublime Aesthetics ◆ 65

Chapter 3: The Middle Ages and the Renaissance ◆ 68
Religion and Biblical Interpretation ◆ 70
Establishing a Canon ◆ 71
Medieval Scholasticism ◆ 72
    The Four Levels of Interpretation ◆ 73
Maimonides and the Jewish Tradition ◆ 76
The Secularization of Interpretation ◆ 77
Boccaccio's Mythological Studies ◆ 78
Humanism ◆ 80
    The Printing Press ◆ 81
    Protestantism ◆ 84
    The Growth of the Vernacular ◆ 85
    New Forms ◆ 86
    New Rules for Writing ◆ 88

Chapter 4: The Enlightenment ◆ 91
Print Culture ◆ 92
Addison and Steele and the Birth of Modern Reviewing ◆ 96
Johnson and His *Dictionary* ◆ 97
The French *Encyclopedia* ◆ 99
Skepticism ◆ 100
Political Revolutions ◆ 101
Abolitionism ◆ 102
Early Feminism ◆ 103
Aesthetic Innovations ◆ 104
Idealism ◆ 106
    Kant's Idealist Philosophy ◆ 107
    Hegel's Ideas of History ◆ 110

Chapter 5: The Nineteenth Century ✦ 114
Romanticism and Nineteenth-Century Poetry ✦ 115
Realism, Nationalism, and the Nineteenth-Century Novel ✦ 120
      Varieties of Realism ✦ 122
Arnold, Taine, and Literary Studies ✦ 125
Decadent Aesthetics ✦ 127
      Poe's Philosophy of Composition ✦ 128
      Art for Art's Sake ✦ 130
Nietzsche's Radical Philosophy ✦ 131
Fin-de-siècle Fictions ✦ 133

Chapter 6: Twentieth- and Twenty-First-Century Formalist Approaches ✦ 135
The Philological Tradition ✦ 137
Saussure and Structuralist Linguistics ✦ 137
Russian Formalism ✦ 140
Anglo-American Formalisms ✦ 142
      Practical and New Criticisms ✦ 143
      Neo-Aristotelianism ✦ 147
Lévi-Strauss and Structuralist Anthropology ✦ 149
Barthes and Structuralist Semiotics ✦ 150
Narratology ✦ 152
Derrida and Deconstruction ✦ 154
      Deconstruction in America ✦ 156
Formalism Today ✦ 158

Chapter 7: Twentieth- and Twenty-First-Century Historicist Approaches ✦ 160
Historicist Criticism in the Eighteenth and Nineteenth Centuries ✦ 161
Historicism to the 1970s ✦ 164
The "New Historicism" ✦ 166
      New Approaches to History and Culture ✦ 167
      Foucault and Discourse ✦ 169
      Greenblatt and the New Historicism ✦ 172
Bourdieu and the Sociology of Culture ✦ 174
From Bibliography to Book History ✦ 176
Digital Humanities ✦ 177

Chapter 8: Twentieth- and Twenty-First-Century Political Approaches ✦ 180
Karl Marx ✦ 181
Early Marxist Theory and Criticism ✦ 186
 The Frankfurt School ✦ 188
 French Marxism ✦ 190
 British Cultural Studies ✦ 192
Later Marxist Theory and Criticism ✦ 193
Postcolonial and Ethnic Studies ✦ 194
 Said and Orientalism ✦ 197
 Later Postcolonial Theory ✦ 199
 Gates and the African-American Tradition ✦ 199
 The Diversity of Literary Traditions ✦ 201
Feminist Theory and Criticism ✦ 203
 Founding Figures ✦ 203
 Later Feminist Theorists ✦ 205
Sexuality and Queer Theory ✦ 207
 Sedgwick and Butler ✦ 208
Disability and Environmental Studies ✦ 209

Chapter 9: Twentieth- and Twenty-First-Century Psychoanalytic Approaches ✦ 211
Freud and Freudian Criticism ✦ 211
Jungian Criticism ✦ 218
Jacques Lacan ✦ 219
 Julia Kristeva ✦ 221
 Heirs to Lacan ✦ 222
Phenomenology ✦ 223
Hermeneutics ✦ 224
Reader-Response Criticism ✦ 226
Cognitive Approaches ✦ 228

Chapter 10: From Theory to Practice ✦ 231
The Example of *Hamlet* ✦ 232
 Hamlet's Organic Unity ✦ 233
 Hamlet's Theatricality ✦ 236
 Hamlet in Literary History ✦ 238
 Hamlet and Class ✦ 240
 Hamlet and Gender ✦ 241
 Hamlet's Melancholy ✦ 242

The Example of *Frankenstein* • 244
    Frankenstein and Narratology • 245
    Frankenstein and History • 248
    Frankenstein and Orientalism • 250
    Frankenstein and Homosociality • 251
    The Sublime, the Abject, the Uncanny • 253
Moving Forward • 254

Glossary • 257

Index • 267

List of Tables and Illustrations

Table 1:   Method and Object of Academic Disciplines ✦ 18
Table 2:   The Enlightenment as an Extension of the Renaissance ✦ 93
Table 3:   Fable and Subject in *Frankenstein* ✦ 246

Figure 1:   Student riots in Paris, 1968 ✦ 25
Figure 2:   Freytag's Pyramid ✦ 59
Figure 3:   Page from the Book of Kells ✦ 83
Figure 4:   Hegel's Dialectic ✦ 112
Figure 5:   A.A. Reformatsky, "An Essay on the Analysis of the Composition of the Novella" [1922] ✦ 141
Figure 6:   Thomas Rowlandson, "Veneration" ✦ 163
Figure 7:   Panopticon ✦ 171
Figure 8:   Poster for John Huston's *Freud* ✦ 213

Acknowledgements

MANY BOOKS ON LITERARY theory have already been written, and many more will be written. In my version of the history of theory and criticism, I have tried to touch upon the points I've found most important in my own training and teaching, but I recognize that my biases will show through and that I've had to leave a tremendous amount out. I'm indebted to the teachers who first exposed me to literary theory and criticism as an undergraduate and later as a graduate student: at the University of Chicago, Beth Ash, Wayne Booth, James Chandler, Bert Cohler, Arnold Davidson, James Lastra, Mark Sandberg, and Katie Trumpener; and at New York University, Margaret Cohen, Troy Duster, Dustin Griffin, Paul Magnuson, Mary Poovey, Kristin Ross, Tim Walters, and many others. I'm equally grateful to the students I've taught, especially the many students in ENG 303, Introduction to Literary Theory and Criticism, at the University of Nevada, Las Vegas, who have been my unwitting guinea pigs for years.

Among the many people I should thank for helping to shape my thinking in this book, first and foremost is my colleague Megan Becker. She first developed the ENG 303 course at UNLV, and our many conversations about the readings and assignments for the class, the history of theory, and other unrelated matters have made this book possible. While working on the project I have benefited from conversations with and emails from Kathy Anders, Andrew Bell, John Bowers, Thomas Breene, Aaron Davis, David Dickens, Ian Dove, Richard Harp, John Hay, Stephanie Hershinow, Ashley Jagodzinski, Todd Jones, Julia Lee, Patricia Matthew, Kelly Mays, Ed Nagelhout, Wendy Nielsen, Molly O'Donnell, Vincent Pérez, Michael Rotenberg-Schwartz, Philip Rusche, Jonathan Sadow, Jessica Teague, Denise Tillery, John Tresch, Mary Vance, James Williams, and others I'm probably forgetting, along with colleagues on Facebook and Twitter, who have all given me food for thought, filled in a detail, suggested readings, or just let me bounce ideas off of them. Thanks to Jay Barksdale and the New York Public Library's Shoichi Noma Reading Room for providing research space and access to the NYPL's collections while completing the manuscript. Ashley Jagodzinski provided research assistance and designed the illustrations of Freytag's pyramid in chapter 2 and the Hegelian dialectic in chapter 4. Finally, thanks to everyone at Broadview Press. Marjorie Mather was willing to take on this project and has been extremely supportive throughout. Thanks also to Michel Pharand, Martin Boyne, Tara Lowes, Tara Trueman, and others at Broadview.

One: Introduction

EVERY DAY WE PERFORM countless acts of reading, writing, interpretation, and evaluation. We read signs, write emails, interpret others' behavior, evaluate our lunch options, or just click "like" on a piece of writing or a photo online. At its most basic level, literary theory provides an opportunity to slow down and to reflect upon these activities. Literary theory provides a vocabulary and tools for thinking about reading, writing, and criticism, both everyday acts of evaluation and more academic studies of literature and culture. It can also help you to place your acts of evaluation into a school of thought with a long historical lineage. In this chapter, I provide a broad overview of literary theory and criticism – its definition, a thumbnail sketch of its history, a summary of some of its major concerns, and a few tips for getting started. I introduce topics here that I explore in more detail in the later chapters of the book.

This book focuses on *literary* theory and criticism, that is, on theoretical and critical issues related to questions of language, literature, writing, and interpretation. In other contexts, you might see the terms **CULTURAL THEORY**,[1] **CRITICAL THEORY**, or just plain theory. Cultural theory can refer to theoretical writings related to culture more broadly – not only literary works but also film, music, advertising, sports, and everyday life. Critical theory or theory usually means theoretical writings, often with a strong philosophical dimension, not limited to those that deal with literary and cultural concerns. Many of these texts deal with the same issues as literary theory and cultural theory, though perhaps with a greater emphasis on abstract, overarching issues and with a more **INTERDISCIPLINARY** focus that draws from different areas of academic study (including political theory, psychology, philosophy, anthropology, and sociology). **LITERARY THEORY**, as opposed to this broader sense of theory, includes more writers and texts concerned specifically with issues related to literature – such as poetic form, author biography, and literary genre – but a survey of literary

---

1 A note on the text: definitions of terms in **SMALL CAPS** can be found in the glossary at the end of the volume.

theory usually does include a number of thinkers, such as Karl Marx (1818–83) and Sigmund Freud (1856–1939), who don't necessarily write about literature but whose ideas have influenced literary study.

A cornerstone of literary theory is a belief in the **CULTURAL CONSTRUCTION** of knowledge. Historical and cultural circumstances shape our ideas about truth, beauty, education, art and literature, food, clothing, and everything else. This may seem like a very obvious point – of course different cultures and historical periods have different standards of beauty or cuisines – but it becomes trickier to keep in mind when it comes to thinking about things that seem natural, such as gender and sexuality, or about one's own most cherished beliefs. Just because something is constructed, though, doesn't mean that it is not real. The houses and apartments that we live in are real, material objects even though they are products of human construction. Similarly, ideas about truth, beauty, and the other matters mentioned above take shape through historical processes, are continually evolving, and vary from one culture to another, but even though they're not universal and unchanging, they still have real effects on the world. Literary theory gives you a way to step back and think about the constructed-ness of culture and to reflect upon your own preconceptions. It can provide you with a greater self-consciousness about your acts as a reader, critic, and member of society. Looking at the history of critical debates and becoming more aware of unspoken presuppositions can help you understand literature, and maybe even the world, a little bit better.

Even everyday conversations can contain fairly complex acts of evaluation that literary theory and a greater degree of self-reflectiveness can help to de-cipher. For example, people often assert that some particular book, movie, athlete, or restaurant is "overrated" or "underrated." Here one word conceals a complicated theoretical framework. To call something overrated implies a comparison between two different acts of "rating" or two different critical stan-dards. Usually these two consist of your own act of evaluation and the rest of the world's: even though everyone else loves X (Cristiano Ronaldo, Chipotle, Disneyland), that acclaim or commercial success isn't really deserved, and actu-ally X should be "rated" much lower (because Ronaldo was disappointing at the World Cup, Chipotle's burritos are soggy, Disneyland is just too crowded). Conversely, saying that X (an independent film or musician, for example) is underrated suggests that you can see merit where others do not, and that the evaluative system of the rest of the world is flawed (maybe because people don't know about the work because of a lack of distribution or promotion, because it goes over the heads of many people, or because it challenges conventional ideas about sex or politics). So the next time you hear someone make a casual remark about something being "overrated," challenge them to slow down and explain why they think that their opinion should be given more weight than that of the rest of the world. Thinking through our too often unreflective acts of judgment is a good way to help develop greater theoretical awareness and thus to become more careful and thoughtful critics. Everyone knows *what* they like and dislike, but theorists reflect upon *why* they like and dislike.

In the broadest sense, literary theory and criticism can include a wide range of activities, such as teaching and studying works of literature, book reviewing, reading groups, and online discussions. The critical assumptions or theoretical perspectives underlying these activities can be more or less obvious, more or less self-conscious. For example, all courses on literature employ one or more critical perspectives, such as formalism or historicism. Sometimes teachers will outline their method and assumptions at the start of a course or will suggest other possible methods of study along the way, but at other times it is up to the students to deduce what type of critical approach they're being presented with. Certain other types of courses, with names such as Introduction to Literary Theory, Literary Methods, or Feminist (or Postcolonial, or Marxist) Theory, study approaches to literature rather than only the literary works themselves. A course on literary theory will tend to focus on the underlying questions of method within literary studies and will read works *about* literature rather than (or in addition to) works *of* literature. A course in literary theory is to a literature major what a statistics class is to a psychology major: it focuses on the methods of study and equips you with some technical tools for pursuing advanced studies in the area.

Most literary theorists don't believe that there's a single, correct interpretation for a given literary work, but instead believe that great works of literature provide ample room for multiple interpretations. That's precisely what makes literature worth studying. Questions of meaning and interpretation in literary studies aren't trivia questions. What matters when you take on the big questions of literary theory isn't so much *what* you answer, but *how* you explore the issue. Because there are no easy answers, making an argument about a literary text involves finding compelling evidence to support your claim and arranging it in the most persuasive way possible. In the process of studying literary theory and using it to make arguments, you can hone your argumentative and critical thinking skills, learn about different cultures and historical periods, witness ongoing debates about key issues, and even be entertained along the way.

Theory vs. Criticism

So what's the difference between literary theory and **LITERARY CRITICISM**? In general, *literary theory* refers to writings that deal with the underlying principles associated with the study of literature, language, interpretation, culture, and all sorts of related issues. Many of the thinkers who have shaped major theoretical approaches to literature come from areas outside the boundaries of traditional literary studies, especially in fields such as philosophy and the social sciences. *Literary criticism* usually refers to analysis of a particular work or works: studies of individual authors, genres, literary movements, and the like.

The two terms are closely related, however, since both literary theorists and literary critics study literary texts using a theoretical framework. One way to conceive of the difference between the two relates to the underlying aims of the writing. A work of literary theory might use literary texts as examples or illustrations in the service of developing a larger theoretical point, while a literary critic might use a theoretical perspective in the service of better understanding a literary text. The distinction is quite subtle and subjective, though, because these two sides – theory and practice – constantly reinforce each other: criticism of works can be used to develop larger theoretical points, while large theoretical points can provide a foundation for analyzing individual works.

In order to better understand this distinction between theory and criticism, I'll use the example of the field known as **QUEER THEORY**, which I discuss in Chapter 8. Queer theory was developed by scholars who study sexuality, gay and lesbian literature, transgender issues, and related matters. Under this larger heading, some of these scholars' works might better be thought of as theory and some as criticism. French historian Michel Foucault's *The History of Sexuality* (1976–84), for example, is a good example of a work of theory. His multi-volume work (left unfinished at his death) examines the ways in which our ideas about sexuality are historically constructed and shaped by the power relations of their time. Although Foucault (1926–84) uses literary texts here and there to illustrate his points, the central goal of his argument is to outline a new way of conceiving of sexuality as culturally constructed rather than biological and unchanging. In contrast, a literary critic might take Foucault's theoretical ideas about the fluidity of sexual identity and apply them to a text such as William Shakespeare's *Twelfth Night* (1601–02), a play that features cross-dressing and same-sex attraction between characters. This hypothetical critic isn't developing his or her own theoretical perspective so much as using Foucault's theories as a means to better understand Shakespeare's play. However, someone like Eve Kosofsky Sedgwick (1950–2009), another founding figure in queer theory, might be said to blur the distinction I'm trying to draw here between theory and criticism. In her book *Between Men* (1985), for example, she studies the phenomenon of **HOMOSOCIAL** relations (non-sexual but emotional relationships between members of the same sex – in a sense, male bonding or "bromance") through case studies of individual authors such as Shakespeare and Charles Dickens. She's both developing a theoretical perspective and applying it to literary texts, and the two activities can't really be disentangled. The theoretical perspective informs the acts of criticism, while the acts of criticism help to develop the theoretical perspective.

In fact, all literary critics – indeed, all readers – possess some kind of theoretical framework. Even a person who claims to read books only "for their own sake," without any kind of theoretical "bias," has a theoretical perspective: the belief that books shouldn't be read for political, ethical, or theoretical issues. Most people, however, are a little more self-aware about their theoretical approaches and underlying assumptions as readers and critics.

Every academic discipline has at least one defined object of study and at least one method for studying it. In the case of certain disciplines, the object and method are right there in the name. The discipline of art history, for example, takes as its object of study works of art, and uses historical methods (chronology, studies of historical periods and artistic movements, studies of influence, and so forth) to examine those works. The case of literary studies is a bit more complicated both in terms of object and method. Obviously literary works serve as one object of study, but literary studies can also include scholarship that focuses on writing, languages, popular culture, and other products of human expression aside from works of imaginative literature. Similarly, literary theory and criticism serves as an umbrella term for the set of methods associated with literary studies and includes everything from author studies to politically motivated analyses of individual works to literary histories. Table 1 details the object and method of literary studies in comparison to a few other academic disciplines.

In the eighteenth and nineteenth centuries, the word *literature* shifted from meaning writing of any type to referring to a narrower category of imaginative literature: poetry, fiction, and drama. As departments of English and other literatures began to take shape in the nineteenth-century university, their object of study tended to be this more restrictive field of imaginative literature. However, non-fiction works have always been part of the object of literary studies, from historical works and biographies to philosophical treatises. Today, scholars within a department of literary studies may include people whose primary expertise is creative writing, composition and rhetoric, popular culture, linguistics, or sometimes even film or journalism. If you have ever heard someone say "such and such doesn't belong in an English department," you can

Field	Method of study	Object of study
Art history	Historical method	Works of art, individual artists, artistic movements
Biology	Scientific method	Living things, the natural world
Anthropology	Field work, ethnographic observation, archaeology	Human culture
Sociology	Statistics, surveys, empirical methods	Human society
Literary studies	Literary theory and criticism: close reading, genre studies, historical contextualization, socio-political analyses, deconstructive readings – multiple methods but all focused on language/human expression	Literary classics, literary history, writing as a practice, language, popular culture, discourses – multiple objects but all products of language/human expression

Table 1: Method and Object of Academic Disciplines

assume that person has a pretty narrow idea of what an English department should be. The field of literary studies has always been a big tent, with all sorts of different subfields and approaches under it.

Close Reading and Literary Studies

The practice of **CLOSE READING** has been at the heart of the discipline of literary studies since World War II or so. Associated both with the formalist American **NEW CRITICS** and the British practice of **PRACTICAL CRITICISM** (see Chapter 6), close reading means an approach to literary texts that pays careful attention to the nuances of their language. To close read a poem or other piece of writing means to consider its word choices, tone, moments of ambiguity and irony, the rhetoric employed, underlying structures such as plot archetypes and genres, allusions to other works, and any number of other matters. Much contemporary literary studies, from published criticism to classroom activities, employs some element of close reading – it's the thing we do that separates us most clearly from historians or biographers. Even when critics move on to discuss longer works and to take into consideration external factors such as author biography or historical context, close reading is still at the heart of what it means to be a literary critic.

Close reading is also one of the key skills developed by students of literature that they can take with them in a variety of career and general life situations. Here are a few examples of ways in which you can employ close-reading skills beyond the classroom and the scholarly essay:

- Close reading can help you to read carefully and follow instructions, for everything from following directions to putting together a piece of IKEA furniture.
- Close-reading skills will help you to pay careful attention to rhetorical structures and how people use words to influence and manipulate, in everything from political rhetoric to advertising to spam emails.
- Many English majors go on to law school and to practice law. You can think of close reading as a kind of cross-examination of a text. Paying careful attention to word choices can serve lawyers well in a variety of contexts.
- Close attention to language is a crucial skill in a range of other careers, such as advertising, public relations, journalism, grant writing, and professional and technical communications.
- Close reading also hones your aesthetic sense by making you appreciate the artistry that goes into a literary work. This can lead to a lifetime of reading but also to careers in cultural criticism and publishing.
- Close reading doesn't even have to be restricted to reading. Careful attention to hidden meanings, complicated plot structures, foreshadowing, and moments of irony can deepen your appreciation of good movies and TV shows as well.

Criticism through the Ages

Though close reading remains central to literary studies to this day, it and literary studies more generally are products of a history that stretches back to ancient Greece. Chapters 2 to 9 explore this history of specific movements in much more detail. In this section, though, I outline some of the highlights to give you a sense of the big picture before delving into individual theorists and issues in the later chapters. Many guides to literary theory and criticism don't cover much material before the twentieth century, because there is so much to cover once you get into the modern era. However, understanding the longer historical tradition of theory and criticism can help to highlight some of its continuities and the issues that recur throughout this long history.

Ever since people began writing things down, other people have arisen to comment on them and criticize them. Treatises on poetry and **RHETORIC** (discussed in Chapter 2) are among the earliest surviving written works from ancient Greece. Before the establishment of the academic discipline of literary studies, literary theory and criticism took place in handbooks for writers, philosophical dialogues, works of theology, critical prefaces to individual works, manifestoes by authors, reviews, and all sorts of other places.

The modern university is structured around academic disciplines with their own courses, curriculum, and faculty. Too often people stay within the confines of their particular discipline instead of making interdisciplinary connections to other areas of study. This modern system of disciplines only came to structure knowledge, however, at the end of the nineteenth century. Prior to that time, thinkers ranged more widely across different areas of inquiry without the benefit of specialized training. Aristotle (384–322 BCE) best exemplifies the wide-ranging nature of intellectual inquiry of these earlier thinkers. Though he is best known as a philosopher, Aristotle's works might be assigned in classes devoted to philosophy, political science, rhetoric, or literary studies. He wrote works in all these areas, as well as works on meteorology, animal anatomy, and dreams. Today for one person to become a respected authority in so many different areas would require decades of advanced training. Because the roots of literary study stretch back so far, to Aristotle and even earlier, its history is inherently interdisciplinary (or predisciplinary) in a way that more modern fields of study such as computer science or electrical engineering are not. The history of theory and criticism that I trace in the next eight chapters will touch upon philosophy, history, political theory, psychology, theology, sociology, anthropology, film studies, and other areas.

Literary Studies Comes to the University

Before the nineteenth century, modern literature was not an accepted university subject. In Britain and America, college education was basically restricted to men (and then, pretty much only white men of a certain economic status), and that education consisted of an intensive study of the Greek and Roman classics. Most jobs didn't require a college degree but were instead learned through apprenticeships and on-the-job training, including fields such as law and medicine. A lot of people didn't have jobs at all in the modern sense, particularly women but also many in the upper classes. Occasionally college students would study other subjects, such as religion or scientific fields, but college mostly consisted of a gentlemanly reading of the classics or perhaps training to become a member of the clergy – a far cry from the specialization and career training of modern universities.

Toward the end of the nineteenth century, the structure of the modern research university began to take shape, originally in Germany and then spreading elsewhere. Universities began to organize themselves around academic departments specializing in different subject areas. Many of the major academic disciplines originated around this time, including fields in the social sciences and the humanities. Literary studies gradually moved from being a gentlemanly pursuit to an academic discipline. Students could now major in English if they wanted to go on to a career in teaching, for example. Advanced degrees (Master's and PhD degrees) became available for those who wanted to teach literature at the college or university level. Additionally, in the early twentieth century as the old classical curriculum disappeared, the study of modern literary texts took its place.

As literary studies made the transition from extracurricular activity to academic discipline, it (along with other new disciplines) had to acquire features associated with the structure of a modern discipline. Scholars pursuing advanced degrees were required to write theses or dissertations in a specialized area, usually concentrating on a particular period of literary history, such as the Middle Ages or Renaissance. Academic journals were established to publish scholarly work in literary studies. Literary studies became a profession and established professional associations, just as other fields were doing at the time. In the US, the Modern Language Association (MLA) was founded in 1883, the American Historical Association (AHA) in 1884, the American Psychological Association (APA) in 1892, the American Anthropological Association (AAA) in 1902, and the American Sociological Association (ASA) in 1905.

Johns Hopkins University in Baltimore, Maryland, became the first modern research university in America, divided into academic disciplines and offering graduate degrees, in 1876. Other universities followed suit, and English quickly became an academic subject. In Great Britain, the old medieval universities, Oxford and Cambridge, did not begin offering courses of study in English literature until the early twentieth century. Newer, secular (non-religious) universities, such as the University of London (established in 1836), offered courses in English slightly earlier. London was also the first British university to admit women on an equal footing as men, in 1878.

As the old classical curriculum gave way to specialized subject areas, in America a system developed where a college degree would consist of both a course of study in a particular major area of specialization and general college courses that provide exposure to different areas of study and basic skills (general education courses). Courses in literature and writing are now typically part of every college student's general education requirements, even if the student is majoring in business or science. The idea that every student needs to study some literature harkens back to the earlier ideal of a gentlemanly education. Students study literature in general education courses in order to gain exposure to different writers, to broaden their horizons, and to hone their reading and critical thinking skills, as well as to get practice at writing college essays, rather than in pursuit of an advanced degree in English.

Although people had been producing works of literary theory and criticism since the ancient Greeks, when literary studies came to the university the climate changed significantly. An academic discipline requires a specialized vocabulary, expertise in a particular subject area, and a scientific or quasi-scientific methodology. Literary studies had to transition into a more scientific mode of investigation in order to fit into the new research university atmosphere and to justify offering specialized degrees in this area.

Obviously the type of work that scholars in literary studies produce isn't analogous to work that comes out of a scientific lab, although some scholars in the areas of digital humanities and cognitive studies (discussed in Chapters 7 and 9, respectively) have made use of technology in new and innovative ways. Still, a scientific, specialized quality to academic work in literary studies marks it as different from non-academic work (such as book reviews in newspapers and magazines). Academic articles in literary studies journals, for example, use technical language, are heavily footnoted, and are peer reviewed (sent out to other specialists in the field for comment prior to acceptance) in the same way that scientific papers are. The earliest academic approaches to literature in the nineteenth century grew out of the discipline of **PHILOLOGY** (which I touch upon again in Chapter 7), which emphasized the study of literature for what it could tell us about the history of language – studying medieval texts for their grammar and vocabulary, for example.

In the early twentieth century, a variety of new methods for studying literature developed, including the close-reading methods discussed above, which emphasize a close attention to literary form rather than a focus on history. From around the 1930s to the 1960s, New Criticism dominated American departments of English, though other approaches, including historical studies, **FREUDIAN** criticism, and **NEO-ARISTOTELIAN** formalist approaches, were also present. In Britain, beginning in the 1930s, a strain of **MARXISM** coexisted in literary studies alongside formalist criticism. I survey some of these developments in more detail in Chapters 6 to 9. For now, the point I want to stress is that "theory" didn't just come to the English department in the 1960s, and that literary studies, in its first hundred years or so as an academic subject, was already a

highly theoretical and complex mode of study, with multiple methods, including formal, historical, psychological, and political approaches, coexisting.

The "Theory" Revolution

Even in the early days of literary studies as an academic discipline, multiple
methods of study coexisted and competed with each other. The most popular approaches in the first half-century or so of academic literary studies were
those that study literature in order to better understand languages (philology),
those that study literature in its historical context (**HISTORICISM**), and those that
look closely at literary technique (**FORMALISM**). However, in the 1960s and 1970s,
academic literary studies received an infusion of new theoretical approaches,
particularly from France, that really changed the landscape of the discipline.

Many histories of literary theory or handbooks of theoretical approaches
begin with the moment in the 1960s when "French theory" came to America. Not
all of these approaches were French, but "French theory" became a convenient
piece of shorthand. On the one hand, characterizing the 1960s as the moment
that literary studies becomes theoretical ignores the fact that people had been
theorizing about literature and writing almost since the invention of the written
word, and some of the earliest texts that have survived in the Western tradition
have to do with poetry and language. On the other hand, since the "theory"
revolution of the 1960s and 1970s, scholars in literary studies have become much
more overtly theoretical and conscious of their critical assumptions. The scope
of literary studies has broadened to include a wider range of authors, texts, and
approaches. These changes in turn reflect the ways in which the university and
the world have changed, becoming more diverse and inclusive.

The most obvious choice of a starting place for understanding the theory
revolution of the 1960s is a single essay, Jacques Derrida's "Structure, Sign, and
Play in the Discourse of the Human Sciences" (1966). Derrida (1930–2004) was a
leading figure in **DECONSTRUCTIONIST** criticism and **POSTSTRUCTURALISM** (both discussed in Chapter 6). His essay began as a speech at Johns Hopkins University
at an academic conference on **STRUCTURALISM**, an intellectual movement interested in the structures underlying language, culture, mythology, and literature
(I discuss structuralism in more detail in Chapter 6 as well). While Derrida
helped introduce American audiences to structuralism, at the same time his talk
critiqued it in a way that came to be called poststructuralist (the *post* part of
the word means that poststructuralism builds upon structuralism rather than
meaning that it merely rejects it). His argument (which is too complex to do
justice to here) focuses on the issues of play within structures. It attempts to
decenter structures of thought by pointing out that the centers which provide

stability for different systems of thought, including "essence, existence, substance, subject ... transcendentality, consciousness, or conscience, God, man," are themselves constructions.[1] Derrida tries to trace the ruptures within systems of thought, the internal contradictions that highlight a structure's lack of a stable foundation, in order to make possible "freeplay" and new ways of thinking.

In a broader sense, Derrida's essay stands in for a range of intellectual approaches that gained popularity in the late 1960s and early 1970s that subverted conventional wisdom, undercut foundations, and in other ways pointed out the social construction of everything from language to ideas about gender and race to systems of Western thought. These poststructuralist approaches didn't all emanate from within literary studies. In fact, many of the key figures come from other disciplines, including anthropology, sociology, history, and philosophy. Structuralism itself originated with a linguist, Ferdinand de Saussure (1857–1913), who studied the structures of languages. Anthropologist Claude Lévi-Strauss (1908–2009) applied Saussure's ideas about language to cultures more generally, creating the field of **STRUCTURALIST ANTHROPOLOGY**. Scholars within literary studies, though, were among the earliest and most enthusiastic to embrace poststructuralism.

It's no coincidence that these revolutionary new approaches to literary studies gained ground in the 1960s and 1970s. The larger cultural shifts that were taking place in this decade (stylishly dramatized in the television series *Mad Men*) are reflected in the changes happening within literary theory and criticism. The turn to theory toward the end of the 1960s coincided with the social and political unrest of the time, and many theoretical movements, such as feminism and ethnic studies, grew out of larger political movements such as the women's movement, the civil rights movement, the Chicano Movement, and the protests against the Vietnam War. In fact, if you have professors of a certain age, there's a good chance they may have been involved in the student movements of the late 1960s.

Nowhere is the connection between political agitation and literary theory better illustrated than in the events of May 1968 in Paris. In the spring of 1968, student protests over university reforms, the Vietnam War, and imperialism began to escalate in France. In May, workers across the country joined students in a strike. On the day of the May 13 general strike, nearly 20 per cent of the French population was on strike, a million people marched in the streets of Paris, and the country was essentially shut down. Photographs from this time, as Figure 1 illustrates, show masses of students and workers protesting in the

---

1   Jacques Derrida, "Structure, Sign, and Play in the Discourse of the Human Sciences," *The Structuralist Controversy: The Languages of Criticism and the Sciences of Man*, ed. Richard Macksey and Eugenio Donato (Baltimore: Johns Hopkins UP, 1970), 249.

Figure 1: Student riots in Paris, 1968. © Hulton-Deutsch / Hulton-Deutsch Collection / Corbis.

streets of Paris, waving flags and holding up signs. The images call to mind those from *Les Misérables* or the Occupy Wall Street movement. Many important French literary theorists, such as Derrida, participated in the strike, while others, such as Foucault, were deeply influenced by it.

Theory and Criticism Today

The theoretical approaches coming out of France (and elsewhere) in the 1960s and 1970s began to reshape literary studies throughout this period and into the 1980s and 1990s. By the 1990s, a course covering literary theory became a standard part of many undergraduate and graduate literature students' training, either as a standalone course or as a unit within an introductory course or courses. Academic conferences and journals devoted specifically to literary theory proliferated.

Almost without fail, however, as something becomes popular and trendy, a backlash follows. The backlash against theory took a number of different forms. Some questioned the importance of "theory" and whether critics were losing sight of "traditional" literary studies, worrying that students weren't studying works of literature any more, only works *about* literature or about other matters entirely. Other more benign forms of backlash included a resurgence of historical studies and a greater emphasis on clarity in academic writing. The anti-theory backlash began in the 1980s and continued into the 1990s and beyond, and it coincided with and was related to debates about the literary **CANON** itself.

Just as Derrida's essay is a watershed moment in the theory revolution, Allan Bloom's book *The Closing of the American Mind* (1987) is a touchstone for this anti-theory backlash. In it, Bloom (1930–92) argues against the **RELATIVISM** or lack of universally accepted values within the university since the 1960s. He points his finger at student radicalism, deconstructionism, and popular culture. In place of this he advocates a course of study in the great books of the Western tradition. In retrospect, some of his worries about popular culture seem rather overblown, as in this passage where he describes Mick Jagger: "A shrewd, middle-class boy, he played the possessed lower-class demon and teen-aged satyr up until he was forty, with one eye on the mobs of children of both sexes whom he stimulated to a sensual frenzy and the other eye winking at the unerotic, commercially motivated adults who handled the money."[1] Despite its sometimes

---

1   Allan Bloom, *The Closing of the American Mind: How Higher Education Has Failed Democracy and Impoverished the Souls of Today's Students* (New York: Simon and Schuster, 1987), 78.

hyperventilating tone, or perhaps because of it, Bloom's book became a best-seller and, along with E.D. Hirsch's *Cultural Literacy* (1987), sparked a series of debates about the great books and the opening up of the canon in the 1980s and 1990s that came to be known as the culture wars or canon wars.

The fact is, though, that theoretical concerns have always been a part of the tradition of literary studies. After the theory revolution, students of literature are now more conscious of the choices they are making as critics through the texts they read, the questions they ask, and the questions they omit. Theory and criticism will be a part of literary studies as long as people continue to read and study literature.

British Marxist critic Raymond Williams (1921–88) had a useful way of thinking about the complexity of any moment in time. Each historical moment contains dominant, emergent, and residual elements. At any given time, multiple generations of people exist at once, and they don't all have the same background and expectations. Even within the same generation, some people are more forward-thinking and some are more traditional or old-fashioned in their ideas. So characterizing a decade or an era as being uniform in its tastes and preferences is inaccurate and misleading. The dominant ideas will be the most central ones, while residual traces from past generations will still be a part of the culture, and emergent ideas that won't come to fruition until later will be present in an early stage. According to Williams, identifying elements that are residues of earlier eras or that are part of some emerging trend helps make sense of history and helps "reveal ... characteristics of the 'dominant.'"[1] In literary studies today, theoretical approaches influenced by poststructuralism are dominant. Yet there are still older scholars writing and teaching who came of age in the 1950s and early 1960s and who represent an earlier, residual approach. Likewise, the method of close reading still used in the classroom is a residue of the heyday of New Criticism. Students of today and younger scholars represent the emergent generation who will be shaping literary studies in the future. We won't know for certain what that future will look like, but some approaches, such as **DIGITAL HUMANITIES, ETHNIC STUDIES, GENDER AND SEXUALITY STUDIES**, and **COGNITIVE STUDIES** (see Chapters 7 to 9), have been emerging for the last few decades.

In the next several sections of this chapter, I outline some of the key issues in literary theory and criticism that have been explored throughout its long history and continue to be important today. Some of these issues have particular theoretical approaches associated with them, while others cut across a variety

---

1   Raymond Williams, *Marxism and Literature* (Oxford: Oxford UP, 1977), 122.

of theoretical movements and historical periods. This list is far from exhaustive, but it should give you a sampling of some of the matters literary theory and criticism grapples with.

Literary Form

All literary works belong to at least one genre or type of writing, and many works participate in multiple genres. No literary work is entirely original; writers begin with some previously existing model for writing, a set of rules or expectations that they can then shape to their own purposes. (An exception can perhaps be granted for the very first human to paint a story about killing a bear on a cave wall.) Knowing the conventions of the form that a writer is working with – whether short story, sonnet, tragedy, biography, or essay – can help readers know what to expect and to see where the work is coming from.

Established conventions for writing help readers to navigate works. Many of these are so firmly established that readers unthinkingly take them for granted. For example, when you pick up a novel, you know to start reading on page 1 rather than page 200, and you read straight through from beginning to end rather than flipping around as you would with an anthology or dictionary. You also know with a work of fiction that when you encounter a name such as "Jay Gatsby" or "Emma Bovary," those words refer to a character that authors have created out of their imagination, not a real person. Other conventions or rules for writing can be much more specific, as in the case of poetic forms such as the sonnet or the villanelle, which have very specific rules for numbers of lines, rhyme schemes, repetition, and subject matter. In order to understand any work of literature, you must first have some idea of the genre or genres it's working within.

Genres can develop over centuries, as in the case of the epic poem, or they can spring up overnight, such as modern-day Internet memes. Literary criticism can provide a framework for studying literary form in a variety of aspects: it can look at the history of particular forms (tracing the history of the ode, for example), explore the way an individual author has worked within the constraints of a form (such as looking at twentieth-century short-story writer Flannery O'Connor's use of the conventions of the gothic), or investigate the underlying essence of a type of writing (studying the techniques and strategies of satire, perhaps). Literary theorists and critics study the craftsmanship that goes into good (and bad) writing of whatever sort – looking at storytelling techniques, figures of speech in poetry, or how a novel is constructed.

Critics often make a distinction between form and content in a work of literature: the content is the subject matter and the form is the manner in which that subject matter is conveyed. The more you think about it, though, the harder it is to disentangle the two. Forms themselves come with meanings already attached to them: the epic poem is associated with heroic stories, the sonnet form calls to mind unrequited love or philosophical musings, and so forth, so the choice of a particular literary form already has content associated with it. Conversely, the content of a work of literature can't be separated entirely from the way in which that content is conveyed. Literary characters aren't real people but merely the sum of the words the author uses to describe them. So while it may be useful to think about certain aspects of a literary work as having to do more with form or with content, keep in mind that you can't have one without the other: there's no contentless form and no formless content.

Literary Characters

Another key issue for literary theorists relates to the invention of characters in poetry, fiction, and drama. Invented characters are not living, breathing individuals, but certain types of texts and characters can provide insight into the human condition. Good literature can explore multiple aspects of human psychology, from the bond between a parent and child to unrequited love to the darkest machinations of a psychopath's mind. Literary criticism can help illuminate the ways in which literature teaches us about human nature, the inner workings of the mind, abnormal psychology, and related matters.

Fictional works take readers inside the minds of literary characters in a particularly rich and immersive way. First-person narrators tell their own stories, as in the case of Charles Dickens's novel *David Copperfield* (1850), the first chapter of which is titled "I Am Born." An omniscient third-person narrator tells stories about characters and can narrate their thoughts and feelings along with their dialogue and action, as in the case of Jane Austen's novel *Emma* (1816), which begins, "Emma Woodhouse, handsome, clever, and rich, with a comfortable home and happy disposition, seemed to unite some of the best blessings of existence; and had lived nearly twenty-one years in the world with very little to distress or vex her."[1] Novelists and short-story writers have employed first-person narration and omniscient narration to give readers insight into the thought processes of children, autistic individuals, criminals, real historical figures, animals, and even gods.

Critics debate the merits of treating fictional characters like real people.

---

1   Jane Austen, *Emma*, ed. Richard Cronin and Dorothy McMillan (Cambridge: Cambridge UP, 2005), 3.

Some emphasize that characters are not people but words on a page that can in the best cases conjure up a mental image of a character. These critics tend to be skeptical of readers who identify too closely with a literary character or get too emotionally invested in a fictional world. Other critics go in the opposite direction, imagining literary characters as real people, as in the case of much psychologically oriented criticism. For example, L.C. Knights critiques this type of approach in an essay called "How Many Children Had Lady Macbeth?" (1933). The title of his essay refers to a note in A.C. Bradley's book *Shakespearean Tragedy* (1904) discussing whether or not Macbeth had children. Bradley's other notes take the form of questions that seem to presume that Shakespeare's characters have an existence outside the text, such as "Where was Hamlet at the time of his father's death?", "Did Lady Macbeth really faint?", and "Did Emilia suspect Iago?"[1] Knights criticizes the practice, associated with Bradley and others like him, of studying Shakespeare for "his characters, his heroines, his love of Nature or his 'philosophy' – with everything, in short except with the words on the page, which it is the main business of the critic to examine."[2] It is easy but dangerous to get swept up into the world of fiction so that you imagine characters as real people with full lives outside the confines of the book.

Because great literature as an art form can place you deep inside another consciousness, readers have a history of becoming so deeply invested in fictional characters that they steal them away from the author's control and make them their own. In the early seventeenth century, Miguel de Cervantes satirized this phenomenon in *Don Quixote*. The first part of Cervantes's novel was so popular and beloved that another author published a continuation of the story without Cervantes's knowledge. When Cervantes came to write his own second part, he had *his* Don Quixote encounter a character who had read the false continuation, so that poor Quixote has to explain the difference between himself and this impostor. Today fan fiction, reimaginings, and continuations carry on this tradition of plucking characters out of their original context in works such as E.L. James's novel *Fifty Shades of Grey* (2011), which was originally conceived as *Twilight* fan fiction, and Seth Grahame-Smith's *Pride and Prejudice and Zombies* (2009), a supernatural take on the Austen classic. One of the most successful examples of this phenomenon is Alan Moore's comic-book series *The League of Extraordinary Gentlemen*, begun in 1999, which features dozens of characters from classic works of literature as time-traveling superheroes.

---

1   See A.C. Bradley, *Shakespearean Tragedy: Lectures on* Hamlet, Othello, King Lear, Macbeth (New York: St. Martin's P, 1992).

2   L.C. Knights, "How Many Children Had Lady Macbeth?," *Explorations: Essays in Criticism Mainly on the Literature of the Seventeenth Century* (London: Chatto & Windus, 1946), 6.

The Importance of Context

Literary works, like all cultural phenomena, are products of their historical moment. Reading a book not only can bring characters to life, but it can also transport you back in time or halfway across the globe. Literary critics who study works and their contexts do so for varied purposes: using a text to better understand a historical period, for example, or conversely using a historical period to better understand a text. In the first case, critics can use a literary work to shed light upon a moment in history. For example, much of what scholars know about Anglo-Saxon culture in the early Middle Ages comes from the study of surviving texts from that era, such as the tenth-century (or so) heroic epic *Beowulf*. In the second case, understanding historical context can also help readers to understand a classic work of literature better: knowing what a mead-hall is and its importance to Anglo-Saxon society, for example, will help us to understand why the first part of *Beowulf* deals with a monster named Grendel attacking a mead-hall (basically a drinking hall, but more importantly the center of Anglo-Saxon social and political life). Just as form and content can only be separated up to a certain point, so too is the case with text and context. You can't understand a text without knowing a bit about the context, and you learn more about the context by reading the text.

Certain critical approaches to literature emphasize historical context, while others bracket it. A certain degree of historical background can aid in understanding a work of literature, but too much history can get in the way of direct appreciation of the more "timeless" aspects of literary works related to literary form, storylines, characters, and emotions. At one extreme, certain theoretical approaches disregard historical context altogether in favor of a focus on language, structure, or psychology, and at the other extreme, certain types of historicist approaches are primarily interested in the text's relationship to history and use literary texts as sources of information about the past in the way a historian would do, without looking at formal or linguistic issues. Most readers tend to fall somewhere between the two poles, and much historically driven criticism these days employs some amount of formalist close reading.

When reading an older work of literature, you generally have a choice of editions of the text. One way to determine which edition is best for you is to think about how much historical background you require and will utilize. A facsimile version of a text reproduces the text as it was originally published, with no explanatory notes, no editorial preface, and with spelling and punctuation as they appeared in the original version. Along with printed facsimile editions, you can get electronic facsimiles of early books online through databases such as Early

English Books Online and Early American Imprints. The downside to reading a facsimile is that you may encounter many unfamiliar words and references and have to struggle to understand antiquated spelling and punctuation. Older books tend to capitalize many more words than modern conventions require, for example, and punctuation, including quotation marks around dialogue, is erratic. If you go back to Renaissance texts you will encounter anarchic spellings, such as the letter *u* used in place of *v*, and vice-versa (or should I say uice-uersa!). In Edmund Spenser's late-sixteenth-century poem *The Faerie Qveene*, for example, *up* is spelled *vp*, *love* appears as *loue*, and *ever* takes the form *euer*. If you don't want to struggle with these historical matters, you probably will prefer a modernized, edited, annotated edition. Some scholarly editions of classic works, though, are so heavily annotated that nearly every sentence contains a reference to a footnote.

The Identity of the Author

Just as it can be helpful to understand something about the historical context of a literary work, it can also be helpful to know something about the life of its author. Most books today come with at least a paragraph of author biography that tells you where authors were born, how old they are or when they died, and other potentially relevant details. The importance of this type of information has been the subject of much debate among literary theorists.

One side of the debate would argue that an author's work should speak for itself, that authors put what they wanted to say into their work, and that we should focus on the work rather than on the author's life story. Authors use their imaginations to create new worlds on the page, and their own life experiences shouldn't matter. The other side of the debate believes that understanding something about an author's life can help us to better appreciate his or her works – understanding their background, education, formative experiences, and so forth. Knowing that an author such as the American fiction writer Tim O'Brien, who was born in 1946 and whose books (such as the 1990 short-story collection *The Things They Carried*) depict the horrors of war, fought in the Vietnam War, for example, lends credibility to his account and perhaps enhances the emotional impact of his works.

The idea of authorship itself is historically constructed, as Foucault argues in a famous essay called "What Is an Author?" (1969). In the Middle Ages, he explains, works of the imagination, such as ballads and romances, did not have author names attached to them, but scientific works did. In more recent times, authors sign their works (and receive royalties and copyright privileges for them), while scientific and medical knowledge has become much less attached to author names. In the eighteenth century a majority of novels were published anonymously, while in the nineteenth century a number of women writers took on male pseudonyms, for example George Sand (1804–76), George Eliot (1819–80), and Michael Field (1846–1914, 1862–1913; the pseudonym for *two* women writing together). These examples illustrate the ways in which conventions of authorship and what Foucault calls the author-function change over time.

Related to the question of the author's identity is the question of his or her intentions. Some critics are very interested in what the author "really meant," and so they study such things as early drafts of works, author interviews, and personal correspondence in order to better determine the true significance of a work of literature. Other critics believe the question of intention is irrelevant. They believe that since one of the most important features of literary works is that they are open to multiple interpretations, they can't be boiled down to merely a simple, straightforward message. If a reader finds meaning in a work that the author didn't "intend" to be there, how valid is it?

Most critics would agree that it's impossible to ever know *exactly* what an author intended. Even if an interviewer asks an author directly regarding the meaning of her or his work, there's always a chance that the author could refuse to answer, answer dishonestly, or not even realize some unconscious level of meaning within that work. In the case of authors from the past, we don't have the luxury of asking them what they meant. This means that readers are always empowered to discover meaning for themselves within a work. However, some meanings are more "meaningful" than others, and knowing something about the background of authors, their other works, or their historical context can make you a more informed reader.

The Role of the Reader

Many of the issues I have outlined so far have to do with authors and their creations, but authors and their books are relevant only because of the active participation of readers. Literary critics have studied readers in any number of ways, from looking at the mental processes that go into reading, to looking at popular taste and sales figures, to examining reader reactions to a work over time.

It can be easy to lose sight of the importance of real readers, because readers are much harder to study than authors. Readers don't always leave a record of what they've read or how they've responded to a text, especially in centuries past. That is changing, though. The Reading Experience Database project

<http://www.open.ac.uk/Arts/RED/> is compiling information on the history of reading from 1450 to 1945, while contemporary readers can rate books they've read and thus provide information for future literary critics on sites such as Goodreads <http://www.goodreads.com/>.

Though we take reading for granted these days, in other cultures and in ages past illiteracy was much more common than literacy. Historians of reading use old records to determine literacy rates – if people could sign their names on a birth certificate or marriage license, they are counted as literate, while if they signed with an "X" or mark or had someone sign for them, they are counted as illiterate. By these rough standards, it's estimated that about 20 per cent of the population of medieval England could read (or at least sign their names). Today, literacy rates are close to 100 per cent in the developed world, but less than 50 per cent in some African countries.

Reading as Education, Reading as Entertainment

In *Ars Poetica* (c. 19 BCE), the Roman writer Horace asserts that the best writing should both delight and instruct readers, that poetry should not merely entertain but also educate its audiences. Literary critics have been debating the balance between these two aims of writing ever since. On the spectrum of instruction versus entertainment, one extreme would be books whose only aim is to provide pure satisfaction to readers – maybe an airport thriller, a joke book, or a steamy romance. The other end of the spectrum would be works that aim only to convey instruction without the slightest concern for engaging a reader's attention – maybe a very dry sermon or a technical manual. Most writing obviously falls somewhere between these extremes, and the best writing can trick the reader into learning something – about a historical period, about human nature, about a different culture – while entertaining them.

Harold Bloom (b. 1930) is one of the most famous living literary theorists. His 1973 book *The Anxiety of Influence* (discussed in Chapter 9) has become a classic of literary theory, discussing how writers have to grapple with the burden of their predecessors in forging a new way forward for literature. In 2003, however, Bloom took aim at a surprising target – J.K. Rowling. In an editorial for *The Boston Globe*, he accused Rowling's beloved Harry Potter series of "dumbing down" readers.[1] He claimed that her writing was full of clichés and

---

1   Harold Bloom, "Dumbing Down American Readers," *Boston Globe* 24 September 2003, http://www.boston.com/news/globe/editorial_opinion/oped/articles/2003/09/24/dumbing_down_american_readers/.

that children should not read her works, precisely because Bloom values reading for its educative properties rather than its entertainment value. It would appear that the millions of readers of Rowling's books would disagree, both with Bloom's claim that Rowling isn't a good writer and with the idea that her writing lacks larger themes and messages.

Related to the issue of the educational role of reading is its role as moral instructor. The best writing can present complex ethical scenarios and generate sympathy by putting readers into the mindset of another individual. Some critics, from Plato (429–347 BCE) to the present day, place the utmost stress on the ethics of literature. Ethical issues can run the gamut from personal morality to social justice to treatment of the environment. Other critics ignore ethical concerns in favor of more formal or structural approaches. Though we tend to think of morality as an old-fashioned topic, controversies have raged in recent years about the moral value of particular texts, particularly in schools. In 2011, a publisher produced an edition of Mark Twain's classic novel *The Adventures of Huckleberry Finn* (1884) that removed offensive racial epithets. While some people celebrated this edition for its elimination of offensive language, others worried that the original effect of the book would be lost if its language were censored. Other books that have inspired controversy include J.D. Salinger's *The Catcher in the Rye* (1951) and Ralph Ellison's *Invisible Man* (1952).

Another question arises related to morality and literature: what sort of moral responsibility does a writer possess? Some critics, such as Oscar Wilde (1854–1900) and other nineteenth-century aesthetes (see Chapter 5), promote the doctrine of **ART FOR ART'S SAKE**. They believe that art and literature have no duty but to be true to themselves. Art should not try to convey a message, a task better left to writers of political treatises and sermons. Counter to this idea is the belief that writers should work to make the world a better place, and that works of literature that promote harmful ideas such as Nazism, violence toward women, or cruelty in any form should not be taught in schools.

Diversity

Diversity has become a more prominent concern for literary critics in the twentieth and twenty-first centuries. Prior to this time, the literature considered to be worthy of study came, for the most part, from dead, white, European men. Literary theorists have been instrumental in enlarging the canon of classic works by bringing in works by women writers, minority writers, gays and lesbians, Third World writers, and other groups previously excluded or marginalized. In 1986, activists at Stanford University staged protests calling for an expanded canon of texts in their Western Civilization courses. (This was merely one of the things that infuriated Allan Bloom so much and ignited the culture wars of the late 1980s.) Today, it would be unthinkable to study American literature before the Civil War without reading a classic slave narrative such as Frederick Douglass's *Narrative of the Life of Frederick Douglass* (1845), or to study the early British novel without reading a female writer such as Charlotte Brontë (1816–55), but this was not always the case. Theorists have helped to rediscover forgotten texts by women and minority writers and to champion new works from former colonies across the globe. In the process, the world of literature has become more diverse, providing more options for excellent texts to read and more accurately reflecting what the modern world actually looks like.

Part of the reason that men dominate the literary canon before the twentieth century is that women authors did not have the same opportunities as men. Most women could not attend universities until the nineteenth century and were severely limited in terms of their freedom. Similarly, in the American context, prior to the Civil War most African-American slaves lacked the time, education, and freedom to write. A few individuals who escaped were able to tell their stories and thus inform the world of the horrors of slavery, but most did not possess the means to even keep a diary, let alone write a book.

Another reason these voices have been left to the margins for so long has to do with the politics and economics of the publishing world. Up until fairly recently, most powerful figures in the literary establishment, such as editors, publishers, and agents, were white men. Every year the organization VIDA: Women in Literary Arts publishes statistics on numbers of men versus women reviewed in prestigious venues. In 2013, for example, 85 per cent of the books reviewed in the *Atlantic Monthly* were by men, 79 per cent of those in the *New York Review of Books*, 77 per cent in the *London Review of Books*, and 74 per cent in the *Times Literary Supplement*. As more attention gets paid to these sorts of disparities, the likelier they are to change. Yet sometimes change in the literary world can happen at a surprisingly slow pace.

The Uses of Theory and Criticism

Studying literary theory and criticism can enhance your reading experience, deepen your appreciation for the craft of writing, and teach you tricks of the trade that you can use in your own writing. Studying literature in an academic setting provides a good set of mental exercises, such as examining the context of a work, analyzing its construction, and teasing out the political implications. Additionally, learning more about different literary traditions, cultures, and historical periods can help you to be open-minded, appreciate ideas that may be different from your own, see the world from other perspectives, and thus learn how your own perspective has been shaped by your culture, upbringing, and historical circumstances. Literature can broaden your horizons and allow you to see things through the eyes of another. Literary theory gives you a vocabulary for talking about literature and a means of understanding others' vocabulary, to see a text and thus the world from multiple points of view. Different critical approaches highlight different aspects of a text, so the more interpretations of a work you encounter, the richer your reading experience will be.

Great works of literature often provoke big, complicated questions. Shakespeare's *Hamlet* (discussed in more detail in Chapter 10) raises a number of undecidable questions. Readers and viewers have to make up their own minds as to the question of Hamlet's sanity, for example – is he really insane, or is he just pretending? Does he really see his father's ghost? Why does he hesitate when he has the opportunity to kill his uncle? Similarly, the two central characters in Mary Shelley's novel *Frankenstein* (1818), Victor Frankenstein and his creation, are both morally flawed, and readers disagree about which character (if either) to sympathize with. Undecidable questions and complex characters provide moments of ambiguity or paradox that create opportunities to delve more deeply into a text and to support your opinion using textual evidence. These moments also provide perennial material for essay and exam questions, not because there's a right answer, but as a way to test your ability to think through a knotty problem and to find evidence to support your interpretation.

If you study literature at a university, you will be trained by professors who were once themselves beginning students encountering texts and critical approaches for the first time. Because the practice of literary studies is constantly evolving, and because the training we receive in undergraduate and graduate studies tends to shape the way we view the world for the rest of our lives, it's likely that your professors' approaches to literature were formed in an earlier phase of literary studies. Understanding more about the history of critical approaches will enable you to identify and appreciate the theoretical approach or approaches your instructors are using as well as those they're excluding. Theory provides you with ammunition to challenge an instructor's way of reading a text by showing you that literary criticism is pluralistic, that multiple interpretations are possible for any given text.

Some professors, if pressed, might say that they "don't do theory" or that they just "study literature" rather than studying theory. As discussed above, rejecting "theory" is itself a theoretical approach. This type of approach might be a little naïve or lack awareness of the longer history of literary studies, but it is certainly a method of studying literature, one that ignores questions of politics and society or of psychology in favor of a close focus on the language of the text.

The choices professors make in the classroom can point to their type of theoretical approach. A professor who presents a lot of background on authors' lives, for example, clearly believes that author biography is needed to understand a text. A teacher who spends much time on meter and rhyme schemes is using a formalist method, while a survey class that covers a lot of historical background is using a historicist approach. Sometimes you can figure out the approach of a professor or course ahead of time simply by looking at the course title or catalog description. A course with gender or sexuality in the title is likely to use an approach influenced by feminist criticism, for example, while a course title or description that mentions poetics or genre will probably use a formalist approach, at least to a certain extent.

Likewise, knowing a bit more about the history of critical approaches to literature can help you to make your way through published scholarship on literature, to recognize at a glance the methodology of a particular book or article, to identify works of criticism that are of interest to you, and perhaps to find a new way to approach an old text. Most good works of literary scholarship will indicate their methodology clearly and don't claim to be providing the final word on a given topic. Instead, scholars think of themselves as entering into an ongoing debate about authors, genres, literary movements, language, interpretation, and all sorts of other issues. Be wary of reference works or websites that attempt to explain a work of literature in a simple way or to provide definitive answers. A better critic recognizes that they are just one voice among many, and that debates about great works of literature will go on for as long as people are reading.

Perhaps most importantly, knowing more about the history of theory and criticism will make you more conscious of your own reading practices. Becoming more self-aware in turn will allow you to be a more thoughtful and careful reader, to pick up on subtexts and allusions, and to be more open-minded and inclusive about different styles of writing. Here are a few questions you might ask yourself as a reader:

- Do you read for the plot? If you love novels with lots of twists and turns, have ever stayed up all night because you just needed to find out how a story wrapped up, or simply appreciate a satisfying ending that ties up the loose ends of a story, you may be interested in the area of literary theory called **NARRATOLOGY**. Narratologists study the dynamics of storytelling, narrative point of view, plot construction, and the ways in which writers play with time and chronology.

- Do you find yourself reading an Austen novel or a medieval romance and wanting to know all about the food, clothing, and customs of the era? If the pleasure you take in reading derives in part from learning more about a different historical period, if reading transports you back in time and around the world, then you may want to learn more about historicism. Historicists investigate literary works as products of their historical moment.
- Do you find yourself lingering over a beautiful descriptive metaphor in a poem? If you love to read poetry for the imagery, the ways in which writers manipulate words, or even just the sounds of the language, **POETICS** is a great field to learn more about. People in poetics study the technical side of poetry (and other forms of writing), looking closely at things such as rhyme and rhythm. Many of the best writers in this area are also poets themselves.
- Have you ever had a dream about a character in a book you were reading? Writers have the ability to bring words on the page to life, to create characters so real that you can imagine their appearances or even dream about them. **PSYCHOANALYTIC CRITICISM** looks at the psychological dimensions of reading and writing, among other things.
- Do you get angry when you read a book that depicts racism, sexism, or injustice? If you think writers have a responsibility to make the world a better place, or are interested in how writers have used literature in the past to comment upon political oppression, economic injustice, war, slavery, and other matters, you might be most interested in political approaches to literature.

Awareness of different ways of reading and interpreting can help you reflect upon your own tastes and acts of judgment. If you say something is "realistic," "a quick read," "boring," "romantic," or what have you, these are all acts of criticism that involve a methodology. Saying a book is boring, for example, implies an expectation that books should *not* be boring but instead should be exciting or engrossing, an idea that was not always the case at various points in history. Even ideas about what "exciting" means have changed over time.

Getting Started

The best way to understand literary theory and criticism is to read it voraciously. Summaries of important theories can help get you started, but reading theorists for yourself is always going to be better. Any summary of a work is also an interpretation of it: even the most faithful summary (such as the ones included in this book) will emphasize certain points, leave others out, and cast some kind of judgment upon the work. Reading and judging for yourself is especially useful when it comes to some of the biggest names in the history of theory, the ones who inaugurated whole schools of criticism.

Karl Marx, for example, is more often talked about than read. If you've never read him before, you might be surprised to discover that he does not advocate censorship, gulags, and other evils associated with the former Soviet Union. The Marxism that V.I. Lenin (1870–1924), Joseph Stalin (1878–1953), and other revolutionaries put into practice in the USSR was itself an *interpretation* of Marx's ideas. Other political manifestations of his ideas include various social democracies in Western Europe and the trade unionism of the early twentieth century (these aren't solely based on Marx's writings but are largely compatible with many of his basic ideas). Much of Marx's writing critiques the capitalist system, advocates for controls upon unfettered capitalism such as protections for workers, and analyzes how economic circumstances shape people's beliefs. Many of his core ideas have become commonplace and form the basis of disciplines such as social history.

Similarly, if you've never read Sigmund Freud, you might think of his ideas as outdated, misogynistic, and phallus-obsessed. That's actually fairly accurate, but you can also find very interesting observations in his writings about how dreams are constructed, the phenomenon of the **UNCANNY** (discussed in Chapter 9), and the relationship of our conscious thoughts to our unconscious desires and wishes. Even though the discipline of psychology has gone beyond Freud's ideas, some of his key concepts have shaped debates about psychology and literature and are still relevant to literary theorists.

Marx and Freud have lent their names to whole fields of theory and criticism. While certain approaches have descriptive names (such as **FEMINISM** or **POSTCOLONIALISM**), others are named after a founding figure. In addition to Marxism and Freudianism, there are also neo-Aristotelian critics, **JUNGIANS** (after psychoanalyst Carl Jung [1875–1961]), **LACANIANS** (after psychoanalyst Jacques Lacan [1901–81]), and many others. These schools aren't named after particular figures because everyone working within the field merely imitates the originary figure, but rather because the ideas of that figure initiated a new line of inquiry that others have taken up. Critics within these traditions don't merely pay homage to these big names but build upon and question them as well.

When reading works of literary theory and criticism, it helps to identify the type of question the critic is asking. If you can identify the underlying critical approach, you will have a better sense of the larger issues at stake. Sometimes you can easily tell what an author's method is, perhaps because the article or book title states it explicitly (e.g., "A Feminist Reading of Chaucer's Wife of Bath"). At other times, keywords can help you determine the critical approach.

Academic books and articles often have long titles and subtitles. But those titles and subtitles provide crucial information about the object and method of study. Sometimes just one word will be enough for the reader to figure out the particular type of approach of an article or book (*postcolonial, sexuality, reception*, or *history*, for example). Taking the time to look up unfamiliar words will expand your vocabulary and help you better understand what you're reading. Dictionaries of literary terms, such as J.A. Cuddon's *The Penguin Dictionary of Literary Terms and Literary Theory* (1977) or M.H. Abrams's *A Glossary of Literary Terms* (1957), can be great resources for understanding the specialized vocabulary of literary studies.

Keywords in the titles of academic articles can tell you the types of critical approaches being employed, and a keyword approach can also give you a quick thumbnail sketch of the history of criticism. To illustrate the effectiveness of looking at keywords, I will look at a few issues of the journal *Publications of the Modern Language Association*, or *PMLA*.

The Modern Language Association (discussed above) is the premier organization for literary studies in America, and *PMLA* is its journal, published four times a year. I've chosen this journal not only because it's one of the most important academic journals in the field, but more crucially because it has been publishing since the late nineteenth century. As a way to illustrate the importance of keywords and how they have changed over time, I've perused the tables of contents of the first issue of *PMLA* for the years 1900, 1950, 1980, and 2000 and provided examples of the prevailing trends for each issue below.

Turning first to the first issue of the twentieth century, issue one from 1900, we find articles with such titles as "Philology and Purism," "Interpretive Syntax," and "Influence of the Court-Masques on the Drama, 1608–15." In each of these titles, one word signals the methodology of the article: *philology, syntax*, and *influence*. Philology is the study of literary texts as a way to understand the history of languages, and syntax is a term from linguistics having to do with word arrangement. So taken together, these three titles suggest that part of the study of literature in 1900 is connected to the study of language and linguistics and to issues of literary history (as the keyword *influence* suggests, especially in combination with a narrow date range of 1608 to 1615).

In the March 1950 issue of *PMLA*, article titles include "Point of View in Dickens," "Hawthorne's Psychology of the Head and Heart," and "Donne's Metrical Practice." Here too, one word in each title tells you the *object* of study (the works of Dickens, Nathaniel Hawthorne, and John Donne, respectively) and another word or phrase signals the *method* (*point of view, psychology*, and *metrical practice*). We can draw a couple of conclusions from this small subset of titles: 1) in 1950 major, canonical (white male) authors ruled the day, so much so that their first names aren't even needed in article titles; 2) one wide area of investigation had to do with literary technique and other issues relating to literary form (*point of view* suggests an interest in fictional technique while *metrical* suggests a focus on poetic meter); and 3) psychological concerns have entered into the realm of literary studies.

Skipping ahead 30 years to the January 1980 issue, article titles include "The Pardoner's Homosexuality and How It Matters," "A Phenomenological Approach to the Theatrum Mundi Metaphor," and "The Works of Ralph Ellison." These three titles suggest that a variety of new concerns have made their way into mainstream literary studies. In the first article title, for example, the word *homosexuality* suggests that we're a long way from the concerns of the 1900 and 1950 issues. Questions of gender and sexuality (here in relation to one of the characters in Geoffrey Chaucer's *Canterbury Tales*, late fourteenth century) have taken on greater importance. The title "The Works of Ralph Ellison" doesn't give you much of a sense of *method*, but here it's the *object* of study that is of interest: Ellison, author of *Invisible Man*, is one of the great twentieth-century African-American writers. The object of literary studies has expanded to include nonwhite authors to a much greater degree than previously. As for the phenomenological approach of the second title, this may require a reference work, where you will learn that **PHENOMENOLOGY** (see Chapter 9) is the philosophical study of consciousness and perception. New philosophical approaches such as phenomenology have entered literary studies by the 1980s.

Finally, article titles in the March 2000 issue include "A Lady Asks: The Gender of Vulgarization in Late Medieval Italy," "Poetic Practice and Historical Paradigm: Charles Baudelaire's Anti-Semitism," and "Who Shall Teach African-American Literature?" With this set of titles it's again easy to pick out keywords: *gender, historical, anti-Semitism,* and *African-American.* In this sampling, historical and socio-political concerns appear to be at the forefront. Literary studies appears to have changed less dramatically between 1980 and 2000 than it did between 1950 and 1980, confirming the hypothesis that the 1960s and 1970s really were a major turning point in the history of literary theory and criticism.

Identifying an author's method through keywords and placing them in their larger historical context will help you to get started reading works of theory and criticism. These texts tend to be complicated, and often with primary texts of literary theory you will need to read them more than once in order to grasp the argument. The first time through you should read slowly, getting a sense of the work, identifying key passages (such as the thesis statement and places where terms are defined), and dwelling over unfamiliar terms or particularly knotty constructions. Once you've read through more slowly, it's often helpful to read straight through a second time in order to get a better sense of the work as a whole, of the dynamics of the author's argument and its larger implications. In a literary theory course, often you won't be assigned too many pages of reading because the works tend to be dense and philosophical and pack a lot into a little space.

Friedrich Nietzsche's 1903 essay "On Truth and Lies in a Non-Moral Sense" (discussed in Chapter 5), for example, takes up only a few pages, but it needs to be read multiple times to be thoroughly understood. In this essay, Nietzsche (1844–1900) outlines his ideas about language, our place in the universe, the role of the artist, and how concepts are formed. He does so through the use of metaphors, anecdotes, and parables that take time to fully comprehend. It can be more rewarding to read Nietzsche's essay five times over than to read something else five times as long, as his short essay contains much thought-provoking material.

There are a number of excellent anthologies of literary criticism and theory, including Vincent Leitch's *The Norton Anthology of Theory and Criticism* (2001), Hazard Adams's *Critical Theory Since Plato* (1971), and David Richter's *Falling Into Theory* (1999). When reading selections in an anthology, it's always a good idea to read the headnote preceding the selection. You might be tempted to skip this section in order to get to the primary text, but usually these headnotes contain invaluable information that will help you to situate the authors: something about their life, their major works, their influence, the key issues they explore, and how the anthology selection fits into the larger framework of their work. Often these headnotes also contain definitions of key terms or suggestions for further reading.

Alongside the reading of primary works of theory and criticism, a number of very useful secondary sources can help to guide you through these works and provide intellectual and moral support:

+ Johns Hopkins Guide to Literary Theory and Criticism (available as an online guide at http://litguide.press.jhu.edu/). This online guide requires a subscription (often available through public and university libraries), but it is well worth the investment. It covers a range of theorists, terms, and critical approaches in a comprehensive manner.
+ Terry Eagleton's *Literary Theory: An Introduction* (1983; rev. ed. 1996). Eagleton's introduction to literary theory doesn't cover developments of the last 20 years or so, of course, but it was a groundbreaking work in its time and contains a good overview of twentieth-century theoretical approaches, particularly structuralism and poststructuralism.
+ Jonathan Culler's *Literary Theory: A Very Short Introduction* (1997). This

short and inexpensive book by one of the leading figures in literary theory highlights in a readable manner some of the key issues at stake in theory.

+ Purdue Online Writing Lab (http://owl.english.purdue.edu). The OWL at Purdue is a great resource for all things related to academic writing. It provides a quick overview of literary theory and criticism in addition to resources on grammar, academic research, and many other topics.

+ Theory.org (http://theory.org.uk). This British website contains some serious and some lighthearted resources for the study of theory, including theorist action figures and trading cards.

+ Wikipedia. There's nothing wrong with getting some quick background information from Wikipedia or other online resources. Just don't use it as your sole source of information, and know that, because anyone can edit a Wikipedia page, sometimes incorrect or biased information can creep in.[1]

Another good way to familiarize yourself with the variety and complexity of literary theory and criticism is to look at a range of interpretations of a single work. Choose a favorite literary text, preferably something published at least 20 years ago and relatively well known, so that you have a lot of criticism to choose from that covers various stages in the history of criticism. Then just sample the critical opinions. For older works, you can find collections of essays that compile the history of critical approaches to a work. Scholarly editions such as Norton Critical Editions (books.wwnorton.com) or Broadview Editions (www.broadviewpress.com) often include major critical reactions to works as well.

Looking at the range of writing on a single canonical text not only can give you a better sense of the varieties of opinions on a single work, but can also showcase the variety of types of studies that are possible for any major work. These may include

+ **biographical studies** that connect the work to the author's life. Biographies of authors often interweave analysis of their major works with the usual contents of a biography. Reading an author's biography can provide new perspectives on the personal dimensions of major publications.

+ **close readings** of the dynamics of a particular theme or literary device.

+ **contextual studies** of the larger historical context of the work. These could include studies of particular historical events (seventeenth-century poetry

---

1   For an example of the limitations of Wikipedia, see E.J. Dickson, "I Started a Wikipedia Hoax," www.dailydot.com/lol/amelia-bedelia-wikipedia-hoax. Dickson and a friend added made-up details to certain Wikipedia pages in 2009 (such as the detail that children's character Amelia Bedelia was based on a maid from Cameroon), and in 2014 discovered that numerous sources had reproduced their invented information as fact.

and its relation to the English Civil War, for example) or social and cultural history more broadly (looking at how debates about immigration shape the early twentieth-century novel, for example).

- **reception studies** that look at the way a text was reviewed, or at audience and reader reactions to it.
- **source studies** that examine the precedents for and influences on a work.
- **comparisons** that look at the work in relation to another work by the same author or to the works of another author.
- **socio-political criticism** that examines the dynamics of race, class, or gender in relation to a work. There's a huge body of criticism that falls under this category.
- studies of cinematic or other **adaptations** of a work. Great works of literature inspire countless adaptations and rewritings. In the field of drama, you can study the history of various performances and stagings, for example.
- and many more approaches, depending on the work.

In Chapter 10, I return to the issue of putting theory into practice by working through how to apply different critical approaches to two canonical works of literature, *Hamlet* and *Frankenstein*. First, however, Chapters 2 to 9 will outline the history of literary theory and criticism in more detail.

Suggestions for Further Reading

Culler, Jonathan. *Literary Theory: A Very Short Introduction*. New York: Oxford UP, 1997.

Eagleton, Terry. *Literary Theory: An Introduction*. 1983. Minneapolis: U of Minnesota P, 2008.

Graff, Gerald. *Professing Literature: An Institutional History*. Chicago: U of Chicago P, 1987.

Underwood, Ted. *Why Literary Periods Mattered: Historical Contrast and the Prestige of English Studies*. Stanford, CA: Stanford UP, 2013.

Williams, Raymond. *Keywords: A Vocabulary of Culture and Society*. New York: Oxford UP, 1976.

Two: The Ancient World

THE HISTORY OF LITERARY theory and criticism in the Western world begins in ancient Greece, the birthplace of Western civilization. India and China have their own traditions of literary theory stretching back to antiquity, but these traditions are outside the scope of the history I am tracing. The authors I discuss in this chapter wrote thousands of years ago in Greek and Latin, but they continue to be important to literary criticism because of their immense influence on later writers and the sheer power of their ideas.

In this chapter, I use the term *the ancient world* to mean primarily ancient Greek and Roman civilization, during about a thousand-year period from the fifth century BCE to the fifth century CE. The earliest writers I discuss, Plato and Aristotle, come from the Classical era of Greek history, which begins around the fifth century BCE. Greek culture spread throughout the Mediterranean region in the following centuries, until the Roman Republic (which later became the mighty Roman Empire) took over control of the region. At its height, in the second century CE, the Roman Empire stretched all the way from Britain in the west to Armenia in the east. The empire finally collapsed in the fifth century, but the writers of Greece and Rome continued to influence European literature and philosophy throughout the Middle Ages and Renaissance. Until the end of the nineteenth century, Greek and Latin formed the substance of a gentlemanly education (as I discuss in Chapter 1), so knowing a bit about the classics – epic poets such as Homer (c. 800–700 BCE) and Virgil (70–19 BCE), philosophers such as Plato and Aristotle, and dramatists such as Sophocles (496–406 BCE) and Seneca (4 BCE–65 CE) – can help you understand not only that time period but also later writing all the way to the start of the twentieth century and beyond.

The printing press wouldn't come to Europe for another millennium, so much of the writing from the ancient world did not survive to the present day, and other texts survive merely in fragments. Many ancient texts are believed to have been lost with the destruction (the exact date of which is unknown) of the great Library of Alexandria in Egypt, the largest library in the ancient world.

Scholars know of the existence of certain now-lost texts because of references to them in other texts; examples include the lost section of Aristotle's *Poetics* (350 BCE) dealing with comedy, as well as many of the plays he discusses. In other cases, scholars have no way of knowing what treasures may have been lost. Classical scholars have had to make do with the manuscripts that have survived, however fragmentary. To this day, they occasionally uncover new texts from the ancient world, as in the 2014 discovery of two new poems by the Greek poet Sappho (c. 620–c. 570 BCE). In this chapter, I will survey some of the most famous and influential figures in literary theory and criticism from the ancient world – Plato, Aristotle, Quintilian, Horace, and Longinus – and highlight some of their most important texts and concepts.

Plato: The First Literary Theorist

Most histories of literary theory and criticism begin with Plato, who lived in the fifth and fourth centuries BCE. A few fragments, but no complete works, survive from pre-Socratic philosophers, writers before Plato who speculated upon the nature of the universe. However, Plato is really where the Western philosophical tradition, and thus the tradition of literary theory, begins. In the discussion that follows, I refer to two distinct figures: Plato himself and Socrates (c. 470–c. 399 BCE). Plato is a philosopher and the author of the dialogues *The Republic* (360 BCE), *Ion* (380 BCE), *Phaedrus* (360 BCE), and many others. He studied philosophy with Socrates, who appears as the main character in these dialogues. Socrates himself never wrote a word, preferring to teach his students through conversation. Most of what we know about Socrates' ideas comes to us through Plato's writings.

Plato's dialogues cover a variety of topics, including government, education, friendship, and religion, and also address issues of poetry, art, and representation. He was quite skeptical about works of the imagination, and even went so far as to ban poetry from his ideal republic, so it's a little ironic that he has become so central to the tradition of literary criticism. Still, he thought carefully and philosophically about how literature and art represent the world, the ethics of representation, the role of inspiration in writing, and the relationship between the written and the spoken word, all issues that have become central concerns for literary theorists.

Plato wrote his philosophical works in the form of dialogues, imagined conversations between Socrates and one or more individuals. Interestingly, Plato himself never appears as a character in any of his 36 surviving dialogues. Instead, Socrates takes center stage and converses with his pupils, who vary from dialogue to dialogue. The Socratic method – teaching through classroom discussion rather than through lecturing – takes its name from this style of philosophical investigation through conversation.

Often Socrates begins with a question or a proposition and walks his conversational partners through a logical process of back and forth, eventually convincing them of his point of view. Occasionally the dialogues begin with a question from someone other than Socrates. The dialogue *Meno* (380 BCE), for example, begins when the title character asks Socrates, "Can you tell me Socrates – is virtue something that can be taught? Or does it come by practice? Or is it neither teaching nor practice that gives it to a man but natural aptitude or something else?"[1] The dialogues often are formatted like a play, with a list of characters at the start and the dialogue labeled by character names. Many of the dialogues are quite short and surprisingly readable, especially when compared to some later, denser philosophical and theoretical works.

Plato's *Republic*

Plato's most famous dialogue is *The Republic*, a long work in which he outlines his ideas about what his ideal society would look like. Plato's republic would be led by philosopher kings, benevolent and educated individuals who would look out for the common good of all. Children in his republic would be raised communally rather than by their fathers and mothers. Because the children of his republic would be educated in common rather than by their parents, Plato spends a large portion of the dialogue discussing education: what sort of education would be allowed in his republic, and what would be forbidden.

In Book 2, Socrates asks his students Glaucon and Adeimantus their opinions about the best way to educate the future rulers of his republic. At first they discuss the idea that the ideal education would include "physical education for the body, and music and poetry for the mind or soul"[2] – the ideal of a sound mind in a sound body. These music and poetry studies would prominently feature Homer's epic poems *The Iliad* and *The Odyssey* (both c. 800 BCE), the best-known works of ancient Greek literature. Almost immediately, though, Socrates expresses doubts about the value of teaching children made-up stories, worrying that this would give children false notions about the world.

In Book 3, Socrates moves on from thinking that fictional stories would be harmful for children's education simply because they present a false picture of the world to thinking that certain truths should be kept out of the hands even

---

1   Plato, *Protagoras and Meno*, trans. W.K.C. Guthrie (Baltimore: Penguin, 1956), 115.

2   Plato, *The Republic*, trans. Tom Griffith (Cambridge: Cambridge UP, 2000), 61.

of the adult citizens of his republic. He gives as an example some lines from Homer in which characters describe the horrors of the underworld. Socrates says that even though these lines contain beautiful poetry, they should be kept away from the citizens of his republic because the words will make people fearful of death and thus less likely to be courageous in battle. He's not contesting the idea that the underworld is an unpleasant place or that soldiers are right to want to avoid being killed, but he still thinks that this type of idea should be censored in order to create his ideal world.

Socrates argues that poetry can corrupt the minds of youths by providing them with either untrue ideas about the world or true ones that will keep them from being the best potential citizens of his utopia. He is also wary of poetry because he sees it as providing pleasure to readers and listeners, and it seems he's not a big fan of people having fun. (In fact, many of his ideas sound like the later Greek Stoic philosophers, who warned of the dangers of indulging in excessive emotions of any kind.) He sees poetry as a seductive force that could lure his imaginary citizens away from the more serious and healthful subject of philosophy. In fact, he goes on to speak about the ancient quarrel between philosophy and poetry. As a philosopher, he's clearly chosen his side in the quarrel.

Most modern readers tend to be horrified initially by Plato's idea of censoring imaginative works and excluding them from his republic. After all, the word *censorship* may conjure up images of book-burnings or totalitarian regimes. However, even today most parents practice some sort of censorship with respect to the kinds of books, films, video games, and TV shows they allow their kids to consume. When Plato as a philosopher king argues that it's okay to keep harmful materials out of the hands of his citizens and even to lie to them if it's for their own good, you might think of him as an overbearing but well-intentioned parent rather than as a totalitarian dictator.

Plato's Theory of Forms

A larger mistrust of representation of any kind underlies Plato's mistrust of poetry. He explores this idea in more depth in Book 10 of *The Republic*, using the example of a couch to talk about the difference between material objects and their ideal forms. At first, Plato's theory of forms sounds rather far-fetched. Yet his theory has influenced the idealist tradition of Western philosophy and literary theory for thousands of years. Later writers such as Immanuel Kant (see Chapter 4), Friedrich Nietzsche (see Chapter 5), and Simone de Beauvoir (see Chapter 8) all reference Plato's **IDEALISM** (a type of philosophy that believes in universal ideals) in different ways – either by building upon it or by critiquing it.

Socrates begins his discussion of representation with the proposition that any group of things that has the same name makes up a single type. Take the category of *dog*, for example. Even though individual dogs can vary a lot in color, size, and personality, everyone has a basic idea of what a dog is, some sense of the essence of "dogness" that might include aspects such as their four legs, the fact that they're kept as pets, their activities of barking and wagging their tails, and so forth. We recognize each individual dog, or even picture of a dog, as a part of this larger category. You can do the same thing with any category, whether a biological species (dogs), a man-made object (table), or an abstract quality (goodness). For Plato, all things that have the same name are part of the same general type, not merely as an agreed-upon social convention but because they are all manifestations of an eternal ideal.

The example that Socrates uses in this section is a couch (or bed in some translations). Even though craftsmen make an individual couch, he says, they don't make the *idea* of a couch – they look to that idea when making their individual product; they make "something *like* the real thing, but not itself the real thing."[1] So Socrates posits that there must be another kind of craftsman, the one who makes the *idea* of a couch: God, for lack of a better name.

Here's where Plato's philosophy starts to get a little odd. He believes that the idea of a couch, of "couchness," just like dogness or goodness, is divinely created rather than a product of human construction. For every individual category in the world there exists a divinely created ideal form. We often refer to this notion as the Platonic ideal – the perfect, theoretical version of a given type. Any individual couch – whether sleeper sofa, sectional, love seat, or patio furniture – is only an imitation of the perfect, real couch, the essence of couchness that God, not humans, invented, and thus one step removed from reality and from perfection.

No individual example of any given thing can ever come close to the ideal that exists only in the realm of forms. The highest-priced designer leather sofa is still not the ideal couch, nor is the dog that wins the Westminster Kennel Club show the ideal dog. Any material manifestation is merely a copy of the ideal and thus inferior. The only way to gain access to the ideal is through philosophical contemplation, not through the observation of the material world at all.

Plato takes his argument a step further in a move that has important implications for theories of art and literature. He shifts from talking about material objects to talking about *pictures* of objects. As you might by now guess, Plato is not very fond of art. If you have a painting of a couch, he says, that is an imitation of an imitation, because the painter is only copying the material form of

---

1   Plato, *Republic*, 315.

a couch rather than looking to its ideal form (which can only be apprehended through philosophy, not through the senses). Thus a painting is two steps away from reality, as is representational art of any sort, such as poetry. While Plato earlier in the dialogue had allowed a limited place for poetry in his republic, by the end of *The Republic* he rejects it and representational art altogether as inferior to philosophy.

The Greek word **MIMESIS** means representation or imitation. Often you will see this Greek word in literary criticism and theory, or its adjectival form *mimetic*, meaning imitative. *Mimesis* is even the title of a very influential book of literary criticism written in 1953 by Erich Auerbach about the representation of reality in literature. While Plato was extremely critical of mimesis, his student Aristotle celebrated it (as I discuss later in this chapter). Plato's ideas also gave rise to the word *platonic*, used to refer to non-sexual love, or friendship. Plato mistrusted physical pleasure and celebrated chaste friendships in a number of his dialogues.

The Allegory of the Cave

Even though Plato is extremely critical of storytelling, in *The Republic* he tells a famous story of his own, which is known as "the allegory of the cave." An **ALLEGORY** is a type of story that uses symbolism to conceal a hidden meaning, like a parable. In allegory, characters and objects in the story have a one-to-one correspondence with something outside the text that is hinted at in the story. C.S. Lewis's children's novel *The Lion, the Witch, and the Wardrobe* (1950) is a famous example of Christian allegory, where the character of Aslan the lion is an allegorical representation of Christ, while Jonathan Swift's *Gulliver's Travels* (1726) and George Orwell's *Animal Farm* (1945) are well-known examples of political allegory.

In order to illustrate his theory of forms, Plato includes his famous allegory of the cave. He asks his listeners to imagine that there are people imprisoned since childhood in an underground cavern. (He neglects to explain exactly how they got there or why they're being held captive.) For some bizarre reason, the captors have bound the prisoners in place so that they can look in only a single direction toward a wall. Behind the prisoners a fire is burning, and their captors project shadow figures onto the wall by placing objects in front of the fire.

It's a rather far-fetched (and dark and twisted) scenario, but it allows Plato to get to his larger point about representation and reality. The shadows on the wall are the only reality the prisoners know, just as for all humans we only know things by what we observe with our senses (our own couches and dogs, for example) rather than knowing the ideal forms of things. So let's say the captors put a block of wood in the shape of a tree in front of the fire and told the prisoners "this is a tree." The prisoners would think that a tree is a tree-shaped shadow, nothing more, because that is the only reality that they have ever known. They have no way of processing the idea of real trees, or dogs, or anything else, because that is beyond the scope of their perception.

In the next stage of his allegory, Plato asks his listeners to imagine that a few prisoners finally break free from their bonds, escape from the cave, and go out into the sunlight for the first time. It would take a long time for the newly freed captives' eyes to adjust to the light, and once they did, they would realize how limited their view of the world had been back in the cave. They would be introduced to a whole new world of objects lit by the light of the sun rather than by the cave-fire. If they were to return to the cave, they would have a hard time adjusting back to the darkness and an even harder time convincing the people they left behind of the reality of what they saw. They would be thought crazy, because the prisoners left behind lack the ability to grasp the idea of anything beyond the cave.

This stage of the allegory corresponds to the process of education through philosophy, of beginning to recognize the realm of the ideal. Leaving the cave symbolizes learning the true, divine nature of the realm of forms, of couchness and all the rest, but more importantly of morality, beauty, goodness, and truth. For Plato, the light of the sun represents goodness, truth, and the divine, while the fire in the cave is an inferior source of light and not a part of the true and the good. Once people achieve this knowledge of the ideal, they have a difficult time returning to the ordinary world of ordinary objects.

The allegory of the cave resonates with the tragic end of Socrates' own life. He was sentenced to death for corrupting the minds of Athenian youth, and a number of Plato's dialogues depict Socrates' trial and death (by drinking poisonous hemlock). So Plato may well have had Socrates' end in mind when he warns of the dangers of trying to share one's philosophical insight with the prisoners in the cave.

Plato's philosophy has had a pronounced influence on modern culture. Andy and Lana Wachowski, directors of the Matrix trilogy (1999–2003), *Cloud Atlas* (2012), and other films, frequently draw upon concepts from literary theory and philosophy in their works. In *The Matrix* (1999), their influential action/science fiction movie starring Keanu Reeves and Laurence Fishburne, the Wachowskis update the image of humans imprisoned in a cave from Plato's allegory to imagine a post-apocalyptic world where machines rule and humans are kept imprisoned to provide the machines with an energy source. These humans are held in pods, their bodies imprisoned but their minds plugged into "the Matrix," a virtual reality world. Just as the shadow figures are the only reality Plato's prisoners know, the imprisoned humans in *The Matrix* know no reality beyond the virtual reality that their consciousnesses experience. The movie's hero, Neo (Reeves), breaks free from his bonds and experiences the real world for the first time, just like Plato's prisoner who sees the sunlight for the first time. A number of literary theorists and philosophers have analyzed the ways in which the Wachowski siblings have used Plato's philosophy in this movie.

Speech vs. Writing

Although *The Republic* is probably Plato's most important dialogue that deals with issues related to literary theory, he touches upon matters related to poetry and writing in a number of other dialogues. The dialogue *Phaedrus*, for example, contains an important discussion of speech and writing. Today, we take writing for granted, but during Plato's time the written word was substantially less common than the spoken word. The Greek alphabet, adapted from the Phoenician, had been around for only a few centuries before Plato, and written works were still fairly scarce. Remember that Socrates himself never wrote anything down but taught his students through dialogue and discussion.

So even though the written word was becoming more important to Greek life during his time, Plato still mistrusts writing in favor of the more immediate sensation of listening to an orator. Much literary life in ancient Greece centered on oral performance, from the poetic performances of trained orators called rhapsodes to the political speeches that were a major part of civic life. In the *Phaedrus*, Socrates argues that speech is superior to writing. After a lengthy discussion of the topic, he concludes that "a written discourse on any subject can only be a great amusement, that no discourse worth serious attention has ever been written in verse or in prose." The best learning, he says, is "truly written in the soul concerning what is just, noble, and good."[1]

In another dialogue, *Ion*, Socrates speaks with a rhapsode named Ion about the latter's performance of Homer's poetry. Socrates contends that true poetry comes from the gods, and that a poet can't write until he is "possessed" and "out of his mind." He downplays the importance of human effort in composing poetry, instead attributing it directly to divine inspiration. He's considerably more sympathetic to poetry here than he is in *The Republic*, but he is still wary of poetry's power to inspire emotion.

---

1   Plato, *Phaedrus*, trans. Alexander Nehamas and Paul Woodruff (Indianapolis: Hackett, 1995), 84. Jacques Derrida, discussed in Chapter 6, presents a very famous critique of Plato's privileging of speech over writing in his 1972 book *Dissemination*.

Plato did not invent the idea of poetry as divine inspiration. Homer's *Iliad* and *Odyssey* both begin with an invocation of the Muse, whereby the poet asks for the aid of the Muses, the goddesses of the arts, in creating their poem. This convention continued not only in Virgil's first-century BCE epic *The Aeneid*, but also in the epic tradition long after people stopped believing in Greek and Roman mythology. John Milton, for example, repeatedly calls for the aid of the Holy Spirit in writing his epic *Paradise Lost* (1667), which was his Christianized form of the ancient epic.

Aristotle

Aristotle was a student of Plato, but his works part ways from his teacher's on a number of issues. Whereas Plato likes to explore issues through a freewheeling dialogue form, Aristotle uses a much more systematic and scientific method. Like Plato, Aristotle wrote on a wide range of topics, including ethics, the law, politics, natural history, and of course literature. His works cover an even wider range of subject areas than Plato's. If you read one work of literary theory, it should probably be Aristotle's *Poetics*, which may be the most important and influential work in the entire history of literary criticism. Its influence can be seen in medieval theology and Renaissance writings on drama, as well as in twentieth- and twenty-first-century studies of narrative and genre.

Aristotle had a famous student of his own – Alexander the Great (356–323 BCE). Alexander's father, Philip of Macedon, hired Aristotle to tutor his son for several years. Alexander didn't go on to be a philosopher, though. Instead, his legendary military conquests extended his empire from Greece through the Middle East and all the way to India. In the process of building this empire, he helped to spread Greek culture and the Greek language throughout this region (a process called Hellenization). The New Testament of the Bible is written in Greek because of Alexander's success at spreading the Greek language through-out the Middle East, even though Judea had been taken over by the Romans by that time.

Aristotle's works are denser and more difficult to read than Plato's because they are written in a very dry, scientific prose rather than in dialogue form. However, this makes his ideas much more organized and easier to follow. Aristotle's thought is extremely systematic – he divides things into numbered parts and works through each part sequentially. He takes this approach wheth-er he's talking about animals or poems.

As with many ancient Greek texts, we don't have the complete text of his *Poetics*. Scholars believe that the surviving text is not even Aristotle's original composition but was reconstructed through notes, and that it is missing a second half that deals with comedy. The surviving text has nevertheless been hugely influential.

Aristotle begins by stating the subject of his treatise: poetry. He divides poetry into different kinds, and then says he wants to discuss each kind in turn. The categories he uses to divide up different types of writing are still applicable: comedy, tragedy, and epic. At first glance, Aristotle's discussion of the ideal tragedy seems to resemble Plato's belief in a realm of ideal forms of things. It would appear that Aristotle is trying to get at the Platonic ideal of the tragedy through philosophical contemplation. Aristotle goes through every part of the tragedy, from plot to scenery, and discusses what the ideal tragedy would be like. As it turns out, his ideal looks a lot like Sophocles' tragedy *Oedipus the King* (c. 429 BCE), which he repeatedly uses as an example. There's a big difference between Plato's method and Aristotle's, however: Plato says that the ideal can be understood only through philosophical contemplation and can never be achieved by any one object, while Aristotle bases his description of the ideal on observation of many individual tragedies and does not rest his notions on a divine realm of forms.

Classification

Aristotle divides tragedy into six parts, which he lists in order of importance:

1. **Mythos** (plot or fable). The events depicted in the drama. Drama, for Aristotle, is all about the story. He believed that a good plot was the most important part of the drama and that everything else had to flow from the plot, and he had very definite ideas about what made up a good plot.

2. **Ethos** (character or manners). The personages depicted in the drama. For Aristotle, character comes second to plot but is also crucially important. Character and plot are intertwined – you can't have actions without characters to perform them, just as you can't have characters who don't do anything. Hypothetically you can, but it doesn't make for very interesting viewing. In the best tragedies, he says, the source of the tragedy comes from a flaw in the central character rather than external circumstances – it's much more moving to see characters brought down because of their own weakness than because of an "act of God."

3. **Dianoia** (sentiment, thought, or theme). The ideas of the drama. This aspect of the tragedy is a little harder to understand, but it concerns the

thoughts that go into the drama in the broadest sense. While *mythos* is what happens and *ethos* is who it happens to, *dianoia* is in a sense everything else: the thematic material, the larger subjects explored, the ideas conveyed through the dialogue of the characters and the telling of the story. Aristotle places this third in importance because he believes that the best tragedies conveyed ideas to the audience through character and plot. Without the storytelling aspect, all you would have would be ideas – a philosophical essay or sermon.

4. **Lexis** (diction or speech). The language of the drama. While *dianoia* has to do with the ideas, *lexis* has to do with the way these ideas are expressed: the words chosen, the author's style, figures of speech, and so forth. Aristotle spends a large part of his treatise going into matters of Greek grammar and figures of speech. These portions of the *Poetics* tend to be the most obscure for non-Greek speakers.

5. **Melos** (music or melody). The musical aspects of the drama. You might be surprised to learn that Greek tragedies were also accompanied by music. A key component of Greek drama is the chorus, a group of actors who sing and dance but also serve as characters in the story. In *Oedipus* the chorus consists of Theban citizens, while Aristophanes' comedy *Frogs* (405 BCE) features a croaking chorus of dancing frogs.

6. **Opsis** (spectacle or scene). The visual aspects of the drama. Aristotle places this last in importance and spends very little time discussing it in the *Poetics*. Nowadays, the visual aspects of stage drama (not to mention film) are crucial; things such as set design and costuming and even special effects have become much more elaborate over the years. The chief visual effect in ancient Greek drama was the mask: actors wore masks that allowed them to portray multiple characters, made their facial expressions easier to see for large audiences, and helped to project their voices.

When Aristotle is discussing tragedy, he has in mind a very specific form: the Greek tragedy of the ancient world, specifically the fifth century BCE. These tragedies were staged before huge audiences for special occasions (religious festivals) and had distinctive features such as the chorus and the use of masks. Some portions of the *Poetics* that don't seem relevant to tragedies such as *Hamlet* or *Death of a Salesman* make a lot more sense if you think about them in relation to these original Greek tragedies.

Narrative Form

Aristotle's analysis of story structure is one of the most influential aspects of the *Poetics*. He discusses the structure of tragedies in particular, but his analysis of the construction of good stories has influenced many storytelling forms, including the novel and the film. A good story, Aristotle says, has a beginning, a middle, and an end. Even though this seems very obvious to us today, Aristotle was the first to elaborate upon the point. In good Aristotelian fashion, I will go through these three parts of the story one at a time:

+ **Beginning.** A good story has a logical starting point, Aristotle says, but that doesn't have to be a chronological starting point. He thinks that a person's life does not necessarily make for a good story, for example, because there are too many conflicts and episodes within a person's life. Instead, a good story will focus on a central event or conflict. Instead of starting with a person's birth, a story might begin by introducing a central problem or question that the story will explore. The city of Thebes is beset with a mysterious plague at the beginning of *Oedipus*, for example, or a couple of young, rich, single men move into the neighborhood of a family with five daughters at the start of Jane Austen's novel *Pride and Prejudice* (1813). Both these starting points immediately raise questions and possibilities that propel their stories forward. What caused the plague? Will romance develop between any of the new neighbors? Beginnings of stories also need to include exposition, the background information a reader or viewer must possess in order to understand the characters and situation. The best dramas weave in exposition naturally and subtly, without having characters come on stage to recite their whole history to the audience. Too much exposition at the outset of a drama can seem artificial and forced, but too little can mean that a reader or viewer won't know the identities of characters or the relationships among them.

+ **Middle.** The crux of the story happens in the middle: characters get developed, situations get complicated, plots get wrinkled. King Oedipus seeks to rid Thebes of the plague and in the process learns a little too much about himself; the Bennet sisters' love lives become messy. In Aristotle's terms, the best tragic plots build up to a turning point around which the plot revolves. Aristotle used two Greek words to describe the ideal turning points for tragedies: *peripeteia* and *anagnorisis*. *Peripeteia*, or reversal, refers to a change in the circumstances of a character, such as a change from good fortune to bad fortune. In the case of *Oedipus*, the reversal comes as

Oedipus goes from being a powerful king with a loving wife to finding out that his wife is actually his mother and that he murdered his father years before; for Elizabeth Bennet in *Pride and Prejudice* her reversal moves her from a state of happy contentment to embarrassment and unhappiness. *Anagnorisis*, or recognition, describes the moment when a character goes from ignorance to knowledge, recognizing something about themselves or the world in a way that has significance for the plot. In the case of Oedipus, he learns something about himself (the fact that he has committed murder and incest) that reverses his fate and leads to his tragic downfall; for Elizabeth Bennet her embarrassment and unhappiness come when she learns that she has misjudged Mr. Darcy's character and her own feelings for him. In both cases the moment of reversal comes through a moment of recognition: Aristotle says that the best turning points are those where recognition and reversal go hand-in-hand.

✦ **End.** After the turning point, the plot has to be resolved at the end of the story. Aristotle doesn't think that stories have to wrap up the fate of every minor character. Instead, a satisfying conclusion is one that brings closure to the central incident of the story that has been introduced in the beginning and developed in the middle. Critics often use a French term, *dénouement* (literally, "unknotting") to refer to the concluding moments of a drama after the climax of the action. The end of *Oedipus* consists of everything that happens after he learns the truth about himself, including the suicide of Jocasta (his wife/mother) and his own self-blinding. The end of *Pride and Prejudice*, like that of so many courtship novels, consists of clearing up misunderstandings, a final declaration of feelings, and a wedding or two.

Gustav Freytag, a nineteenth-century German critic, diagrammed Aristotle's idea of story structure visually. This diagram, known as Freytag's pyramid, illustrates the workings of a typical narrative. Critics often talk about the "story arc" of a movie or play, but in Figure 2 it's pictured as more of a triangle.

Hollywood films provide a perfect way to think through Aristotle's ideas about storytelling. In fact, many screenwriting manuals allude directly to the *Poetics* and use Aristotelian terms to talk about cinematic structure. Think of your favorite movie, in any genre — romantic comedy, action, horror, sci-fi, whatever. Next think through how the plotline is structured: usually you get some set-up and exposition in the first 15 minutes or so, a conflict is introduced and complicated, which leads to a turning point and moment of crisis, and in the end everything is wrapped up, either happily or not so happily. Even

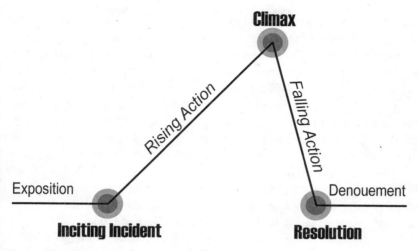

Figure 2: Freytag's Pyramid (image by Ashley Jagodzinski).

filmmakers who take liberties with chronology and storytelling structures, such as Quentin Tarantino, do so against the backdrop of our expectations of how a film's story should unfold.

Another important aspect of Aristotle's analysis of drama is his belief in the unity of a dramatic work. He believes that every incident in the story should follow from what came before, and that in a good tragedy nothing could be taken out without harming the meaning of the overall work. Speaking of plot, he says that it should be "a unitary and indeed whole action; and the component events should be so structured that if any is displaced or removed, the sense of the whole is disturbed or dislocated: since that whose presence or absence has no clear significance is not an integral part of the whole."[1] Every scene, character, exchange of dialogue, or incident should be carefully chosen and crucial for advancing the central storyline or thematic content of the play. This belief in the unity of a good work of art influences Western beliefs about good storytelling profoundly. Later critics such as Samuel Taylor Coleridge (see Chapter 5) and the New Critics (see Chapter 6) emphasize the ORGANIC UNITY of a work of art.

Mimesis

While Plato mistrusts works of literature and art because he sees them as mere copies of copies of the ideal forms of things, his student Aristotle celebrates the way in which art reflects the world. Near the start of the *Poetics*, Aristotle states

---

1   Aristotle, *Poetics*, trans. Stephen Halliwell (Cambridge, MA: Harvard UP, 1995), 59.

that representation is natural to human beings: "It is an instinct of human beings, from childhood, to engage in mimesis (indeed, this distinguishes them from other animals)."[1] Not only does Aristotle believe that representational art is a part of what makes us human, he also believes that it is beneficial to society. Tragedy in particular provides audiences with a moment of **CATHARSIS**, a Greek word meaning cleansing or purgation. Watching a tragedy produces strong emotions in audience members, especially pity and fear for the fate of a tragic hero. Audiences who experience pity and fear through fictional characters are thus cleansed of some of their negative emotions and are able to lead happier lives. You can really see how far Aristotle has come from his teacher Plato here. Plato mistrusted any kind of representational art or mimesis and any kind of strong emotions; Aristotle, on the other hand, sings the praises of both, believing that art (not only philosophy) makes the world a better place.

Even though Aristotle believes that art imitates the world, he does not believe that it should limit itself to ordinary, everyday occurrences. He allows room in his *Poetics* for the extraordinary, the fantastic, and the supernatural in literature. He says that poets have the ability to describe impossible occurrences, as long as they do so in a believable way, and that in fact it is preferable to show things that are impossible but believable than things that are possible but unbelievable. Showing supernatural creatures or the impossible feats of superheroes is fine, as long as the work makes it plausible within the confines of the fictional world that the poet has created by depicting the supernatural elements in a believable framework. He says that presenting fantastic but plausible occurrences is superior to depicting things that are within the realm of human possibility but that audiences would find implausible, such as rich characters giving away all their money out of the kindness of their heart, or a completely flawless, unselfish, virtuous individual.

Rhetoric

Aristotle's *Poetics* has influenced a range of literary approaches, particularly **FORMALIST** approaches (see Chapter 6) that focus on literary technique, studies of individual genres, and **NARRATOLOGY** or the study of how narrative works. Another of his treatises, the *Rhetoric* (350 BCE), also influenced literary theorists greatly. **RHETORIC** is the study of language as a means of persuasion, and this treatise has influenced rhetorical theory all the way up to the present day.

In the twenty-first century, rhetorical studies reside in the academy in a number of fields. Some universities have separate departments of rhetoric, while

---

1   Aristotle, *Poetics*, 37.

others include the fields of rhetoric and composition within English depart-ments or include scholars of rhetoric in communications studies departments. Scholars of rhetoric study the persuasive aspects of language and communi-cation in a wide range of venues: political speech, visual rhetoric, advertising, technical communication, and many other areas. Using the tools that Aristotle and other ancient rhetoricians helped to develop, these scholars explore the ways in which arguments are constructed.

In the *Rhetoric*, Aristotle touches upon a range of topics, including the uses of rhetoric, the components of a good argument, and rhetorical figures or figures of speech. Aristotle's method involves classification, so much of his work tries to systematize rhetoric. For example, he divides "rhetorical speeches" into three types: "deliberative, forensic, and epideictic."[1] Deliberative speeches include political debates and private advice, forensic rhetoric has to do with legal cases, and epideictic rhetoric aims to give praise or blame. Many of Aristotle's ideas would be pursued by later classical writers on rhetoric, including the Romans Cicero and Quintilian (discussed below), as well as by writers in the Middle Ages and Renaissance.

In one of the most influential portions of the *Rhetoric*, Aristotle details the three key ways in which orators can make appeals to their audiences. Here he's talking specifically about delivering speeches (which is the original meaning of *rhetoric*), but these terms can be applied equally to other forms of communication:

1. ***Ethos*** **(character).** *Ethos* concerns the person or persons delivering the speech. Do they have credibility? Are they credentialed to speak upon this topic? Sometimes who is speaking carries as much weight as what that person is saying. A good way to think about *ethos* is to think about celebrity endorsements – companies hire famous athletes and actors to endorse their products because of the *ethos* of the speaker. Having an athlete like Usain Bolt or a pop star like Taylor Swift extol the virtues of your product carries more persuasive effect than merely having a random person deliver the same speech. And when a famous figure falls out of favor, as in the case of golfer Tiger Woods, that person's *ethos* disappears as a result and the endorsements stop.

2. ***Logos*** **(logic).** *Logos* has to do with the content of a persuasive speech: what facts are included? How are they organized? Are they convincing? Do they

---

1   Aristotle, *The "Art" of Rhetoric*, trans. John Henry Freese (Cambridge, MA: Harvard UP, 1926), 33.

anticipate any objections that could be raised to the argument? In order to persuade a listener of your point of view, whether giving a political speech or writing an essay, your facts need to be accurate and organized. Thinking of advertising again, *logos* may be more or less important depending on the ad. In an ad for a new prescription allergy medication, for example, the commercial might include information about the drug's effectiveness in treating a variety of allergies, its lack of side effects such as drowsiness, or its benefits in comparison to the existing products on the market.

3. ***Pathos* (emotion)**. *Pathos* means an appeal to the emotions of the audience. Think about political speeches – politicians can speak endlessly about some particular policy they wish to enact, but appealing to the emotions by telling the story of a single mother that the policy could help often can produce a greater effect than the most thorough listing of facts.

The best orators will balance all three types of appeal, using each when appropriate to make the most convincing argument possible.

Horace's Poetic Art

Although Plato and Aristotle are by far the biggest names in ancient literary theory and criticism, a number of other important figures are worth mentioning. Much literary criticism in the ancient world consisted of guides for writing, such as handbooks for poets or for orators. These how-to books help us to see a bit more of what ancient writers valued and how they constructed their works. They also helped to establish much of the vocabulary for literary criticism for centuries to follow. In the final sections of this chapter, I will discuss three important ancient literary theorists: Horace, Quintilian, and Longinus. While Plato and Aristotle were Greek, the authors discussed in these sections come from Rome or from the larger ancient world during the period of the Roman Empire.

Horace was one of the most important and celebrated Roman poets. He lived in Rome in the first century BCE and wrote poetic epistles (letters) and satires on numerous topics. Together with another Roman writer, Juvenal (c. 55–c. 140 CE), he is considered one of the founding figures in the tradition of satire. His major contribution to literary theory was his last work, *Ars Poetica or The Art of Poetry* (c. 19 BCE), a poem that instructs readers on how to write good poetry. Alongside Aristotle's *Poetics*, this is one of the two ancient works of criticism that have had the most continuous influence upon the tradition of theory and criticism from the Middle Ages onward.

In the *Ars Poetica*, Horace stresses that the best poetry should be unified and consistent rather than discordant. He begins the poem by asking readers to imagine that "a painter starts from a human head, he joins to it a horse's neck, he inserts a variety of feathers on limbs assembled from any and everywhere, and so, repulsively, a woman of appealing form above ends in a black fish."[1] He then compares this bizarre and grotesque image to writing that mixes up all sorts of conventions. The best writing, Horace says, should be unified.

Like Aristotle, Horace sings the virtues of clarity and simplicity above over-elaborate writing. Some of his recommendations are very specific, such as his advice that plays should all be five acts long. Other advice is more universal, like his very famous suggestion that good poetry should both delight and instruct audiences, providing both pleasure and some kind of edification. Unlike Plato, who believed that poetry was merely divine inspiration, Horace believes that good poems come from both art and nature and that they should unite instructive and pleasing content.

Horace's *Ars Poetica* is one of the first and most important poems about poetry, but it is certainly not the last. He helped to inspire a whole range of poets who talk about what good poetry should be by demonstrating it through their poem. Famous examples of this genre include Alexander Pope's *An Essay on Criticism* (1711), Marianne Moore's "Poetry" (1924), and Archibald MacLeish's "Ars Poetica" (1926).

Quintilian's Figures of Speech

Quintilian (35–100 CE) was Rome's first professor of rhetoric, and his major work *Institutio Oratoria* or *The Orator's Education* (95 CE) is a guide for aspiring orators. Everything an aspiring Roman politician would need to know about rhetoric can be found here, from guides to spelling and grammar to recommendations for great orators of the time. Literary theorists are most interested in the portions of this long book that discuss good diction and style and define and analyze figures of speech. Quintilian is not the first or the last writer to name and discuss rhetorical figures or figures of speech, but his discussion is a good example of the type of language that can be found in a classical work of rhetoric. (Other noted works on the topic include the many writings of the Roman statesman and philosopher Cicero [106–43 BCE].)

---

1   Horace, "The Art of Poetry, a Prose Translation," trans. James Hynd, *The Art of Poetry*, ed. Burton Raffel (Albany: SUNY P, 1974), 43.

Quintilian discusses figures of speech, or tropes, as devices whereby artists or orators use a word in an unusual way to embellish their speech. Here are a few of the figures he discusses, many of which are central to the study of poetics and rhetoric to this day:

+ **Simile and metaphor.** A simile compares two things using *like* or *as*, whereas a metaphor leaves out the comparison word. Quintilian uses the example of "he is like a lion" as a simile and "he is a lion" as a metaphor. The metaphor is more powerful because it is more direct, and Quintilian further praises metaphors that produce surprising connections or that bring action to life. Poets use metaphors all the time, but so too do politicians – from the "ship of state" to political "gridlock." Quintilian and other rhetoricians make it easier to identify when figures of speech are being used to persuade.

+ **Synecdoche and metonymy.** These figures involve substitution, as do metaphor and simile, but in a more specific way. A synecdoche substitutes a part of something for the whole, as when workers are called *hands* or a ship a *sail*. Hands are just one part of a worker, and a sail just one part of a ship, but synecdoches that substitute a part can highlight particular aspects of the whole (the part of the body that performs the work, the part of the ship that creates motion). A metonymy substitutes something associated with the thing for its name, such as saying *crown* instead of king or *the White House* instead of the president. Often metonymies and synecdoches can harden into clichés, as in the above examples, but writers can also use them to create new and surprising connections.

+ **Irony.** Irony in its most basic sense is when a speaker says one thing but means the opposite, as when speakers praise someone they dislike as "excellent" or say something is "fun" when it isn't (like waiting in line at the post office or having dental work done). Irony depends a lot on contextual clues such as tone of voice or an understanding of the underlying beliefs of the speaker. Quintilian also speaks about a whole life being colored with irony, as in the case of Socrates, because he was so wise but took on the role of a man who knew nothing.

Quintilian names many more figures of speech in his treatise, including *hyperbaton* (switching around the expected order of words), *catachresis* (applying a word in an unusual or unexpected context), and *metalepsis* (a far-fetched association). He stresses that these figures can add to oratory "when deployed at the right moment," but that they "are utterly inept when they are too much sought after."[1] So if you're looking to impress your friends and teachers with some vocabulary words, try some figures from Quintilian, but don't overdo it.

Longinus's Sublime Aesthetics

Scholars know very little about one of the most important names in ancient literary theory: Longinus, author of the treatise *On the Sublime*. He is known only for this one work, and critics aren't certain exactly when he lived or even if Longinus was really his name. All we know is that he wrote in Greek, came from the Hellenistic world (the part of the ancient Middle East that Alexander the Great conquered), and wrote in the first century or so. There is another Longinus who wrote in the third century, and who is not the author of *On the Sublime*, so sometimes you see the author of *On the Sublime* listed as "Longinus" in quotation marks or as Pseudo-Longinus. In order to keep things from being needlessly complicated, I'm just going to call him Longinus.

While the works of Plato, Aristotle, and Horace influenced writers throughout the Middle Ages and Renaissance, Longinus's treatise fell out of circulation for a long time after it was written, reappearing only in the seventeenth and eighteenth centuries. When it did come back, it came back strong, changing the shape of aesthetics by promoting Longinus's concept of the SUBLIME (which I discuss again in Chapter 4).

So what, exactly, is the sublime? Longinus explores this question over the course of his work, but he never defines it simply and straightforwardly, in part because it is a complicated notion. The closest he comes is early on in the treatise, when he calls it "a consummate excellence and distinction of language."[2] But sublimity isn't just any old excellence; a work that is sublime produces a feeling of wonder, astonishment, and ecstasy in the listener or reader. Longinus compares the beauty of the sublime to a wild and untamed horse, a destructive whirlwind, and a kind of madness, using powerfully sublime metaphors in order to illustrate the phenomenon he's talking about. According to him, the greatest works of literature produce almost a loss of control, because a listener gets so carried away by their beauty and sublimity.

Longinus lists five sources of the sublime in literature:

---

1   Quintilian, *The Orator's Education Books 9–10*, trans. Donald A. Russell (Cambridge, MA: Harvard UP, 2001), 161.
2   Longinus, *On the Sublime*, trans. W.H. Fyfe (Cambridge, MA: Harvard UP, 1995), 163.

1. **Grand conceptions**. A sublime work of art must be about an important subject, containing serious and weighty thoughts. Sublime works of literature explore themes of passion, conflict, and suffering rather than the mundane stuff of ordinary life.

2. **Vehement emotion**. Sublime works also engage the reader's or listener's emotions. Longinus quotes a passage from the Greek poet Sappho that illustrates the madness of being in love as an example of how sublime literature engages the emotions. A poem merely expressing pleasure in another person's friendship or appearance isn't sublime until it brings in strong, turbulent emotions.

3. **Well-chosen figures of speech**. Like Aristotle, Longinus believes that form and content must go together. It's not enough to have important thoughts or to tug on a reader's emotions if this is done in clichés. Thoughts and emotions must be expressed well in order to achieve true sublimity.

4. **Good diction**. By this, Longinus means well-chosen words and metaphors, going along with his third component. Writers need to think carefully and select exactly the right word to express their meaning. Here he doesn't mean choosing only long and obscure words, but rather the best words to suit the writer's purpose.

5. **Elevated word arrangement**. A sublime work will sound sublime in the way the words are arranged, in the style of the author. Longinus doesn't advocate overly elaborate word arrangements, however. He says the best art will look like nature, meaning that you get lost in the artist's work and don't even notice the effort and craft that went into it. Similarly, he says that nature is best when it has "concealed art" within it – a winding path through the forest that is manmade but feels natural might be an example of this.

In another important section of *On the Sublime*, Longinus discusses genius versus mediocrity. He argues that it is better to be great at some things even if your writing has some faults than to be good overall but without any touches of genius. A true genius makes mistakes. He also singles out Plato's writing for its sublimity, saying that Plato "had striven, with heart and soul, to contest the prize with Homer."[1] Given Plato's disparagement of poetry and of Homer

---

1   Longinus, *On the Sublime*, 213.

in particular in *The Republic*, I am not sure if he would have taken Longinus's description of him as an aspiring poet as a compliment.

The contrast between Horace and Longinus illustrates the variety of opinions expressed within ancient literary criticism. Both writers are concerned with giving advice to writers on how to achieve excellence, analyzing what makes writing good in the style of a practitioner's manual rather than a historian. Their recommendations, though, are quite different: Horace emphasizes correctness and consistency while Longinus pushes writers to be bolder, perhaps at the expense of correctness. Taken together, the literary theorists of the ancient world set the tone and direction for future literary criticism. Because the study of the classics was the main form of literary education throughout the Middle Ages and Renaissance and all the way to the end of the nineteenth century, classical ideas about literature predominate in the history of criticism for a couple of millennia at least.

Suggestions for Further Reading

Kennedy, George Alexander, ed. *The Cambridge History of Literary Criticism: Volume 1: Classical Criticism.* Cambridge: Cambridge UP, 1990.

Murray, Penelope, and T. Dorsch. *Classical Literary Criticism.* New York: Penguin, 2004.

Preminger, Alex, O.B. Hardison, Jr., and Kevin Kerrane. *Classical and Medieval Literary Criticism: Translations and Interpretations.* New York: F. Ungar, 1974.

Russell, D.A., and M. Winterbottom. *Ancient Literary Criticism: The Principal Texts in New Translations.* Oxford: Clarendon P, 1972.

Three: The Middle Ages and the Renaissance

THIS CHAPTER SURVEYS DEVELOPMENTS in literary theory and criticism from the fall of the Roman Empire in the fifth century through the end of the seventeenth century. Often surveys of literary theory and criticism skip over this period altogether, especially the medieval era (the years between approximately 500 and 1400), since the history of theory and criticism in this period can seem less eventful than in later periods such as the Enlightenment and the nineteenth century (covered in Chapters 4 and 5). Still, some very important things happened during this long span of time: the writings of the ancient world received new attention in the Renaissance, theologians developed elaborate systems for interpreting the Bible, the printing press allowed for the publication of monumental works of literature and the more rapid transmission of knowledge, European voyages of discovery began, and Martin Luther and other Protestant reformers established new churches.

"The Dark Ages" is an outdated term for the period between the fall of the Roman Empire and the rebirth of classical learning in the Renaissance. Italian poet Petrarch (1304–74) first used the term as a way to contrast the "light" of his era with the "darkness" of the centuries that preceded him. Today scholars no longer consider the Middle Ages a period of darkness, but instead argue for the importance of these centuries in terms of the establishment of European monarchies, the growth of cities, and the creation of scholarly and religious works. After a weakened Roman Empire fell to the forces of invading Germanic tribes in the fifth century, the various areas formerly under the control of the Empire established their own forms of government. Early medieval Europe was an interesting hodge-podge of different monarchies and systems of government:

+ After the Romans left Great Britain, Germanic groups, such as the Angles, the Saxons, and the Jutes, invaded England, pushing the native

Britons to the west and north. Anglo-Saxon England was a collection of small kingdoms (the heptarchy) until united in the tenth century. In 1066 William of Normandy invaded from France and thereafter became known as William the Conqueror, establishing a Norman French ruling elite, who eventually blended with the Anglo-Saxons. (The modern English language is a fusion of Anglo-Saxon and French, with some Viking and Latin words thrown in.) The Normans also assumed an uneasy control of Ireland in the following century.

* In the Middle East, the Prophet Muhammad established the Islamic religion in the Arabian Peninsula in the seventh century. He and his followers established Islamic *caliphates* (the term for an Islamic state led by a *caliph* or successor to Muhammad) that quickly gained control of large portions of the Middle East, Central Asia, and North Africa.

* In Spain, the Germanic tribes who assumed control of the region after the fall of the Romans were themselves in turn conquered by Islamic invaders from North Africa in the eighth century. Muslims controlled portions of Spain and Portugal for centuries to follow, until the fifteenth century. In southern Spain in particular one can still see traces of Islamic influence in the architecture and language.

* In France, the Germanic Franks established a kingdom that lasted until their king, Charlemagne, became the Holy Roman Emperor in the year 800. The Holy Roman Empire covered an area that includes much of modern-day France, Germany, and Italy. During the Middle Ages the Pope, the head of the Catholic Church, also wielded significant political power. From the eleventh to the thirteenth centuries, various popes sent armies of Crusaders to do battle with Muslim armies for control of the Holy Lands in the Middle East.

* The Byzantine Empire, headquartered in Constantinople (now called Istanbul) was the eastern portion of the Roman Empire and continued to hold sway until the fifteenth century. The boundaries of the Byzantine Empire ebbed and flowed, covering modern-day Turkey and Greece and at times large areas of territory beyond that.

Medieval Europe consisted of an assortment of different cultures, monarchies, religions, and languages. This can make it a difficult period of time to study, especially because documents from those times can be hard to access and are written in archaic languages. The foreignness of the medieval past and its rich variety of cultures and religions have also made it a tempting source of material for fantasy writers. J.R.R. Tolkien's Middle Earth (in *The Lord of the Rings* trilogy, 1954–55) and George R.R. Martin's Westeros and Essos (in *A Song of Ice and Fire*, 1996-present, and its television adaptation *Game of Thrones*) both present fantastic versions of medieval Europe.

In this chapter, I outline major developments in the history of theory and criticism in the Middle Ages and Renaissance. First I look at the interpretive strategies developed for studying the Bible and later applied to more secular texts. Then I discuss key developments that mark the Renaissance as a distinct period of literary history, including the invention of printing and the Protestant Reformation. Finally, I summarize the works of a few key Renaissance literary theorists.

Religion and Biblical Interpretation

The Christian religion first started to spread across Europe and the Middle East during the latter days of the Roman Empire, and by the fourth century the Roman emperor Constantine the Great had ceased persecuting Christians. It took a while for this new religion to become accepted, but eventually most of Europe became converted to Christianity from various pagan religions (non-Christian, polytheistic belief systems) by the end of the first millennium. As Christianity spread, it developed a whole range of institutions and rituals, the most important of which include the establishment of the pope as head of the Church in Rome and the development of religious orders (monks and nuns).

The pagan religions of pre-Christian Europe included Norse mythology in the Scandinavian countries and Druidism among the inhabitants of Britain. Because these cultures tended not to write a lot down, what we know of these early religions is fragmentary but intriguing. Scandinavia was one of the last places in Europe to adopt Christianity, so we know quite a bit about its gods (for example, Thor and Loki). Much less is known for certain about the pre-Christian beliefs of the Britons.

After the Church became established, much of the intellectual work in medieval Europe took place under the auspices of the Catholic Church and for religious purposes. Many medieval monasteries possessed massive libraries of manuscripts prior to the invention of print. The works of the ancient Greek and Roman writers that survived did so because they were kept alive and copied either by Christian monks or by the scholars of the Islamic world.

Medieval religious scholars helped to shape the practice of literary criticism through their development of methods and terminology for interpreting the Bible. The Bible was the most important book to European medieval thinkers, and the methods that theologians developed to interpret it helped reshape the history of literature by establishing a canon of texts and developing methods for interpreting biblical passages on multiple levels.

Establishing a Canon

In the early years of Christianity, one of the first tasks the Church had to undertake was to decide upon the contents of their new holy book, eventually known as the New Testament of the Bible. One important thinker who helped in this debate was St. Augustine of Hippo (354–430), a North African bishop. At this time, the writings that depicted Jesus's life and the lives of his followers consisted of a variety of fragmentary manuscripts written in multiple languages. Early theologians were faced with the task of trying to determine which of these texts was really the word of God and which weren't. One of the problems they encountered was the question of how to interpret texts that were cryptic, nonliteral, or contradictory.

The term for the list of books that the Church eventually recognized as the genuine word of God or the official Bible is *canon*. The books that were labeled non-authentic or not part of the official scripture are referred to as *apocryphal*. Much later, the word *canon* was applied to non-religious texts to mean a set of books accepted as important or as classics, the kind of things that make it into anthologies and course syllabi. Today you're much more likely to hear someone speak of a canonical text as meaning an established classic (such as Emily Dickinson's poems or Herman Melville's fiction) than as referring to controversies over establishing the biblical canon. However, the newer, secular sense of a literary canon still carries traces of the original religious sense. We venerate canonical texts, hold them in high regard, and scrutinize them closely.

In works such as *On Christian Doctrine* (397 CE), Augustine helped develop a theory of signs, which in turn aided in the process of establishing a biblical canon and interpreting those contradictory or cryptic passages. He classified some signs as natural, such as smoke being a sign of fire or an animal track as a sign of an animal, and others as conventional, meaning that they are agreed-upon conventions, such as the human names for things. Smoke will signify fire or a bear track danger to anyone regardless of what language they speak, while the word *fire* is a sign of the concept of fire only to those who understand English (or *fuego* for Spanish speakers, *Feuer* for German speakers, *ignis* for Latin speakers, and so on).

Later thinkers about language such as Ferdinand de Saussure (see Chapter 6) extended Augustine's idea of conventional signs much further to argue for the arbitrary nature of language. Not only are signs human names for things and not universal but rather merely agreed-upon conventions; there is also no necessary connection between a thing and the name humans give it. Augustine addresses the question of why humans all give different names to things using the biblical story of the Tower of Babel. In this story from the book of Genesis, the people of the world were trying to build a tower that could reach Heaven, and God punished them by making them all speak different languages so they could no longer conspire together. Thus the variety of languages spoken in the world originates as a punishment from God.

In another important passage, Augustine discusses how to make sense of scriptures that contradict each other or don't seem to follow God's teachings. In this case, he says, those passages should not be taken literally but instead should be interpreted metaphorically. He provides a general guideline: "Anything in the divine discourse that cannot be related either to good morals or to the true faith should be taken as figurative."[1] This raises a further set of issues, for how do we learn about the moral lessons or principles of faith except through reading scripture? How do we sort out the literal from the metaphorical? How are people supposed to know the passages that shouldn't be read literally if all they have is the Bible as their source? This type of circular proposition opened a space for specialists in biblical interpretation. These later theologians would build upon Augustine's foundation while refining his method. Later medieval scholars pored over the Bible, trying to unlock hidden and esoteric meanings available only to those initiated into the mysteries of biblical interpretation.

Medieval Scholasticism

Augustine wrote at a time when Christianity was just beginning to gain ground. Several hundred years later, Christianity had become firmly established throughout Europe, great cathedrals and monasteries dotted the landscape, and the Christian canon had been settled. In the eleventh and twelfth centuries, a new intellectual movement called **SCHOLASTICISM** developed in monasteries and universities. Scholasticism was a Christian intellectual movement that used rigorous philosophical methods to study the Bible, theological issues, and other matters.

---

1   Augustine, *De Doctrina Christiana*, trans. R.P.H. Green (Oxford: Clarendon P, 1995), 147.

The scholastics were associated with the earliest universities, such as those at Paris, Oxford, and Cambridge, all established in the eleventh to thirteenth centuries. If you've ever had a chance to visit one of these institutions, you will know that many of their buildings date back to the Middle Ages and are beautifully ornate, with Gothic arches, gargoyles, great oaken dining halls, and other features.

Medieval university students did not have quite the same choice of majors as students do today. In fact, they didn't have any choice at all in what they studied. The medieval curriculum consisted of the seven liberal arts, divided into the three-subject trivium (logic, rhetoric, and grammar) and the four-subject quadrivium (geometry, astronomy, music, and mathematics). The trivium was the more important of the two, and consisted of training in reading, writing, and philosophy, while the quadrivium dealt with more scientific matters.

St. Thomas Aquinas (1225–74), the most famous of the scholastic philosophers, was an Italian priest and the author of over 50 works of philosophy and theology. He modeled his method on Aristotle (see Chapter 2), taking his lead from Islamic scholars' Aristotelian studies, and applied Aristotelian ideas to Christian subject matter. Just as Aristotle liked to classify his objects of study in a very scientific manner, so too did Aquinas and other Scholastics. The Scholastics are also sometimes called the Schoolmen and are in many ways the forerunners of modern academics.

The Four Levels of Interpretation

The most relevant part of Aquinas's voluminous works in terms of literary criticism is his model of a fourfold method of interpretation, which he outlines in a portion of his 22-volume *Summa Theologica* (1265–74). Aquinas builds upon the earlier ideas of Augustine about hidden meanings in the Bible, turning biblical interpretation into a much more rigorous and scientific affair.

One of the issues that Aquinas and other medieval theologians had to grapple with was the relationship between the Old and the New Testaments. Christianity grew out of Judaism, and the early Christians chose to retain the Hebrew Bible for their new faith, renaming it the *Old* Testament while adding a *New*. In many places the Old and New Testaments contradict each other: for example, where the Old Testament advocates "an eye for an eye" (calling for direct retaliation for wrongs done to you), the New Testament instructs one to "turn the other cheek" (advocating forgiveness and discouraging retaliation).

One way to reconcile these types of apparent contradiction is through a practice known as **TYPOLOGY**, where an Old Testament story can be read as an allegory for a New Testament one. That is, because Christians believe that the

New Testament and Christ's teachings supplant the old Jewish laws, they read the older books of the Hebrew Bible as containing hidden Christian messages and allegories. Ultimately, Aquinas and other theologians developed a four-level system of biblical interpretation. They believed that the Bible is polysemous, that is, it has more than one meaning at the same time. Any passage in the Bible can be read on more than one level, and many can be read on four. The four levels of interpretation Aquinas outlines are the following:

1. **Literal or historical**. At the most basic level, Aquinas believes that the Bible tells a literal story, meaning that the people described really lived and the events narrated really took place. When the book of Genesis says that Noah built an ark and placed two of every animal upon it, this is recounting a historical event that really happened. In a sense, the literal level is the most important because it comes first and all other senses grow out of it. Even as theologians developed elaborate systems of allegorical interpretation, these were always grounded in a literal reading of scripture.

2. **Allegorical or typological**. Moving beyond the literal, a biblical story can be interpreted on a second and deeper level as having a one-to-one correspondence with a hidden, symbolic dimension. For Aquinas, this means typological readings of Old Testament stories, which he interprets as corresponding to something in the New Testament. Thus a story such as that of Noah's ark might be literally true, but it also allegorically corresponds to a New Testament story at the same time (here, perhaps, Noah's saving of the animals prefigures Jesus's saving of humanity through his death and resurrection, so that Noah is both a real historical figure and a typological figuring of Jesus).

3. **Tropological or moral**. This level has to do with the moral lessons to be learned from a story: a message about how best to live one's life, honor the Ten Commandments, or in other ways live out Jesus's teachings here on Earth. Moral lessons are sometimes stated directly in the Bible, but at other times they have to be uncovered through learned interpretation. Theologians believe in the unity of the Bible as emanating from God and containing important lessons for us, so even passages that don't seem to contain a moral could be revealed to have one upon close scrutiny (by a trained professional, of course – until the Protestant Reformation, Christians weren't supposed to read and interpret the Bible for themselves; see below).

4. **Anagogical or spiritual**. The anagogical is the trickiest and most hidden level, because it deals with mystical or spiritual matters. Aquinas defines this sense as relating to "eternal glory," or matters of heaven and the after-life. So while the moral sense of a biblical story relates to what you need to do to get to heaven, the spiritual sense explores what happens once you're there.

Not all four of these levels can be found in every passage from the Bible, but all passages have at least a literal sense and one or more other senses in which they can be read. Keep in mind that when medieval theologians argued about the correct interpretation of the Bible or claimed that it is a polysemous text containing multiple meanings, they absolutely did not mean that everyone should interpret the Bible for themselves in whatever manner they saw fit. Only priests and monks could perform these interpretive tasks after training in biblical exegesis or interpretation. However, the development of biblical criticism did pave the way for people to begin wanting to read scripture and interpret it for themselves rather than leaving it to priests and monks, thus preparing the ground for the Protestant Reformation (discussed below).

Italian humanist Dante Alighieri's "Letter to Can Grande" (1317) provides a good example of how to apply Aquinas's four-level interpretive scheme. Can Grande was Dante's patron, and in this famous letter Dante (1265–1321) discusses how to interpret his *Divine Comedy* (discussed below). Dante chooses as his example this biblical passage: "When Israel went out of Egypt, the house of Jacob from a barbarous people, Judea was made his sanctuary, Israel his dominion."[1] On a literal level, he says, this passage is about the Israelites leaving Egypt. It recounts a real event in the history of the Jewish people. On a typological level, Dante interprets this passage allegorically to refer to Christians being saved through Christ (he doesn't go into detail in the letter, but presumably Moses would stand typologically for Christ and the Israelites for those that Christ/Moses saves). The moral sense of the passage, Dante says, has to do with a soul going from a state of imprisonment through sin to freedom. So the journey of the Israelites can be read as an allegory for the journey that every human soul must take from being imprisoned in sin to being freed through Christ. This sounds similar to the typological level, but with the difference that the moral sense has to do with the state of an individual's soul and the typological with humanity in a broader sense. Finally, at the spiritual level the story signifies to Dante the soul going from the imprisonment of this world to the

---

1   Dante Alighieri, "The Letter to Can Grande," *Literary Criticism of Dante Alighieri*, trans. Robert S. Haller (Lincoln: U of Nebraska P, 1973), 99.

freedom of heaven. As with the moral level, on the spiritual level the Israelites symbolize a human soul, but here the journey takes on a different significance related to the afterlife rather than life on earth.

As can ideally be seen in such a brief illustration, the four levels are all interrelated. All have to do with freedom from imprisonment, and the three non-literal levels all have to do with Jesus saving humanity. Each sense reinforces the others, so that all four levels taken together make up a very rich and resonant passage rather than contradicting each other.

Maimonides and the Jewish Tradition

While Christian theologians were developing methods for interpreting the Christian Bible, Moses Maimonides (1135–1204) and others were doing the same thing for the Hebrew Bible. Maimonides was a rabbi born in Spain while it was under Islamic control. For a time, Muslims, Jews, and Christians peacefully (and often not so peacefully) coexisted in medieval Spain, and as a product of that multicultural atmosphere Maimonides was exposed to a variety of linguistic, religious, and philosophical traditions.

Maimonides published many works on philosophy, medicine, and biblical interpretation, the most famous of which is called *Guide of the Perplexed* (1190). He states that the purpose of his treatise is to explain obscure portions of the Bible to those who are perplexed, but that he expects his readers will already have a background in philosophy and theology. Thus his guide doesn't teach the fundamentals of Judaism but focuses on the deeper interpretive questions raised by reading scripture.

Maimonides stresses that the hidden meanings behind biblical parables are not meant to be accessible to all. He compares the flashes of insight achieved through interpretation to lightning flashes: "You should not think that these great *secrets* are fully and completely known to anyone among us. They are not. But sometimes truth flashes out to us so that we think that it is day, and then matter and habit in their various forms conceal it so that we find ourselves again in an obscure night, almost as we were at first."[1] Maimonides' interpretive method reads scriptural passages allegorically, using Aristotle's philosophy. If this sounds like Aquinas, it's because Maimonides provided Aquinas with a model for how to apply Greek philosophy to religious studies. Maimonides is not as frequently recognized as part of the critical tradition as are Aquinas and

---

1   Moses Maimonides, *The Guide of the Perplexed*, trans. Shlomo Pines (Chicago: U of Chicago P, 1963), 7.

Augustine, but scholars recently have begun rectifying that by paying closer attention to his influence.

Although he was born in Spain and was of Jewish descent, Maimonides wrote neither in Spanish nor Hebrew but in Arabic. At this time, scholars from the Arabic-speaking world far outpaced Christian writers (who, like Aquinas, wrote in Latin) in terms of their knowledge of ancient Greek philosophy. The Spanish Islamic philosopher Averroes (1126–98), for example, wrote commentaries on Aristotle and Plato in the twelfth century that helped to bring these philosophers to the attention of scholars writing in Latin.

The Secularization of Interpretation

Medieval Europe was extremely religious, which is why this chapter has focused on religion up to this point. However, as we move into the fourteenth century, Europe saw the beginnings of what would come to be called the Renaissance, a period when religion ceased to be the be-all and end-all of learning, art, and literature, and when secular (non-religious) subject matter became more important for all forms of art and inquiry. There is no universally accepted date when the Middle Ages ended and the Renaissance began, and in fact the cultural movement associated with the Renaissance happened at different times in different parts of Europe. One of the most significant aspects of this process of secularization as it relates to literary criticism came when people took the interpretive methods developed for studying the Bible and began to use them both to interpret texts other than the Bible and as the basis for constructing original and often secular works of literature.

The undisputed master of medieval literature is Dante, who lived in Italy in the late thirteenth and early fourteenth centuries. His great work, *The Divine Comedy* (1308–21), describes in beautiful Italian verse a journey in three parts from hell (*Inferno*) to purgatory (*Purgatorio*) to heaven (*Paradiso*). As we have seen, Dante admired Aquinas's four-level model of interpretation. In his letter to Can Grande (mentioned above), after discussing the four levels of interpretation in relation to the Bible, Dante goes on to state that his *Divine Comedy* is likewise polysemous, meaning that it has several senses. This doesn't seem such a radical notion today, but remember that he is adopting this idea of polysemy from theology, so he is basically comparing his writings to the word of God.

In the letter, he then applies each of Aquinas's four levels to his own work. This is fitting, since a work as complex as the *Divine Comedy* is meant to be read on more than one level. In the *Inferno*, for example, Dante describes his journey to the underworld, guided by the Roman poet Virgil. They descend further and further into the depths of hell, seeing its organization into different circles for the torment of different types of sinners. On the literal level the plot unfolds, describing the many circles of hell. Within different episodes Dante includes coded references to political figures of his time, which represents the second, allegorical level. At the third, moral level, the stories of sinners receiving their punishment in hell clearly contain moral lessons about how to behave on Earth in order to avoid eternal damnation. His famous story of Paolo and Francesca, for example, warns against the dangers of lust, since these adulterous lovers end up in hell as a result of their actions. (They're on one of the higher levels of hell, though, so they are clearly not as evil as those punished for greed or treachery.) The scope of the work as a whole depicting a soul's journey from earth to heaven clearly points to the work's spiritual meaning, the fourth level of interpretation. All four levels are present at once, but a reader doesn't need to read each passage for each of these four levels.

Many other works of medieval literature employ **ALLEGORY** and symbolism, so much so that allegory becomes one of the defining characteristics of medieval literature. Medieval romances, such as the anonymous *Sir Gawain and the Green Knight* (late fourteenth century) and Guillaume de Lorris and Jean de Meun's *Roman de la Rose* (1275), overtly signal their symbolic and allegorical dimensions. The "rose" of the romance is a central symbol, while a gigantic green knight – who gets beheaded and then picks up his head – riding a green horse can easily be interpreted symbolically.

While the four-level interpretive method can help make sense of medieval writers like Dante, you can also adapt it to interpret more modern works that employ allegory or symbolism. The basic idea that writers construct literary texts to contain more than one level of meaning or that these texts are open to multiple interpretations is a cornerstone of modern literary criticism. Any good work of literature should be able to be read for its basic story, for larger symbolic or thematic significance, for moral or ethical lessons, and for larger philosophical or spiritual questions. One thing to remember, though, is that the literal dimension of the story always comes first and can't be neglected. If a story doesn't function on the literal level and must be interpreted symbolically to be understood, what you have is less a work of literature than a code or a puzzle.

Boccaccio's Mythological Studies

While Dante's *Divine Comedy* is obviously a deeply religious work, dealing with matters of heaven and hell, a slightly later Italian writer, Giovanni Boccaccio

(1313–75), went in a more strictly secular direction in his writing. Boccaccio's most famous work is the *Decameron* (1353), a long prose work that consists of a collection of entertaining short stories (many of them extremely risqué) framed by a story about a group of men and women who go to a country house to escape an outbreak of the plague and tell each other stories to pass the time. The ten exiles, seven men and three women, each tell a story a day for 10 days, so that the collection consists of 100 stories altogether.

Boccaccio wrote many other works, including romances, a biography of Dante, and a critical work, *Genealogy of the Pagan Gods* (1360). In the latter, he applies the allegorical method of interpretation (developed by Aquinas and extended to non-biblical subjects by Dante) to ancient Greek and Roman mythology. Using texts such as Ovid's *Metamorphoses* (8 CE), a collection of stories based on Greek myths of transformation, as his source material, Boccaccio delves beneath the surface to find hidden, often Christian, allegorical levels of significance. Here's an example of his method from early in the book:

> Perseus, the son of Jupiter, killed the Gorgon in the poetic fiction, and, victorious, he flies up into the air. When one reads this in the literal sense, it offers historical meaning. If one seeks a moral understanding from a reading, it reveals how the prudent conquer vice and accede to virtue. If we wish to treat it allegorically, it means that by spurning earthly delights the pious mind ascends to the heavens. In addition, an anagogical interpretation would say that the fable reconfigures the ascension of Christ to the Father after overcoming the ruler of the world.[1]

In his work he also includes a long discussion of poetry, defining its uses in a theoretical way that would influence later Renaissance writers on poetry such as Sir Philip Sidney (see below).

Boccaccio uses allegorical interpretation in order to promote the study of pagan myth for a Christian audience. Even though ancient writers were not Christians, he says, their works contain important moral and spiritual lessons to those trained in allegorical interpretation. By promoting the value of these pre-Christian works, Boccaccio helped to set the stage for the explosion of interest in classical antiquity associated with the Renaissance.

Another fascinating allegorical text from the Middle Ages is the Italian writer Christine de Pizan's *The Book of the City of Ladies* (1405). Written in French, this work depicts the main character, Christine, being visited by three

---

1   Giovanni Boccaccio, *Genealogy of the Pagan Gods*, vol. 1, trans. Jon Solomon (Cambridge, MA: Harvard UP, 2011), 51.

female figures: Lady Reason, Rectitude, and Justice. These allegorical figures instruct her in how male authors have slandered women in the past and show her examples of female excellence and virtue. She begins the work by wondering "how it happened that so many different men – and learned men among them – have been and are so inclined to express both in speaking and in their treatises and writings so many devilish and wicked thoughts about women and their behavior."[1] The bulk of the work then goes on to discuss notable women from history, the Bible, and myth in order to counter male writings on the wickedness of women. Coming centuries before an organized feminist movement, the work is now considered one of the earliest works of feminist criticism.

Humanism

Dante, Boccaccio, and de Pizan are forerunners of the transition from the Middle Ages to the Renaissance. The term Renaissance literally means rebirth, so called because the period is associated with the rediscovery of classical learning. In a broader sense, though, a number of interrelated factors help to differentiate the Renaissance from the Middle Ages: the humanist movement, the invention of printing, the Protestant Reformation, the "discovery" of the New World, and the development of all sorts of new genres of writing. The Renaissance took hold in different parts of Europe at different times, although Italy is generally considered to be its starting point, which makes sense since Rome was the center of the old classical world.

The term "Renaissance man" describes someone who excels in a variety of arenas, perhaps someone who is a star athlete, an inventor, and also writes children's books, if such a person existed. Leonardo da Vinci (1452–1519) is the most celebrated Renaissance man: he painted great masterpieces of art, studied anatomy, invented remarkable devices, and was a brilliant engineer. Da Vinci and other Renaissance men were **HUMANISTS**. Humanism was a movement to revive the study of ancient Greek and Roman classics that began in Italy in the fourteenth century and later spread throughout Europe to Germany, France, Britain, and elsewhere. You've already been introduced to two key humanist figures: Dante and Boccaccio. Other important humanists include the poet Francesco Petrarca or Petrarch, political theorist Niccolò Machiavelli (1469–1527), and classical scholar Desiderius Erasmus (1466–1536).

Humanists studied earthly rather than spiritual matters, marking an

---

1   Christine de Pizan, *The Book of the City of Ladies*, trans. Earl Jeffrey Richards (New York: Persea Books, 1998), 3–4.

important shift away from the religiosity of much medieval scholarship, art, and literature. Humanists also helped to set up academies across Europe devoted to the study of the ancient Greek and Latin classics. They didn't reject Christian beliefs and start worshiping Zeus and Athena and other Greek gods, however. Instead, they tried to take the best of the classical era and synthesize it with Christian ideas. In so doing the humanists paved the way for more radical critiques of religion, including **SKEPTICISM**, **DEISM**, and **ATHEISM** (see Chapter 4).

Humanist has two different but related meanings. In this section, I am discussing the historical phenomenon of humanism during the Renaissance, involving a rediscovery of classical learning and secularization of the arts. Today, when people refer to themselves as humanists, they don't usually mean that they are fourteenth-century Italians. Instead, today a humanist is someone who studies a field within the broad heading of the humanities, a group of academic disciplines devoted to the study of the human arts and culture: languages and literature, philosophy, art, history, and so forth.

The Printing Press

In China, technologies for printing had existed since at least the third century, but this technology never made it to the West. Instead, historians tend to credit the invention of printing in the Western world to a German, Johannes Gutenberg (c. 1398–1468), in 1450. His first major printed work was his famous Gutenberg Bible (copies of which are now priceless). This new technology of printing rapidly reshaped the Renaissance world. Before printing, the only way to make multiple copies of a text was by hand, a task that kept countless medieval monks occupied for centuries. Individual manuscripts tended to be held either in monasteries or in the private libraries of wealthy individuals, so very few people had access to the knowledge contained therein. In fact, only a very small portion of the population of medieval Europe could read or write.

Imagine the world of medieval peasants, if you will. They cannot read or write, and never have occasion to – no bookstores, no periodicals, not even a Bible at home. Recording technology doesn't exist, either, so all these peasants' information about the world has to come from direct interactions: listening to a priest deliver a sermon, talking to fellow laborers, or perhaps listening to an oral performance of a song or watching a puppet show or other type of performance. The world is incredibly small for peasants, who lack knowledge of other cultures and religions, or of anything beyond their own village. The technology of printing therefore changed the shape of the world by opening up new avenues of information, at first just for the elite but eventually even for the rural peasantry and urban workers.

The printing press enabled a variety of new types of publications:

+ **The Bible.** The fifteenth-century world was still deeply religious, and the printing press now allowed people to have their own copies of the Bible and to read it for themselves. This had profound effects on the history of religion, leading to the Protestant Reformation (see below).

+ **The classics.** Humanists championed the works of the Greek and Roman writers, and now these works could be reproduced either in their original languages or in translation into French, Italian, English, German, and other languages. These translated classics inspired a wave of imitations and adaptations of classical forms.

+ **Manuscript works.** Works of medieval literature that had previously existed only in manuscript could now be mass-produced and could reach a much wider audience. While manuscripts circulated in copies among only noble and learned circles, now anyone with a few shillings and the ability to read (though still a very small and elite group) could buy a copy of a book. Geoffrey Chaucer's great collection of stories *The Canterbury Tales* (late fourteenth century), for example, was one of the earliest books printed in England. Turning manuscripts into printed books led to new problems, though. Each manuscript of a work was unique because it was handwritten. In the case of Chaucer's work, he left it unfinished at his death, and individual manuscript copies arranged the various pilgrims' tales in different orders. Printers and editors had to determine which order, if any, was the one that Chaucer intended.

+ **School books.** Printing also made it much easier to create school texts for students (mostly boys at this time). Grammar books, editions of the classics, religious catechisms, and all kinds of other texts could be printed for the first time.

Education became much easier and more widespread with the invention of printing. Compared to later centuries, books were still luxury items, and literacy rates were still very low, especially among women and the lower classes. But the impact of the printing press cannot be overstated. The modern world would be unimaginable without the printed word.

Medieval manuscripts aren't merely paper copies of texts; they are often gorgeous works of art as well. Medieval scribes used parchment or sometimes vellum (animal skin), and embellished their texts with ornate illuminations

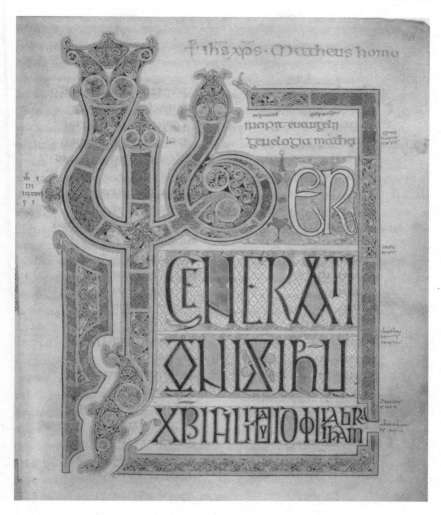

Figure 3: Page from the Book of Kells.

(illustrations), often using bright colors and even gold leaf. The Irish Book of Kells, a ninth-century Latin book of Gospels, is one of the most beautiful and famous examples of an illuminated manuscript (see Figure 3).

Gutenberg's printing press was a far cry from today's printing technology. His press used moveable type, metal sets of individual letters of the alphabet that a printer would compose into lines of text. The typeset text was then inked and pressed onto a sheet of paper. It was still very time-consuming, but easier than writing by hand, and with the advantage that multiple copies of a work could be produced with ease. William Caxton (c. 1415–c. 1492) set up England's first printing press in the late fifteenth century. Early printed books from Caxton and others can be quite difficult to read, because the blackletter typeface that they used looks a lot different from modern fonts (it looks like calligraphy and is most often seen today on beer labels and heavy metal album covers). Over the centuries, printing continued to expand, and the technology of printing became easier to use, more mechanized, and less expensive. The material used also changed. Early paper was made from old clothes and rags (you can sometimes see colored fibers if you look closely at the pages of early printed books), and it wasn't until the nineteenth century that wood pulp became the main ingredient in paper, which contributed to reducing book prices.

Protestantism

In Western Europe, the Catholic Church, centered in Rome, was the dominant religion throughout the Middle Ages (while the Orthodox Church reigned supreme in Eastern Europe, as did Islam in the Middle East). Splinter groups with names such as the Lollards and the Waldensians challenged the Church's authority in the twelfth to fourteenth centuries but did not succeed in establishing new, fully fledged religions in the years before the printing press.

The Protestant Reformation of the sixteenth century would not have been possible without the technology of printing, which helped to disseminate new ideas and make copies of the Bible available for people to read for themselves. In 1517, a German priest named Martin Luther (1483–1546) composed a world-changing document, in Latin, the *Disputatio pro declaratione virtutis indulgeniarum* (commonly known as the *Ninety-Five Theses*), protesting against the abuses of the Catholic Church. In it he questions the authority of the pope and encourages his followers to read scripture for themselves, stressing the importance of individual faith over doctrine handed down from authority figures.

Luther's ideas formed the basis of the new Protestant sect of Lutheranism. Other Protestant sects followed soon thereafter, including Calvinism (named after Protestant reformer John Calvin [1509–64]) and Presbyterianism (which became popular in Scotland). In England, King Henry VIII (1491–1547) famously broke with the pope in the sixteenth century and established the Church of England (also called Anglicanism or Episcopalianism) so that he could divorce his first wife, Catherine of Aragon, and marry Anne Boleyn.

The Protestant Reformation provided a catalyst for two centuries of religious wars in Europe, where Catholics and Protestants struggled for dominance. Knowing something about this backdrop of religious conflict can help you to understand Renaissance literature a little better. In a broader sense, the

Reformation extended the developments of the Renaissance that asked people to think for themselves, placing an even higher premium on reading and interpretation. Many of the best-selling early English books were Protestant texts such as the Anglican *Book of Common Prayer* (1549), *Foxe's Book of Martyrs* (1563), and John Bunyan's *The Pilgrim's Progress* (1678).

Voyages of exploration across the globe began in the fifteenth and sixteenth centuries, involving Spanish, Portuguese, French, Dutch, and English explorers voyaging to the Caribbean, the Americas, and elsewhere. The encounters with the indigenous peoples living in these places were brutal and bloody, as European explorers claimed these territories for their home countries through conquest and oppression. These encounters did help to expand the worldviews of some Europeans, however, by exposing them to cultures utterly unlike their own. Various important Renaissance works show the influence of these New World encounters, including Thomas More's *Utopia* (1516), Shakespeare's *The Tempest* (1610–11), and Michel de Montaigne's *Essays* (1580). Colonies in America also provided a haven for religious refugees. The Pilgrims who landed in America in the seventeenth century were seeking a place to practice their religion (a different, dissenting form of Protestantism) away from the authority of the Church of England.

The Growth of the Vernacular

Latin was the language of the Roman Empire. After the Empire fell, Latin continued to be the international language of the Catholic Church, politics, and learning. In fact, Latin is still the official language of Vatican City. Latin ceased to be a language of everyday speech, however, as the languages that people actually spoke in their day-to-day lives evolved. We call these languages vernaculars, from a Latin word meaning native or indigenous. Because Latin was still the language of learning, and a gentleman's education consisted of heavy doses of Latin study, writers continued to compose literary, philosophical, and scientific works in Latin into the seventeenth century. In the late Middle Ages, though, writers began defending the practice of composing works in their native tongues rather than in Latin.

The areas closest to Rome, the center of the empire, developed dialects of Latin that evolved into new languages. These Romance languages (so called because they developed from the Roman Empire, not because they're "romantic" in a Valentine's Day sense) include Italian, Spanish, French, Portuguese, and Romanian. In northern Europe, the Roman Empire was less firmly established and the languages spoken there were not as closely related to Latin but instead evolved from the languages of the tribal groups the Romans conquered.

These language families include Germanic (English, German, Dutch, the Scandinavian languages), Celtic (Irish, Welsh, Breton), and Slavic (Russian, Czech, Polish).

One of the first defenses of writing in vernacular languages rather than Latin came from Dante, in a work (ironically enough, composed in Latin) entitled *De Vulgari Eloquentia* or *On Eloquence in the Vernacular* (c. 1302). Dante composed his poetry in the Italian vernacular, so in this essay he defends this practice, arguing that vernacular languages can be as eloquent and expressive as Latin.

In the sixteenth century, Joachim du Bellay (c. 1522–60) wrote a similar defense of the French vernacular in his work *The Defense and Enrichment of the French Language* (1549). In this work, du Bellay worries that the French language does not have as rich a vocabulary as Greek and Latin, and that works written in French could be considered "barbarous." Rather than advocating for writing in Latin, though, he encourages French writers to translate and emulate classical authors and thus enrich French by adding new words to the language and creating new models for writing: "Let him who would enrich his language devote himself to the imitation of the best Greek and Latin authors and aim, as at a sure target, the point of his stylus at all their greatest strengths. For there is no doubt that the largest part of artfulness is encompassed in imitation."[1] While today we tend to think of works of art that too closely imitate a model as unoriginal or inferior, for the writers of the Renaissance imitation was considered a quality of good writing.

While du Bellay and Dante encourage learned writers to use vernacular languages like French and Italian in order to rival the ancient Greek and Roman greats, one area where vernacular composition was already thriving was oral folk poetry. French troubadours, English minstrels, and Irish bards all composed and performed poems and songs in vernacular languages in the Middle Ages. These works range from love songs to ghost stories to adventurous tales of heroes like Robin Hood to accounts of major battles and other historic events. Many of these oral compositions weren't collected and printed until much later, but they survived for centuries as forms of oral literature even after the invention of the printing press.

New Forms

In part because of historical factors such as the invention of printing and the renewed interest in classical literature, many new or revived genres flourished in

---

1   Joachim du Bellay, *The Regrets*, trans. Richard Helgerson (Philadelphia: U of Pennsylvania P, 2006), 338.

the Renaissance. Among some of the more notable are the following:

* **The tragedy.** The only plays performed in the Middle Ages in Europe were morality plays, religious plays often staged for holy days that either reenact biblical scenes or tell simple allegorical religious lessons. The most famous morality play, the anonymous *Everyman* (late fifteenth century), tells the story of a character named "Everyman" as he makes his last reckoning before death. The characters are all one-dimensional, and there's not much suspense or action, merely a lot of sermonizing. Morality plays were associated with the Catholic Church, so after the Reformation Protestant audiences in England and elsewhere needed to find a new form of entertainment. Writers looked back to Greek and (especially) Roman models for inspiration, and in the process created some of the greatest works of English literature, including plays by Shakespeare, Christopher Marlowe (c. 1564–93), and Ben Jonson (1572–1637).

* **The comedy.** Though we tend to think of tragedies first when we think of Renaissance drama, the writers of this time, including Shakespeare and Jonson, also produced classic comedies. The first English comedy, by Nicholas Udall, was *Ralph Roister Doister* (1553), a play that hasn't really stood the test of time.

* **The sonnet.** The sonnet form originated in Italy. Petrarch popularized it in the fourteenth century, and Thomas Wyatt (1503–42) and Henry Howard, Earl of Surrey (1517–47), imported it into English in the sixteenth century. The sonnet is a perfect embodiment of Renaissance literature: it's a very strict poetic form of fourteen lines, with rules regarding rhyme scheme and meter. Within those constraints, great poets showcased some of the best poetry the world has ever seen. Nearly all great Renaissance poets tried their hand at the sonnet form.

* **The epic.** Renaissance writers looked back to the ancient epics of Homer and Virgil for inspiration and adapted the form for their time. Among the major Renaissance epics are John Milton's *Paradise Lost* (1667), which retells the story of Adam and Eve, and Luís de Camões's Portuguese epic *Lusiads* (1572), about Vasco da Gama's voyages of exploration.

* **The essay.** One new Renaissance form that didn't derive from a classical model was the essay. The name comes from the French *essai*, which means "an attempt." Montaigne popularized the form in short prose pieces that

discussed a particular idea or train of thought. Later writers, such as Francis Bacon (1561–1626), emulated Montaigne and helped to establish this genre devoted to intellectual inquiry. These early essays were often freewheeling and exploratory, very unlike the structured essay form modern students must master in college.

These are just a few of the many new genres that flourished in the Renaissance. Others include pastoral poetry (which celebrates country life) and the prose novel (see Chapter 4).

New Rules for Writing

With all of these new genres, more people reading, and a new technology making writing more widely available than ever before, it's no surprise that literary criticism flourished in the Renaissance. A lot of Renaissance criticism looks back to classical models, especially Aristotle and Horace (see Chapter 2). This **NEOCLASSICAL** approach to literature influenced both the construction of new works and the direction of literary criticism.

One extreme version of neoclassicism can be found in seventeenth-century French writer Pierre Corneille's essay "Of the Three Unities of Action, Time, and Place" (1660), where he outlines the principles that he believes good dramas should follow:

1. **Unity of action**. This principle derives directly from Aristotle's *Poetics*, which states that a good play recounts a single plotline with a beginning, a middle, and an end. The neoclassical ideal was for unified storytelling; digressions and subplots were discouraged in favor of telling a single story on the stage.

2. **Unity of time**. This principle comes from Aristotle, too, though Aristotle doesn't place much emphasis on it. He merely says that plays tend to take place over a 24-hour period, describing the way that Greek tragedies were structured. Neoclassicists like Corneille made this a maxim, requiring that the action of a play should take place within a single 24-hour span.

3. **Unity of place**. Corneille admits that he can "find no rule concerning it in either Aristotle or Horace."[1] Nonetheless, neoclassical drama requires

---

1   Pierre Corneille, "Of the Three Unities of Action, Time, and Place," *The Continental Model: Selected French Critical Essays of the Seventeenth Century, in English Translation*, ed. Scott Elledge and Donald Schier (Minneapolis: U of Minnesota P, 1960), 128.

that plays take place in a single location. This doesn't mean they have to use the same set for the entire play, but that the action should take place in the same geographical vicinity (within greater Paris or London, for example).

The belief in the unities was at its height in the seventeenth century to such an extent that later writers reworked Shakespeare's plays to conform to the unities. The most famous example of this is John Dryden's *All for Love* (1678), a rewriting of Shakespeare's *Antony and Cleopatra* (1606). Shakespeare's play takes place over the span of many years, with several subplots, and different scenes set all over the ancient world. Dryden's rewrite concentrates on the final day of the lives of the hero and heroine, with the rest of Shakespeare's story either eliminated or recounted through exposition. Some people actually think Dryden's rewriting is superior to Shakespeare's because his simplification of the story makes the plot easier to follow and highlights the central tragic love story.

Another major work of Renaissance criticism is sixteenth-century poet Sir Philip Sidney's *A Defence of Poetry* (1579). Sidney (1554–86) was a nobleman, a dashing military hero, and the author of one of the great Renaissance sonnet sequences, *Astrophil and Stella* (c. 1580s). In his work of literary criticism, he defends poetry against such charges as the Platonic idea that poets are just liars and religious attacks on poetry as sinful or a waste of time. He draws heavily upon Aristotle's *Poetics* and other classical works to make his case for the usefulness of poetry. The text is a good example of the way in which Renaissance critics celebrated imaginative writing while drawing upon ancient authorities.

Many other Renaissance writers similarly promoted the value of poetry and of imaginative writing more generally. They also developed technical language for talking about English verse forms and meter, thus helping to establish thorough studies of the form of poetry. They adapted terms from classical rhetoric and the study of classical poetry for the purposes of studying vernacular English writing. As the emphasis turned from the divine to the secular in Renaissance writing, these types of defenses laid the foundations for secular literary criticism and for the serious study of literature, something Enlightenment writers would take even further, as discussed in the next chapter.

Suggestions for Further Reading

Alexander, Gavin, ed. *Sidney's "The Defence of Poesy" and Selected Renaissance Literary Criticism*. New York: Penguin, 2004.

Eisenstein, Elizabeth L. *The Printing Press as an Agent of Change: Communication and Cultural Transformations in Early-Modern Europe*. 2 vols. Cambridge: Cambridge UP, 1979.

Hardison, O.B., Jr. *Medieval Literary Criticism: Translations and Interpretations*. New York: F. Ungar, 1974.

Four: The Enlightenment

WHEN SCHOLARS REFER TO the Enlightenment, they usually mean a period of about 100 to 150 years, from the middle of the seventeenth century to the end of the eighteenth century. Like the periods before and after it, those of the Renaissance and Romanticism, the Enlightenment doesn't have universally agreed upon start and end dates. All three of these periods are actually better thought of as intellectual movements that emerge in one or more places (such as Italy for the Renaissance, France for the Enlightenment, and Germany for Romanticism) and then spread elsewhere. Scholars who want to refer to these intellectual movements in the more neutral language of time periods (in order to emphasize the years spanned rather than particular intellectual and artistic developments) use *early modern* instead of Renaissance, *the long eighteenth century* instead of the Enlightenment, and *Romantic era* instead of Romanticism.

During the Enlightenment, the world changed rapidly and dramatically – new colonies sprang up around the globe, populations migrated from the countryside to cities, education became more accessible, and experimental science was born. Because of all these changes, the writers and thinkers of this time thought of themselves as living in an enlightened age, where civilization was making continual progress toward knowledge, freedom, and prosperity. It's no coincidence that the word *optimism* was coined in the Enlightenment. In this chapter I highlight some of the major developments in literary theory and criticism during the Enlightenment. These developments range from new types of publications and new audiences for books, to groundbreaking philosophical movements such as skepticism and idealism, to the political revolutions in France and America that shaped the modern world. Many of the debates that are still important to literary theory and criticism originated in this revolutionary time.

Print Culture

Although many great writers produced novels, poetry, drama, and criticism during the Enlightenment, the period isn't dominated by a few towering figures along the lines of Dante for the Middle Ages or Shakespeare for the Renaissance. Instead, large numbers of individuals contributed to advancing knowledge in a variety of ways, from developing new scientific theories, to creating great works of history, to writing political treatises supporting women's rights or the abolition of the slave trade.

In the middle of the twentieth century, media theorist Marshall McLuhan (1911–80) popularized the term **PRINT CULTURE** to characterize the monumental shifts that took place after the introduction of the technology of printing. He modeled his study on an important book by Albert B. Lord called *The Singer of Tales* (1960), which examines Homer's epic poems as a product of an earlier oral culture before the invention of writing. Just as the shift from an oral to a written culture brought with it all kinds of new ways of viewing the world, so too did a shift from manuscript to print culture in the Renaissance and Enlightenment. McLuhan was ahead of his time in thinking about the waning of print and the advent of new media: "We are today as far into the electric age as the Elizabethans had advanced into the typographical and mechanical age."[1] Before the invention of the printing press, knowledge had to be transmitted through handwritten manuscripts. This manuscript culture coexisted alongside newer printed books throughout the Renaissance. By the late seventeenth and early eighteenth centuries, though, print had won out. New types of publications and new modes of inquiry are associated with print culture in this period.

Many of the major features of the Enlightenment built upon the upheavals of the Renaissance. As Table 2 summarizes, the developments of the Renaissance were extended in new ways, both good and bad, during the Enlightenment. The initial promise of religious liberty associated with Martin Luther and the Protestant Reformation led to lengthy and bloody conflicts between Catholics and Protestants on the European continent and, in Britain, between the Protestant Church of England and the Puritans who dissented from the established Church. Similarly, the original excitement of the discovery of new lands during the Renaissance led to the growth of colonies in the Americas and the expansion of the transatlantic slave trade to supply cheap labor to the colonies, at a tragic cost.

In terms of literary theory and criticism, the invention of printing technology

---

1   Marshall McLuhan, *The Gutenberg Galaxy: The Making of Typographic Man* (Toronto: U of Toronto P, 1962), 1.

enabled many new types of publication and the possibility of making a living as a writer. The move away from Latin as the universal language of scholarly and literary works to writing in vernacular languages such as French, Italian, and English in turn made the writing world less international through the development of specific national traditions of French literature, Italian literature, English literature, and so forth. In philosophy, the humanists' turn from a focus on church teaching and spiritual matters to a focus on the human concerns of this world was extended into a deeply radical skepticism that called into question every piece of established thinking and conventional wisdom, including the nature of reality itself.

Renaissance		Enlightenment
Invention of printing	➡	Growth of print culture
More people writing	➡	Writing becomes a profession
Protestant Reformation	➡	Religious conflicts
"Discovery" of New World	➡	Growth of colonies, slave trade
Vernacular literatures	➡	Development of national canons
Humanism	➡	Skepticism

Table 2: The Enlightenment as an Extension of the Renaissance

During the Enlightenment, both the number of readers and the number of publications dramatically increased. Although the printing press was a fifteenth-century innovation, books did not become widely available to a large array of readers until the end of the seventeenth century. More and more people learned to read during this time, including more women and working-class people. Reading became more than just the province of aristocrats and scholars; it became a way for all kinds of people to while away a spare hour or to learn about the world. Publishers catered to these new readers with a wide range of new types of reading material:

- **The novel**. The novel took on a more modern form and grew tremendously in popularity during the Enlightenment. Unlike the stories of kings and heroes in earlier fiction, these newer novels often focus on more ordinary individuals in realistic, modern settings. Novelists wanted to appeal to these new readers who were more middle-class or even working-class and more likely to be female. The novelists themselves were often women and working-class writers. Samuel Richardson's *Pamela; or, Virtue*

Rewarded (1740) is one of the most popular and influential novels of the Enlightenment and a good illustration of its features. Richardson (1689–1761) was a printer by trade and a dissenting Protestant. In this his first novel (written when he was 51 years old), he selects as his heroine an ordinary, working-class English girl, a 15-year-old servant for the "B" family. (Early novels often use this convention of blocking out family names, perhaps to create the illusion that they are referring to a real family whose name needs to be protected.) The story consists of a series of letters that Pamela writes to her parents, worrying about the unwanted advances of her master, Mr. B. It's filled with ordinary domestic detail and is very sympathetic toward the heroine, who, though of humble origins, appears as an equal to the upper-class Mr. B.

+ **Reference books**. To appeal to new readers in search of practical knowledge, reference works of all sorts grew in popularity, including dictionaries, encyclopedias, atlases, travel guides, textbooks, cookbooks, and how-to manuals. Booksellers set up shop in major cities to offer their wares. Another Enlightenment innovation, the circulating library, offered readers the opportunity to borrow books and periodicals (including novels) for a fee.

+ **Newspapers**. The first newspapers began to be published across Europe and the Americas in the seventeenth century. The earliest papers were usually only a single sheet or two containing the latest information about wars and other notable occurrences. Newspapers became bigger and more established in the eighteenth century. As more and more people gathered in cities rather than being scattered in the countryside, new markets sprang up for daily publications containing the latest information about war, commerce, foreign affairs, and even gossip. Eighteenth-century newspapers, like those of today, also included advertisements listing items for sale, announcements about events, and personal ads.

+ **Magazines**. Magazines were another new Enlightenment genre. Just like modern magazines, these publications targeted particular audiences. Among the more notable British periodicals of this time were the *Gentleman's Magazine* (begun in 1731), the *London Magazine* (1732), the *Lady's Magazine* (1770), and *Philosophical Transactions* (1665). This latter work was a more scholarly publication that printed scientific papers by members of the Royal Society of London, the first modern scientific society.

+ **Pamphlets on all topics**. Pamphlets – short, inexpensive publications that could be produced quickly – became a very popular form of communication in the Enlightenment. Pamphlet wars raged as writers debated the latest political and social issues, such as the American and French Revolutions, which provided endless fodder for pamphlet-writers.

+ **Editions of older works**. Just as Renaissance writers helped to rediscover the works of ancient writers such as Plato and Aristotle, Enlightenment writers looked back to the Middle Ages and Renaissance and attempted to establish a canon of the best works of earlier ages. During this time, William Shakespeare and John Milton came to be considered modern classics, analogous to earlier authors such as Sophocles and Homer. The canon as initially established has remained in place ever since, even as it has expanded to include newer and more diverse writers.

Copyright protection has expired for most books published before the twentieth century. That means that most works of the types described above are now available in free electronic editions. Websites such as Project Gutenberg, Google Books, and the Internet Archive feature downloadable editions of both classic works and lesser known pamphlets and reference works. Where once researchers had to travel to a good reference library to investigate the history of Enlightenment print culture, now all you need is a laptop and a wireless connection, or even just a smartphone, to get started.

As the reading public grew, publishing became a lucrative business. Printers, booksellers, and even authors could now make a living through the book trade. Prior to this time, writers had to court the favor of aristocratic patrons. Playwrights such as Shakespeare made money through ticket sales, but poets and other writers had to find a wealthy aristocratic patron to dedicate their work to in order to survive, or had to find other sources of income. This situation changed in the Enlightenment, as writing became a viable profession for those in need of an income. This led to all sorts of new people entering the republic of letters, hoping to make a living through their words. This also provoked much anxiety about the types of works these so-called "Grub Street hacks" – Grub Street was a working-class street in London where many professional writers lived – were producing. Satirists Jonathan Swift (1667–1745) and Alexander Pope (1688–1744), for example, worried about unqualified writers entering the republic of letters and flooding the market with inferior publications. They turned these anxieties into classic works of satire, including Swift's *The Battle of the Books* (1704), in which he imagines the ancient and modern books in St. James's Library coming to life and battling for supremacy, and

Pope's *The Dunciad* (1728), a mock-heroic poem satirizing the dunces of the modern London literary scene.

Despite Swift's and Pope's worries about the influence of commerce on writing (and they themselves certainly benefitted from the new market for publications), the new professional writing classes produced some important works. Without the Grub Street writers we wouldn't have the novels of Daniel Defoe (1660–1731), for one, or the voices of talented women writers like Eliza Haywood (c. 1693–1756). At a time when very few career paths were open to women, writing was one place where they could make a living and have a voice.

Addison and Steele and the Birth of Modern Reviewing

Joseph Addison (1672–1719) and Richard Steele (1672–1729), friends and collaborators, both wrote poetry and plays but are most famous for their periodicals the *Tatler* (begun in 1709) and the *Spectator* (1711). Like newspapers, these appeared daily, in large numbers, and at a very minimal cost. Unlike newspapers, however, they weren't always filled with "news." Instead, Addison and Steele wrote on everyday topics, such as etiquette, fashion, the custom of settling one's differences through duels, and the latest publications.

The titles of these periodicals refer to the imaginary figures behind them. Steele says he named the *Tatler* after the "fair sex," who were more interested in "tattle" about fashion and gossip than in serious news. Addison and Steele invented the character of "Mr. Spectator" for their next venture, a detached figure who considers himself to be rather "a Spectator of Mankind, than one of the species" and who thus sees himself as qualified to comment upon society rather than participate in it actively.[1] Thus Addison and Steele's papers were forerunners of modern magazines, with their interest in female readers, popular entertainment, and fashion, and their editorial detachment (rather than being closely associated with a single viewpoint or political position). Among the notable features of their work are the following:

+ Establishing a middle-class taste in all sorts of matters, but especially when it comes to pastimes and entertainment. They condemn the brutality of spectacles like bear baiting in favor of more respectable forms of entertainment such as musical performances and the theater.

---

1   Joseph Addison, *Spectator* 1, *The Commerce of Everyday Life: Selections from* The Tatler *and* The Spectator, ed. Erin Mackie (Boston: Bedford/St Martin's: 1998), 81.

+ Celebrating the pleasures of the imagination. In a series of papers, Addison discusses the imagination, exploring the principles of beauty and art in accessible language. This writing helped pave the way for later Romantic writers such as William Wordsworth and Samuel Taylor Coleridge, who celebrate the imagination.

+ Distinguishing between true and false wit. In another series, Addison discusses things he considers false wit: overly clever poetry that contains difficult puzzles for readers, puns, or complicated figures of speech. In its place, he celebrates clarity, sincerity, and simplicity, echoing classical writers such as Horace and Quintilian.

Addison and Steele shaped English taste and helped set standards for good and bad writing. In their wake, book reviews became increasingly important in informing readers of new works and recommending or critiquing them. Publications in Britain, such as the *Monthly Review* (begun in 1749), the *Critical Review* (1756), and the *Edinburgh Review* (1802), critiqued all the latest publications, from the most elevated works of history and philosophy to the lowly novel. Reviewers could be incredibly mean-spirited, too, destroying anything that didn't strike their fancy. What they lacked in manners, however, these reviewers made up for in terms of helping to sort the quality from the questionable works and to establish rules for various literary forms.

Johnson and His Dictionary

Samuel Johnson (1709–84) was one of the most important and prolific literary figures of the Enlightenment in England. Like Addison and Steele, he produced periodical essays on a variety of topics in his publications *The Idler* (1750–52) and *The Rambler* (1758–60). In these essays, Johnson notably discusses the morality of literary works, stressing that writers have a responsibility to make the world a better place rather than merely to entertain readers. In addition to these papers he also produced drama, fiction, poetry, a collection of biographies of major poets (*The Lives of the Poets*, 1779–81), an important edition of Shakespeare, and a travel narrative, to name just a few of his accomplishments. Even after his death, he continued to contribute to English literature; James Boswell (1740–95) celebrates his friend in *The Life of Samuel Johnson* (1791), which is often cited as the first modern literary biography.

Arguably Johnson's most important work is his *Dictionary of the English Language* (1755). Previous English dictionaries had merely collected difficult and obscure words, but Johnson undertook the much bigger task of defining *every* word in the English language. Critics speak about two different ways to approach the task of writing a dictionary: prescriptivism and descriptivism. A prescriptive approach prescribes particular rules for spelling, grammar, and usage, establishing a correct way to use the language; a descriptive approach simply describes the way speakers actually use a language, mistakes and all. In fact, most dictionaries (including Johnson's) try to balance these two approaches, taking into account the ways languages change over time as new words enter a language and older rules fall out of favor. For example, the distinction between *who* and *whom* originates in a time when English contained many more grammatical declensions than it now does. Those declensions derive from English's Germanic origins, but contemporary speakers don't always recognize how to use them because they no longer serve an important grammatical function in the language. In fifty years' time, linguists predict, this rule will be obsolete. A prescriptivist might try to insist upon the correct occasions when *whom* should be used, but if no one can keep track of the rule any longer, a descriptivist would argue that this rule no longer applies and thus is no longer a part of the living language.

Before Johnson's dictionary, no one had attempted to standardize English spelling. The same word could be spelled in multiple ways, often within the same work. One of Johnson's purposes in writing the dictionary was to "fix" the language so that it would remain more consistent. In France, *L'Académie française* (the French Academy), established in 1635, serves this function of overseeing the French language, but the English-speaking world does not have an equivalent institution. Johnson knew that he couldn't stop the language from evolving, but he did slow that process down and created more consistent spellings and definitions for words. Alongside his clear definitions of ordinary words, Johnson famously sprinkled in some more whimsical entries:

- Lexicographer: "A writer of dictionaries; a harmless drudge, that busies himself in tracing the original, and detailing the signification of words."

- Oats: "A grain, which in England is generally given to horses, but in Scotland supports the people."

- Pension: "An allowance made to anyone without an equivalent. In England it is generally understood to mean pay given to a state hireling for treason to his country."[1]

---

1   Samuel Johnson, *A Dictionary of the English Language: An Anthology*, ed. David Crystal (New York: Penguin, 2006), 348, 403, 428–29.

A little later, in 1806, Noah Webster would attempt to standardize American English by publishing a specifically *American* dictionary of English. The differences between British and American spellings of common words such as *flavor/ flavour, tire/tyre,* or *center/centre* originate with Webster and his dictionary. His choice of a particular American spelling for certain words helped to set the course of American English as a dialect distinct from British English.

The French Encyclopedia

The hugely important Enlightenment project the *Encyclopédie* (*Encyclopedia*), was produced between 1751 and 1765 by some of the leading figures of the French Enlightenment, including Jean-Baptiste le Rond d'Alembert (1717–83) and Denis Diderot (1713–84). Just like modern encyclopedias, this work attempts to collect in one place all important knowledge, in alphabetical order. The word itself means *a circle of learning*.

The *Encyclopedia* was the quintessential Enlightenment project: utterly ambitious, aimed at the democratic spread of knowledge, politically radical, and, as the name suggests, entirely encyclopedic. It provided a model for all future encyclopedias, from the *Encyclopedia Britannica* to Wikipedia. By bringing all aspects of knowledge together in one place and attempting to debunk "superstitions," the *Encyclopedia* also became a source of inspiration for the French Revolution.

D'Alembert describes the project of the *Encyclopedia* as utterly empirical, materialist, and secular: "All our direct knowledge can be reduced to what we receive through our senses; whence it follows that we owe all our ideas to our sensations."[1] These Enlightenment thinkers believe that we learn about the world through observation rather than through Platonic preconceived concepts (see Chapter 2) or divine revelation. In this way, then, the *Encyclopedia* can be seen as an alternative to scripture – here's what you need to know about the world, they say. It's a collection of scientific and historical information available to all.

---

1   Jean-Baptiste le Rond d'Alembert, *Preliminary Discourse to the Encyclopedia of Diderot*, trans. Richard N. Schwab (Indianapolis: Bobbs-Merrill, 1963), 6.

Skepticism

Writers of the Enlightenment such as the French *encyclopédistes* continually question authority and orthodoxy about religion, government, social status, the role of women, the definition of beauty, and other matters. This type of philosophical **SKEPTICISM** leads to all sorts of revolutionary developments in the era, including political revolutions, the birth of feminism, the beginnings of the abolitionist movement, and groundbreaking scientific discoveries. In his essay "What Is Enlightenment?" (1784), philosopher Immanuel Kant (1724–1804) says that the motto of the Enlightenment is "Have courage to use your own reason!"[1] – and that is exactly what Enlightenment thinkers did: they thought for themselves, and in the process they changed the world.

Some of the most important issues for the history of literary theory and criticism arose out of Enlightenment skepticism. One of the defining characteristics of literary theory is not taking things at face value, but rather questioning the underlying assumptions of a work and digging beneath the surface. Literary theorists take inspiration from the skeptical attitude of the Enlightenment and have the courage to use their own reason.

The tradition of philosophical skepticism, like so much else, goes all the way back to the ancient Greeks. Socrates very famously declared, "All I know is that I know nothing." This type of skepticism about the certainty of knowledge came back into prominence during the Enlightenment. During a time when knowledge was advancing on every front, thinkers questioned assumptions and challenged orthodoxies. As both Socrates and the Enlightenment skeptics illustrate, it takes a very intelligent person to admit to knowing nothing.

Enlightenment thinkers questioned the authority of the Church and religious figures, sometimes even questioning the value of religion altogether. The Protestant Reformation of the Renaissance opened the doors for all sorts of new religious movements. In Europe, reformers Martin Luther and John Calvin established the Protestant sects Lutheranism and Calvinism. Similarly, as travel and exploration became more common, people were more likely to encounter religious ideas very different from their own. Western Europeans encountered Muslims in the Ottoman Empire and a range of wildly different belief systems in the Americas.

As their horizons broadened in the Enlightenment, some individuals began questioning the very value of religion. Voltaire (1694–1778) and David Hume

---

1   Immanuel Kant, "What Is Enlightenment?," *Foundations of the Metaphysics of Morals* and *What Is Enlightenment?*, trans. Lewis White Beck (New York: Macmillan, 1990), 83.

(1711–76) derided all religions as "superstition" and called attention to the violence that was taking place in the name of religion, such as the Catholic Church's Inquisition and the wars of religion that raged throughout this period. Voltaire, who attacks the Inquisition directly in his satirical novel *Candide* (1759), faced continual persecution and censorship for his writings. Indeed, it took a lot of courage to speak out against religion at this time: freedom of the press didn't yet exist, and writers could be censored or imprisoned for their opinions. Some of Hume's most controversial writings weren't published until after his death, while Jean-Jacques Rousseau (1712–78) went into exile for questioning religious authority.

While a few Enlightenment thinkers could be called ATHEISTS, meaning that they rejected the notion of any higher power, more of them are better described as DEISTS. One early deist text, for example, John Toland's *Christianity Not Mysterious* (1696), argues that everything within the Christian gospels can be explained through reason rather than faith. DEISM is a kind of middle ground between accepting Christian orthodoxy and fully embracing ATHEISM or skepticism. Deists believe that a higher power created the universe, and then left it alone. They don't believe in a higher power that takes an active role in interfering in the workings of the world. Deists place more faith in science and reason than in church teachings. Many of the American Founding Fathers held deist beliefs, at least to a certain extent.

Political Revolutions

As might be expected, the Enlightenment habit of questioning authority culminates in some major political revolutions. The two biggest revolutions of the Enlightenment were the American Revolution of 1776 and the French Revolution of 1789. In the case of America, revolution meant breaking free from the colonial rule of King George III of Great Britain and establishing a free American republic. In France, the people had to depose their king and queen, Louis XVI and Marie Antoinette, eventually beheading them during the Reign of Terror in 1793.

These political revolutions grew out of revolutionary philosophical writings, especially the ideas of Voltaire, John Locke, and Rousseau. In his writings on government, for example, Locke (1632–1704) argues that all people are born free, and that every man is entitled to life, liberty, and property (which the American founders altered to "life, liberty, and the pursuit of happiness"). Locke believes that the power of the government must come from the will of the people. Similarly, Rousseau begins his book *The Social Contract* (1762) by asserting that "man was born free, but is everywhere in bondage."[1] Rousseau believes that free individuals enter into a "social contract" for the greater good, and that governments that do not provide for the greater good of their people could be rightfully dissolved. These ideas were in sharp contrast to earlier notions of the divine right of kings, the belief that God had placed monarchs on their thrones to be God-like authorities on earth.

The details of the French Revolution in particular can get very complicated. France didn't become a democracy overnight in 1789, just as the American republic followed a slow path toward inclusion and opportunity. The French revolutionaries executed their King and established a rule of the people led by figures such as Maximilien de Robespierre (1758–94). Later the French made a military leader, Napoleon Bonaparte (1769–1821), their emperor. After Napoleon's defeat at the Battle of Waterloo, the French reestablished the monarchy, and then after another failed attempt at revolution made Napoleon's nephew emperor again, until finally arriving at a king- and emperor-free form of government at the end of the nineteenth century.

Abolitionism

As the colonial enterprise expanded during the Enlightenment, so did the slave trade. In order to justify the forcible enslavement of millions of Africans, theories of racial inferiority developed after the fact. Slave traders could argue that their cruel practices were justified if they believed Africans were "naturally" inferior and subordinate to Europeans. At the same time that these discourses about race were developing, they were simultaneously being called into question by Enlightenment thinkers who believed in the principle that "all men are created equal." Ironically, the author of that famous assertion of universal human rights in America's Declaration of Independence, Thomas Jefferson (1743–1826), was himself a slave-owner.

The transatlantic slave trade continued from the Renaissance until the nineteenth century, and during that time over 10 million Africans were forcibly transported to the New World as slaves. As the slave trade grew, so did its critics. In her early English novel *Oroonoko* (1688), Aphra Behn (c. 1640–89) tells the story of an African prince who is tricked into slavery and sent to South America, where he then leads an uprising. In the form of a novel, a woman writer was questioning the justice of slavery long before political debates to end the slave trade had begun.

---

1   Jean-Jacques Rousseau, *The Social Contract*, trans. Willmoore Kendall (Chicago: Henry Regnery, 1954), 2.

By the middle of the eighteenth century, abolitionist movements calling for the end of the slave trade sprang up in Britain, though slavery didn't end in America until the Civil War (1861–65). Abolitionist societies also promoted the publication of writings by those who had suffered under slavery, such as Olaudah Equiano (c. 1745–97) and Phillis Wheatley (c. 1753–84), in order to raise awareness of the cause. Often these societies were associated with Dissenting Protestant sects such as the Quakers. Inspired by the French Revolution, slaves in Haiti organized a rebellion in the 1790s. Under the leadership of former slave Toussaint L'Ouverture (c. 1743–1803), the rebellion was successful, slavery was abolished, and Haiti became an independent republic in 1804.

Early Feminism

Women, too, began questioning their subordinate status more insistently during the Enlightenment. In 1701, Mary Astell (1666–1731) called for a greater emphasis on female education in her treatise *A Serious Proposal for the Ladies*. Closer to the end of the century, Mary Wollstonecraft (1759–97) called for greater equality for women, especially in terms of education. Women at this time were not allowed to attend universities, hold political office, vote, or in most cases even own property. Very few jobs – other than wife and mother, servant, or prostitute – were open to them. These early feminist thinkers began questioning this state of affairs, calling for greater equality in marriage and increased opportunities for women to receive an education.

Although women could not receive the same kind of education as men, many women made a name for themselves as writers during this time. In France, both women and men would meet in female-led literary salons to discuss matters ranging from politics to literature to philosophy. Many women writers were associated with these salons, producing important works of fiction, poetry, and drama. Notable *salonnières* include novelist Madeleine de Scudéry (1607–1701) and novelist and playwright Françoise de Graffigny (1695–1758). In Great Britain, educated women (nicknamed "bluestockings") produced works of poetry, drama, history, travel writing, philosophy, and fiction throughout the century. One such work is Catharine Macaulay's multi-volume *History of England from the Accession of James I to that of the Brunswick Line* (1763–83).

Wollstonecraft's *A Vindication of the Rights of Woman* (1792) grew out of debates regarding the French Revolution. Thomas Paine's pamphlet *The Rights of Man* (1791) argues in support of the French Revolution, and Wollstonecraft extends Paine's arguments about the rights of men to include women as well. She says that young women are taught to value beauty alone as a means of getting a husband, because no other opportunities are open to them. She calls for "a revolution in female manners – time to restore to them their lost dignity – and make them, as a part of the human species, labour by reforming themselves to reform the world." She concludes, "Let women share the rights, and she will emulate the virtues of man; for she must grow more perfect when emancipated."[1] Wollstonecraft uses the language of rights, emancipation, and revolution here and elsewhere, linking her calls for female equality in education to both revolutionary and abolitionist ideas of the time. Although it took another few decades for an organized women's movement to really get underway, Wollstonecraft's *Vindication* is recognized as one of the founding texts of **FEMINISM**.

Aesthetic Innovations

While Enlightenment thinkers were questioning received wisdom about everything from organized religion to the role of women, they also questioned preconceived notions about the definition of beauty and the rules of art. The era is known for its neoclassical literature and art, art that looks back to the Greeks and Romans for inspiration. **NEOCLASSICISM** tends to be very polished, elegant, and refined in its aesthetic – think white marble, Grecian columns, and simple drapery. While the neoclassical aesthetic reigned supreme, at the same time other writers were bringing in a wide range of new perspectives, including

+ **"Outsider" artists.** During this period a cult of the self-taught writer developed, especially in poetry. Readers enjoyed poems by thresher Stephen Duck (c. 1705–56), milkwoman Ann Yearsley (1753–1806), and washerwoman Mary Collier (c. 1688–1762), celebrating their simple language and perspective. The most famous of these writers was Robert Burns (1759–96), the Scottish poet best known for the New Year's anthem "Auld Lang Syne" (1788). Burns had a bit more education than some of these other self-taught writers, but he benefitted from the vogue for naïve art.

+ **Experimental forms.** Some of the wildest and most innovative texts in the history of literature come out of this period. Laurence Sterne's novel *Tristram Shandy* (1759–67) is the most famous experimental novel of the time. It's been described as the first **POSTMODERN** work, in part because of

---

1   Mary Wollstonecraft, *A Vindication of the Rights of Woman*, ed. Mary Warnock (London: J.M. Dent, 1992), 51, 215.

the way Sterne manipulates the chronology of his story. Tristram, the narrator, sets out to tell his life story. Before he can do this, he says, you have to understand his parents' relationship, his eccentric Uncle Toby, and dozens of other matters. In the process, he digresses so much that he's not even born until the fourth volume of the novel. Russian Formalist critic Viktor Shklovsky (see Chapter 6) praises *Tristram Shandy* as the most "typical" novel in the world because of the way it lays bare the conventions of writing, exposing its construction.[1]

* **Hybrid works**. Many great works of the Enlightenment combine elements of different genres or fields of study, often in surprising ways. Bernard Mandeville's *Fable of the Bees* (1714), for example, is a short allegorical poem about bees supplemented by a long philosophical essay about economics (in the form of footnotes to the poem). Erasmus Darwin (1731–1802), Charles Darwin's grandfather, produced long poems that double as scientific treatises, such as *The Loves of the Plants* (1791), which explains plant reproduction through the conventions of love poetry. Meanwhile, Enlightenment readers enjoyed georgic poems that provided instruction on agricultural matters such as making cider and raising sheep.

Hume's essay "Of the Standard of Taste" (1757) illustrates how Enlightenment writers questioned ideas about literature. In this short essay, Hume asks if one can establish universal rules for defining good and bad writing. He believes "it is natural for us to seek a *Standard of Taste*; a rule, by which the various sentiments of men may be reconciled; at least, a decision, afforded, confirming one sentiment, and condemning another."[2] On the one hand, he admits that taste is relative and that beauty is in the eye of the beholder. Even when individuals use the same word, such as *beauty* or *excellent*, they have different ideas in their mind about what those concepts represent. On the other hand, Hume remarks that people do tend to agree much of the time on excellence in literature. People everywhere, he argues, have praised Homer's epics. In the end, Hume thinks through the issues but doesn't resolve the question, leaving it for readers to use their own reason and come up with their own conclusion.

Hume was one of the leading figures of an intellectual movement called the Scottish Enlightenment. Centered mainly in Edinburgh, the Scottish

1 Viktor Shklovsky, "Sterne's *Tristram Shandy*: Stylistic Commentary," in *Russian Formalist Criticism: Four Essays*, trans. Lee T. Lemon and Marion J. Reis (Lincoln: U of Nebraska P, 1965), 57.
2 David Hume, "Of the Standard of Taste," *Essays: Moral, Political, and Literary*, ed. Eugene F. Miller (Indianapolis: Liberty Classics, 1985), 229.

Enlightenment consisted of a group of writers who explored a huge range of subjects including history, social theory, and philosophy. Along with Hume, one of the other notable figures of this group was Adam Smith (1723–90), whose *Wealth of Nations* (1776) was a groundbreaking work of economic theory and a foundational work for the analysis of modern capitalism. In it, Smith celebrates the division of labor and analyzes how the capitalist system works at an early stage of its development.

Idealism

The philosophical movement known as **IDEALISM** comes on the heels of, and is closely related to, skepticism. The most important idealists of this period were a group of German philosophers, the most famous of whom were Kant and G.W.F. Hegel (1770–1831). Kant's and Hegel's philosophies are notoriously complex yet extremely important in the development of later literary theory. Nearly every literary theorist of the twentieth century owes a debt to Kant and Hegel.

The roots of idealist philosophy can be traced back to Plato's theory of forms. Plato believed that there was an ideal type of every object or concept (the Platonic ideal, discussed in Chapter 2). God created this ideal, and every individual example of a thing is merely a copy of the ideal, perfect form of the thing. Later **EMPIRICIST** philosophers challenge this theory of forms, arguing that there are no innate categories in the human mind but that individuals learn about the world through observation. In Locke's empirical philosophy, for example, the human mind is a *tabula rasa* or blank slate that gets filled in through observation, experience, and education. This basic debate about experience versus innate categories runs throughout the history of theory and criticism.

It is important to distinguish between the philosophical idealism of the late eighteenth century (often labeled German idealism) and the ordinary meaning of the word *idealism*. In ordinary speech, an idealist is a dreamer, someone who believes the best of everyone and who strives toward a lofty-minded goal or set of ideals. In philosophy, an idealist is someone who believes that the way we perceive reality stems from the human mind, that reality isn't "out there" as much as it is in our own heads. An anecdote from Boswell's *Life of Johnson* illustrates the objections many people have to philosophical idealism. George Berkeley (1685–1753), a radical idealist, believed that there was no way for an individual to definitively know that what he or she perceived was "real" in a universal sense. We have no way of getting outside our own mind and our own perceptions, so we can never truly "prove" that anything truly exists (and instead we must rely on faith). Boswell describes Johnson's response to Berkeley's philosophy:

> After we came out of church, we stood talking for some time together of Bishop Berkeley's ingenious sophistry to prove the non-existence of matter, and that every thing in the universe is merely ideal. I observed, that though we are satisfied his doctrine is not true, it is impossible to refute it. I never shall forget the alacrity with which Johnson answered, striking his foot with mighty force against a large stone, till he rebounded from it, "I refute it *thus*."[1]

Delving into the world of philosophy can be daunting for a student of literature, but a little bit of knowledge can be useful since literary theory has borrowed so liberally from philosophical debates and terms over the centuries. One helpful set of terms to know relates to the various branches of philosophy: **EPISTEMOLOGY** is a branch of philosophy that studies questions of knowledge, **ETHICS** means philosophy that deals with questions of morality and right and wrong, **METAPHYSICS** grapples with the big issues of the nature of reality and being, and **AESTHETICS** is philosophy that wrestles with questions of art and beauty. Today, academic philosophers also distinguish between Continental philosophy and analytic philosophy. Kant and Hegel are key figures in the Continental tradition, which tends to be more prevalent on the European continent (as opposed to in Britain) and deals with issues of metaphysics, among other things. There's a great deal of crossover between Continental philosophy and literary theory, beginning in the Enlightenment and continuing down through French and German thinkers of the nineteenth and twentieth centuries. In contrast, analytic philosophy is more prominent in Britain and America, and studies issues related to logic, language, and science in a very precise, almost scientific manner. Important early figures in analytic philosophy include the early-twentieth-century thinkers Bertrand Russell (1872–1970) and Ludwig Wittgenstein (1889–1951).

Kant's Idealist Philosophy

Kant's philosophy can be summed up in a single word: reason. He believed in the power of human reason to solve every human problem, and he applied his reasoning skills to nearly every big philosophical question of the time, including man's place in the universe, the existence of God, how people should treat each other, and how to define the beautiful. He believed that this faculty of reason

---

1   James Boswell, *The Life of Samuel Johnson, LL.D,* 10 vols. (London: John Murray, 1839), 2:262–63.

LITERARY THEORY AND CRITICISM

was superior to empirical observation. He put this into practice in his own life and never traveled more than ten miles from home. Legend has it that he was so methodical in his daily life that his neighbors could set their watches by the timing of his daily walks. He truly lived a life of the mind, believing that walking around thinking through big abstractions was a better way to learn about the world than by traveling or gathering scientific evidence.

Kant writes about a range of concerns, always emphasizing the importance of reason. His writings are extremely challenging and dense, written in a rigorous philosophical style typical of German philosophers. Even so, his ideas have been extremely influential. In England, one of the first writers to popularize Kant's ideas was Coleridge (see Chapter 5), who writes about Kant and other German idealists in his critical works. Among Kant's key ideas are the following:

+ **Noumena** and *phenomena*. Kant distinguished between *noumena*, or categories determined through pure reason, and *phenomena*, or individual instances of a larger category that can be apprehended through empirical observation. He called *noumena* "things-in-themselves" to distinguish them from the phenomenal objects we can see, hear, and touch. This distinction goes back to Plato's theory of forms: while people can observe individual examples of objects or categories (a bed, a child, goodness), the larger ideal or *noumenon* can be perceived by the mind alone. No one couch or example of something beautiful will contain the perfect specimen of all couches or all aspects of beauty – only philosophers can achieve the ideal through imagination and reason. Twentieth-century phenomenology (see Chapters 6 and 9) concentrates on Kant's phenomena as a way to study perception.

+ *A priori* and *a posteriori*. In a similar way, Kant distinguishes between *a priori* knowledge that comes through pure reason and *a posteriori* knowledge that comes through the senses. *A priori* means before the senses – this is how you achieve knowledge of things-in-themselves or *noumena*: through reason rather than the *a posteriori* method of appealing to the senses.

+ **Categorical imperative**. In ethics, Kant applies the principles of *a priori* reasoning to come up with a universal law of ethics. He wanted to see if he could use pure logic to come up with an ethical system that would apply to all cultures regardless of the laws of individual countries or religious systems. He calls the result of his experiment the categorical imperative. This imperative or command (which had to be obeyed categorically) states that you should "act only according to that maxim by which you can at the same time will that it should become a universal law."[1] In other words, Kant is saying that you should do unto others as you would have them do unto you. By proceeding through pure reason in an *a priori* manner, however, Kant attempts to prove that the Golden Rule of the Bible shouldn't just be obeyed because religious authorities command you to do so, but because it is universally true and logical for all people and times.

Of all of Kant's wide-ranging ideas, he most directly touches upon literary concerns in his writings about aesthetics, especially about the **SUBLIME**. He distinguishes between the beautiful and the sublime in his *Critique of Judgment* (1790). Art and nature, he says, can produce both beautiful and sublime sensations, the former produced by an object with "definite boundaries," while the latter is produced by a "formless object" that creates a sensation of "boundlessness" or the infinite.[2]

Years earlier, and in less abstract terms, Irish politician and writer Edmund Burke (1729–97) had explored the theory of the sublime in his *Philosophical Enquiry into the Origin of Our Ideas of the Sublime and Beautiful* (1757), which influenced Kant's thinking. In this short work, Burke distinguishes between beauty, a pleasing sensation caused by harmony, symmetry, grace, and pleasure, and a darker but more intense sensation of the sublime – which produces fear, awe, and even pain alongside the pleasure. Burke summarizes the differences: "Sublime objects are vast in their dimensions, beautiful ones comparatively small; beauty should be smooth, and polished; the great, rugged and negligent … beauty should not be obscure; the great ought to be dark and gloomy; beauty should be light and delicate; the great ought to be solid, and even massive."[3] Looking at the rolling hills and meadows of the English countryside might produce a sensation of beauty, for example, while standing on top of a jagged mountain peak would produce a feeling of sublimity, a more profound and frightening sensation.

Kant and Burke both derived their theories of the sublime from the treatise *On the Sublime* by Longinus (see Chapter 2). Though Longinus had published during antiquity, his ideas were lost for many centuries during the Middle Ages. They found a new audience when they were translated from Greek into French and English at the end of the seventeenth century.

The concept of the sublime influenced the development of Romanticism and

---

1   Kant, *Foundations*, 38.
2   Immanuel Kant, *Critique of Judgment*, trans. J.H. Bernard (New York: Hafner, 1966), 82.
3   Edmund Burke, *A Philosophical Enquiry into the Origin of Our Ideas of the Sublime and Beautiful*, ed. James T. Bouldon (Oxford: Basil Blackwell, 1987), 124.

Romantic aesthetics. Toward the end of the eighteenth century, writers turned to darker subject matter and celebrated the sublime in art. This can be seen clearly in the popularity of the gothic novel at this time. Readers sought out the terrifying sensations produced by gothic novelists such as Ann Radcliffe (1764–1823) and Matthew Lewis (1775–1818). These gothic novels are the forerunners of the modern horror genre. Similarly, Romantic poets such as Percy Shelley (1792–1822) and Wordsworth (Chapter 5) depict sublime landscapes such as the Swiss Alps and sensations of terror and awe in their poetry.

Hegel's Ideas of History

Among the many figures associated with German idealism, Hegel is the next really big name in German philosophy after Kant. Like Kant, he was a philosophical idealist who believed in the power of his own reason and philosophical system to explain the world. He built upon Kant's ideas and developed new ideas of his own, especially about history. Like Kant, too, Hegel presents a challenge for a layperson to read because of the difficulty of his language and ideas. Yet his philosophical theories helped to shape later traditions of literary theory, especially influencing the ideas of Karl Marx and of historicist critics (see Chapters 8 and 7, respectively).

Like other Enlightenment thinkers, Hegel believes strongly in the concept of progress, that humanity was becoming more enlightened with each era. He asserts that "world history is the progress of the consciousness of freedom," that humanity is advancing towards a freer and freer state.[1] In a series of lectures printed after his death, he develops a philosophy of history, a philosophical system to explain how history works, which studies the progress of this freedom from the ancient world to modern society, culminating of course with his own moment in time. For Hegel, history isn't shaped by human decisions and actions so much as by the underlying workings of the World Spirit (discussed below). He labels Julius Caesar and Napoleon as world-historical individuals – these figures shaped the course of history by serving as the agents of the underlying Spirit, without necessarily being conscious of this fact.

Rather than individual actions, the engine that moves civilization and history forward in Hegel's philosophy is *Geist*, a German word sometimes translated as "spirit" and sometimes as "mind" (the word is etymologically related to the English word *ghost*). This spirit, also called the Ideal or the Idea, is Hegel's extremely abstract, philosophical version of God. Spirit becomes conscious and

---

1   G.W.F. Hegel, *Reason in History: A General Introduction to the Philosophy of History*, trans. Robert S. Hartman (New York: Macmillan, 1985), 24.

reveals itself through the unfolding of history. Each historical period has its own spirit, which manifests itself in all aspects of life, including the form of government, religion, literature, art, and even mundane matters of food and clothing. Hegel characterizes this spirit as a **TOTALITY**, the essence that produces the underlying unity of an age. The idea of a spirit of the age or a zeitgeist, an underlying spirit that characterizes a particular culture at a particular moment in time, comes from Hegel. His ideas shape the larger intellectual movement known as **HISTORICISM**, whose proponents believe that each historical period has its own identity and must be judged in relation to its own moment.

A key to understanding Hegel's ideas and his influence on later writers is his concept of the **DIALECTIC**. He uses a German word to describe this process, *Aufhebung*, which means both to raise something up and to cancel something out. It's often translated as "sublation." The dialectic drives history forward and shapes individual self-consciousness.

One of the most famous and influential passages in Hegel's writings, particularly for twentieth-century literary theory, is a section of *Phenomenology of Mind [Geist]* (1807) where he discusses what is now often referred to as the master-slave dialectic. (The translation I'm using employs the terms *lordship* and *bondage* rather than *master* and *slave*.) Hegel believes that every thesis implies an antithesis and every self implies an other. His discussion begins, "Self-consciousness exists in itself and for itself, in that, and by the fact that it exists for another self-consciousness; that is to say it *is* only by being acknowledged or 'recognized.'"[1] That is, individuals can become conscious of themselves only by recognizing another being recognizing them. You can't have a sense of yourself until you see yourself being seen. Similarly, you can't have independence without dependence. In this way, a master is just as dependent upon the slave as the slave is upon the master – one needs the other to exist. Through a recognition of this dependence on the other, spirit can come to greater self-consciousness and history can progress toward greater freedom. Master and slave can recognize their dependence on each other and transcend their differences. Though abstract, Hegel's discussions of self-consciousness, identity, and the other were embraced by a number of French existentialist thinkers, including Jean-Paul Sartre, Simone de Beauvoir, and Frantz Fanon (all discussed in Chapter 8).

Later commentators on Hegel elaborate upon his model of the dialectic. For every thesis, a proposition or entity, there exists an antithesis, an opposing force that originates within spirit as a contradiction. The way history moves forward

---

1   G.W.F. Hegel, *The Phenomenology of Mind*, trans. J.B. Baillie (New York: Harper & Row, 1967), 229.

is for thesis and antithesis to come into conflict, resolve the contradiction, and create a synthesis, a combination of the best of both thesis and antithesis. The synthesis cancels out or gets rid of the bad parts of thesis and antithesis and raises the best parts to a new level. The synthesis then becomes the new thesis, and the whole process starts all over again. Figure 4 illustrates the process of this dialectic.

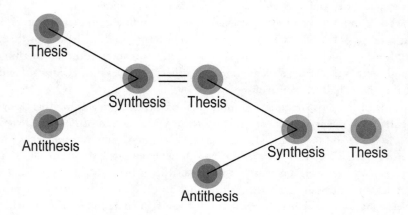

Figure 4: Hegel's Dialectic (image by Ashley Jagodzinski).

Hegel's ideas about the movement of Spirit through history provide an influential model for thinking about historical change during an age of revolution. Marx claimed that he was standing Hegel's upside-down dialectic on its feet when he developed his own theory of history. In Marx's model, economic systems rather than a disembodied Spirit underlie each era of civilization, and conflict comes through contradictions within an economic system, such as the conflict between capitalists and workers under capitalism. For Hegel, the end of history comes when Spirit becomes completely conscious of itself, whereas for Marx the end of history comes with the establishment of a Communist utopia and the end of capitalist exploitation and class conflict. Though many no longer fully endorse either of these ideas, Hegel's and Marx's description of history as a process of conflict and resolution remains extremely influential. I return to Marx's use of Hegel in Chapter 8 on political approaches, but first I turn to other nineteenth-century developments in the history of theory and criticism in the next chapter.

Suggestions for Further Reading

Butler, Marilyn. *Romantics, Rebels and Reactionaries: English Literature and Its Background 1760–1830*. New York: Oxford UP, 1982.

Donoghue, Frank. *The Fame Machine: Book Reviewing and Eighteenth-Century Literary Careers*. Stanford, CA: Stanford UP, 1996.

Schmidt, James, ed. *What Is Enlightenment? Eighteenth-Century Answers and Twentieth-Century Questions*. Berkeley: U of California P, 1996.

Thomas, Hugh. *The Slave Trade: The History of the Atlantic Slave Trade 1440–1870*. London: Picador, 1997.

Five: The Nineteenth Century

IN THIS CHAPTER, WE edge ever closer to a more recognizably modern world. Many of the developments discussed in the previous chapter on the Enlightenment, themselves extensions of Renaissance developments, were further extended during the nineteenth century. The abolitionist movement, for example, succeeded in abolishing slavery (though only after a bloody civil war in the United States). The first inklings of the women's movement helped to bring about the 1848 Seneca Falls Convention for women's rights. The Enlightenment political upheavals of the American and French Revolutions spawned a wave of revolutions across Europe and the globe in the nineteenth century, perhaps the most important of which was the Industrial Revolution, which led to the growth of factories and later gave rise to the Labor movement. The Enlightenment spirit of scientific inquiry flourished in this century as well, leading to Charles Darwin's revolutionary theory of evolution and to important medical discoveries. Finally, the European exploration of the globe, begun in the Renaissance, in the nineteenth century developed into European conquest and colonization throughout Africa, Asia, and elsewhere.

In terms of the history of literary theory and criticism, some of the most significant nineteenth-century developments have to do with education and literacy. Educational opportunities expanded greatly, as public libraries, schools, and universities grew in numbers. As discussed in Chapter 1, universities took on their modern form during this time, and literary studies became an academic discipline. NATIONALISM, a complex concept relating to the belief in the importance of nations and nationalities in shaping culture and politics, became increasingly important. On a geopolitical level, ideas of nationalism provided the impetus for German and Italian unification (and lay the groundwork for twentieth-century Nazism and Fascism). Less sinister, perhaps, in the context of national traditions, was the interest in the literary traditions of different nations and the organization of literary studies around national and linguistic lines: German literature, French literature, English and American literature, and so forth. A number of important nineteenth-century endeavors developed out of this desire to write a history of national literary traditions, including the collecting of folklore and fairy tales by the Grimm brothers (and others), the monumental *Oxford English Dictionary* (a historical dictionary of the English language, first published in 1884), and the *Dictionary of National Biography* (a compilation of biographies of notable figures in British history, first published in 1885).

The nineteenth century was a transitional moment in the history of literary theory. Many of the most important foundations of current-day literary theory come from nineteenth-century thinkers. I will discuss many of them in this chapter, while reserving discussion of Karl Marx and Sigmund Freud for Chapters 8 and 9, respectively, because of their direct impact on the traditions of Marxist and psychoanalytic thought in the twentieth and twenty-first centuries. I will concentrate in this chapter on the key developments in literary theory and criticism, especially as they relate to the work of three clusters of mostly creative writers: Romantic poets of the early part of the century, realist novelists of the mid-century, and end-of-the-century **DECADENT** writers and philosophers.

Romanticism and Nineteenth-Century Poetry

The literary movement known as Romanticism can be a slippery concept to define precisely. Check ten different reference books and you'll get ten different definitions of Romanticism, with ten different starting and ending dates. At the time they were writing, authors we now call Romantics wouldn't have used that label to describe themselves, just as Renaissance writers wouldn't have used the term *Renaissance* (though Enlightenment writers did embrace the term *Enlightenment*, as in the example of Immanuel Kant's "What Is Enlightenment?" [1784]). In any case, though, Romantic-era writers were aware that they were living in a remarkable and turbulent period of history. For the writers of that time, the French Revolution was the event that sparked an entire age of revolution, even though some aspects of what we now think of as a part of the Romantic movement originated before the storming of the Bastille in 1789.

Although there are no hard and fast dates for Romanticism (roughly the last third of the eighteenth century through the first third of the nineteenth century can serve as a good ballpark figure), most scholars can agree on a few of the basic features of the movement. The term itself derives from the word *romance*, not in the sense of a love story but in the sense of the genre of medieval romance (like *Sir Gawain and the Green Knight*). Many Romantic writers turned away from modern rationality and looked back to medieval romance for inspiration. Romanticism is especially associated with poets such as John Keats (1795–1821), Lord Byron (1788–1824), and William Blake (1757–1827), though today the canon of Romanticism has broadened to include more women writers and writers of prose.

Many major Romantic poets also wrote literary criticism and theory. Although Romanticism was an international movement (begun in Germany and Great Britain and then spreading to France, America, and elsewhere), in the following section I discuss three British theorists – Samuel Taylor Coleridge, William Wordsworth, and Percy Shelley – whose critical writings highlight three key Romantic-era concerns: the imagination, nature, and politics.

Romanticism in its broadest sense can be seen as a response to certain aspects of the Enlightenment (see Chapter 4). In particular, Romantic writers were reacting against the Enlightenment ideals of **NEOCLASSICISM** and rationality, instead embracing the irrational, the irregular, the gothic, the **SUBLIME**, the fragmentary, and the natural. Like Enlightenment thinkers, though, Romantic writers were still interested in issues of political revolution. That's why figures such as Mary Wollstonecraft and Olaudah Equiano, mentioned in the last chapter, could just as easily fit into the discussion here and are now considered as Romantic writers in terms of courses and anthologies.

Rather than thinking of Romanticism purely as a reaction *against* Enlightenment, it's best to think of it as an *extension* of the Enlightenment, just as the Enlightenment itself can be seen as an extension of the Renaissance. Romantic writers didn't actually want to go back to the Middle Ages or to abandon the scientific and political progress made in the eighteenth century. Now that some progress had been made, though, they looked back nostalgically on the past and embraced cultural phenomena that were fading away while also calling attention to some of the darker aspects of progress.

The movement to collect oral traditions like ballads and folklore is a good illustration of the Romantic attitude toward the past. Over the course of the eighteenth century, more and more people were moving to cities to work in the factories that were springing up because of the growth of industrial manufacturing brought about by the Industrial Revolution. Literacy rates climbed, and a lot of the old traditions of the rural peasantry were fading away as people moved out of rural villages to new industrial centers such as Manchester, Sheffield, and Bradford in the north of England. So toward the end of the eighteenth century, scholars began to take steps to preserve such fading oral traditions as folk ballads and fairy tales. The Grimm brothers of Germany (Jacob, 1785–1863, and Wilhelm, 1786–1859) are the most famous of these types of collectors. In 1812 they published their first collection of folktales, which included many stories now familiar to most children, such as Snow White and Sleeping Beauty. The Grimm brothers did not want the peasantry to go back to their rural villages and a state of illiteracy and poverty, but they did want to make sure that these oral traditions were not lost. German Romantic writers E.T.A. Hoffmann (1776–1822) and Ludwig Tieck (1773–1853) then wrote new stories that took their inspiration from German folklore.

Many of the central critical ideas that shaped the Romantic movement came out of Germany. Immanuel Kant and G.W.F. Hegel, discussed in the last chapter, are only two of the most famous German writers of these years; others include Friedrich Schiller (1759–1805), Johann Gottlieb Fichte (1762–1814), August and Friedrich Schlegel (1767–1845, 1772–1829), and Johann Wolfgang von Goethe (1749–1832). Many of the most important ideas coming out of late-eighteenth- and early-nineteenth-century German writing made their way to English readers and a wider audience through the work of the English poet Samuel Taylor Coleridge (1772–1834). Best known for his poems "The Rime of the Ancient Mariner" (1798) and "Kubla Khan" (1816), Coleridge was also an influential literary critic. *Biographia Literaria: Biographical Sketches of My Literary Life and Opinions* (1817), his most important critical work, popularizes (and often outright plagiarizes) from a range of German Romantic writers.

One central idea that Coleridge stresses is the role of the imagination in literary creation. He characterizes the imagination as an "esemplastic" power, coining that word from a Greek root meaning "molding" or "unifying" and adapting it from a German word in Friedrich Schelling's *Lecture on the Philosophy of Art* (1802–03): *Ineinsbildung*, or forming into one. Coleridge believes that the imagination has the power to shape disparate materials into a unified work of art. A good work of art, shaped by the imagination, "contain[s] in itself the reason why it is so, and not otherwise." That means that a work of art is like an organism – all the parts work together to function as a whole, and you cannot change one part of a work (removing the rhyme from a poem, for example) without changing the unity of the whole as shaped by the imagination of the author. A few thousand years earlier, Aristotle had made a similar argument in the *Poetics* (see Chapter 2). The key difference is that while Aristotle focuses on the structural integrity of good storytelling, Coleridge's discussion of the power of the imagination has a more spiritual dimension. He defines the imagination as "the living Power and prime Agent of all human Perception, and as a repetition in the finite mind of the eternal act of creation in the infinite I AM."[1] Thus all poetic inspiration ultimately comes from the "infinite I AM," or

---

1   Samuel Taylor Coleridge, *Biographia Literaria, Coleridge's Poetry and Prose*, ed. Nicholas Halmi, Paul Magnuson, and Raimonda Modiano (New York: W.W. Norton, 2004), 493, 488.

God, an idea not that far removed from Homer and other epic poets' calls for the Muses to aid them in their work.

In the *Biographia* Coleridge also coins the phrase "willing suspension of disbelief" to describe how readers must approach works of literature. Calling it "poetic faith," he suggests that readers or audiences for fictitious works should suspend their doubts about the possibilities of supernatural occurrences in order to enjoy a work of art. This is a very Romantic notion, since the object of a work of art here is to elevate the soul or to create beauty, not to teach a lesson.

William Wordsworth (1770–1850), Coleridge's friend and collaborator and one of the most important of the English Romantic poets, included a preface to the second edition of their coauthored volume of poetry, *Lyrical Ballads* (1800), which became extremely influential in the history of criticism. Explaining his purpose in writing the volume, Wordsworth overstates the originality of his work while downplaying the contributions of Coleridge to the first edition (1798) of the volume. Despite this, Wordsworth's preface has become one of the most frequently anthologized and cited works of Romantic literary theory.

In both his poetry and his criticism, a key concept for Wordsworth is nature. He says that his poems depict the rural poor in the Lake District of England primarily because readers can see the workings of human nature more clearly in "simpler" people. Even though Wordsworth was highly educated, he says that he uses the simpler language of the peasantry in order to convey emotion more clearly. In his preface he also rejects overly complicated poetic language and figures of speech such as personifications in favor of simpler and more direct language.

He calls poetry the "spontaneous overflow of powerful feelings; it takes its origin from emotion recollected in tranquility; the emotion is contemplated till by a species of reaction the tranquility gradually disappears, and an emotion, kindred to that which was before the subject of contemplation, is gradually produced."[1] The poet experiences an emotional moment, and then reflects upon it and shapes it into verse. Wordsworth's interest in human nature, the natural world, and a more natural-sounding poetic language all influenced generations of writers to come.

Wordsworth and Coleridge began their careers in the 1790s and are considered to be of the first generation of British Romantics. Writers of the second generation, such as Shelley and Keats, were deeply influenced by the first generation writers but also were disappointed that those writers moved away

---

1   William Wordsworth, Preface, *Lyrical Ballads*, 2nd ed., ed. Michael Mason (Harlow, England: Pearson Longman, 2007), 82.

from their early embrace of radical political causes in favor of the less politically charged concerns of nature, the imagination, and spirituality.

Percy Shelley's major critical work, *A Defence of Poetry* (a title deliberately similar to Sir Philip Sidney's, discussed in Chapter 3) was written in 1821 but not published until 1840. In it, Shelley (1792–1822) displays a more overtly political and even radical dimension of Romanticism. Like Coleridge, Shelley emphasizes the importance of the imagination in creating poetry. But he takes these ideas about the importance of poetry a step further by calling poets the "founders of civil society" and the "unacknowledged legislators of the world." He believes that poets have a social role to play, but that their role has nothing to do with religion or morality. While critics such as Plato (see Chapter 2) and Samuel Johnson (see Chapter 4) believe that poets have a moral obligation to improve the world, Shelley is not at all concerned with morality. He chooses two deeply religious poems, Dante Alighieri's *Divine Comedy* (1308–21) and John Milton's *Paradise Lost* (1667), and reads these texts against their overt moral messages, saying that Milton was not a moralist because his Satan is such a compelling character: "Milton has so far violated the popular creed (if this shall be judged to be a violation) as to have alleged no superiority of moral virtue to his God over his Devil. And this bold neglect of a direct moral purpose is the most decisive proof of the supremacy of Milton's genius."[1] (Another radical Romantic, Blake, also saw Satan as the hero of Milton's epic.) Instead of a moral role, Shelley believes that poets should play a more political role in promoting liberty and fighting oppression. He reads Milton as a political radical and anti-monarchical figure rather than as a deeply devout Puritan, even though in reality Milton was both.

Shelley's political and religious views were daring for his time: he was a vegetarian, believed in free love, and supported political revolution. Some of his poetry, such as the sonnet "England in 1819" (1819), is extremely critical of the King and supports a violent overthrow of the government. As we move further into the nineteenth century, class unrest spurred by economic inequality and political oppression becomes more and more common, giving rise to political rebellions across Europe in 1848 (which I discuss in more detail in relation to Marx in Chapter 8).

---

1   Percy Bysshe Shelley, *A Defence of Poetry, Shelley's Poetry and Prose*, ed. Donald H. Reiman and Sharon B. Powers (New York: W.W. Norton, 1977), 508, 498.

Realism, Nationalism, and the Nineteenth-Century Novel

Though many writers produced great novels during the Romantic era, including Jane Austen and Mary Shelley, for better or worse we tend to think of the Romantic era as one dominated by poetry. A little later in the century, this emphasis shifted, and the novel now commands the most attention in the literary histories of the period. Across Europe and America, some of the greatest achievements of nineteenth-century literature were big, sprawling, realistic novels. In Britain and America alone, the nineteenth century produced many novels now considered classics, including Herman Melville's *Moby-Dick* (1851), Nathaniel Hawthorne's *The Scarlet Letter* (1850), Mark Twain's *The Adventures of Huckleberry Finn* (1884), George Eliot's *Middlemarch* (1874), Charlotte Brontë's *Jane Eyre* (1847), and Charles Dickens's *Great Expectations* (1860).

The novel was an international form in the nineteenth century: successful novels were translated into many languages, and genres such as the realist novel, the *Bildungsroman* or novel of education, and the historical novel became widespread. Novels also became even easier and cheaper to obtain during this time as paper and book prices decreased, economies of scale in publishing took effect, and lending and public libraries made borrowing books ever more convenient. Newspapers and magazines became an important new venue for consuming fiction, both through the flourishing new genre of the short story and through the process of serialization, with novelists such as Dickens, Wilkie Collins, and others publishing long works in monthly installments in periodicals. A telltale sign of a nineteenth-century novel that was originally serialized is when every chapter or section ends on a cliffhanger, which was a way to get people to keep anticipating the next installment. As train travel became popular beginning in the 1830s, novels provided a way for readers to pass the time as they moved from one place to another. Even while they provided entertainment and escape, nineteenth-century novels strove for greater realism in their depictions of history, society, and character psychology.

In contrast to earlier Romantic and later **AESTHETICIST** notions about the autonomy of art, the idea that works of art should merely provide beauty to the world, realist writers were concerned with art's relationship to the real world and the way in which literature – and particularly the novel – can teach us about society, history, and humanity. The idea of literary works imitating the real world can be seen as far back as the discussions of **MIMESIS** in Plato's *Republic* and Aristotle's *Poetics* (see Chapter 2), but in the nineteenth century mimesis took on a more explicitly political and utilitarian dimension. Nineteenth-century **UTILITARIANISM**, a philosophical movement associated with Jeremy Bentham (1748–1832) and John Stuart Mill (1806–73), contends that the best actions are those that result in the greatest good for the greatest number of people. A utilitarian would view the novel as useful to society in promoting social reform or conveying information to the public. Later decadent and aestheticist writers such as Théophile Gautier (1811–72) and Oscar Wilde would react strongly against the utilitarian notion that art and literature could be "useful."

The slave narrative and abolitionist novel traditions provide clear examples of writers using their words to protest injustice, reach a wider audience, and enter into political debates. Autobiographies of former slaves, such as Frederick Douglass's *The Narrative of the Life of Frederick Douglass* (1845), Solomon Northup's *Twelve Years a Slave* (1853), and Harriet Jacobs's *Incidents in the Life of a Slave Girl* (1861), and novels such as Harriet Beecher Stowe's *Uncle Tom's Cabin* (1851–52), became bestsellers. These works did not only tell entertaining or informative stories; in addition to delighting and instructing (in Horace's terms), they aimed to persuade readers. They used both narrative and rhetoric – story and argument – in order to inform readers of the horrors of slavery, the moral degradation of slave-owners, and the crimes committed under the auspices of a slave-owning society in order to convince readers that the institution of slavery needed to be abolished in the US. Similarly, in Britain, "Condition of England" novels such as Elizabeth Gaskell's *North and South* (1854–55), Charles Dickens's *Hard Times* (1854), and Charlotte Brontë's *Shirley* (1849) used the novel form to call attention to the impoverished conditions of industrial workers in the north of England, the exploitative practice of child labor, and growing class disparities and social unrest.

The realist novel also played an important role in shaping national identities. Political theorist Benedict Anderson has discussed the importance of nationalism in nineteenth-century political and intellectual history. He calls nations "imagined communities" – new formations that people think of as very old. In the nineteenth century, nationalism is one of the most important ideological movements. Spurred by the ideology of nationalism, Germany and Italy became unified nations during the century. Instead of viewing themselves as members of small principalities or large empires, people increasingly began to see themselves as members of a nation united through a national language, a cultural and literary tradition, and even a shared racial and ethnic heritage. Literary traditions and especially the novel can serve the same kind of role as national flags, national anthems, and national sports teams in uniting a group of people. Even today one can find images of writers on the currency of some countries. In one sense, nationalism can be seen as a positive force that brings together people who share a common language and heritage. The darker side of nationalism, however, created the ideologies of Nazism and Fascism in the twentieth century and underlies the horrors of genocide and ethnic cleansing to this day.

Varieties of Realism

Historical novels – novels that dramatize events and figures from the past – became very popular during the nineteenth century following the international success of Sir Walter Scott's Waverley novels (1814–32). Historical novels depicting major historical events (such as wars and revolutions) in various national histories flourished in an age of growing nationalism and political revolution. One of the greatest historical novels, and certainly a candidate for one of the greatest novels ever, is Leo Tolstoy's *War and Peace* (1869). This massive book depicts Napoleon Bonaparte's invasion of Russia in 1812 and features numerous characters and a sweeping plot. One of the most important aspects of the novel, and one that has been a major influence on literary theory, is Tolstoy's philosophical musings about the nature of history. His novel features multiple plots and multiple perspectives on a single event as a way to illustrate the complexity of history. The story he tells isn't merely the story of great men or Hegelian world-historical individuals like Napoleon, but of countless individuals with their own experiences and perspectives. To Tolstoy, those individuals shape history just as much as the famous names do: "It was necessary that millions of men in whose hands lay the real power – the soldiers who fired, or transported provisions and guns – should consent to carry out the will of these weak individuals, and should have been induced to do so by an infinite number of diverse and complex causes." Later in the novel he generalizes about the laws of history: "To study the laws of history we must completely change the subject of our observation, must leave aside kings, ministers, and generals, and study the common, infinitesimally small elements by which the masses are moved."[1] This turn toward individual experience perfectly suits the novel form, which allows readers access to everyday life and interior experience. Through these means, historical novelists such as Tolstoy help to complicate and democratize our understandings of the past.

Many nineteenth-century novelists set out to depict their society, but no one was more ambitious about it than French writer Honoré de Balzac (1799–1850). His *La Comédie humaine* (*The Human Comedy*) is a multi-volume series of novels and stories revolving around a large cast of characters. A single character, such as Eugène de Rastignac, can appear in dozens of Balzac's works, sometimes as the central figure, as he does in the novel *Le Père Goriot* (1835), and at other times as only a peripheral one. Through recurring characters, Balzac manages to create the entire French society of his day in miniature.

---

1   Leo Tolstoy, *War and Peace*, trans. Aylmer and Louise Maude (New York: W.W. Norton, 1966), 669, 919–20.

Balzac was not modest, as seen in his grandiose ambition to create an entire world in his novels. Luckily, most critics agree that he achieved his aim and became one of the most influential realist writers of all time. In the "Avant Propos" or preface to his works (1842), Balzac describes the epic scope of his project, and this document showcases the scientific and literary ambitions behind many nineteenth-century realist novelists. Balzac begins by saying that the idea for his project "came from the study of human life in comparison with the life of animals."[1] Just as zoologists divide the animal kingdom into different species, Balzac says that his novels do the same for the different types of people in society, since society is what "makes the man." Within the *Comédie humaine*, he divides its volumes into "Scenes from Private Life," "Scenes from Political Life," "Scenes from Country Life," and so forth, creating a taxonomy of his own works just as he is trying to create a taxonomy or classification of different social types.

As a realist, Balzac strives to put humanity under the microscope, like a scientist, examining the social forces that shape people's identities and daily lives. Another signature of his style is his extensive use of visual description and inclusion of details of daily life. Perhaps the most famous passage in all of Balzac's works is the opening of *Le Père Goriot*, where he describes the interior of a Paris boarding house in exhaustive detail. By documenting microscopically what French people's lives were like in the first half of the nineteenth century, Balzac claims that he is writing the history that historians leave out, the history of everyday life. Just as Tolstoy says that historical events aren't exclusively created by "great men" but by the forgotten little people of history, Balzac is interested in telling ordinary stories of everyday life.

While Balzac's novels depict French society in minute, realistic detail, another French novelist, Gustave Flaubert (1821–80), made his name by delving into the inner workings of the human mind in a detailed and realistic way. His most famous novel, *Madame Bovary* (1857), has been celebrated for its psychological realism and particularly for its use of a technique called free indirect style.

Flaubert did not invent free indirect style: you can find examples of it in novels by much earlier (often women) writers, such as Mme de Lafayette's *La Princesse de Clèves* (1678) and Eliza Haywood's *Love in Excess* (1719). Jane Austen, too, was a master of the technique in her six novels. Briefly, free indirect style is a way for authors to put readers into the heads of characters without readers necessarily knowing that they're doing it. That is, instead of saying

---

1   Honoré de Balzac, *La Comédie humaine*, vol. 1, trans. Katharine Prescott Wormeley (London: Downey & Co., 1898), v.

"Elizabeth Bennett thought," the author blends the voice of a narrator with the interior thoughts and feelings of a character, so you can't always tell where one ends and the other begins. Here's an example of free indirect style from *Madame Bovary*, giving us Emma Bovary's thoughts: "She was not happy; she had never been happy. Why had her life been such a failure? Why did everything on which she leaned crumble immediately to dust?"[1] "She was not happy" can be read as an objective statement of a fact, provided to us by the narrator. What follows, though, is clearly inflected by Emma's own thoughts, even though not presented as direct quotation or interior monologue. Emma is the one who thinks her life is a "failure," and readers are led to sympathize with her by seeing her own perception of herself.

Although Flaubert might not have thought of himself as a realist in the mold of Balzac, his detailed depiction of his characters' inner lives, presented without judgment and without commentary, marks an important development in the history of the realist novel. In fact, because of his frank presentation of Emma's infidelity and lack of editorial commentary, Flaubert was accused of obscenity by the French government. His realistic depiction of character psychology and sexuality made Flaubert a favorite of later modernist writers Henry James (1843–1916), Marcel Proust (1871–1922), and Virginia Woolf (1882–1941).

Another French novelist, Émile Zola (1840–1902), builds upon the realism of his predecessors Balzac and Flaubert. Zola's style of realism is called naturalism because he uses the methods of natural science to study people. Balzac in his preface compared his method to a scientist, but Zola's version of scientific realism is influenced by the newer evolutionary ideas. Darwin's *Origin of Species* (1859) had a huge impact not only on the world of science but on all sorts of other fields as well, including social science and literary studies. In this work, Darwin develops the evolutionary ideas of earlier scientists who posited that life on earth developed over a long geological span of time (rather than being created in six days, as in the Bible). Higher forms of life, such as primates, evolved from simpler species over millions of years. The process driving evolution forward in Darwin's theory is natural selection (often popularly termed "survival of the fittest"), a process whereby the individuals best adapted to conditions such as climate and avoiding predators are likeliest to survive and to pass on inherited characteristics that equip their offspring for survival.

In his essay "The Experimental Novel" (1880), Zola calls his type of novel "a consequence of the scientific evolution of the century."[2] A key word for

---

1   Gustave Flaubert, *Madame Bovary: Life in a Country Town*, trans. Gerard Hopkins (Oxford: Oxford UP, 1998), 260.

2   Émile Zola, *The Experimental Novel and Other Essays*, trans. Belle M. Sherman (New York: Haskell House, 1964), 19.

naturalists is *determinism*. Just as Darwin contended that all life is a product of natural selection rather than a divine plan, Zola says that individual human life is determined by the struggle for existence and the economic and social environment in which a person develops, rather than by some master plan. He used his novels, as did other naturalist writers such as the American novelist Theodore Dreiser (1871–1945) and Norwegian playwright Henrik Ibsen (1828–1906), to look at the cold hard facts of existence (as a scientist would study nature) and to depict the struggle for survival.

Arnold, Taine, and Literary Studies

While nineteenth-century novelists were theorizing about the relationship between art and life – whether by depicting major historical events (Tolstoy), producing a taxonomy of social types (Balzac), delving into character psychology (Flaubert), or showing the struggle for existence (Zola) – literary critics were also concerned with these issues. In the nineteenth century, as literary studies was in the process of becoming a university discipline, these issues being debated by critics and scholars helped shape the way in which literature would be studied at universities and even in secondary schools.

Poet Matthew Arnold (1822–88) was one of the most influential nineteenth-century British critics, and his essay "The Function of Criticism at the Present Time" (1864) is a good place to start to understand why he was so influential. In a frequently quoted passage, he defines criticism as "a disinterested endeavour to learn and propagate the best that is known and thought in the world."[1] Because the passage is so famous, it's worth spending a moment isolating its component parts:

+ **a disinterested endeavour**: Disinterestedness defines what Arnold thinks criticism should be. "Disinterested" critics aren't bored (that would be "uninterested"); by this word he means that critics should be neutral observers. Critics should not be affiliated with a particular political position and should stand above the practical, everyday concerns of the world, aiming for objectivity (in another famous phrase he says that critics should "see the object as in itself it really is"). Many nineteenth-century British reviews had partisan affiliations, but Arnold wants critics to transcend partisanship and focus on the more timeless aspects of literature. He also believes in the ideal

---

1   Matthew Arnold, "The Function of Criticism at the Present Time," *Matthew Arnold's Essays in Criticism*, ed. G.K. Chesterton (London: Everyman's Library, 1964), 32.

of a liberal education, training in the liberal arts (such as literature, history, and philosophy) rather than vocational training for a particular profession.

+ **to learn and propagate**: Here Arnold doesn't explicitly say that literary studies should be solely the province of academics rather than journalists and reviewers, but that idea is certainly implied. Literary studies was about to get a new home at the modern research university, and the idea that a critic's function is to "learn and propagate" has a very educational ring to it.

+ **the best that is known and thought**: As discussed in Chapter 4, during the Enlightenment a CANON of great writers was emerging, a modern analogue to the Greek and Roman classics. By the time Arnold was writing, the English had pretty well agreed upon their canon, with Chaucer, Shakespeare, and Milton occupying a prominent place. Although our canon has changed a bit in the intervening years, we still devote much more critical and classroom time to those historically agreed-upon "bests" than we do to non-canonical authors.

+ **in the world**: Here's where Arnold diverges from the conventional wisdom of his time. As critics and scholars were focusing more and more on specific national traditions of literature, Arnold explicitly says that criticism should *not* respect national boundaries. He says that English critics "must dwell much on foreign thought," because "the best" isn't confined to England alone.[1] In his desire for an international literary climate rather than one confined to national boundaries, Arnold expresses sentiments similar to Goethe's call for a world literature or a global literary tradition.

A critic whose work helped to shape the nationalist as opposed to the internationalist side of literary studies was literary historian Hippolyte Taine (1828–93). Though he was French, Taine's most important work was his *History of English Literature* (1863). Previous histories of English literature had been produced since the eighteenth century, but Taine's distinctive feature was his focus on what he calls, in a famous phrase in French, *race, milieu, moment* ("race, environment, epoch"). He posits that a nation's literature is a product of its geography, its history, and the race of its people. Marx (see Chapter 8), a contemporary, also put forward a model for understanding literature as a product of its history, contending that works of literature are determined by their economic and social circumstances. For Taine, however, the nineteenth-century

---

1   Arnold, "Function," 32.

conception of race is the determining factor. He calls race "the innate and hereditary dispositions which man brings with him into the world, and which, as a rule, are united with the marked differences in the temperament and structure of the body." So for him, English literature is racially *Anglo-Saxon* literature (as opposed to French, Russian, or Japanese) – there's a national disposition or character that's determined by the geography and history of a place and that's reflected in its literature. He begins his history of English literature by discussing the weather – because the English climate is foggy and cold, the Anglo-Saxon disposition is gloomy and thus English literature is also gloomy. He lists the characteristics of the Saxon race: "Huge white bodies, cool-blooded, with fierce blue eyes, reddish flaxen hair; ravenous stomachs, filled with meat and cheese, heated by strong drinks; of a cold temperament, slow to love, home-stayers, prone to brutal drunkenness: these are to this day the features which descent and climate preserve in the race."[1]

This racially determinist model that sees national characters as growing out of the soil of a place, as it were, and as unchanging, obviously does not factor in migration, cross-cultural influences, or variations among individuals. As mentioned earlier, the nineteenth-century "science" of race that tried to prove that there are essential biological differences between groups of people developed as a way to justify slavery, colonialism, and white supremacy and has since been discredited. Though Taine's racialized literary history seems benign in comparison to other products of theories of race, such as segregation and lynching, it is racist nonetheless. Though distasteful to modern sensibilities, Taine's ideas about race and climate were extremely influential at the time. He helped to develop historical criticism (see Chapter 7) by examining literature as a product of its time and circumstances. His focus on the unity of national literary traditions became part of the foundation of much university literary studies, where scholars often specialize in one national tradition rather than in a more Arnoldian canon of "the best that is known and thought in the world."

Decadent Aesthetics

The word **DECADENCE** in the late nineteenth century evoked the idea that the world was not improving but getting worse. Though many social critics worried about this, a few creative writers embraced the more hedonistic aspects of the decline of traditional values. Late-nineteenth-century decadent writers such as

---

1   Hippolyte A. Taine, *History of English Literature*, vol. 1, trans. H. Van Laun (New York: Frederick Ungar, 1965), 17, 41.

Charles Baudelaire (1822–67) and Oscar Wilde actually have much in common with 1960s and 1970s countercultural figures (from poets like Allan Ginsberg to rock stars like David Bowie), reveling in sex, drugs, rock and roll, outrageous fashions, and especially beauty in all its forms.

Though they anticipated the 1960s generation, this group of writers also looked backwards to the Romanticism of the first part of the nineteenth century (discussed at the beginning of this chapter). They take inspiration from Romantic figures like Keats, who famously celebrated beauty in art in poetic lines such as "A thing of beauty is a joy for ever" and "Beauty is truth, truth beauty."[1] Wordsworth and Coleridge provided them, likewise, with notions about the importance of the creative imagination and the organic unity of a work of art.

In championing beauty and the ideal of **ART FOR ART'S SAKE**, these decadent writers were reacting against some of the ideas discussed in the previous section, particularly realism, utilitarianism, and nationalism. They didn't want art to be realistic, but instead to provide an escape from the everyday world. They hated the idea of the usefulness of art, saying, in Wilde's words, "All art is quite useless."[2] In search of pleasure and beauty, they crossed national boundaries and transgressed social taboos. Their pursuit of pleasure and interest in fashion and beauty reflected the growth of consumer capitalism during this time, as shopping and luxury goods became more and more popular, while their avoidance of politics may suggest a turning away from the same social unrest that the realists commented upon. While writers such as Dickens saw the child labor and factories of their day as something to make readers aware of, these later writers avoided such topics altogether.

Poe's Philosophy of Composition

The name Edgar Allan Poe (1809–49) conjures up images of ravens squawking "nevermore," crumbling castles, and premature burials. Poe is one of the great masters of gothic horror, and his work also paved the way for science fiction and detective fiction. He never received much recognition for his work during his lifetime, but since his death in 1849 his reputation has continued to grow. As a struggling writer, Poe wrote for a variety of American magazines and newspapers. Alongside his famous short stories, he also wrote a number of influential pieces of criticism that borrow from some of the British Romantic

---

1   John Keats, *Endymion* 1.1; "Ode on a Grecian Urn" l. 49, *Complete Poems*, ed. Jack Stillinger (Cambridge, MA: Harvard UP, 1982).
2   Oscar Wilde, *The Picture of Dorian Gray* (New York: Signet, 1995), 18.

writers, especially Coleridge. The best illustration of his critical principles can be found in his seminal essay, "The Philosophy of Composition" (1846).

Poe describes, somewhat tongue-in-cheek, how he came to write his most famous poem, "The Raven" (1845). He says his process of composition began at the end, that he wrote "backwards," starting with the effect he wished to achieve and then working backwards to figure out how to achieve that effect through every aspect of the poem (length, subject-matter, rhyme scheme, and so forth). First, he says, he decided that his aim was to achieve the effect of beauty. Then he asked what the "*tone* of its highest manifestation" was, answering that "melancholy is thus the most legitimate of all the poetical tones." After deciding that he wanted a repeated refrain word to create a melancholy effect, he then considered not the *meaning* of the refrain word but its sound. He decided that the long *o* is the saddest vowel and *r* the saddest consonant, so he needed a word that contains those sounds. "In such a search," he says, "it would have been absolutely impossible to overlook the word 'Nevermore.'" Finally he settles upon the speaker of the refrain, quite naturally a talking raven, and on the topic of this melancholy poem, "the death ... of a beautiful woman ... the most poetical topic in the world."[1] Though he's almost certainly half joking when he turns the creation of his beautiful poem into a math problem, Poe is completely serious about the underlying principles of his essay:

1. the purpose of art is to create beauty, nothing else;

2. works of art are organic unities, with all aspects of a piece of writing working together to achieve an effect; and

3. the role of criticism is to determine the effect a work is aiming for and to study the unity of a work of art in all its aspects.

Poe's ideas, which draw upon Aristotle, Kant, Coleridge, and other authors, made their way to France and helped to shape an emerging literary movement there. (Though Poe didn't live to see his French success, he would have loved it.) Although American, he always thought of himself as writing for an international rather than a specifically American audience. In fact, he rejected calls for American literary nationalism made by American writer Ralph Waldo Emerson (1803–82) and others.

---

1   Edgar Allan Poe, "The Philosophy of Composition," *Literary Criticism of Edgar Allan Poe*, ed. Robert L. Hough (Lincoln: U of Nebraska P, 1965), 24–26.

Art for Art's Sake

One of the most important ideas of the decadent writers was the concept of art for art's sake, meaning that the purpose of art and literature is to *be* artistic and literary, to provide beauty and pleasure, rather than to produce social commentary or engage in political debates. French philosopher Victor Cousin (1792–1867) first used the phrase (in French, "l'art pour l'art") in an 1818 essay, where he was drawing upon the philosophy of Kant (see Chapter 4).

In the preface to his novel *Mademoiselle de Maupin* (1836), French novelist Théophile Gautier elaborates upon the idea that art should not be useful. He famously says, "There is nothing truly beautiful but that which can never be of any use whatsoever; everything useful is ugly, for it is the expression of some need, and man's needs are ignoble and disgusting.... The most useful place in a house is the water-closet [toilet]."[1] So Gautier considered books that tried to make a difference in the world through social commentary as ugly but useful – like a toilet.

Probably the most famous name associated with the art for art's sake movement and literary decadence is the French poet Baudelaire, who admired both Poe and Gautier and borrowed liberally from them. He also translated Poe into French, helping to make him one of the most beloved writers in France after his death. Baudelaire celebrates the evil, bizarre, and grotesque in art and believes that all of these things could be sources of great beauty and originality.

In one of his most famous essays, "The Painter of Modern Life" (1863), Baudelaire touches upon nearly all of the key points that make him such an important figure for the decadents. He takes a Poe story called "The Man of the Crowd" (which he had translated) and uses it to discuss the modern artist as a "passionate spectator," an urban wanderer (or *flâneur*), and a lover of fashion (or dandy). He describes this perfect *flâneur*: "To be away from home and yet to feel oneself everywhere at home; to see the world, to be at the centre of the world, and yet to remain hidden from the world." He says dandyism is "the last spark of heroism amid decadence," and includes a whole section praising women who wear heavy make-up ("In Praise of Cosmetics") to enhance their artificiality.[2]

All of these ideas connect back to the decadents' central ideas about art and literature: they prefer writing to be beautiful but detached from real-life

---

1   Théophile Gautier, *Mademoiselle de Maupin: A Romance of Love and Passion* (Paris: Société des Beaux-Arts, 1905), xxvii–xxviii.
2   Charles Baudelaire, "The Painter of Modern Life," *The Painter of Modern Life and Other Essays*, trans. Jonathan Mayne (London: Phaidon, 1995), 9, 28–29.

concerns, extremely modern and daring in its ideas but without promoting a particular social or political agenda. Though so far decadence sounds like an extremely French movement, one of its greatest practitioners was in fact an Irishman, Oscar Wilde, a detached, urban dandy who celebrated the uselessness but beauty of art.

Wilde admired and emulated the French decadent writers. His novel *The Picture of Dorian Gray* (1890), for example, contains a tribute to the most famous of French decadent novels, J.-K. Huysmans's *Against Nature* (1884). Another formative influence on his pronouncements about art was his teacher at Oxford, Walter Pater (1839–94). We find in the preface to *Dorian Gray* a few of Pater's key concepts. Where Wilde writes, "From the point of view of form, the type of all the arts is the art of the musician," Pater had written, "All art constantly aspires towards the condition of music."[1] That is, good art is about producing beauty through its form rather than about conveying a particular message, just as music is a nonrepresentational art form. Similarly, Wilde echoes Pater's **IMPRESSIONISTIC** critical approach. For Pater, the purpose of art is to produce an impression in the mind of the spectator or reader, and the role of the critic is to render that impression, to describe the effect the work of art had on him or her rather than strive for Arnoldian objectivity. Criticism is thus subjective rather than scientific, an idea that twentieth-century theorists would both challenge and echo in a variety of ways. I.A. Richards's practical criticism (see Chapter 6), for example, develops as a response to Paterian impressionism, while later reader-response critics such as Stanley Fish (see Chapter 9) resume Pater's concern with the minds of individual readers.

Nietzsche's Radical Philosophy

Even if you've never read or even heard of German philosopher Friedrich Nietzsche, you probably are already acquainted with some of his words and concepts. Versions of his aphorism *"From life's military school. – What doesn't kill me makes me stronger"* have inspired t-shirts and song lyrics, including hits by Kanye West ("Stronger," 2007) and Kelly Clarkson ("Stronger [What Doesn't Kill You]," 2011).[2] His notion of eternal recurrence has inspired the reincarnation plot of David Mitchell's novel *Cloud Atlas* (2004) (and its film

---

1   Wilde, *Picture*, 18; Walter Pater, *The Renaissance. Three Major Texts*, ed. William E. Buckler (New York: New York UP, 1986), 156.

2   Friedrich Nietzsche, *Twilight of the Idols or, How to Philosophize with the Hammer*, trans. Richard Polt (Indianapolis: Hackett, 1997), 6.

adaptation) and the philosophical spoutings ("Time is a flat circle") of Matthew McConaughey's character Rust Cohle in the HBO program *True Detective* (2014). Nietzsche's pronouncement "God is dead" (repeated often in his works) has become notorious – even inspiring the plot of a Christian movie about an atheistic philosophy professor (*God's Not Dead*, 2014) – and he also famously coined the word *Superman* (*Übermensch*, or "Overman," in German).

Because much of his writing is cryptic, fragmentary, and epigrammatic, it's endlessly quotable and open to a variety of interpretations. His ideas provided inspiration for both the racial theories of Adolf Hitler and the Nazis and the anti-fascist ideas of existentialists such as Simone de Beauvoir and Jean-Paul Sartre. His anti-foundationalist ideas have also inspired many of the most important thinkers in twentieth-century literary theory, such as Jacques Derrida and Michel Foucault, both of whom cite Nietzsche as a formative influence on their thought.

Nietzsche was trained as a classical philologist, a scholar of language and literature, and in his first book (*The Birth of Tragedy*, 1872), which examines ancient Greek drama, he distinguishes between the Apollonian and Dionysiac tendencies in Greek art. Apollo and Dionysius were Greek gods of the arts, but Nietzsche associates Apollonian art more with rationality, visuality, and language, and Dionysiac art with music and revelry (Dionysus is also the god of wine). The full title of the work, *The Birth of Tragedy from the Spirit of Music*, suggests which side Nietzsche is on. He believes that music comes before language and resists being put into words. Music for him is the highest form of art because it can't be reduced to rational ideas, and that escape from language helps people to forget the miseries of human existence. (Pater and Wilde express similar ideas about music as the highest form of art.)

Nietzsche's essay "On Truth and Lying in a Non-Moral Sense," written in 1873 but not published until 1903, after his death, elaborates upon *The Birth of Tragedy* and gives a fuller picture of his ideas about language and epistemology. Nietzsche was a philosophical skeptic in the tradition of Enlightenment skeptic David Hume (see Chapter 4). In fact, his skepticism is so extreme it's often called **NIHILISM**. The root word *nihil* is Latin for "nothing," so nihilism is thus a philosophy of nothingness, one that asserts that life has no inherent meaning.

He begins the essay by asserting the insignificance of humanity within the vastness of the universe, calling humans arrogant for thinking that they matter. He says that people have to cling to lies and deceptions in order to keep going in the face of this insignificance. For Nietzsche all words and concepts are fundamentally lies, human creations that bear no relation to any kind of timeless, transcendent reality. He takes Plato's idea about forms (see Chapter 2) and turns it on its head. Plato says that concepts come from God; they are eternal, perfect, and unchanging, and all individual examples of an entity (such as various couches) are merely pale imitations of the ideal form. Nietzsche reverses this formulation, arguing that humans observe individual things (he uses the example of leaves), forget the individuality of each thing by "making equivalent that which is non-equivalent," create a category that these things all fit into, and eventually forget that they have created the category and instead think of it as something real and scientific.[1] For him, all so-called "truths" are only illusions and metaphors that humans use to make sense of the world. He believes, like linguist Ferdinand de Saussure (see Chapter 6), that languages divide up the world in arbitrary ways.

However, the arbitrariness of language and meaninglessness of life for Nietzsche are cause for celebration, not despair. He promotes Dionysiac, abstract, experimental art that liberates individuals from rationality and realism. In that way, his ideas echo those of the aestheticist and decadent thinkers discussed above. Though he's coming from a philosophical rather than a literary background, he arrives at the same place: questioning conventional morality and reveling in art for its own sake.

Fin-de-siècle Fictions

The reaction against nineteenth-century realism takes on many forms, from the decadence of Baudelaire to the nihilism and celebration of experimentalism of Nietzsche. In the popular novel, the last decade of the nineteenth century (called the fin-de-siècle or "end of the century") was a time of the revival of romance and a turn to new strains of fiction. Here are a few examples of the notable fictions of the tail end of the century:

+ **Gothic, with a twist:** Bram Stoker's *Dracula* (1897) popularized the vampire story but incorporated newer technologies such as the telegram and sound recording.

+ **Science fictions:** H.G. Wells and Jules Verne, among others, wrote novels about journeys to outer space and under the sea, invisible men and time machines, which helped establish science fiction as a major and enduring genre.

---

1   Friedrich Nietzsche, "On Truth and Lying in a Non-Moral Sense," *The Birth of Tragedy and Other Writings*, ed. Raymond Geuss and Ronald Speirs (Cambridge: Cambridge UP, 1999), 145.

+ **Detective stories:** Though he wasn't the first literary detective, Arthur Conan Doyle's Sherlock Holmes character was more popular than any of the detectives who preceded him, and detective fiction exploded in popularity as a result.

+ **Film:** The motion picture camera, a late-nineteenth-century invention, was about to reshape popular culture in fundamental ways in the twentieth century. It seems impossible to imagine modern life without film technology.

On the eve of the twentieth century, the world was infinitely more complex, thanks to the growth of new technologies for transportation, communication, entertainment, and warfare. Likewise, the world of literary theory and criticism became increasingly more intricate as literary studies was established as an academic discipline. Chapters 6 to 9 will examine twentieth- and twenty-first-century theory and criticism (with some forays back to the nineteenth century and earlier), but from this point the book will break away from strict chronology in order to group certain strands of theoretical approaches together: formalist, historical, political, and psychological approaches. These strands overlap, interfuse, and recombine, but I will look at each separately before bringing them together again in the conclusion.

Suggestions for Further Reading

Anderson, Benedict. *Imagined Communities: Reflections on the Origins and Spread of Nationalism.* 1983. London: Verso, 2000.

Benjamin, Walter. *The Writer of Modern Life: Essays on Charles Baudelaire.* Ed. Michael W. Jennings. Cambridge, MA: Harvard UP, 2006.

Day, Gary. *Literary Criticism: A New History.* Edinburgh: Edinburgh UP, 2008.

Habib, M.A.R. *The Cambridge History of Literary Criticism.* Vol. 6. Cambridge: Cambridge UP, 2013.

Hustvedt, Asti, ed. *The Decadent Reader: Fiction, Fantasy, and Perversion from Fin-de-Siècle France.* New York: Zone Books, 1998.

Weinstein, Leo. *Hippolyte Taine.* New York: Twayne, 1972.

Wellek, René. *A History of Modern Criticism: 1750–1950.* 5 vols. New Haven, CT: Yale UP, 1965.

Six: Twentieth- and Twenty-First-Century Formalist Approaches

IN THIS CHAPTER, WE now enter the era of literary studies as a university subject and an academic discipline. Universities proliferated in the twentieth century, and a whole range of new fields of study came into their own, including sociology, anthropology, and other social science fields. The university went from being a place of gentlemanly, liberal education in the classics to a more democratic institution where students can specialize in a variety of fields and receive training for numerous careers and vocations.

In America, higher education expanded dramatically in the years following World War II, in part because of the GI Bill, which provided funding for returning veterans to attend college. The numbers of students attending college keeps rising: in 1947, 2.3 million students were enrolled in American institutions of higher education, and by 2010 that number had increased to 21 million. At the same time, the demographics of the student population have changed: 29 per cent of those 1947 students were women, as compared to 56 per cent of the 2010 students.[1] The student population has become much more diverse in terms of race and ethnicity as well.

Prior to the twentieth century, literary theory and criticism had been the province of philosophers, humanists, critics, and "men of letters." As it moved into the university context and as universities expanded, literary studies became a job: one that could be trained for by getting a PhD. Because of this, there's simply *more* theory and criticism to deal with after 1900. For that reason, I've divided my discussion of theory and criticism since 1900 into four separate

---

1   US Department of Education, Digest of Education Statistics: http://nces.ed.gov/programs/digest/.

chapters. These chapters will look at the institutional age of literary theory and criticism by subdividing it into four interrelated types: formalist, historical, political, and psychological. Grouping approaches in this way will help to pinpoint some lines of influence and affiliation among the theorists I discuss, but readers should keep in mind that these groupings are for the purposes of organization only. The boundaries among the four types I outline are porous, and many critical approaches combine aspects of more than one of these types of concerns as well as from the theorists discussed in Chapters 2 to 5. Because the history I trace in these chapters is much more recent and thus likely to be more familiar territory for readers, I will discuss major events since 1900 only where relevant, rather than include a detailed chronological account of the century. World War I, World War II, the civil rights movement, the women's movement, new technologies such as television and the Internet, the rise and fall of the Soviet Union, the Cold War, decolonization, global migration, changing demographics – all these factors and many more have shaped theory and criticism in the modern era.

In this chapter, I look at a set of critical traditions that are not always grouped together in histories of literary theory. The range of approaches I'm calling FOR-MALIST here are united by an interest in literary form and literary language. Over the course of this discussion I will try to make clear both what these approaches have in common and where they diverge. Of course, literary critics have always studied literary form in a variety of ways, from Aristotle's interest in genres to Longinus's study of the sublime to Quintilian's rhetorical approach to medieval allegory and beyond. More immediately, twentieth-century formalist approaches are particularly informed by Romantic ideas about the organic unity of a work of art (especially Coleridge's) and aestheticist ideas of art for art's sake. Twentieth- and twenty-first-century formalist critics study language, poetic devices, narrative strategies, genres, style, and a range of other matters, but what unites them is a foregrounding of the *formal* aspects of literature as opposed to matters of history, politics, or psychology (though I touch upon those concerns throughout this history). Most approaches to literature today involve at least some element of formalism, and certainly the way most contemporary students study literature in the classroom includes some degree of attention to matters of form, craft, and textual analysis. In this chapter, I trace the formalist tradition from nineteenth-century philology through Russian formalism and New Criticism, to more recent structuralist and poststructuralist approaches, including narratology.

The Philological Tradition

The first type of formalism in the institutional age of literary criticism was philology, the historical study of languages. The origins of philology go back to late-eighteenth-century Germany, when German scholars (such as the Grimm brothers, mentioned in Chapter 5) developed methods for studying the history of languages, etymology, grammar, and other matters. If you study the history of languages to this day you'll encounter something called Grimm's Law, a principle describing how consonant sounds in certain languages shifted over time as languages evolved. The Grimm of the law is the same Grimm (Jacob) who collected all those famous fairy tales, as the philological study of languages was intertwined with studies of folklore and the oral tradition.

The idea of the modern research university also originated in Germany, so as universities restructured themselves or were newly created along German principles in the late nineteenth century, they imported Germanic methods for studying literature and other subjects. Philology was already the method for studying the Greek and Roman classics, so as modern languages began to become a part of the university curriculum, philological approaches were the first to be adopted.

What did it mean to be a philologist at the start of the twentieth century? As discussed in Chapter 1, philologists read literary texts in order to learn about the history of languages. The works of Geoffrey Chaucer, for example, could serve as a source of information about verb formations in Middle English, or Christopher Marlowe's plays could be used to study syntax in the late sixteenth century. What the words were actually saying mattered much less than the grammar, syntax, vocabulary, and other linguistic aspects of texts. Clearly this was not a recipe for a vibrant and long-lasting academic discipline (the English major would probably now be defunct if all it ever did was look at verb conjugations), but the decisive break with philology didn't take place in Anglo-American universities until after World War I. After a long and bloody war with Germany, American and British scholars felt it was their patriotic duty to develop some homegrown methods of studying English literature. Various new types of formalist approaches were some of the first to be developed.

Saussure and Structuralist Linguistics

While Anglo-American critics would develop a range of formalist strategies to replace philology in literary studies, within the study of languages themselves came another set of challenges that would reshape the field of linguistic study and also profoundly inspire literary critics. Ferdinand de Saussure is the founding figure of modern linguistics. His ideas influenced both the Russian Formalists of the 1910s and the **STRUCTURALIST** and **POSTSTRUCTURALIST** theorists of the 1950s and later. Oddly enough, his reputation rests mostly on a single text, one that he didn't write and that wasn't published until after his death.

Saussure was a professor of philology at the University of Geneva. From 1906 to 1911 he gave a series of lectures that would revolutionize twentieth-century thought, but he died in 1913 before he had a chance to publish his research. Luckily his students were good note-takers. His ideas were reconstructed by collecting and comparing various students' notes from the lectures and were published in 1916 as *Course in General Linguistics*. In this work, Saussure begins by discussing the history of philology, the way it developed in late eighteenth-century Germany initially focusing on classical languages. He then goes on to distinguish his approach, linguistics, from philology, saying that while philology studies the history of languages, his method is to study languages as structures.

Many terms and concepts taken from Saussure have made their way into literary theory and criticism. Here are some of the most important ones:

+ **Language (*langue*) vs. speech (*parole*)**: By language (the French word *langue*), Saussure means the "system of signs" that make up a particular language.[1] This includes vocabulary, grammatical rules, and common expressions. He opposes language to speech (*parole*), which is the infinite number of acts of speaking by individual speakers of a language. His interest is in the underlying structure of language rather than in individual texts or speakers.

+ **Signified, signifier, sign**: Saussure writes that "a linguistic sign is not a link between a thing and a name but between a concept [signified] and a sound pattern [signifier]" (66). For Saussure, as for Nietzsche, words don't give names to preexisting things but create concepts that shape the way we view the world. The **SIGNIFIER** is the word itself, and the **SIGNIFIED** is the "meaning" of the word. Taken together, signifier and signified make up the **SIGN**. Signifier and signified are inextricably linked, like two sides of a sheet of paper; you can't separate them. That is, for an English speaker the word *tree* brings to mind the image of a tree, and seeing a tree brings to mind the word *tree*. We view the world through the words available to us.

---

1   Ferdinand de Saussure, *Course in General Linguistics*, trans. Roy Harris (La Salle, IL: Open Court, 1986), 14. Subsequent references will appear in parentheses within the text.

- **The arbitrary nature of the sign**: There is no *necessary* connection between signifier and signified, even in cases of onomatopoeia (words that sound like the thing they're describing, such as animal noises) or interjections (exclamations such as *argh*). This is why different languages have different words for the same concept (*tree* vs. *arbor*) and even different words for animal noises (English roosters say "cockadoodledoo" while French ones say "cocorico," for example). Additionally, the way concepts divide up the world is also arbitrary: "If words had the job of representing concepts fixed in advance, one would be able to find exact equivalents for them as between one language and another. But this is not the case" (114–15). Different languages conceive of time, familial relations, and other matters differently.

- **Synchronic linguistics**: the study of language as a system or structure. This is opposed to diachronic linguistics, the study of a language as it evolves in time (such as philology). You can't do both at the same time. To study language synchronically a linguist must take a snapshot of a particular moment in the life of a language. The structure itself is constantly evolving. Today, for example, the *who/whom* distinction and the subjunctive formation *if I were* are both fading from the rules of English as a language, while new words such as *selfie* and *hashtag* enter the language and are added to dictionaries every year.

- **Value**: The value of a sign comes from its relation to other signs in the language system. The little slice of the chaotic world of thought that a sign denotes is distinguished from all other signs that designate different portions of thought. Saussure uses the example of *mouton* in French, which has two equivalents in English: *sheep* (the animal) and *mutton* (the meat). The value of *mouton* in French is different than the value of *sheep* in English, since it signifies a larger concept (both animal and meat as opposed to just the animal). The same can be said for phonemes (sounds) and letters of the alphabet. English distinguishes between the phonemes represented by *t* and *th* but some other languages don't, so English speakers can "hear" that distinction while speakers of languages without that distinction have more difficulty. Likewise, letters signify through their distinction from other letters. Many letters in the Roman alphabet consist of a circle with a line attached to it, but the relation of circle to line creates the difference between *q*, *p*, *b*, and *d*.

- **Syntagms**: These are two or more consecutive units within a language. Syntagms are combinations of words that belong to language as a structure rather than to individual speakers – common phrases, idioms, and clichés. Saussure's point about syntagms is that there is no clear border between what belongs to language as a collective structure and what is the creation of an individual speaker. We all use a combination of creativity and habit in producing new utterances, working within the structures we inherit from language.

Saussure's interest in language as a system of signs, his distinction between signifier and signified, and his emphasis on the arbitrary nature of the sign all became foundational concepts within linguistics, which fairly quickly took over from philology as the academic discipline that studies languages. His ideas also helped to shape the movement known as Russian Formalism in the 1910s and 1920s. His most significant impact on literary theory, however, wouldn't happen for another couple of decades and would take place outside of literary studies, with the creation of structuralist anthropology (see below).

Russian Formalism

The first group of critics to use Saussure's ideas to break away from philology lived in Russia, which was soon to become the Soviet Union. In 1915–16, the Moscow Linguistic Circle formed as a group of like-minded scholars who were influenced by Saussure's revolutionary structuralist linguistics. The Russian Formalists, as they came to be known, used Saussure's ideas about linguistic structure as a way to study literary texts and literary language. The Russian Formalist Boris Eichenbaum (1886–1959) outlines the movement in a 1926 essay, saying that Formalists want to "create an independent science of literature" by turning away from history and psychology and instead taking inspiration from linguistics.[1] Beginning in 1916, members of the circle began to publish essays on formalist topics, particularly about poetry and **POETICS**.

The Russian Formalists did not believe in a distinction between form and content in a work of literature, because they conceived of works of literature as pure form. In other words, the meaning of what's being said cannot be separated from the ways in which it's being said. Earlier versions of this idea can be found throughout nineteenth-century criticism, from Coleridge's insistence on the organic unity of a work of art to Pater's declaration that all art aspires to the condition of music, or pure form (see Chapter 5). Yet never before had

---

1 Boris Eichenbaum, "The Theory of the 'Formal Method,'" *Russian Formalist Criticism: Four Essays*, trans. Lee T. Lemon and Marion J. Reis (Lincoln: U of Nebraska P, 1965), 103.

these ideas been framed in such a scientific manner. The Russian Formalists developed rigorous procedures for studying poetic language and narrative structures, and some of their publications can almost look a bit like math problems, as Figure 5 demonstrates.

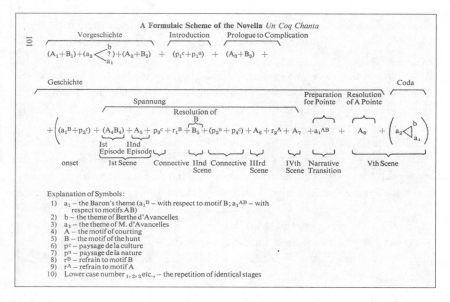

Figure 5: A.A. Reformatsky, "An Essay on the Analysis of the Composition of the Novella" [1922], *Russian Formalism: A Collection of Articles and Texts in Translation*, ed. Stephen Bann and John E. Bowlt (Edinburgh: Scottish Academic Press, 1973), 101.

A key concept for the Russian Formalists is **DEFAMILIARIZATION**, in Victor Shklovsky's words the idea that art "makes the familiar seem strange."[1] Shklovsky praises writers such as Laurence Sterne, author of the eighteenth-century novel *Tristram Shandy* (see Chapter 4), who lay bare their technique. Like Sterne, the Formalist critics attempted to make familiar literary devices and structures "strange" by analyzing their workings in detail. Rather than treating literary works as mystified works of art emanating from God-like imaginations, they dissected texts as though they were puzzles to be solved. They favored experimental writers and avant-garde techniques that allowed readers to peer behind the curtain to see how literature gets made.

After the Russian Revolution in 1917, the newly formed Soviet Union became a Communist state, ideologically inspired by the writings of Karl Marx

---

1   Victor Shklovsky, "Art as Technique," *Russian Formalist Criticism*, 13.

(see Chapter 8). The Communists increasingly wanted to monitor literature and scholarship to make sure it adhered to Marxist principles. The first attack on the Russian Formalists came in 1923, when Leon Trotsky (1879–1940) critiqued the Formalist method for ignoring social and historical forces. By the end of the 1920s, after Joseph Stalin came to power, Soviet authorities cracked down on Formalist criticism because they believed it didn't adhere to Marxist ideas about art being shaped by social and economic forces. One of the key Formalists, Roman Jakobson (1896–1982), who was only 19 years old when he helped found the Moscow Linguistics Circle, had already left for Prague, where he founded an influential school of linguistics named for that city. The Russian Formalists who remained in the Soviet Union had to shift to more historically based studies to conform to Stalinist dictates.

Russian Formalism as an organized literary movement lasted less than two decades, and for a long time its works were unknown in the non-Russian-speaking world. However, the influence they would have on later twentieth-century formalist approaches is immense. Through Jakobson they provided inspiration for French structuralism, while Tzvetan Todorov and Julia Kristeva renewed interest in their works in the 1960s, leading to the creation of the field of **NAR-RATOLOGY**. They also inspired the field of **STYLISTICS**, which takes a linguistic approach to the study of literature. I discuss the influence of the Russian Formalists on structuralism and narratology later on in the chapter.

Anglo-American Formalisms

While Russian Formalists Shklovsky and Eichenbaum were developing a linguistically based "science of literature," at nearly the same time, but independently, British and American critics were attempting a similar project. Russian and Anglo-American formalisms both strove for a less subjective, more empirical approach to literature to replace philology. Both groups rejected philological and historical studies in favor of close examination of literary form: "the text itself" rather than such external factors as historical context or author psychology. Eventually these two movements would meet, particularly through the efforts of René Wellek (1903–95), but initially language, geography, and politics separated them. Wellek was a member of Jakobson's Prague Linguistic Circle. When he came to America, he met the New Critic Austin Warren (1899–1986) in 1939, and they found much common ground in their approaches and later collaborated on a book called *Theory of Literature* (1949), an important formalist study.

Russian and Anglo-American formalisms differ in a number of key ways. Among the most important is the type of texts favored by each group. The

Russians loved experimental, self-conscious writing that defamiliarized literary conventions by highlighting the text's status as a constructed artifact. The British and Americans tended to look to older texts, particularly the canon of English poetry. The Russians were also much more influenced by linguistics and a more scientific approach to literature, while their Western counterparts built upon the tradition of literary criticism and reviewing linked to people such as Matthew Arnold. Politically, too, there were major differences, the American New Critics in particular being a much more conservative and religious group than the Russians.

Practical and New Criticisms

The most famous twentieth-century formalist approach is American **NEW CRITICISM**, which is often distinguished from British **PRACTICAL CRITICISM**. The histories of the two formalist movements are intellectually intertwined, however, even though geographically separated, and are best thought of as a transatlantic critical movement. The epithet "New Critics" came from a 1941 book by John Crowe Ransom entitled *The New Criticism*, though *The New Criticism* had previously been the title of a 1910 lecture by J.E. Springarn at Columbia University. In his book, Ransom traces the formative influences on his critical school and begins with British critic I.A. Richards (1893–1979), the founder of practical criticism. Richards and other British critics in turn had been inspired in part by the essays of T.S. Eliot (1888–1965), born in America but later to become a British citizen, so this period of the history of literary criticism truly is transatlantic.

Richards taught at Cambridge University and began his career as a philosopher of language. An early publication, *The Meaning of Meaning* (1923, coauthored with C.K. Ogden), explores the ways in which language conveys meaning. Other language philosophers of the time, such as Ludwig Wittgenstein and Bertrand Russell, were exploring similar questions in their works, which would become central to the field of analytic philosophy. Analytic philosophy is a more scientific branch of philosophy and is dominant in American universities today; it examines questions of language, logic, and meaning. It's distinguished from Continental philosophy, a tradition that derives from French and German thinkers (such as Kant and Hegel, discussed in Chapter 4, and Heidegger and Derrida, discussed below).

In *The Principles of Literary Criticism* (1924), Richards builds upon his work on language and meaning and calls for a more scientific form of criticism. He characterizes the current state of critical theories about literature as "chaotic" and asks, "Why is one opinion about works of art not as good as another?"[1] If criticism is purely relative, and one person's reading of a poem is as good as anyone else's, that is, then how can literary criticism be an academic discipline? He's responding here to Walter Pater's **IMPRESSIONISM**, discussed in Chapter 5, the idea that critics should describe the impression a work of art has on them rather than strive for objectivity. Richards's most famous book, *Practical Criticism* (1929), tries to answer this question by showing how certain opinions about literature are better than others. In this book he describes a procedure whereby he distributed poems to students without including any author information and asked them to comment on the poems. He then analyzed the student responses, pointing out how they misunderstood or misread the texts. In the second half of the book he calls for better training in careful critical reading for students as a way of preventing misreading. This idea of a correct way to read a poem would prove extremely important for the American New Critics.

Another British critic, William Empson (1906–84), studied with Richards and put his teacher's ideas about critical reading into practice in his own important studies. In his first major book, *Seven Types of Ambiguity* (1930), Empson conducts close, line-by-line readings of poems in order to classify different modes of ambiguity in poetic language. He credits this method to an earlier work, the poets Laura Riding and Robert Graves's *A Survey of Modernist Poetry* (1927). Riding and Graves in turn credit Edgar Allan Poe (see Chapter 5) and the French symbolists as models for their interpretive strategies and close attention to language. Other important British formalists include F.R. and Q.D. Leavis (1895–1978, 1906–1981), who edited a journal called *Scrutiny* for two decades beginning in 1932. The journal's title suggests its close attention to language, something shared by all these critics.

Alongside a close attention to language, a characteristic of practical criticism is its lack of attention to the author. In a 1919 essay, "Tradition and the Individual Talent," T.S. Eliot suggests that critics should focus on the poem rather than the poet. He calls poetry an impersonal art form because poets don't express their personalities in their writing, but instead take part in a long poetic tradition where they subsume their individuality to the larger medium. He calls this process depersonalization.

The American New Critics used Eliot's idea of depersonalization and Empson's method of **CLOSE READING** in order to establish an American variant of a more objective type of criticism of the type that Richards (and the Russian Formalists) had called for. As a group, the New Critics tend to be associated with universities in the US South, such as Vanderbilt University in Tennessee

---

1   I.A. Richards, *Principles of Literary Criticism*, ed. John Constable (New York: Routledge, 2001), 7.

and Louisiana State University, though a number of them later moved to northern universities such as Yale University in Connecticut. Their ideas helped shape twentieth-century literary studies in profound ways. Two textbooks by New Critics Cleanth Brooks and Robert Penn Warren, *Understanding Poetry* (1938) and *Understanding Fiction* (1943), promulgated New Critical methods of reading across American colleges and high schools, so much so that New Criticism became the dominant form of criticism in the US in the 1940s and 1950s. Every time teachers assign a close reading of a short story or poem, they are indebted to the New Critics for that concept.

Many guides to literary theory posit the New Critics as the antithesis to theory, suggesting that close reading is a natural or unsophisticated approach to literature while "theoretical" approaches add something more to close reading. Yet close reading and the practices of Anglo-American formalism were themselves built upon theories of interpretation (the idea that interpretation is not merely subjective but can be objective), authorship (the theory that poets lose their personalities in writing and that critics should pay attention to language over author), and reading (the notion of close reading stresses rereading and attention to the nuances of language). The New Critics privileged certain types of texts and certain types of questions, linguistically complex works of poetry and fiction, mostly by white male authors.

The New Critics became notorious for their pronouncements on literary studies. In a number of key books and essays, they declared the right and the wrong way to read literature, judging certain practices to be "heresies" or "fallacies." Here are a few of their key ideas:

- **"close reading"**: a method of literary analysis that privileges literary form over questions of history, intention, politics, or psychology. The New Critics paid close attention to literary expression and especially to moments of irony, ambiguity, and paradox in a text. One early New Critical manifesto is Ransom's "Criticism Inc." (1937). In it he calls for criticism to be more scientific by focusing on close readings of texts instead of focusing on personal response, history, linguistics, or morality.

- **"the heresy of paraphrase"**: This phrase, from Brooks's *The Well Wrought Urn* (1947), means that literary language can never be simplified into paraphrase and is always richer than any one interpretation. Brooks concentrates on moments of paradox in his close readings of poems, places where texts can't be simply paraphrased because they contain two contradictory meanings at the same time. For the New Critics, paradox is the essence of good literature.

+ **"the intentional fallacy"**: This phrase, the title of a 1946 essay by W.K. Wimsatt and Monroe Beardsley, refers to the idea that we can never know, and shouldn't try to determine, what an author intended. All we can go on are the words the author wrote and the effect they have on the reader. They argue that even if you were to ask authors point blank what they meant by a piece of writing, you couldn't trust their reply. An author's work should speak for itself. In a larger sense, this downplaying of authorial intention connects to a larger lack of interest in author biography and to Eliot's notion of depersonalization. A great work of literature, they believe, shouldn't be a piece of autobiography, but should have larger, impersonal artistic aims.

+ **"the affective fallacy"**: This is another Wimsatt and Beardsley phrase and the title of a 1949 essay cautioning readers not to confuse a text with their emotional response to it. Here they're arguing against Walter Pater's impressionistic approach to literary analysis in favor of something much more objective and scientific.

A number of the New Critics were associated with a movement called Southern Agrarianism. Ransom, Allen Tate, and Robert Penn Warren were among the "Twelve Southerners" who contributed to a collective volume called *I'll Take My Stand* (1930), whose title comes from a line in the Confederate anthem "Dixie." This manifesto in support of a "Southern way of life" is both anti-industrial and deeply racist. Warren, for example, in an essay called "The Briar Patch," defends segregation and calls for African Americans to stay in the rural South sharecropping rather than migrating to industrial jobs in the North. He ignores the realities of lynching and racial violence, treating African Americans as inherently inferior to whites. (He later recanted these views.) Within this Southern Agrarian context, the ideas of the New Critics can take on a sinister note. The turn away from formalism in the 1960s toward approaches that deal with race, class, and gender (see Chapter 8) is in part a response to this side of the New Critics. As literary studies has expanded to include more women and people of color (as scholars, students, and writers to be studied), the New Critics' isolation from context, emphasis on a white male canon, and racist past have become ever more dated.

Neo-Aristotelianism

While the New Critics were becoming entrenched at southern institutions from the 1930s to 1950s, a group of critics came together at the University of Chicago in the 1930s as their rivals. This group, the Chicago School or the Chicago NEO-ARISTOTELIANS, never became as dominant as the New Critics but consistently challenged them. R.S. Crane (1886–1967), Elder Olson (1909–92), and Richard McKeon (1900–85), among others, produced a more philosophical strain of formalism, inspired in large part by the works of Aristotle, especially the *Poetics* (see Chapter 2). While the New Critics looked to Coleridge and Eliot, the Chicago School engaged with a much longer critical tradition, discussing Longinus, medieval rhetoric, and Samuel Johnson, among other things.

The neo-Aristotelians wanted to reconcile differences among critical schools and castigate the New Critics for being too single-minded in their creation of heresies and fallacies. In an influential collection of essays, Crane accuses the New Critics of not paying enough attention to the generic context of a work (whether an author is writing in a didactic or satirical mode appropriate to a particular genre, for example). Instead of paying attention to the particular genres of individual poems, he says, the New Critics "read all poems as if their authors had constructed them on identical principles."[1] The Chicago critics brought an interest in genre and classification (Aristotle's specialties) back into literary studies.

They also revived an interest in RHETORIC, particularly through the writings of one of their most famous members, Wayne Booth (1921–2005). Booth was a student of Crane and later became his colleague at Chicago, where he taught for most of his long career. Through another of his teachers, Kenneth Burke (1897–1993), Booth became interested in rhetoric. In his books *A Grammar of Motives* (1945) and *A Rhetoric of Motives* (1950), Burke urges critics to pay attention to the rhetorical aspects of texts – the way in which works of literature aim to persuade – rather than to study them merely for their aesthetic or formal qualities.

In his first book, *The Rhetoric of Fiction* (1961), Booth combines Crane's attention to genre and speaking situation and Burke's interest in looking at literary technique in terms of rhetorical strategies to take on some conventional wisdom about fiction. He begins with the maxim that good novelists "show, don't tell" – the idea that good fiction should dramatize situations rather than speak directly to the reader. Booth's earlier work had been on the type

---

1   R.S. Crane, Introduction to *Critics and Criticism: Ancient and Modern*, ed. R.S. Crane (Chicago: U of Chicago P, 1952), 15.

of self-conscious narration where narrators directly address readers (a kind of "breaking the fourth wall"), particularly in relation to eighteenth-century novels, such as Henry Fielding's *Tom Jones* (1749) and Sterne's *Tristram Shandy*. The common critical view in the earlier part of the century, inspired by Henry James's pronouncements on the novel and the Flaubertian ideal of detachment, held that the author should be "objective" and should not editorialize or tell readers what to think. Booth counters this by pointing out that all novels express the viewpoint of their author, whether directly through a narrator or indirectly through characters. A reader can always detect an **IMPLIED AUTHOR** behind the characters and narrator with discernable values and views, and good readers must be alert to the rhetorical strategies and devices emanating from the implied author but expressed through narrators and characters.

Booth's concept of an implied author is a clever way around the New Critics' intentional fallacy – instead of talking about what the author intended, a critic can look at the implied author created by a text, the author's "second self." Implied authors are *not* the flesh and blood authors but versions of themselves that they put into their writing. In this way, Booth was able to analyze the ethical and rhetorical issues within a text rather than merely remain on the level of form. In order to discern the implied author's views, Booth studies the degree of distance between the narrator and the implied author. He classifies different types of narrators that an author can use (such as whether they're a character in the story or are conscious of the fact that they're telling a story). Booth calls the most extreme version of a narrator whose views are at odds with the implied author's an **UNRELIABLE NARRATOR**: "I have called a narrator *reliable* when he speaks for or acts in accordance with the norms of a work (which is to say, the implied author's norms), *unreliable* when he does not."[1] Extreme cases of narrative unreliability include narrators who are insane, naïve, or who lie to readers. Booth studies the ways in which readers are able to discern the rhetorical strategies behind such unreliable narrations so that we don't read Vladimir Nabokov's *Lolita* (1955) or, more recently, Alissa Nutting's *Tampa* (2013), as texts promoting pedophilia, and don't take the narrator of Jonathan Swift's "A Modest Proposal" (1729) at his word when he advocates eating babies. With his interest in narrative point of view and storytelling, Booth bridges the gap between the Anglo-American formalisms of the first half of the century and the narratology of the second half.

---

1   Wayne C. Booth, *The Rhetoric of Fiction* (Chicago: U of Chicago P, 1983), 158–59.

Lévi-Strauss and Structuralist Anthropology

I now turn from the English-speaking world back to Continental Europe to pick up the thread of structuralism. Structuralists, as the name suggests, study structures: the structure of language, the conceptual structures that underlie cultures and myths, and literary structure. Structuralism isn't necessarily merely formalist in its orientation, however: in later chapters I discuss structuralist historians such as Michel Foucault (Chapter 7), structuralist Marxists such as Louis Althusser (Chapter 8), and structuralist psychoanalytic critics such as Jacques Lacan (Chapter 9).

The story of how structuralism came to reshape twentieth-century thought begins during World War II. During the war, a French anthropologist named Claude Lévi-Strauss was teaching at the New School for Social Research in New York. In 1941 he met another wartime exile, the Russian Formalist critic Roman Jakobson (see above), who introduced him to Saussure's *Course in General Linguistics*. This reading sparked Lévi-Strauss's interest in structuralist linguistics, and he took Saussure's ideas and put them to use in his anthropological work.

Lévi-Strauss's book *Structural Anthropology* (1958) collects papers he had published between 1944 and 1957 and helped to make his name internationally. Lévi-Strauss's method breaks aspects of culture, such as myth and kinship structures, into their smallest possible structural elements (akin to the phonemes of a language) and then studies the entire cultural system as a structure akin to Saussure's *langue*. These cultural structures, he argues, are built upon underlying mental structures. He characterizes members of primitive cultures as *bricoleurs*, a French word meaning a tinkerer or improviser. While a scientist builds a system based on large concepts, a *bricoleur* improvises with whatever is at hand. Myth is thus a form of *bricolage* that primitive cultures assemble from the materials around them, and it can be analyzed to get at its underlying structures. For example, in his influential essay "The Structural Study of Myth" (1955), Lévi-Strauss takes Saussure's ideas about language and speech to analyze the common underlying structures across a range of mythologies, from the Oedipus myth to Zuni trickster stories. Though these cultures assemble different types of stories, their underlying structures are consistent. Similarly, in his discussion of kinship systems, he breaks down the entire set of kinship relations from a number of cultures into their smallest components such as brother-sister, maternal uncle-child, and so forth, in order to ascertain that the incest taboo is at the heart of all varieties of kinship systems. When Jacques Derrida talks about structures in his essay "Structure, Sign, and Play in the Discourse of the Human Sciences" (see Chapter 1), he uses Lévi-Strauss's discussion of the incest taboo at the heart of myth and kinship systems as an example of a structural *center* that he wants to *decenter*.

In another work, *The Savage Mind* (1962), Lévi-Strauss examines how different cultures classify plants and animals, showing that humans have a need to classify things to make sense of the world. Studying a variety of cultures, he identifies the underlying binaries that structure classification systems: male-female, human-animal, clean-unclean, high-low, edible-inedible, black-white, right-left, and so on. He writes that "all classification proceeds by pairs of contrasts."[1] This notion of binaries is crucial to understanding the transition from structuralism to poststructuralism. While structuralists look at how cultures are constructed upon binary oppositions, poststructuralists look to undo and subvert those binaries.

Barthes and Structuralist Semiotics

Lévi-Strauss's work on structure, classification, and binaries influenced thinkers in a number of different fields in the 1950s and 1960s, such as the aforementioned Foucault, Lacan, and Althusser. The most specifically literary application of his ideas initially can be found in the works of French thinker Roland Barthes (1915–80). Barthes's work isn't merely structuralist or formalist but touches upon many different strands of twentieth-century literary theory, as his ideas evolved throughout his career. The course of his career clearly illustrates the continuities between structuralism and poststucturalism.

His first book, *Writing Degree Zero* (1953), was influential, but the structuralist element in his work can be seen more clearly in a slightly later book, *Mythologies* (1957). This work collects short essays published between 1954 and 1956, wherein Barthes analyzes a range of aspects of French culture, from children's toys to laundry detergents to steak to wrestling. He looks at these phenomena as myths in the same way that anthropologist Lévi-Strauss was studying the myths of "primitive" cultures. Barthes calls his method **SEMIOLOGY**, or the science of signs. Semiologists look at cultural objects as signifiers, in Saussure's sense of the word, and they try to discern the signified content behind them. For Barthes the "Caesar" haircut in gladiator movies signifies "Romanness," roses signify love, eating steak signifies strength, and so forth. Barthes's approach influenced later semiotic theory, including the works of his student Julia Kristeva (see Chapter 9), the Italian semiotician and novelist Umberto Eco, and others.

---

1   Claude Lévi-Strauss, *The Savage Mind* (Chicago: U of Chicago P, 1969), 217.

In the late 1960s, Barthes began to push the insights of structuralism further in a way that would come to be called poststructuralism. As previously mentioned, poststructuralism is best thought of as an *extension* rather than an outright *rejection* of structuralism. Barthes's essay "The Death of the Author" (1968) is one of the most frequently cited and anthologized pieces of twentieth-century literary theory and a good illustration of the new turn his thought was taking at the end of the decade. The death of the author, he says, means the birth of the reader. Rather than focusing on a single line of authorial meaning in his reading of texts, he emphasizes the "play" of the reader and the **INTERTEXTUALITY** of a text, the way in which it forms a part of larger linguistic and cultural structures beyond the control of a single author. (It was in fact Kristeva who coined the term *intertextuality* in an essay on Mikhail Bakhtin in 1966.) The emphasis on play and on the lack of a single, stable meaning echoes the thinking of poststructuralist and deconstructionist thinkers like Derrida. Barthes says that a text is "not of a line of words, releasing a single 'theological' meaning (the 'message' of the Author-God), but of a multi-dimensional space in which are married and contested several writings, none of which is original: the text is a fabric of quotations, resulting from a thousand sources of culture."[1]

The confluence of structuralist analysis and poststructuralist play can be seen most vividly in what is perhaps his masterpiece, *S/Z* (1970), a book based on a seminar he taught in 1968–69 at the Collège de France. The book consists of an extremely close, line-by-line examination of Honoré de Balzac's short story "Sarrasine" (1830). Barthes identifies five different "codes" within the text corresponding to the different functions of a text: to tell a story, raise questions in readers' minds, develop themes, allude to authorities, and so on. He focuses on the ways in which a single text can be infinite because language is infinite, saying that a work of literature is an "entrance into a network with a thousand entrances." The book concludes with Barthes discussing the ways in which stable systems of language and gender break down in the story. What had seemed like a story about a man and a woman turns out to be about a man and a castrato (a young man castrated at an early age to retain his high voice for performance in opera), and that confusion of genders "represents the very confusion of representation, the unbridled (pandemic) circulation of signs, of sexes, of fortunes."[2] An analysis of the underlying structures of the text leads Barthes to dismantle those structures in favor of a free play of signs. This would in turn become one of the hallmarks of deconstruction.

---

1   Roland Barthes, "The Death of the Author," *The Rustle of Language*, trans. Richard Howard (New York: Hill and Wang, 1986), 52–53.
2   Roland Barthes, *S/Z*, trans. Richard Miller (New York: Hill and Wang, 1991), 12, 216.

Narratology

In its examination of the underlying structure of a narrative work, *S/Z* also participates in another 1960s offshoot of structuralism, narratology. Todorov, a Bulgarian who studied in Paris with Barthes, coined the term in a 1969 book on Giovanni Boccaccio to describe the work he was doing using Russian Formalist and structuralist principles to study how narratives operate. Earlier he helped to popularize Russian Formalist ideas among the French through a 1965 anthology of Russian Formalism that he edited.

The most relevant Russian Formalist work to narratologists is Vladimir Propp's *The Morphology of the Folktale* (1928). In this structural analysis of Russian tales, Propp (1895–1970) examines the characters in folk tales in terms of their narrative functions, such as hero, villain, helper, and magical agent. He then analyzes how different functions are connected through actions: the hero leaves home, the hero acquires a magical agent, the hero and villain fight, the villain is defeated, the hero returns home. These elements combine in different ways in different tales but suggest an underlying structure or "morphology" of fairy tales. Propp's work influenced Lévi-Strauss's work on myth and the writings of Todorov, both of whom were interested in narrative structures.

Another foundational text for narratologists is Gérard Genette's *Narrative Discourse* (1972). Genette (b. 1930) was a friend and associate of Todorov, and in 1970 they founded the journal *Poétique* with Hélène Cixous (see Chapter 8). In *Narrative Discourse*, Genette takes Todorov's initial application of grammatical concepts to discuss how narratives work and builds it into a very influential system. The book studies Marcel Proust's *Remembrance of Things Past* (1913–27) throughout, dividing the discussion into five chapters using the grammatical categories of order, duration, frequency, mood, and voice. Order is the arrangement of events within a text, including the use of flashback and foreshadowing. Duration is the "speed" at which events happen in a story, the way a text can speed up or slow down rather than move merely at a steady pace. Frequency refers to repeated events and the ways in which they get narrated in a story (a character may wake up every morning, but each time doesn't necessarily get described in a text). Mood is the distance from and perspective on events, including narrative focalization, discussed below. Finally, voice has to do with the narration of events, including the "person" of the narrator (first-person versus third-person narration, for example) and the time of narration (the distance between the events and their narration).

Narratology is a still-vibrant subfield of literary criticism that comes with its own extensive set of terminology. Narratologists have given names to narrative devices, aspects of storytelling, points of view (like Booth's unreliable narrator), and other things related to storytelling. Here are a few other key terms from the field of narratology:

+ *fabula* and *syuzhet*: The Russian words **FABULA** and **SYUZHET** can be translated in different ways, but their closest English analogues are "fable" and "subject." For the Russian Formalists, the fable means the raw material of the story, the events of the story chronologically arranged, and the subject refers to how the writer shapes and presents these materials. In the detective novel, Todorov says, the reader deals with only subject for most of the reading experience and doesn't learn the complete fable till the very end, when the detective solves the mystery, reconstructing the events that led up to the crime. So narratologists examine the ways in which writers play with chronology, the ways in which readers have to reconstruct the events of a story, and other such matters. They tend to be especially interested in texts that use a nonlinear arrangement, multiple points of view, or in other ways play with readerly expectations.

+ **fabula, story, text**: In her book *Narratology* (1985) Dutch narratologist Mieke Bal added a third term to the earlier fable/subject distinction. For her, fabula is still the raw material of the story, including the chronological events and the actors within it. Story then is the events as they're told, the way an author arranges them chronologically but also how they're presented in terms of point of view. Finally, text refers to the telling of the story, including style and description. Bal builds upon the Russian Formalist foundations but adds new complexity to their distinctions.

+ **focalization**: Rather than only talking about first-person versus third-person point of view, narratologists tend to discuss narrative in terms of focalization. The focalizer of a story is the character or narrator whose perspective on events the reader gets. A text can have multiple focalizers if the viewpoint shifts from one character's consciousness to another's using the device of free indirect style (see Chapter 5). A focalizer provides the eyes through which a reader "sees" the events of a story.

+ **paratexts**: Another influential concept that originates with Genette, **PARATEXTS** are the elements of a text that stand outside of the story itself, including prefaces, titles, chapter epigraphs, indexes, and any number of other things. Though not a part of the narrative proper, paratexts can profoundly influence how readers experience texts.

This list is just the tip of the iceberg: narratology even has its own separate dictionary of terms (Gerald Prince's *A Dictionary of Narratology*, 1987). Today the field has grown to include scholars who work on film, television, biography and memoir, medical narrative, and a range of other areas. Wherever stories are being told, in whatever form, narratologists will be there to study them.

Derrida and Deconstruction

At the same time that Todorov and Genette were developing the field of narratology upon the foundations of structuralism, other French thinkers, especially Jacques Derrida, were extending the insights of structuralism in a movement that would come to be called **DECONSTRUCTION**. Deconstruction differs from previous formalist approaches such as Russian Formalism and New Criticism, but it also resembles them in a number of ways. Deconstructive critics tend to be interested in the play of language and of form and tend not to pay as much attention to issues of historical context. Derrida's version of deconstruction is also much more deeply grounded in philosophical concerns than in the linguistic and literary concerns of some of the other formalists, and his later works take a turn toward **ETHICS** and the political.

Derrida trained as a philosopher, and the major influences on his work include Friedrich Nietzsche's questioning of our ideas about truth and language (see Chapter 5), the phenomenology of Edmund Husserl (1859–1938), and the existentialism of Martin Heidegger (1889–1976). Derrida's first publication was a translation of and commentary on Husserl's *The Origin of Geometry* (1962). The branch of philosophy called **PHENOMENOLOGY** traces its roots back to Immanuel Kant's distinction between *noumena* and *phenomena* (see Chapter 4), things in themselves versus things as we perceive them (which in turn echoes Plato's theory of forms). For Kant, though we can only perceive *phenomena*, philosophers can use pure reason in order to talk about *noumena*, or things in themselves. Later phenomenologists like Husserl turned their attention to perception or the way we know things. We can't truly "know" anything but our own perceptions, since we're all trapped inside our own heads, so Husserl studied perception itself as a way to get at big questions of knowledge and truth, such as the geometry that was the subject of the book Derrida translated.

Heidegger, a contemporary of Husserl in Germany, was interested in big questions of existence. In his major work, *Being and Time* (1927), Heidegger asserts that there is no pre-given *essence* of human life, but rather that *being* or human existence unfolds in time. He critiques the Western philosophical tradition since Plato for focusing on being as a substance or presence rather than looking at its temporal dimension. Heidegger characterizes his method as *Destruktion*, a German word that he uses to mean his way of questioning received notions by showing their constructedness. Derrida's term *deconstruction* harkens back to Heidegger's *Destruktion*. The French philosopher Jean-Paul Sartre (see Chapter 8) introduced French readers to Heidegger's ideas in his book *Being and Nothingness* (1943) and helped to popularize existentialism. The existentialist maxim "existence precedes essence" means that humans are the sum total of their actions, rather than having innate, pre-given essences.

Derrida can be thought of as a radical phenomenologist, or an heir to the existentialists, as well as a poststructuralist. His work combines a phenomenological interest in truth-claims, a Heideggerian critique of the philosophical tradition and of presence, and a structuralist interest in examining the underlying structures of thought. He first came to prominence in 1966 with his Johns Hopkins talk (see Chapter 1). At that conference, devoted to structuralism, Derrida discussed and critiqued structuralist anthropologists such as Lévi-Strauss by celebrating the play of signifiers within structures rather than grounding them in a center (like the incest taboo). The following year two of his major works, *Writing and Difference* and *Of Grammatology*, were published in France and gained him a wider audience.

These works aim to deconstruct the philosophical tradition and its notions of presence, in Heidegger's sense of the word. As Derrida puts it, "Play is the disruption of presence."[1] *Play* is a key term for him, and consequently his writings use wordplay and experimentation, which make them difficult to summarize. The French philosopher Alain Badiou (b. 1937), in a eulogy for Derrida, defined his notion of deconstruction as

> an indication of a speculative desire, a desire for thought…. Derrida accepted that the experience of the world is always an experience of discursive imposition. To be in the world is to be marked by discourses, marked even in our flesh, body, sex and so on. Derrida's thesis, Derrida's conclusion, the source of Derrida's desire is that, whatever form that discursive imposition may take, there is a point that escapes that imposition, and that we can call a vanishing point…. Derrida un-closes closed matters.[2]

Derrida terms that "vanishing point" **APORIA**, a Greek word meaning an unresolvable contradiction or moment of undecidability. *Aporia* is a gap that

---

1   Jacques Derrida, *Writing and Difference*, trans. Alan Bass (Chicago: U of Chicago P, 1978), 292.
2   Alain Badiou, *Pocket Pantheon: Figures of Postwar Philosophy*, trans. David Macey (London: Verso, 2009), 132–33, 138.

reveals the underlying structure, and many of Derrida's works attempt to find a moment of *aporia* that helps to subvert the binary oppositions that structure thought. Lévi-Strauss talked about the human impulse to classify the world using binaries, such as male-female, clean-unclean, left-right, and so on. For his part, Derrida finds a moment of *aporia* or undecidability that opens up a space to show the constructedness and artificiality of the binary opposition, the ways in which the privileged term shouldn't necessarily be privileged. The most famous example of Derrida's method is his discussion of the opposition of writing and speech in *Of Grammatology*. He says that speech is thought of as "present," as superior to writing, and that writing is thought of as merely an inferior transcription of speech. Derrida contends that rather than simply reversing the binary or saying that writing is more present than speech, he wants to say that speech isn't present to begin with.

Critics of deconstruction often accuse Derrida of denying that language has any meaning. This is clearly a misreading, since if he really believed that language was meaningless, he would not have tried to get his ideas across through lectures and publications. Rather, Derrida's model of language builds upon Nietzsche's and Saussure's ideas about the arbitrary nature of language. Language consists of an endless chain of signifiers, and we follow signifiers along the chain because meaning or the signified is endlessly deferred. We desire, but never achieve, true presence, because we can't get beyond language. Words are human creations rather than standing in for pre-existing concepts, as both Saussure and Nietzsche argued, and thus we can never get to an ultimate "truth" through language, since language is always provisional.

Deconstruction in America

Derrida's critique of presence and philosophical undoing of binaries found its first and most enthusiastic audience not among the French or among other philosophers but in certain American departments of literary studies, particularly at a few elite east-coast institutions. One of the people who attended the 1966 Johns Hopkins conference was a Belgian scholar named Paul de Man (1919–83), who went on to do a great deal to promote deconstruction in America. De Man had come to America in 1948. He began his academic career doing New Critical-style close readings but tinged with European phenomenology. After the 1966 conference Derrida became his friend and a major influence on the direction of his later work.

De Man was at Yale University and became known as one of the Yale Critics who popularized deconstruction in America. The other Yale Critics included Harold Bloom, Geoffrey Hartman, and J. Hillis Miller (see Chapter 9), who also shared de Man's initial interest in phenomenology. De Man's first book, *Blindness and Insight* (1971), collects his essays and is a good example of his version of deconstruction. In these essays and elsewhere, he focuses on acts of reading, producing a version of close reading but one stripped of the New Critical idea of objectivity or scientificity. In place of objective truth-claims, de Man asserts the radical indeterminacy of literary language. After his death in 1983, in 1987 a Belgian researcher discovered that de Man had written for Belgian pro-Nazi newspapers during World War II. This revelation overshadowed his reputation and led to a very public backlash against deconstruction. The anti-foundational, relativist tendencies of deconstructive thinkers leave the door open for a lack of concern for all sorts of abuses, such as those who would deny the truth of the Holocaust. Making matters worse, a Nazi streak runs through the philosophical underpinnings of deconstruction, from the Nazis' embrace of Nietzsche's philosophy to Heidegger's membership in the Nazi party.

Despite these later revelations, during his lifetime de Man was an influential theorist and teacher. Many of his Yale students went on to popularize and modify deconstructive strategies. The writings of these deconstructive critics have a well-deserved reputation for difficulty. The writings of Derrida and of those influenced by him are marked by wordplay, unconventional structures, very close reading, numerous allusions to the philosophical tradition, and much terminology taken from Heidegger, speech-act theory (a branch of philosophy of language), and Derrida's own coinages. One of the most readable of the American deconstructionists is Barbara Johnson (1947–2009), who translated Derrida, studied with de Man, and was deeply indebted to both men for her critical approach. Each essay in her first collection of essays, *The Critical Difference* (1980), reads the way in which a text sets up a network of differences through binary oppositions, such as masculine-feminine, science-literature, or prose-poetry. Through her close, careful readings Johnson dismantles these differences in a deconstructive manner. In later writings, Johnson adapts the deconstructive approach to foreground **FEMINIST** and other politically motivated concerns. She critiques her own earlier essay collection, taking herself to task for not discussing female authors, characters, or critics in *The Critical Difference*, saying that "like others of its type, the Yale School has always been a Male School."[1] Others among de Man's students, such as Gayatri Spivak, have gone on to shape **POSTCOLONIAL** studies (see Chapter 8) and in other ways bring political, historical, and ethical concerns to bear upon their scholarship.

---

1   Barbara Johnson, "Gender Theory and the Yale School," *A World of Difference* (Baltimore: Johns Hopkins UP, 1987), 32.

Formalism Today

Formalism pervades literary studies to this day. If literary scholars didn't pay attention to the formal aspects of texts, including poetic devices, narrative structures, genre conventions, and stylistic particularities, we would be merely historians. In classroom study of literature, close reading still plays a central role, as it does in much literary scholarship. However, pure close readings are no longer as prominent in academic publications as they once were. The institutional reasons for this change are clear.

The central mission of research universities is to produce knowledge. Universities are divided into disciplines with different ideas about what research means; scientific inquiry looks very different from artistic production, for example. A professor of art might stage a gallery exhibition of his or her work that would count as scholarship, while a professor in the sciences might discover a gene. Literary studies falls somewhere between artistic production and scientific inquiry – it involves some degree of creativity and subjectivity but also an aspect of making discoveries and of producing new knowledge. Types of literary scholarship that share features with the sciences – earning external grant money, producing new empirical discoveries – tend to flourish among university administrators, which is why digital humanities (see Chapter 7) and cognitive studies (see Chapter 9) are two of the most celebrated recent movements within literary studies.

Many formalist approaches to literature made claims that were too small (a close reading of a single poem in the case of Cleanth Brooks) or too grandiose (Derrida's attempt to unravel the foundations of Western metaphysics). Today you're much more likely to find formalism combined with historical, political, or psychological concerns. In the next three chapters, I discuss these other matters and the ways in which they intersect with formalism.

Suggestions for Further Reading

Baldick, Chris. *The Social Mission of English Criticism 1848–1932*. Oxford: Clarendon P, 1987.

Bann, Stephen, and John E. Bowet, eds. *Russian Formalism: A Collection of Articles and Texts in Translation*. New York: Barnes and Noble, 1973.

Erlich, Victor. *Russian Formalism: History-Doctrine*. 1955. New Haven, CT: Yale UP, 1981.

Fludernik, Monika. *An Introduction to Narratology*. Trans. Patricia Häusler-Greenfield and Monika Fludernik. London: Routledge, 2006.

Kurzweil, Edith. *The Age of Structuralism: Lévi-Strauss to Foucault*. New York: Columbia UP, 1980.

Lentricchia, Frank. *After the New Criticism*. Chicago: U of Chicago P, 1980.

Seven: Twentieth- and Twenty-First-Century Historicist Approaches

MOST FORMS OF LITERARY criticism and theory contain at least a dash of formalism, that is, some attention to matters of language, style, genre, or structure. Similarly, historical concerns pervade a great many subfields and aspects of literary studies, since by its very nature the study of literature is the study of the past. The approaches discussed in this chapter foreground issues related to history over and above questions of form or psychology. There's a significant amount of overlap between the theorists discussed in this chapter and those discussed in Chapter 8 on political approaches, since both historical and political criticisms are concerned with the way texts relate to their social, cultural, and historical contexts.

In literary studies, **HISTORICISM** is the belief that works of art and literature are products of an underlying spirit of the age, and that in order to understand a text you must understand its historical context. Historicism developed in late-eighteenth-century Germany; G.W.F. Hegel's philosophy (see Chapter 4) provides a good example of the outlines of historicist thinking. Much eighteenth- and nineteenth-century criticism uses a historicist framework, including the works of German Romantic scholars and the racialized literary history of Hippolyte Taine (see Chapter 5). Another nineteenth-century thinker, Karl Marx (see Chapter 8), turns Hegel's historical determinism into economic determinism, the idea that works of literature are products of the material relations of production or economic systems rather than just a disembodied spirit of the age, while Michel Foucault's version of historical determinism (discussed below) theorizes about discourses and power shaping literary works.

Many of the formalist studies discussed in the last chapter concentrate on a single text: the individual chapters in Cleanth Brooks's *The Well-Wrought*

Urn (1947) each focus on a single poem, Gérard Genette's *Narrative Discourse* (1972) is a study of Marcel Proust, and Barbara Johnson's essays in *The Critical Difference* (1980) focus on single texts, for example. Rather than looking closely at individual texts, historical studies work to make connections

+ between an author and a text through author biographies and biographical studies
+ between texts and their contexts in historicist and sociological studies
+ between a text and previous texts in source studies
+ between a text and subsequent texts in influence studies
+ among many texts from the same period in literary histories
+ among different versions of a single text in scholarly editing.

In this chapter I survey some of the major twentieth- and twenty-first-century methods of studying literature historically, including historicisms old and new, the sociology of literature, bibliography and book history, and digital humanities.

Historicist Criticism in the Eighteenth and Nineteenth Centuries

Before the twentieth century, historical literary studies, including the writing of literary histories and biographies and the practice of textual editing, took place mostly outside the confines of the university. Like literary studies, history writing went from being the province of "men of letters" such as Edward Gibbon (1737–94) and David Hume in the eighteenth century to being an academic discipline located in the modern research university at the end of the nineteenth.

Much of the historical investigation of the eighteenth and nineteenth centuries grew out of the context of antiquarianism, the study of antiquities or material relics of the past. Antiquaries collect and study visible remains of the past, such as ruins, artifacts, manuscripts, and old books. The practice of antiquarianism originated during the Renaissance, when renewed interest in ancient Greek and Roman cultures led to new investigations into the remains of those eras. As antiquarianism spread from Italy to other parts of Europe, it also expanded to include the study of more periods of history beyond classical antiquity. Seventeenth-century antiquaries tended to be gentlemen collectors who amassed cabinets of curiosities, including both historical artifacts and objects taken from newly explored parts of the world, from exotic flora and fauna to such curiosities as shrunken heads.

In 1717 a group of London antiquaries founded the Society of Antiquaries. The Society was meant to be a companion organization to the Royal Society of London, a group founded in 1660 to pursue scientific studies (which in turn help to develop protocols of modern experimental science). Members of the new antiquarian society included lawyers, politicians, members of clergy, gentlemen, merchants, and professors. Famous members included the gothic novelist Horace Walpole (1717–97) and American founding father Benjamin Franklin (1706–90). At their meetings members would usually bring an artifact or old book to show, or would read papers investigating a topic of antiquarian concern. The range of eighteenth-century antiquarian interests includes topics now part of such fields as archaeology, art history, social history, literary studies, material culture studies, and linguistic studies.

Satirists and caricaturists at the time often mocked antiquaries for focusing too closely on small details and insignificant artifacts without seeing the bigger picture. Thomas Rowlandson's (1756–1827) satirical print "Veneration" (1800), for example, caricatures a bespectacled antiquary peering into a cracked chamber pot (see Figure 6).

Admittedly, collections of antiquarian papers from this time do include some rather minute investigations of archaeological remains and historical papers. However, some figures associated with antiquarian societies or antiquarian methods produced work that takes a much wider view and that synthesizes studies of individual historical relics into a larger narrative. Among the achievements of literary antiquaries in eighteenth-century Britain are Thomas Percy's *Reliques of Ancient English Poetry* (1765), a collection of medieval ballads that uses them as a source of information about everyday life in the Middle Ages, and Thomas Warton's *History of English Poetry* (1774–81), the first important history of English literature. Both Warton and Percy were members of the Society of Antiquaries. Outside the Society, however, other scholars of the time produced historical studies with an antiquarian flavor. The Society was strictly for men only, but outside the Society some female scholars did participate in the antiquarian enterprise by reading and publishing antiquarian works and corresponding with members. Elizabeth Elstob (1683–1756), for example, produced pioneering work on the Anglo-Saxon language, while Clara Reeve's (1729–1807) *The Progress of Romance* (1785), a history of fiction from antiquity to the eighteenth century, is a fine example of the type of work being done by female literary historians. Though she couldn't join the Society, Reeve in her later years corresponded with the Irish antiquary Joseph Cooper Walker (1761–1810) about her work.

Antiquarianism continued into the nineteenth century (and indeed to this day), though some would-be antiquarian work migrated into more formal

Figure 6: Thomas Rowlandson, "Veneration."

academic contexts. More than a few traces of antiquarianism remain in present-day literary studies, however. The journal *Notes and Queries*, for example, was founded in 1849 and is still being published. Its original subtitle, "A Medium of Inter-Communication for Literary Men, Artists, Antiquaries, Genealogists, Etc.," indicates that its audience comprised both amateur and professional students of literature. Though much has changed in literary studies since 1849, the longevity of *Notes and Queries* indicates a degree of continuity between popular antiquarianism and academic literary studies, between the past and the future of the field.

Historicism to the 1970s

In the early years of academic literary studies in the late nineteenth century, the philological methods imported from Germany dominated. As discussed in Chapter 6, philologists study texts as resources for learning about the history of languages: their grammar, syntax, and vocabulary. At this time, too, the discipline of literary studies began to be organized around specialization in particular periods (rather than genres or methods of study). That is, people pursuing PhDs in English literature, for example, would focus on a single period, such as the Renaissance or the eighteenth century. Departments of English would then hire specialists in each period of literary history, and those professors in turn would teach courses covering the period of their expertise. This underlying structure of English departments hasn't much changed in the intervening years – most English doctoral students specialize in a particular period, such as Modernism or Romanticism, and a large proportion of academic jobs continue to be advertised by period designations, even as new theoretical methods and new understandings of particular periods have developed.

Because the discipline is structured around periodization, historical studies have always been an important part of academic literary studies. As the philologists' power began to wane at the end of the nineteenth and beginning of the twentieth century, historical scholars took their place. The historical studies of the generation following the initial philologists analyzed texts in order to learn about more than merely the history of languages. These scholars produced literary histories, scholarly editions, source studies, historicist readings of texts, and other such projects grounded in making connections. The NEW CRITICS' focus on the text itself and their lack of attention to things like author biography are a response to the dominance of historicist approaches at the time when they began championing close readings as an alternative. Austin Warren and René Wellek's *Theory of Literature* (1949), for example, promotes close reading as an *intrinsic* method of studying literature, as opposed to *extrinsic* studies that examine author biography or historical context.

In the first part of the twentieth century, the New Critics attacked the works of early historicist scholars as extrinsic, and in the second half the new historicists attacked these same studies for being insufficiently theoretical. Yet many of these works are impressive achievements in the history of criticism and are under-recognized for their achievements. Here are just a few examples that showcase the range of "old historicist" studies:

+ John Livingston Lowes's *The Road to Xanadu* (1927) is a 600-page study of the sources for just two famous poems: Samuel Taylor Coleridge's "Kubla Khan" (1816) and "The Rime of the Ancient Mariner" (1798). Lowes thoroughly studies Coleridge's notebooks and goes back and reads the works Coleridge read as he was composing these poems, such as the travel literature he drew upon to depict the Mariner's voyage.

+ J.M.S. Tompkins's *The Popular Novel in England, 1770–1800* (1932) is a stellar example of the thorough, well-researched work of the old historicists. In it, Tompkins examines popular fiction of the last three decades of the eighteenth century, including a wide range of forgotten authors. More recently scholars such as Franco Moretti (discussed below) have promoted the study of forgotten figures in literary history, but Tompkins's book and others like it show that this type of work was being done much earlier (and without the aid of electronic resources!).

+ Arthur Lovejoy's *The Great Chain of Being* (1936). Lovejoy, a historian, is the founder of a field known as the history of ideas. In 1923 he founded a History of Ideas club at Johns Hopkins University. His method was to break apart larger abstractions (such as idealism or Romanticism) into smaller elements or unit-ideas in order to trace the history of the way people think. His most famous work examines the notion of a hierarchical chain of being running from God to man to nature and how that concept develops from antiquity to the nineteenth century.

+ E.M.W. Tillyard's *The Elizabethan World Picture* (1943). Tillyard, a Cambridge literary critic, adopts Lovejoy's history of ideas method. In this book, which began as a study of Shakespeare's history plays, Tillyard traces the Elizabethan conception of cosmic order, calling it "a chain, a set of correspondences, and a dance."[1] He says that his task is to reconstruct ideas about the world that Elizabethan writers would have taken for granted but that underpin their works. Later new historicists often single out Tillyard's work as an example of the limitations of the old historicist scholarship – too broad in its scope, making grand generalizing claims – yet it remains an impressive piece of scholarship.

---

1   E.M.W. Tillyard, *The Elizabethan World Picture* (London: Chatto and Windus, 1960), v.

✦ Richard Altick's *The English Common Reader* (1957). In this influential study, Altick surveys the growth of the reading public in Britain in the nineteenth century. He studies literacy rates, the growth of public libraries, the newspapers and bestsellers of the time, and reading societies. His work helped spark interest in the history of reading and of the working classes.

The works of old historicists, historians of ideas, and textual editors produced great achievements in the twentieth century, including literary biographies, anthologies, scholarly editions, and historical studies. Because these works tend to be on more circumscribed topics instead of making larger theoretical claims, they often don't get the recognition they deserve in histories of literary theory. I also see much more continuity between this type of work and newer historical approaches than is often acknowledged. In certain historical subfields of literary studies, such as medieval studies or eighteenth-century studies, despite the efforts of the New Critics, historical approaches have persisted. Some of the underlying assumptions and scholarly conventions may change, but it may be best to see the new historicism of the 1980s and after as a refinement upon and revival of rather than a break with earlier historical scholarship, just as poststructuralism is less a rejection than an extension of structuralism.

The "New Historicism"

The movement that we now call **NEW HISTORICISM** (sometimes capitalized) coalesced in the 1970s. It didn't have a name until 1982, when Stephen Greenblatt referred to "the new historicism" in "The Forms of Power and the Power of Forms in the Renaissance," his introduction to a special issue of the journal *Genre*.[1] A few years later, in 1986, J. Hillis Miller, in his presidential address to the Modern Language Association (MLA), described a sudden turn away from language and toward history that had taken place in the last few years. This historical turn in literary studies caught on quickly and continued to gain momentum into the next decade.

What makes new historicism *new* isn't its historicism; historicist work continued to be produced throughout the peak periods of New Criticism and **STRUCTURALISM**. Instead, the *new* of Greenblatt's phrase refers to the *types* of historical approaches seen in the contributions to that special issue of *Genre*. These scholars are more political, more theoretical, and more self-conscious than the previous generation of historicist critics. New historicism positions

---

1   Stephen Greenblatt, "Introduction," *Genre* 15 (Spring-Summer 1982): 5.

itself as an alternative to the formalisms of New Criticism and **DECONSTRUCTION**, while absorbing some of the same theoretical influences coming out of France as the latter group. While the patron saint of deconstruction was Jacques Derrida, new historicists prefer Michel Foucault. In the following sections I outline some of the key theoretical influences that new historicists absorb from history, anthropology, and **CULTURAL STUDIES**, including the work of Foucault, before returning to literary studies proper.

New Approaches to History and Culture

New historicists tend to be much more self-conscious about their investigations of the past than old historicists. They are wary of making big truth-claims and stay away from grand narratives in favor of smaller claims and anecdotes. Instead of talking about the spirit of the age or the world picture they use metaphors of circulation, negotiation, and exchange as a way to create a more complicated, nuanced, provisional picture. In Louis Montrose's phrase, new historicists are interested in the "historicity of texts" and the "textuality of history": how texts relate to their historical context as well as how our knowledge of the past depends on literary means of expression.[1] Much new historicist thinking about history draws upon theoretical work within historical studies itself.

One important proponent of this type of self-reflective historical thinking is the historian Hayden White (b. 1928). In his book *Metahistory* (1973), White analyzes the underlying literary structures of some famous nineteenth-century historical works. He looks at how historians take the raw materials of history, the chronicle of events, and shape them into very different types of stories, structured around the genres of romance, tragedy, satire, and comedy. (His interest in these four underlying genre archetypes derives from the work of Northrop Frye, discussed in Chapter 9.) White considers historians to be storytellers who make choices about which events to emphasize, where to attribute causes, and so forth, rather than as scientists discovering the truth about what really happened in the past. White himself was influenced by philosopher of history R.G. Collingwood (1889–1943), whose book *The Idea of History* (1946) studies different concepts of history from the ancient world to the twentieth century.

Another concept that influenced new historicist thinking came from the Italian historian Carlo Ginzburg (b. 1939), who popularized the term *micro-history*. Ginzburg's method of microhistory focuses on the very small, on particulars and individuals rather than on creating a grand narrative. Works of microhistory tend to study ordinary individuals and folk beliefs rather than

---

1   Louis A. Montrose, "Professing the Renaissance: The Poetics and Politics of Culture," *The New Historicism*, ed. H. Aram Veeser (New York: Routledge, 1989), 20.

only looking at political and military history. Natalie Zemon Davis's *The Return of Martin Guerre* (1983), a narrative history about the case of one sixteenth-century French impostor, is a celebrated example of this type of work.

Microhistorians in many ways work like anthropologists: they study how individuals behave and what they believe through close observation rather than taking a more sweeping view. So it makes sense that work coming out of anthropology would be an influence on new historicists, particularly the work of American ethnographer Clifford Geertz (1926–2006). From Geertz's *The Interpretation of Cultures* (1973) the new historicists borrowed the concept of thick description, of looking at small anecdotes rather than beginning with large premises, using something small to reveal larger cultural logics.

Geertz in part was reacting to the methods of **STRUCTURALIST ANTHRO-POLOGISTS** such as Lévi-Strauss (see Chapter 6), who attempted to deduce the underlying structures of phenomena such as kinship systems, myth, and classification systems in a variety of cultures in order to make broad, universal claims about "the savage mind" or the incest taboo. Geertz instead recommended a method of ethnographic thick description, where an anthropologist would study and observe how people behave within a culture and how people within a culture interpret their own behavior. Anthropologists should look at how people in a society answer their own questions rather than try to speak for them, Geertz argued. The most famous essay in the collection is his account of cockfighting in Bali. He describes the betting practices around the fights and the way in which the men identify with their birds, saying "societies, like lives, contain their own interpretations."[1] Similarly, new historicists pay attention to how writers of earlier historical periods would have understood the world and themselves, instead of trying to impose an explanation upon them.

Along with their borrowings from history and anthropology, new historicists owe a major debt to **MARXISM**, and some of the more politically engaged work of new historicists (and offshoots such as **POSTCOLONIAL** studies) will be discussed in the next chapter. In critical discussions new historicism is often paired with **CULTURAL MATERIALISM**, its British counterpart. This term is taken from the work of British Marxist theorist Raymond Williams and refers to different types of socio-political cultural analysis. Jonathan Dollimore and Alan Sinfield, two Shakespeare scholars who popularized the term within Renaissance studies, state that cultural materialism "studies the implications of literary texts in history."[2] Other varieties of Marxist theory, including the ideas

---

1   Clifford Geertz, *The Interpretation of Cultures* (New York: Basic Books, 1973), 453.
2   Jonathan Dollimore and Alan Sinfield, Preface to *Political Shakespeare: New Essays in Cultural Materialism* (Ithaca, NY: Cornell UP, 1985), viii.

about **HEGEMONY** of Antonio Gramsci, the **DIALOGISM** of Mikhail Bakhtin, and the cultural theorizing of the Frankfurt School, all play a role in shaping new historicist thought, as does **FEMINIST** theory.

Foucault and Discourse

Michel Foucault was arguably the most significant influence on new historicism. Though he had been writing and publishing since the 1950s, Foucault's influence on Anglo-American literary studies became prominent after the psychoanalytic theorist Leo Bersani invited him to give a series of guest lectures at the University of California, Berkeley, in 1975. Though he was already a bestseller in France, Foucault's work wasn't as well known in the English-speaking world. Foucault loved California and returned to Berkeley, Stanford, and other parts of America many times before his death in 1984. In California he influenced new historicist thinking about history, power, and truth.

Foucault's name is often paired with Derrida's in discussions of **POSTSTRUC-TURALISM**. Derrida attended Foucault's seminars while a student at the École Normale Supérieure in the early 1950s, and the two explored similar issues (though they were critical of each other's work), Derrida from the standpoint of a philosopher and Foucault as a historian. In the 1950s and 1960s, structuralist anthropology's attempts to identify the underlying structures of various cultural phenomena dominated French intellectual life. Derrida's response to this was to point out the constructedness of those structures, to undo the hierarchies of those binary oppositions that Lévi-Strauss was so fond of, and to celebrate the play of language. Foucault's response was to bring the history of ideas and the history of science to bear upon structuralism in order to show the element of time at work within structure by suggesting that the thought of different historical periods is constructed upon different foundations.

Foucault's book *The Order of Things* (1966) illustrates his relation to both structuralism and the history of ideas. In this work, he studies the history of the human sciences from the sixteenth to the nineteenth centuries. He focuses on three areas of study: how people understand the natural world, how they study money and the economy, and how languages are understood. Rather than writing separate histories of botany, economics, and linguistics, he looks at the underlying assumptions and rules about how knowledge is produced in each of these areas. He calls these underlying assumptions the *episteme* of a period, and says that there are ruptures or shifts between different periods. In emphasizing discontinuity and rupture in the history of thought, Foucault borrows from the work of French historians of science. In an introduction to Georges Canguilhem's *The Normal and the Pathological* (1966), Foucault credits

Canguilhem (along with Gaston Bachelard and Alexandre Koyré) with taking up "the theme of 'discontinuity'" in the history of biology, seeing that the history of science isn't "a history of the true, of its slow epiphany."[1]

In a later book, *The Archaeology of Knowledge* (1969), Foucault explains his method in *The Order of Things*. He clearly owes a debt to structuralism in his interest in deep underlying structures, but he stresses that his work breaks from structuralists in some important ways. Likewise, he differentiates his work from traditional history of ideas. He calls for historians of ideas to get rid of ideas about worldviews, a spirit of the age, influence, tradition, development, and evolution – all the things that characterized old historicist work. He also calls for scholars to do away with disciplinary boundaries and for them to think of books as nodes within larger networks of discourse rather than as unified and self-contained objects (much as Barthes had theorized about **INTERTEXTUALITY** in "The Death of the Author," discussed in Chapter 6). Whereas Barthes's intertextuality celebrates the free play of signifiers, Foucault uses the notion of intertextuality as a way to look at the rules that allow statements to be made or the "law of what can be said."[2] He uses the example of madness, the subject of one of his earlier books, to illustrate his model. Foucault's study of discourses about madness examines medical writings, laws relating to insanity, and representations of madness in works of literature and art. It also considers who has the authority to speak about madness and the role of institutional sites such as madhouses and prisons. In so doing, Foucault is reaching for the idea that madness isn't something that is just given, but that different time periods thought about sanity and insanity in very different ways, and that our own ideas are just as historically conditioned as those of previous eras, which believed in demonic possession or bodily humors.

In his later works *Discipline and Punish* (1975) and *The History of Sexuality* (1976–84, discussed in Chapter 8), Foucault examines the topics of criminality and sexuality to examine how these phenomena are historically constructed and to raise the possibility that they could be thought of differently. He also introduces some new terms and issues that became widely used in literary theory, including *bodies, power,* and *surveillance. Discipline and Punish* examines the shift from an older mode of punishing criminals based on public executions and spectacle to a modern system based on surveillance. His emblem of the modern surveillance state is the **PANOPTICON**, a structure devised by nineteenth-century Utilitarian thinker Jeremy Bentham (see Figure 7).

---

1 Michel Foucault, Introduction to *The Normal and the Pathological* by Georges Canguilhem, trans. Carolyn R. Fawcett and Robert S. Cohen (New York: Zone, 1989), 13–14.
2 Michel Foucault, *The Archeology of Knowledge and the Discourse on Language*, trans. A.M. Sheridan Smith (New York: Vintage Books, 2010), 129.

Figure 7: Panopticon.

A panopticon (Greek for "all-seeing") is an architectural model structured around a central watchtower. In a panoptic prison, prisoners' cells all face the tower, but the prisoners can't see whether a guard is in the tower at any given time. For Bentham, this was a model of efficiency: prisoners would have to behave, because they knew they might be watched at any time, but the state would not necessarily have to man the tower at all times, thereby saving on labor costs. Today surveillance cameras serve an analogous function. In a metaphoric sense, Foucault says, this is how power operates in the modern state: it's everywhere and nowhere. We behave not because there's someone giving us orders to fall in line but because we've internalized a sense of right behavior, both in a legal and a religious sense. Foucault compares schools, factories, and military barracks to prisons, suggesting that power operates upon individual human bodies in all these sites. Power produces knowledge for Foucault, so this same idea of power shapes the conditions of what we think possible at any given moment.

As Foucault says in a later work, the point of his project is "to learn to what extent the effort to think one's own history can free thought from what it silently thinks, and so to enable it to think differently."[1] Like Derrida, he wanted to "deconstruct" or decenter commonly held assumptions about truth, language,

---

1   Michel Foucault, *The History of Sexuality, Volume 2: The Use of Pleasure*, trans. Robert Hurley (New York: Vintage Books, 1990), 9.

and knowledge. For Foucault the political stakes are much more pronounced: he wants to point out that things have been different in order to make room for change. He calls this method genealogy, in homage to Friedrich Nietzsche's use of the term in *The Genealogy of Morals* (1887). In his lifetime Foucault advocated prison reform, and since his death from complications related to AIDS, activists have used his work on the history of sexuality to advocate for marriage equality and other issues.

Greenblatt and the New Historicism

As mentioned earlier, Stephen Greenblatt gave the new historicist movement in literary studies its name in 1982. He also co-founded its most important academic journal, *Representations*, in 1983 with a group of like-minded scholars. Greenblatt's career stretches back before new historicism emerged. He received his PhD from Yale in 1969, writing a dissertation on Sir Walter Ralegh that used the phenomenological ideas of Georges Poulet (see Chapter 9). He began teaching at Berkeley, where he joined another Renaissance scholar, Stephen Orgel. In a footnote to a 1971 article, Orgel thanks Greenblatt for bringing a passage in a 1944 *Journal of the History of Ideas* article to his attention, suggesting that from the start there were at least some linkages between old and new historicism.[1]

During the 1970s, Greenblatt, Orgel, Montrose, and other Renaissance scholars on the west coast began to assimilate some of the interdisciplinary influences described above into more traditional literary studies. The change in Greenblatt's work can be seen in his book *Renaissance Self-Fashioning* (1980), which examines a group of sixteenth-century men (including Thomas More, Thomas Wyatt, and Shakespeare) and their acts of self-fashioning. Greenblatt uses Geertz and cultural anthropology to examine how these men shaped themselves while being shaped by their culture, calling his approach a poetics of culture.

Greenblatt's work became even more theoretical, and more influential, in *Shakespearean Negotiations* (1988), which discusses the processes of social circulation that take place across literary and nonliterary texts. Individual chapters discuss social circulation by pairing non-literary discourses with a Shakespeare play: a treatise on hermaphrodism and *Twelfth Night*, an account of exorcism and *King Lear*. Though initially this may seem somewhat reminiscent of old historicist source studies, such as *The Road to Xanadu*, or history of ideas such as *The Elizabethan World Picture*, Greenblatt says that he doesn't want to treat

1   See Stephen Orgel, "The Poetics of Spectacle," *New Literary History* 2 (Spring 1971): 367–89.

the canonical literary texts as primary and the sources as secondary. He is interested in circulation as a reciprocal process, rather than in models of source and influence that merely point in one direction. New historicists don't try to discover sources for canonical literary texts, that is, but instead try to reconstruct the discourses that make texts of a given moment possible. Greenblatt argues that "history cannot simply be set against literary texts as either stable antithesis or stable background, and the protective isolation of those texts gives way to a sense of their interaction with other texts and hence of the permeability of their boundaries."[1] Adapting Foucault's ideas about discourses and their relationships to power, Greenblatt introduces terms such as *containment* and *subversion* to illustrate issues of power and language in the Renaissance.

This interest in Foucault and in historicist literary studies soon spread to other subfields beyond Renaissance studies. The titles and subjects of a few books from this time indicate their debts to Foucault's interest in prisons and bodies: D.A. Miller's *The Novel and the Police* (1988) looks at issues of discipline and surveillance in the nineteenth-century novel, John Bender's *Imagining the Penitentiary* (1989) looks at eighteenth-century texts in relation to prisons, and Mary Poovey's *Making a Social Body* (1995) uses a Foucauldian framework to study the social body in such areas as Victorian efforts to regulate sanitation and the poor. Certain areas of study that had been especially resistant to historical approaches gradually absorbed new historicist ideas. British Romanticism, for example, had been a bastion of formalism and "high theory" (meaning, primarily, philosophically inflected deconstruction) in part because it was Paul de Man's specialty and in part because Romantic poems are well suited to both New Critical close reading methods and philosophical deconstructions. Nowadays the boundaries of Romanticism have expanded to include a wider range of historical approaches and a much wider range of authors and texts.

Studies of American literature, in contrast, have been more consistently historical. After English became a discipline, it took some time before American literature came into its own as a field of study. The American Studies movement began in the 1930s with scholars interested in the New England Puritans. Perry Miller, author of a number of influential studies on the Puritans in the 1930s, and others created a program in the History of American Civilization at Harvard University in 1936, and many other programs followed in the 1930s and 1940s, along with the creation of the American Studies Association in 1951. American Studies brings together historians and literary scholars and tends to have a more historical focus. Though it originates with Puritan studies,

---

1   Stephen Greenblatt, *Shakespearean Negotiations: The Circulation of Social Energy in Renaissance England* (Berkeley: U of California P, 1988), 95.

American Studies today is a highly interdisciplinary field that has broadened to include scholars in ethnic studies, cultural studies, hemispheric studies (studies of the literature of the Western hemisphere, including Latin America), and other areas.

Bourdieu and the Sociology of Culture

Another influential French theorist of Foucault and Derrida's generation, Pierre Bourdieu (1930–2002), popularized a method of studying literature through the lens of sociology. A long tradition of using sociology to study aspects of literature, including reading practices, cultural production, and publishers, can be traced back through the Frankfurt School of critics to the ideas of Karl Marx, all of which I discuss in the next chapter. Bourdieu, however, does not emerge from an explicitly Marxist context. A friend and colleague of Foucault, Bourdieu began his career as a structuralist anthropologist. Like Foucault and Derrida he breaks from structuralism while being shaped by it. While Foucault used historical inquiry to analyze the underlying epistemological structures of different eras, Bourdieu became interested in the *mental* structures that shape people's perceptions and taste. What makes us like the things we like? Why do some people prefer action movies and others independent films? What difference do our tastes make in the world? Bourdieu introduced a whole new vocabulary to the sociology of culture to speak about taste. Some of his key concepts include the following:

+ **Habitus: HABITUS** is the underlying mental structure that determines how people act, what they like, and how they perceive the world. It develops in childhood and is socially and culturally determined rather than innate. Habitus determines our taste. Your taste for food, music, clothing, furniture, and everything else is socially determined, and in turn it helps to determine your social position. As he says in his book *Distinction* (1979), a monumental study of French people's taste and its relation to social and economic factors, "Taste classifies, and it classifies the classifier. Social subjects, classified by their classifications, distinguish themselves by the distinctions they make."[1] He also calls taste a "match-maker," because couples come together through common tastes in movies, music, hobbies, and other matters.

---

1   Pierre Bourdieu, *Distinction: A Social Critique of the Judgement of Taste*, trans. Richard Nice (London: Routledge, 1994), 6.

◆ **Cultural capital:** Taste can function as a type of currency, which he
calls **CULTURAL CAPITAL** (as opposed to economic capital). Having refined
tastes, such as a preference for abstract art, classical music, or fine wine,
distinguishes you as a member of an elite group and can in turn lead to
social advancement. Conversely, a taste for monster trucks and Budweiser
might mark you as someone with "lowbrow" tastes and can lead to social
scorn among the "highbrow." In his study, Bourdieu tracks the correlation
of economic and cultural capital. Some groups, such as teachers, possess
high cultural capital but low economic capital, while others possess high
economic capital but low cultural capital, such as successful shopkeepers.

◆ **Fields:** **FIELDS** are places of competition, like a battlefield or a playing field,
with their own rules and their own sets of competitors. Bourdieu analyzes
the literary field as one such place, "an independent social universe with its
own laws of functioning, its specific relations of force, its dominants and its
dominated."[1] Within a field actors take positions organized around binary
oppositions (such as left-right or high-low). These position-takings depend
on the positions of all the other actors on the field, and the arrival of a new
competitor rearranges the positions. People with high economic and cultural capital are more likely to seek out new positions in art and literature.

Bourdieu often studies the literary field of nineteenth-century France, and
in particular the **ART FOR ART'S SAKE** movement (see Chapter 5). To show how
to put Bourdieu's ideas to work, I will use the example of the history of literary theory in the twentieth century. In the 1930s, the New Critics entered the
theory field by staking out a position in opposition to the dominant mode of literary studies at the time, historicism. As well-established scholars, they already
possessed the symbolic capital (or credentials and status) needed to stake out
an oppositional position. When they entered the field, the other players had to
rearrange their positions and upend hierarchies. Historical studies continued,
but became less prestigious and less visible as the virtuoso New Critics received
greater attention and accolades. The Chicago **NEO-ARISTOTELIANS** then entered
the field by taking a position opposed to the New Critics (critiquing them for
not paying enough attention to genre, among other things) but also distinct
from the historical critics.

Similarly, the later generation of new historicists came along and staked
out a position opposed to deconstruction and other formalisms. Even though

---

1   Pierre Bourdieu, *The Field of Cultural Production: Essays on Art and Literature*, ed. Randal Johnson
    (New York: Columbia UP, 1993), 163.

they shared many of the same theoretical concerns, the differences between the approaches was framed as oppositional in J. Hillis Miller's MLA address (mentioned above). New historicism accrued prestige while deconstruction, once cutting edge, came to seem old hat. The de Man revelations of 1987 sped the demise of deconstruction, but the field had already changed with the entry of the new historicists. The close readings of deconstruction went from being a display of virtuosity to a sign of insularity, while historical research became the new display of virtuosity.

In the last several decades, Bourdieu's terms have entered the vocabulary of literary scholars. John Guillory's *Cultural Capital* (1993), for example, uses Bourdieu in order to investigate issues related to canon formation. Janice Radway's *A Feeling for Books* (1997) builds on Bourdieu's *Distinction* to study the Book-of-the-Month Club and its role in shaping American middlebrow literary taste. Her earlier *Reading the Romance* (1984) also uses sociological methods (but not Bourdieu) to study popular romance novels. In it, she both studies the romance publishing industry and employs ethnographic observation and sociological questionnaires with a group of women readers in a Midwestern town. Another interesting work that uses Bourdieu's terminology is James English's *The Economy of Prestige* (2005), which examines literary and cultural prizes such as the Booker Prize and the Nobel Prize.

From Bibliography to Book History

A related area of literary studies influenced by sociology is the field originally called bibliography and now known as **BOOK HISTORY**. Some of the aforementioned scholars, such as Radway, work within this area, which overlaps significantly with the sociology of literature. Influential book historian D.F. McKenzie defines bibliography as "the discipline that studies texts as recorded forms, and the processes of their transmission, including their production and reception" or "the sociology of texts."[1] Book history has its origins in the late nineteenth century and is one of the historical methods that came into literary studies as philology fell out of favor, though antiquaries such as Thomas Dibdin (1776–1847) had been doing bibliographic work prior to this time earlier in the century. In 1892, the London-based Bibliographical Society, associated with the British Museum, was founded. Three men associated with that society are often credited with creating modern bibliographic studies: Sir Walter Wilson Greg (1875–1959), R.B. McKerrow (1872–1940), and A.W. Pollard (1859–1944).

---

1   D.F. McKenzie, *Bibliography and the Sociology of Texts* (Cambridge: Cambridge UP, 1999), 12, 13.

Their works include scholarly editions of Shakespeare, thorough bibliographies of printed books, and historical dictionaries of printers. They helped to establish more rigorous standards for textual editing and focused on the material conditions of the production of texts, right down to the study of paper and typefaces. McKerrow's *An Introduction to Bibliography* (1927) catalogs a number of areas of study for bibliography: printing, paper, book illustration, editions, and fakes and forgeries.

Book history gained new momentum in the 1980s, in part because of French scholars such as Roger Chartier's work on the history of the book and in part because of an increasing interest in historical and textual matters, leading to the creation of the Society for the History of Authorship, Reading, and Publishing (SHARP) in the early 1990s. Scholars in this field today study many of the same areas as the old bibliographers: printing, material editions of books, and textual editing. They bring to this work a new degree of methodological self-awareness, influenced by a range of theoretical approaches that include the sociology of literature, **MARXIST** criticism, **FEMINISM**, and cultural studies. Today the field has significant overlap with the emerging field of **DIGITAL HUMANITIES**.

Digital Humanities

As I discussed in Chapter 4, media theorist Marshall McLuhan's concept of **PRINT CULTURE** is a useful way of thinking about the cultural changes brought about because of the new technology of print in the early modern era. McLuhan distinguishes print culture from its predecessor, manuscript culture, and from the even earlier oral culture before the invention of writing. Each era involves its own ways of communicating, though earlier technologies don't necessarily go away. People didn't stop speaking once writing was invented, though certain aspects of oral cultures, such as a reliance on memory and the proliferation of legend and folklore, became less prominent. Similarly, the printing press enabled ideas to spread much more widely, even while manuscript circulation still continued. Today we've moved into an age of digital culture, but the old cultures still survive: we still have speech, manuscripts, and print, and have added new digital methods of writing and communication. Since the advent of the computer, a new type of literary studies has been developing in response to the growth of digital technologies.

The field now commonly known as digital humanities grew out of what used to be called humanities computing and refers to the use of digital technologies to aid in literary studies and other areas of the humanities. The earliest efforts to use computers in humanistic inquiry go back to the 1940s and 1950s and to projects at Brown University beginning in the 1960s. These projects involved the old, room-sized computers, punch cards, and other obsolete computing technologies. With the advent of the personal computer many more scholars were able to use computers in their own work without access to a mega-lab. By the 1980s, George Landow and others at Brown were working on hypertext projects, ways to create links within electronic texts. Reading a text online and clicking on a link today is natural, but in the 1980s it was a revolutionary concept that changed the way people read. Landow connected his theory of hypertext back to the theories of intertextuality of Barthes and Foucault, the idea that a text is a node within a network and that the boundaries of a text are never clear-cut.

While Landow and others were working on hypertext projects and theorizing about it, at the same time in the 1980s and 1990s the field of media theory was developing a rich body of scholarship. Building upon the earlier media theories of McLuhan and others, these scholars explore issues related to media, technology, and communication. German media theorist Friedrich Kittler, for example, analyzes the role of discourse networks and technology in *Discourse Networks 1800/1900* (1985) and *Gramophone Film Typewriter* (1986). In America, N. Katherine Hayles and Donna Haraway are two of the leading scholars in this area. Haraway's influential "A Cyborg Manifesto" (1985, republished in her book *Simians, Cyborgs, and Women*, 1991) combines technology studies and feminism. Hayles began her academic career writing about Shakespeare, but has gone on to be a major figure in science fiction studies and studies of literature and science. Her book *How We Became Posthuman* (1999) studies new media and technology in relation to issues such as cybernetics and virtual reality.

Humanities computing came into its own in the early 1990s with the launch of the World Wide Web (now simply called the Internet). Pioneers of humanities scholarship online include Jerome McGann, who began working on an online hypermedia archive of the works of the Victorian artist and poet Dante Gabriel Rossetti (1828–82) in 1993, and Alan Liu, who created the Voice of the Shuttle website, a collection of online resources for humanities study, in 1994. Many other digital projects were launched during this time, including the creation of numerous digital editions of texts and the assembly of databases for literary studies.

Another theorist associated with digital humanities is the Italian sociologist of literature Franco Moretti, who founded the Stanford Literary Lab in 2010. The work of the Stanford lab and of Moretti is different from projects involving hypertext or the creation of digital editions. Instead, the Stanford group uses digital tools to analyze things such as literary genres and stylistic devices.

Moretti coined the phrase "distant reading" to describe this type of work (which doesn't necessarily need to be digital). Distant reading is the opposite of close reading, focusing on "units that are much smaller or much larger than the text: devices, themes, tropes – or genres and systems."[1] Moretti's own scholarship uses tools such as maps and graphs to see texts in new ways, studying the role of clues in the development of detective fiction or mapping the settings of Gothic novels. Moretti's method of distant reading has been critiqued for ignoring the text and for working in broad strokes, though others have built upon his approach in more circumscribed and thorough studies.

Today digital humanities is a varied and thriving field that encompasses a huge range of projects. Humanities computing work initially was relatively marginal to the discipline of literary studies, but it has become increasingly prestigious and prominent in recent years. Digital humanities has brought new life to old subjects by allowing researchers to ask new questions using such techniques as data mining and encoding, for example, to trace word usages in an author or time period, citational networks, networks of influence among authors and texts, or just to create searchable, annotated editions of classic works. As universities in the twenty-first century have placed greater emphasis on interdisciplinary collaborations and in research projects that bring in grant money (see the end of Chapter 6), the presence of digital humanities in literary studies is only likely to increase.

Suggestions for Further Reading

Delany, Paul, and George P. Landow, eds. *Hypermedia and Literary Studies*. Cambridge, MA: MIT P, 1991.

Feather, John. *A Dictionary of Book History*. New York: Oxford UP, 1986.

Hamilton, Paul. *Historicism*. London: Routledge, 1996.

Rowe, John Carlos, ed. *A Concise Companion to American Studies*. Malden, MA: John Wiley and Sons, 2010.

Veeser, H. Aram, ed. *The New Historicism*. New York: Routledge, 1989.

---

1   Franco Moretti, *Distant Reading* (London: Verso, 2013), 48–49.

Eight: Twentieth- and Twenty-First-Century Political Approaches

In this chapter, I turn to theory and criticism engaged with political issues. A number of the theorists and critics I discussed in previous chapters were interested in literature's social and political implications, beginning with Plato and Aristotle. However, nineteenth-century German philosopher and sociologist Karl Marx gave literary studies a whole new vocabulary for talking about the relationship between literature and politics. In an early work called "Theses on Feuerbach" (1845), Marx described his break from the German philosophical tradition in which he was trained: "Philosophers have only *interpreted* the world in various ways; the point is to *change* it."[1] Many of the approaches discussed in this chapter share common ground with the historical approaches discussed in Chapter 7. The difference is that while historicist critics interpret texts in their social and historical contexts and make historical connections, the political critics discussed here do so in order to create change, in the service of particular political agendas.

From Marxism to queer theory, all the approaches in this chapter grow out of political activist movements. Marxism is not merely a set of philosophical concepts but a political movement advocating workers' rights, social reform, and, in some cases, political revolution. Similarly, postcolonial studies, ethnic studies, and gender and sexuality studies all develop out of twentieth-century grassroots movements, such as the civil rights and women's movements and the struggle against European colonialism. Politically minded literary critics use literary studies as a way to critique capitalism, patriarchy, imperialism, white privilege, homophobia, and other forms of oppression.

---

1   Karl Marx, "Theses on Feuerbach," *The Portable Karl Marx*, ed. Eugene Kamenka (New York: Penguin, 1983), 158.

Over the past fifty or so years, these approaches have radically overhauled the terrain of literary studies. New courses, departments, and programs have been created in African-American studies, women's studies, cultural studies, and other fields. The profession of literary studies, formerly the terrain almost exclusively of white men, has become increasingly diverse, and more women than men now study literature at every level. Within the classroom, the canon of texts studied has opened up to include women, minority, and international writers.

This chapter covers a range of approaches to literature that are concerned with politics. I begin by outlining some of Marx's key concepts. Even though Marx wrote very little about literature specifically, his ideas influenced an entire tradition of literary theorists. From there I survey some key developments in Marxist thinking in the twentieth century. Then I turn to race and ethnicity studies, including postcolonial theory. The chapter concludes with gender and sexuality studies and a brief look at ecocriticism.

Karl Marx

Karl Marx was born in 1818, so he could have been discussed in Chapter 5. However, his ideas reshaped twentieth-century intellectual and political life to such a degree that it makes more sense to discuss him here. Marx trained as a philosopher at a time when Hegel's ideas (see Chapter 4) dominated in German universities. Marx's key innovation was to take Hegel's theories of history but to ground them in the material world. Hegel's dialectical theory posits that *Geist* or spirit drives history forward, and the shape of each historical era emanates from that spirit striving to become conscious of itself. To Marx, a world spirit is just a frivolous, religious notion. Marx says that his project is to take Hegel's ideas, which are standing on their head, and put them back on their feet by grounding them in the real world and replacing the idea of an abstract spirit with economics. Marx's most famous work, *The Communist Manifesto* (1848), was published while he was in Paris right before a failed revolution attempt. Marx then became involved with another failed revolution in Germany as part of a wave of popular revolutions in Europe in 1848. The following year he was exiled to London because of his political involvement. While there, he continued to publish and to collaborate with his friend Friedrich Engels (1820–95), writing his masterpiece *Capital* (1867) in the British Library. As the labor movement grew after 1848, his publications became more widely circulated, including in Russia, where they would inspire a Communist revolution in the twentieth century.

Marx didn't write very much specifically about literature, though he did write poetry himself and admired nineteenth-century novelists Balzac and Dickens. His theories of historical materialism have been influential in literary studies as well as in many other fields. As his most famous work, the *Communist Manifesto*, was written to agitate a popular audience on the brink of revolution, scholars tend to look to his other works for more thorough explanations of his ideas. His key ideas are scattered throughout his many writings on ideology and political economy. Here are some of the most important terms for understanding Marx's ideas, especially as they relate to literary theory and criticism:

+ **Political economy**: the study of political and economic systems. Marx combines economic study with the German philosophical tradition and an element of direct activism.

+ **Mode of production**: another way of saying economic system. In his philosophy of history, Marx identifies different historical periods by their different modes of production. For example the feudal mode of production of the Middle Ages is based on an agricultural economy, while the capitalist mode of production that develops in the eighteenth century is based on the manufacture and sale of goods. Marx hoped that revolution would bring about a communist mode of production, where all workers would hold the means of production (factories, farms, etc.) communally. Though several nations attempted to enact communism on a grand scale in the twentieth century, none succeeded in bringing an end to history the way that Marx had predicted communism would.

+ **Materialism**: A materialist is the opposite of an idealist. Philosophical idealists such as Hegel, Kant, and Plato believe in a spiritual realm, whether Hegel's *Geist* or Plato's realm of forms. Materialists reject the ideal and instead focus on the material world. A materialist historian, for example, studies the ways in which economic conditions determine history and looks at the real conditions of human existence.

+ **Dialectic**: In Hegel's dialectic, spirit manifests itself in a particular historical moment but then runs into an antithetical force, a contradiction within that force. Thesis and antithesis collide and produce a synthesis, which raises up the best portions of both thesis and antithesis and cancels out the rest. That synthesis produces the next manifestation of the world spirit in history, becoming the new thesis that will then encounter an antithesis. Marx's dialectical (or historical) materialism replaces spirit with economics.

Thus an economic system contains internal contradictions that will then produce conflict and lead to the next stage of history: feudalism gives way to capitalism, which eventually will give way to socialism through class conflict.

+ **Base and superstructure**: In the preface to *A Contribution to the Critique of Political Economy* (1859), Marx outlines his theory of base and superstructure. He states that when people form a society and an economic system, they enter into relations of production with each other, based on systems of exchange. These relations (such as a capitalist economy or a feudal system) form the economic base of a society, the economic system taken as a whole. Upon this economic base a superstructure (ideology, political structures, a legal system, scientific ideas, religion, culture, art) develops. The base determines the particular forms that the superstructure takes, so that feudal art and culture look different from capitalist art and culture, for example. In Marx's famous formulation, "The mode of production of material life determines the social, political, and intellectual life process in general. It is not the consciousness of men that determines their being, but, on the contrary, their social being that determines their consciousness."[1] We are all products of our economic systems and historical circumstances. The base/superstructure model is central for Marxist critics, who study the ways in which literary works are products of their times and circumstances.

+ **Ideology**: For Marx, ideology, or the ideas, beliefs, and dogmas of a society, is produced by economic systems; that is, certain belief-systems come into being in order to support the status quo. Religion, for Marx, is nothing more than an ideology or false consciousness that allows people to accept their exploitation. Racism is another form of ideology. Concepts of different biological "races" of people, and particularly a hierarchy of races, developed as a way to support the slave trade as it expanded in the eighteenth and nineteenth centuries. The ideology of race, developed to justify the enslavement of people of African descent, became so firmly ingrained in thought by the nineteenth century that people believed it to be a scientific reality. Similarly, the ideology of consumerism bolsters commodity capitalism today. Fashion, the idea that you need to buy new clothes in order to keep up with what's trendy, at its root derives from the capitalist system's need for you to keep buying things to keep the whole system running. So even though ideologies are fictions, they're difficult to eradicate. Racism is

---

1   Marx, Preface to *A Contribution to the Critique of Political Economy*, *Portable Karl Marx*, 160.

still with us long after the abolition of the slave trade, and consumerism has spread across the globe.

+ **Historical determinism**: A central issue for Marxist thinkers is how much free will individuals have if they're merely historically determined products of their mode of production and slaves to ideology. Marx seems to suggest that people have some degree of control over their own destiny while still being products of their historical circumstances. As he says in *The Eighteenth Brumaire of Louis Bonaparte* (1852), "Men make their own history, but not spontaneously, under conditions they have chosen for themselves; rather on terms immediately existing, given and handed down to them."[1] If escape from ideology were entirely impossible, revolution of the type Marx proposes would be unthinkable. Historical contradictions make it possible for people to see through the blinkers of ideology to at least a certain extent.

+ **Bourgeois and proletarians**: In the capitalist mode of production the bourgeoisie are the middle and upper classes who own the means of production; the proletariat are the workers. Capitalists are members of the bourgeoisie who control the capital or means of production – factory owners, shop owners, employers rather than employees. In Marx's version of Hegel's dialectic, the dynamic of a contradiction between thesis and antithesis leading to a synthesis is given material form as the class struggle. The proletariat is the antithesis of the capitalists: the capitalists have everything while the workers have nothing. This encapsulates the central contradiction of capitalism: a few individuals (what today we call "the 1 per cent") accumulate all the wealth while the masses ("the 99 per cent") suffer and starve. Marx thought that this contradiction would lead to a revolution and thus to socialism where people would hold the means of production in common. While the biggest socialist experiment in the Soviet Union ended up failing, many of the points Marx advocated were adopted in many parts of the world in the twentieth century, including trade unions, limits on the workday, free public education, and universal voting rights.

+ **Alienation**: the state of modern people under capitalism. Workers are alienated from the products of their labor because they are producing commodities for others, not for themselves. Work isn't fulfilling for them but only a means of earning income. A number of other nineteenth-century

---

1   Marx, *The Eighteenth Brumaire of Louis Bonaparte*, Portable Karl Marx, 287.

thinkers characterized modern life as a state of alienation: for Nietzsche (see Chapter 5), we all are alienated from the truth that human language and concepts are just metaphors and not real, while Freud (see Chapter 9) builds his theories of psychoanalysis on the idea that humans are alienated from their unconscious desires.

+ **Surplus value**: the way in which capitalists make profits, by exploiting the labor of workers in order to produce commodities that they can sell for a profit. The more labor capitalists obtain from workers and the less they pay those workers, the greater the surplus value and, hence, profit.

+ **Use-value and exchange-value**: The use-value of an object is its purpose or its usefulness – the use-value of a pair of shoes is to protect your feet. The exchange-value of an object is its price, what it can be exchanged for in a capitalist economic system. Marx believes there is no necessary and inherent connection between the two: wildflowers you pick for yourself can be just as beautiful and fragrant as a bouquet purchased from a flower shop, but only one has any exchange-value. Some of the most useful things in life, like air and sunshine, have no exchange value. In the capitalist system, money serves as the universal exchange-value, reducing all things to their prices.

+ **Commodity fetishism**: Marx develops his theory of the fetishism of the commodity in *Capital*. A commodity is an object for sale in a capitalist mode of production. Specifically, Marx means products of factory labor. Because in a capitalist economy we think of commodities in terms of their prices, we forget that they are the products of human labor and that the cost of an object comes at the expense of human suffering. By turning relations between people into relations between things (exchanging money for goods instead of thinking about the work that you've done to earn the money being exchanged for the products of other people's work), we fetishize those products. A simple commodity such as a t-shirt conceals a complex set of social relations: the farm laborers who planted and picked the cotton, the laborers who turned the raw materials of the cotton plant into cotton fabric, the people involved with turning the fabric into a shirt, the shippers and distributors who got the shirt to the store, and the sales and marketing people who convinced you to buy the shirt. An entire global network can be contained in a shirt, but we forget those relations and think of it only in terms of its price.

Early Marxist Theory and Criticism

Marx and Engels reshaped twentieth-century thought. Their ideas inspired Vladimir Lenin and others to lead the Russian Revolution in 1917. After the establishment of the Soviet Union, **MARXIST** thought spread as a political movement all over the world, including China, which followed the Soviet Union in ushering in a communist state. Marx's influence on intellectual history is hard to overstate, not only for literary theory but also for such fields as history, sociology, and anthropology. In his essay "What Is an Author?" (1969), Michel Foucault discusses Marx (and Freud) as more than an author but a founder of new discourses, making possible new ways of thinking. Within literary studies, European critics developed Marxist cultural theory in the 1920s and 1930s. Russian, Italian, and German critics, often affiliated with communist or socialist political parties, elaborated upon Marx's analysis of the cultural superstructure. Marxist thought was much slower to take hold in American universities, in part because of US-Soviet tensions during the Cold War, while in Britain scholars outside the confines of Oxford and Cambridge were the first to develop Marxist literary studies.

Antonio Gramsci (1891–1937) was one of the earliest important Marxist cultural theorists. Gramsci was a member of the Italian parliament for the Communist Party when the Fascist leader Benito Mussolini (1883–1945) came to power in the 1920s. Mussolini soon imprisoned his political enemies, including Gramsci. While in prison from 1929 to 1935, Gramsci wrote voluminously. These notebooks, later published, elaborate upon Marx's ideas about ideology, the class struggle, and the role of intellectuals in society. Gramsci uses the term **HEGEMONY** to describe the power a dominant group has over **SUBALTERN** groups who don't hold power. Hegemony is different from direct domination through military or judicial force but instead refers to intellectual and moral control. It's close to Marx's notion of ideology, but with an added element of power and control and with a sense of resistance built into it. Intellectuals can promote the hegemony of the dominant group through their writings and teachings. Gramsci hoped that organic intellectuals from the subaltern or non-dominant groups would develop to oppose the force of political hegemony. His own incarceration and inability to publish his works illustrate the difficulties organic intellectuals faced at this time.

While Gramsci was writing in prison, in the Soviet Union Mikhail Bakhtin (1895–1975) was developing his own version of Marxist literary criticism. Bakhtin trained as a philologist and came out of the same context as the Russian Formalists (see Chapter 6), but he was interested in history and in Marxist ideas in a way the Formalists were not. His first book, *The Problems of Dostoevsky's Poetics* (1929), introduces his concept of dialogism, the idea that different voices can come into dialogue in the novel. In his work on the novel, Bakhtin characterizes the genre by its heteroglossia, a word meaning "another's speech in another's language."[1] He sees the novel as a space where different languages come into contact with each other. These languages can be the vocabularies of different social classes, professions, or generations. In big, sprawling novels, such as Fyodor Dostoevsky's *Crime and Punishment* (1866), characters from all strata of society interact, each speaking their own distinct language. The novelist can take these different languages and put them into dialogue with each other, and in that way can break down class barriers and other obstacles that prevent people from understanding each other.

While writers were allowed relative freedom of expression during the first years of the Soviet Union, after Joseph Stalin's rise to power Bakhtin had a harder time getting published and had to spend six years in exile in Kazakhstan as a result of Stalin's purges of writers and dissidents. Upon his return, he wrote a dissertation on the sixteenth-century French writer François Rabelais, which his advisors did not approve. Eventually published as a book, *Rabelais and His World* (1965) has been very influential. It examines Rabelais's satirical works *Gargantua and Pantagruel* (c. 1532–64) in the context of medieval carnival (the festival right before Lent, like Mardi Gras today). During carnival the expected social order gets jumbled up, social ranks disintegrate, the fool becomes king, and laughter becomes universal. Bakhtin characterizes Rabelais's work as carnivalesque, while also noting its grotesque focus on bodily functions. Bakhtin celebrates the transgressive, radical possibilities of the grotesque and the carnivalesque to undo hierarchies and thus open up new possibilities.

Hungarian thinker Georg Lukács (1885–1971) began his career under the influence both of German sociologists Georg Simmel (1858–1971) and Max Weber (1864–1920) and of Hegel's philosophy. After World War I and the Russian Revolution he began to study Marx and Marxist thought seriously. His influential essay "Reification and the Consciousness of the Proletariat" (1922) begins with Marx's concept of commodity fetishism, the way relations between people begin to look like relations between things (*rei*, from *res*, is Latin for thing, so **REIFICATION** means "thing-ification"). He elaborates upon Marx's discussion of the alienation of workers under capitalism, describing reification in terms of the fragmentation of knowledge into individual disciplines, the division of labor and specialization of the workforce, and the destruction of images of society as a whole or **TOTALITY**. He suggests that art can be one way to grasp the totality

---

1   M.M. Bakhtin, *The Dialogic Imagination: Four Essays*, trans. Caryl Emerson and Michael Holquist (Austin: U of Texas P, 1981), 324.

and thus to advocate social change. We can't actually see the way all the parts of a society fit together because it's just too vast, but we can get a sense of the whole through artistic concentration, compression, and typification.

In the 1930s Lukács lived in the Soviet Union, where he produced a number of studies of realism. He saw the realistic novel as an art form with the potential to capture the social and historical totality, and he championed nineteenth-century writers Walter Scott and Balzac for their ability to do so. These writers portray characters as individuals who also possess the key features of larger historical movements and social classes. These typical individuals "conjure up a world of illusion which requires ... a very limited number of men and human destinies to arouse the feeling of the totality of life."[1] Scott's historical novel *Ivanhoe* (1819), for example, won't give the reader a comprehensive picture of medieval life, but by selecting a few vivid characters representing different strata of medieval society (from serfs to crusading knights), Scott provides readers with a better sense of the historical process and their own place in history. Lukács contrasts the realism of Scott and Balzac with Zola's naturalism (see Chapter 5), which he says focuses too closely on particulars and thus can't see the forest for the trees. In critiquing naturalism, Lukács was critiquing (in a coded way) the doctrine of socialist realism that had become the official artistic style of the USSR in the 1930s. Lukács's writings on realism are often critiqued for being unsympathetic to naturalism and too narrowly prescriptive in their focus, but they were very influential on later Marxist literary critics.

The Frankfurt School

A group of Marxist cultural theorists called the Frankfurt School coalesced in 1920s Germany, at the same time that Gramsci, Bakhtin, and Lukács (who was acquainted with them) were writing. They were associated with the Institute for Social Research, founded in Frankfurt in 1923 on Marxist principles. Members of the institute included Max Horkheimer (1895–1973; who became director in 1930), Theodor Adorno (1903–69), and Herbert Marcuse (1898–1979), while other theorists such as Walter Benjamin (1892–1940) were associated with but not official members of the Institute. Many of these men were Jewish, and after Hitler came to power the Institute and its members relocated to New York in 1934. Benjamin stayed in Europe, committing suicide in 1940 while fleeing the Nazis.

The critical theory of the Frankfurt School (they were the first to coin that phrase) was less interested in the creation of a communist state and more

---

1   Georg Lukács, *The Historical Novel*, trans. Hannah and Stanley Mitchell (Lincoln: U of Nebraska P, 1962), 92.

interested in using Marxist ideas to critique capitalism and the West. They're especially known for their critiques of popular culture and what they call the culture industry. During World War II, Adorno and Horkheimer spent some time in exile in California, and while there they developed a trenchant critique of the Hollywood culture industry in their book *Dialectic of Enlightenment* (1947). Adorno summarizes their argument: "The total effect of the culture industry is one of anti-enlightenment, in which ... enlightenment – that is, the progressive technical domination of nature – becomes mass deception and is turned into a means for fettering consciousness."[1] They critique Hollywood films, popular music, and even Disney cartoons as capitalist tools that brainwash the masses so that they can't think for themselves. In other writings, Adorno promotes the avant-garde and experimental classical music as alternatives to the "mass deception" of popular culture. It's difficult to imagine the masses of the 1940s giving up Hollywood movies for atonal classical composers, and often Adorno's writings can sound elitist and judgmental, but his and Horkheimer's analysis of the culture industry helped to highlight the ideological dimension of seemingly benign pop culture artifacts and was a formative influence on later cultural studies.

Benjamin's writings are brilliant but enigmatic and often fragmentary. He sometimes seems like a Marxist of the Frankfurt School, yet at other times includes elements of Jewish messianism and apocalyptic thinking. Some of Benjamin's best essays, which Adorno compiled in the 1950s, theorize modernity in both its positive and negative aspects. "The Storyteller" (1936), for example, characterizes the modern age as one of information, which has replaced older storytelling. In "The Work of Art in the Age of Mechanical Reproduction" (1936), he discusses the new technologies for reproducing works of art, including sound recording, photography and film, and lithography. Before mechanical reproduction, he says, individual works of art possessed an aura because they were unique. You have to be physically present to see a sculpture or painting or to hear a musical performance, and he ties that sense of aura to religious rituals. Mechanical reproduction means that anyone can see the Mona Lisa, and in the case of photography and film the idea of a single, original work of art disappears altogether: there is nothing but reproduction. He discusses both the democratic possibilities of this state of affairs and its abuses in the hands of Fascists.

---

1   Theodor Adorno, "The Culture Industry Reconsidered," *Critical Theory and Society: A Reader*, ed. Stephen Eric Bronner and Douglas MacKay Kellner (New York: Routledge, 1989), 135.

French Marxism

Before World War II, Marxism made its biggest impact in Germany, Italy, and the USSR rather than in France or England. But after the war Marxism entered French intellectual life via the most famous literary celebrity of the time: the philosopher, novelist, and playwright Jean-Paul Sartre (1905–80). Sartre popularized the existentialist ideas of Martin Heidegger (see Chapter 6) in his influential *Being and Nothingness* (1943). The fundamental principle of existentialism, the proposition that existence precedes essence, contains radical political potential. If there's no predetermined essence, but instead humans are the sum of the choices they make and the actions they perform, then we all have the ability to transcend inequality and oppression. Frantz Fanon (1925–61) built upon Sartre's existentialist ideas to develop postcolonial theory, while Simone de Beauvoir (1908–86) developed a feminist existentialism that posits that there's no universal essence of femininity.

After the war, Sartre turned to Marxism and to more direct political engagement. His book *What Is Literature?* (1947) discusses the political commitments of writers, using African-American novelist Richard Wright (1908–60) as an example of a writer addressing himself to a particular group of people at a particular moment in time, but through that audience aiming at the universal. Wright had joined the Communist Party in the 1930s, and his novel *Native Son* (1940) addresses political issues directly. After the war Wright moved to Paris, where he befriended Sartre. Like Wright, Sartre argues that a writer needs to be situated in a context, which does not detract from the quality of the writing. In making this argument, he's rebutting the idea, coming out of the doctrine of **ART FOR ART'S SAKE**, that politically motivated writing is somehow less artistic, that politics and art are mutually exclusive.

In addition to influencing postcolonialism and feminism, Sartre's existentialism directly influenced a variety of mid-century French thinkers, including Jacques Derrida and Michel Foucault, neither of whom are considered Marxist thinkers (though Foucault's works in particular contain a strong but perhaps under-acknowledged element of Marxism). The philosopher Louis Althusser (1918–90), however, is probably Sartre's most direct successor in terms of developing a French version of Marxist theory. Althusser was a politically committed member of the French Communist Party and a major influence on French intellectual life in the mid-twentieth century. Althusser contends that Marxism is scientific thinking, and he separates Marx's thought from the historicism and humanism of Hegel by stressing the importance of economic determinism. He also includes some concepts from the psychoanalytic theories of Sigmund

Freud and Jacques Lacan (see Chapter 9) in order to analyze Marx's thinking and to develop a Marxist theory of power.

In his essay "Contradiction and Overdetermination: Notes for an Investigation" (1962), Althusser examines Marx's model of base and superstructure, the basis for all subsequent Marxist investigations of literature and culture. Althusser argues that the base doesn't simply determine superstructure; it's overdetermined. He borrows the concept of **OVERDETERMINATION** from Freud's model of dream interpretation, where a single dream may stem from multiple sources. Similarly, historical events, superstructural cultural phenomena, and the historical contradictions that lead to revolution can be overdetermined by multiple causes. From psychoanalytic thinking Althusser also borrows the concept of a **SYMPTOMATIC READING**. Just as psychoanalysts can learn as much from what their patients *don't* tell them as from what they *do*, Althusser contends that critics should look not only at what's in a text but also what's left out, what's missing, the silences and gaps. Those silences and omissions can be symptoms of repression, and recognizing the repressed material can be a way to get at what's really important. Althusser didn't write very much about literature, but his student Pierre Macherey (b. 1938) put Althusser's model of symptomatic reading into practice, analyzing authors such as Jules Verne in *A Theory of Literary Production* (1966).

In a later essay, "Ideology and Ideological State Apparatuses" (1970), Althusser develops the concept of **IDEOLOGICAL STATE APPARATUSES** (ISAs), which influenced Foucault's thinking about power. Here he systematizes Gramsci's discussion of hegemony, listing a number of ISAs that work to maintain state power: the religious ISA, the educational ISA, the family structure, political parties, and the media. All of these ISAs work to maintain the capitalist status quo and reproduce society as it already exists. He theorizes that ideology interpellates people, turning them into subjects (of the state). Interpellation, the process of being "hailed," of acknowledging when someone says "hey, you there!" or of answering the door, happens before an individual is even born. We're always-already subjects: children are born possessing their father's last name, making them subject to the patriarchal familial ISA. The concept of interpellation in part is a response to existentialism. Existence may precede essence, but ISAs can keep us from transcending our circumstances. Like Foucault's idea of power being dispersed rather than centralized, and Gramsci's notion of hegemony as something different from direct domination, ISAs are harder to escape because they are everywhere. You could work to bring down an oppressive dictator, but how do you fight interpellation that happens before you're even born? Althusser's theories present a bleak picture of social change.

British Cultural Studies

A slightly more optimistic, yet at the same time distinctly British, strain of Marxism called **CULTURAL STUDIES** developed in the 1930s to 1960s. The figures associated with it worked in the field of adult education rather than at the elite medieval universities of Cambridge and Oxford. Teaching classes for working-class adults rather than upper-class traditional-age students required a different approach. Rather than teaching practical criticism of the I.A. Richards variety, these teachers (often from working-class backgrounds themselves) sought to engage their students by bringing in popular culture, working-class traditions, and social issues.

After Hitler came to power in Germany, Britain (like America) received an influx of European intellectuals. Karl Mannheim (1893–1947), another member of the Frankfurt School, was among them and inspired a British variant of Marxist theory. Mannheim's book *Ideology and Utopia*, published in English in 1936, is a groundbreaking work in the sociology of knowledge. Influenced by Marx's ideas about ideology, Mannheim discusses the social origins of the ways people think. Specifically, he examines how different groups of people possess different mental structures. Rather than a unified zeitgeist, people from different social classes, generations, and geographic regions have different ways of seeing the world. As these people come into contact with each other, particularly through geographic migration, different ways of seeing the world come into conflict. Mannheim's goal was to make the social origins of knowledge more visible in order to get people to stop "talking past" each other and instead to recognize the grounds of their disagreements. With Hitler ascending to power and the ideology of Nazism on the rise, one understands Mannheim's interest in this issue.

In London, Mannheim got involved in adult education. There, his ideas influenced British academics such as Raymond Williams, E.P. Thompson (1924–93), Richard Hoggart (1918–2014), and Stuart Hall (1932–2014) – leftist, often working-class intellectuals, who were involved in adult education. These thinkers used Mannheim's ideas about the social origins of knowledge as a way to study working-class culture. Rather than dismissing the culture of their students and their families, they tried to understand where this culture came from and to make working-class life visible to upper-class academic readers. In this way they succeeded, at least in part, in breaking down the elitism of British academia and making working-class culture and popular culture a viable subject of academic study, not only in Britain but across the world.

Two books from the 1950s serve as the cornerstones of cultural studies. The first is Hoggart's *The Uses of Literacy* (1957), a study of twentieth-century working-class British culture that examines daily life, popular magazines, pulp fiction, songs, and the author's own working-class upbringing. The following year, Williams's *Culture and Society* (1958) called for a revision of cultural history to include class issues, literacy, and education. He writes that cultural studies should include history, philosophy, music, literature, and daily life. Williams consistently thinks historically about large concepts like art, literature, and culture, a project he expands upon in *Keywords* (1976). Thompson's *The Making of the English Working Class* (1963) would later study the development of the working class during the Industrial Revolution in great detail.

In 1964, Hoggart founded the Birmingham Centre for Contemporary Cultural Studies. Hall joined him there at the outset and became the Centre's second director in 1968. The Centre was devoted to the study of all aspects of popular culture. Hall's work in particular helped to develop a Marxist version of media studies. Written with Paddy Whannell, Hall's *The Popular Arts* (1964), for example, advocates the use of popular film, television, and music in the classroom as a way to engage students. This idea, radical at the time, is now commonplace. Likewise, cultural studies has grown into an academic discipline in its own right. Some variants of cultural studies, influenced by Adorno and Horkheimer, take a more critical view of popular culture, while others look at the subversive and potentially liberating aspects of mass culture.

Later Marxist Theory and Criticism

In the latter part of the twentieth century, Marxist ideas influenced a variety of different approaches to literary studies. Via British cultural studies, Marxism shaped new historicist thinking, while much postcolonial theory drew upon Marxist ideas, and Slavoj Žižek (see Chapter 9) blended Lacanian psychoanalysis with Marxism. Two important figures who helped popularize Marxist ideas within literary studies are Terry Eagleton (b. 1943) and Fredric Jameson (b. 1934). Eagleton studied with Raymond Williams at Cambridge and has written extensively on Marxist theory in *Marxism and Literary Criticism* (1976), *Criticism and Ideology* (1976), and elsewhere. American literary critic Jameson's *Marxism and Form* (1972) raised awareness of continental Marxist thought among American academics.

In the 1980s, Jameson's writings focused on **POSTMODERNISM**, a highly contested term that can refer to either a historical period or an artistic movement, or both. His celebrated essay "Postmodernism, or the Cultural Logic of Late Capitalism" (1984) uses Marxist economist Ernest Mandel's concept of late capitalism, the global stage of capitalism that began after World War II, as a way to characterize the recent past. The literature and culture of the postmodern era, which really comes into its own in the 1960s, is signaled by its lack of grounding in the real, its nostalgia for a past that never existed, a schizophrenic breakdown of signification, fragmentation, consumerism, and the commodification of art. Because global capitalism lost its grounding in manufacturing and agriculture and now has more to do with abstract information economies, culture became abstracted from its grounding in material life. In Jameson's account, this led to the schizophrenic, fragmented quality of postmodern art, architecture, and literature.

Debates about postmodernism became central to certain areas of literary studies in the 1980s, following the work of Jameson and of other French theorists of the postmodern, such as Jean-François Lyotard (1924–98), Gilles Deleuze (1925–95) and Félix Guattari (1930–92), and Jean Baudrillard (1929–2007). Though some of the writings on postmodernism from the 1980s now seem as dated as the decade's fashions, music, and videogames, at the time they were cutting edge. Marxist thinker David Harvey (b. 1935), for example, produced *The Condition of Postmodernity* in 1989. More recently Harvey has popularized the concept of **NEOLIBERALISM**, which appears to be gaining ground on postmodernism for Marxist theorists of contemporary culture. Neoliberalism is a doctrine that promotes the idea that "human well-being can best be advanced by liberating individual entrepreneurial freedoms and skills within an institutional framework characterized by strong private property rights, free markets, and free trade."[1] Associated with privatization, the declining power of labor unions, and the deregulation of industry and the financial sector, neoliberalism arose in the late 1970s and early 1980s and is associated with politicians Ronald Reagan in the US and Margaret Thatcher in the UK. The free-trade principles of neoliberalism have been used as a framework for studying everything from the global market for popular culture to the corporatization of the university.

Postcolonial and Ethnic Studies

I now turn to a group of interrelated fields within literary studies: **POSTCOLONIAL** studies, critical race theory, African-American studies, Latino/a studies, Native American studies, Asian-American studies, comparative **ETHNIC STUDIES**, and other areas. At the very start of the twentieth century, African-American theorist W.E.B. Du Bois (1868–1963) postulated that "the problem of the Twentieth

---

1   David Harvey, *A Brief History of Neoliberalism* (Oxford: Oxford UP, 2005), 2.

Century is the problem of the color line."[1] The theorists discussed in this section bear out Du Bois's assertion. These various fields share common roots in the struggle for civil rights and against racism and colonialism. In a variety of ways, scholars in these areas explore cultural identities, the dynamics of the oppressed versus the oppressors, inequality, the self-expression of oppressed groups, and the fictions of race and nation.

In order to understand the conditions that made possible the rise of these approaches, we need to begin in the fifteenth century and briefly review the history of colonialism and the slave trade:

+ **Fifteenth century**: At the very end of the century, Europeans made contact with the "new world" of the Western hemisphere. In short order, the Portuguese began the trade of slaves in West Africa, resulting in over 10 million African slaves being brought to the New World before the slave trade was abolished, with many more dying en route on the Middle Passage across the Atlantic.

+ **Sixteenth century**: The Spanish conquered the Aztecs in Mexico and the Incas in Peru as a Spanish and Portuguese empire was established in North and South America, with Christianity spreading alongside empire. Meanwhile, the English began to establish colonies in North America, starting a process of colonization whereby they took the land and forced out, conquered, or killed its inhabitants (through violence or through the introduction of diseases previously unknown on the continent).

+ **Seventeenth century**: The North American and Caribbean slave trade expanded among the Dutch, French, and British colonial powers after the establishment of sugar, cotton, and tobacco plantations. Looking to the east, the English and Dutch set up companies for the spice trade with the East Indies (Indonesia and India). Even further east, Europeans made contact with Australia for the first time.

+ **Eighteenth century**: British imperialism expanded, with the establishment of a penal colony in Australia and the acquisition of Canada after a war with the French. However, the British also lost a significant portion of North America when the American colonies declared their independence in 1776.

+ **Nineteenth century**: European colonialism in North and South America

---

1   W.E.B. Du Bois, *The Souls of Black Folk* (New York: Signet, 1995), 41.

was significantly reduced after revolutions across Latin America led to independence from Portugal and Spain. In 1867, Canada became an independent dominion within the British Empire. At the same time, European colonialism expanded across Africa and the Middle East. South Africa and the Middle East came under British control and North Africa under French control. In 1858, power over India was transferred from the East India Company directly to the British crown. In 1885 the Indian National Congress started the organized resistance to British rule that led to Indian independence in the twentieth century. America got into the imperialism game, too, purchasing or taking Alaska, Hawaii, Puerto Rico, and the Philippines (previously part of the Spanish Empire). In the 1880s Leopold II of Belgium (1835–1909) incited a European "scramble for Africa." By the early twentieth century most of Africa was under European control, with Belgium, France, Great Britain, Germany, Italy, Spain, and Portugal all establishing colonial administrations.

- **Twentieth century**: After World War I, the territories that made up the Ottoman Empire were partitioned into new Middle Eastern states, often under European control. After World War II decolonization began, with Europeans leaving the Middle East. In 1947 India and Pakistan gained independence from British rule. Indonesia became independent from the Dutch in 1950, Vietnam got rid of the French in 1954, while European colonialism across Africa ended in the 1960s, for the most part. The last vestige of European colonialism in Africa ended in the 1990s in South Africa, when that country finally abandoned the segregationist policy of apartheid.

Postcolonial theory grew out of twentieth-century struggles against European colonialism and deals with the legacy of that era of history. Aimé Césaire (1913–2008), born in the French colony of Martinique in the Caribbean, is one of the founding figures of postcolonialism. Like many French colonial subjects, he went to study in Paris, where he wrote a thesis on the writers of the Harlem Renaissance. In the 1930s Césaire and other black colonial subjects studying in Paris developed a movement they called *Négritude* (French for "blackness"), a poetic and artistic movement opposed to colonialism and racism, taking inspiration from Harlem Renaissance writers Langston Hughes (1902–67) and Claude MacKay (1889–1948). Césaire and others promoted solidarity across the African diaspora, the people of African descent who could be found scattered throughout North and South America, the Caribbean, Europe, and Africa. A series of Pan-African Congresses, organized initially by Du Bois beginning in 1919, brought together people in America struggling for civil rights with people in Africa seeking independence from European colonialism. Césaire's *Discourse on Colonialism* (1950) developed out of this context. In this brief essay he critiques European colonialism as morally bankrupt and calls on the colonized people of the world to rise up against their oppressors.

One of Césaire's students in Martinique, Frantz Fanon, developed Césaire's ideas in new directions. Fanon fuses Césaire's anti-colonialism, Sartre's existentialism, and his own training as a psychiatrist in his book *Black Skin, White Masks* (1952) to survey the state of black people under colonialism. He uses Sartre's discussion (in *Being and Nothingness*) of the way in which individuals become conscious of themselves through the eyes of the other. In Sartre's formulation, which derives from Hegel's discussion of the master-slave dialectic (see Chapter 4), only when we are recognized by another person and see ourselves being seen by them do we come to self-consciousness and thus into being. Fanon takes this framework and applies it to the way in which black people come to recognize their status as black only in relation to being seen by white people. In essence, they see themselves through the eyes of the other and thus internalize the negative stereotypes that white colonialists have developed to justify their oppression of black people. Fanon describes his own experience of being seen, and thus of seeing himself in another's eyes: "I discovered my blackness ... and I was battered down by tom-toms, cannibalism, intellectual deficiency, fetishism, racial defects, slave-ships."[1] Only after he sees white people seeing him as black and thus as Other does he begin to internalize stereotypes about black inferiority.

In a later work, *The Wretched of the Earth* (1961), Fanon calls for third-world people across the globe to rise up against colonialism (as many were in the process of doing). He says that Europe owes its wealth and power to the slave trade and colonialism, that the Third World created Europe. He calls for colonial people to break from Europe, violently if necessary, and to create their own states and own cultures not modeled on European principles. Fanon's ideas influenced the Black Power and Black Arts movements in the US, other struggles against oppression, and later postcolonial thinkers.

Said and Orientalism

Edward Said's (1935–2003) writings helped to establish the vibrant field of postcolonial literary theory in the 1970s and beyond. Said grew up in Palestine and Egypt under British imperialism and had a personal interest in issues related

---

1   Frantz Fanon, *Black Skin, White Masks*, trans. Charles Lam Markmann (New York: Grove Press, 1967), 112.

to the British Empire. In 1964 he completed a Harvard dissertation on Joseph Conrad (1857–1924), whose novella *Heart of Darkness* depicts the imperialist scramble for Africa. (Nigerian novelist Chinua Achebe famously critiques the racism of Conrad's novel in his 1977 essay "An Image of Africa.") In *Orientalism* (1978), Said uses the ideas of Foucault, Gramsci, Althusser, Williams, and others to study the relationship between the West and "the Orient." The subject of the book, Orientalism, refers to European/Western understandings about the Orient, particularly the Near and Middle East. (He doesn't deal with East Asia.) He uses Foucault's concept of discourse and his theorizing about the interrelations of power and knowledge to explain how knowledge about the "Orient" was put in the service of imperialism and of European control of the region. Reversing Fanon's assertion that the Third World created Europe, he asserts that "the Orient was almost a European invention, and had been since antiquity a place of romance, exotic beings, haunting memories and landscapes, remarkable experiences."[1] By making the Orient into an exotic, romantic locale, European imperialists justified their domination of the region.

One of the most significant moments in Said's work is found in his book *Culture and Imperialism* (1993). In it he takes his interest in British colonialism and empire and turns his attention to a text you might not immediately think of in that regard: Jane Austen's novel *Mansfield Park* (1814). Much of Austen's novel is set at the country estate of the Bertram family. The Bertrams own a plantation in Antigua that is the source of their wealth, and several characters travel there over the course of the novel. The point of view of the novel does not travel with those characters, however, and the events at the plantation are not discussed much in the text, though readers of the time would have been aware of the recent Haitian revolution (see Chapter 4). When the heroine tries to bring up the topic of slavery she is silenced. Said uses this as a way to analyze how issues of imperialism have been relegated to the margins, and brings out a dimension of the text that would have been apparent to Austen's initial readers but that modern readers might not notice as much. He makes the argument not to condemn Austen but to understand her in a new way: "Yes, Austen belonged to a slave-owning society, but do we therefore jettison her novels as so many trivial exercises and aesthetic frumpery? Not at all, I would argue, if we take seriously our intellectual and interpretive vocation to make connections."[2] Said contends that in order to understand the West we have to understand its relation to its colonial others.

---

1   Edward Said, *Orientalism* (New York: Vintage, 1978), 1.
2   Edward Said, *Culture and Imperialism* (New York: Knopf, 1993), 96.

Later Postcolonial Theory

Fanon, Said, and other thinkers such as Albert Memmi pioneered postcolonial studies, while later thinkers developed a range of other terms and concepts used to study imperialism and literature. Gayatri Chakravorti Spivak (b. 1942), for example, turned to postcolonialism in the 1980s. She began her career as a deconstructive theorist, having studied at Cornell with Paul de Man and translated Derrida's *Of Grammatology* in 1976. In the 1980s, she became involved with a group of Indian scholars, mostly historians, called the Subaltern Studies collective. The group, which included historians Ranajit Guha and Dipesh Chakrabarty, used Gramsci's concept of the subaltern as a way to examine various oppressed or non-dominant groups, especially in relation to India. Spivak's essay "Can the Subaltern Speak?" (1988), now a classic of postcolonial theory, explores the idea of attempting to recover the voices of the peasantry and is a product of her involvement with the Subaltern Studies collective. (A word of caution: her background in deconstruction makes her writing notoriously difficult to read.)

Another Indian postcolonial thinker with a difficult writing style is Homi Bhabha (b. 1949). His essay "Signs Taken for Wonders," published in a 1985 special issue of the journal *Critical Inquiry* edited by Henry Louis Gates, Jr., illustrates his central concepts. The essay, whose argument relies upon Fanon and on deconstructive theorists, discusses issues of identity under colonialism. His central terms are hybridity and mimicry. Colonial subjects hybridize aspects of the colonizer and the colonized, native culture and European power (he borrows here from Fanon's *Black Skin, White Masks*). One response to this can be mimicry, a hybrid form of resistance and obedience, taking on the voice of the oppressor but with elements of parody or resistance. Contemporary postcolonial scholars use such concepts as Orientalism, the subaltern, hybridity, and mimicry to study earlier literature in the context of empire (like Said's analysis of Austen) as well as to study emerging literatures of the Third World and ex-colonies across the globe.

Gates and the African-American Tradition

African-American writers Du Bois, Hughes, Wright, and James Baldwin (1924–87) played a role in shaping postcolonial theory from the outset. Within the US the African-American experience has its own distinct set of scholars, issues, and texts, and has developed into a vibrant field of study. Although Princeton University had admitted African-American student John Chavis in 1792, for the most part higher education remained racially segregated in

America until well into the twentieth century. Several institutions of higher learning for African Americans had been set up prior to the Civil War, and many more were established in the years following. These institutions are now called historically black colleges and universities (HBCUs): Howard University in Washington DC, founded in 1869, is among the most famous.

Debates about education for black Americans in the early twentieth century centered on a debate between Booker T. Washington (1856–1915), who advocated vocational training for African Americans, and Du Bois, who called for a liberal education for a "talented tenth" and the creation of a black intelligentsia. Following Du Bois's lead, HBCUs developed courses in black history and literature in the first decades of the twentieth century, but much of the theorizing and criticism of African-American literature occurred outside the academy, in the writings of the Harlem Renaissance and the Black Arts Movement. The Black Arts Movement, the artistic counterpart of the Black Power movement, was led by Larry Neal and Amiri Baraka and sought to find a black aesthetic independent of the dominant white aesthetic. The civil rights struggles of the 1960s led to the integration of higher education, a slow process that remains incomplete. After the Civil Rights Act of 1965, greater numbers of minority students were admitted to formerly all-white institutions. Student demonstrations led to the creation of the first Black Studies department in the US, at San Francisco State University, in 1968. Many other schools followed their example over the next several years.

Henry Louis Gates, Jr. (b. 1950), is one of the leading figures in African-American studies in the academy (other influential African-American theorists include Houston Baker, Jr., Hazel Carby, and Cornel West). An American, Gates received his PhD from Cambridge University in 1979, where he studied with the Nobel Prize-winning Nigerian writer Wole Soyinka. Gates has said that he was the first black graduate student in Cambridge's English department, or at least the first anyone could remember. His contributions to African-American literary studies have been varied: as a theorist, an editor of the *Norton Anthology of African American Literature*, and as a prominent public intellectual who has produced a number of television programs on the African-American experience. In his work Gates utilizes literary theory while acknowledging the racism of much of the tradition (in figures such as Hippolyte Taine and the Southern Agrarians) and translating theory to an African-American context.

Gates's book *The Signifying Monkey* (1988) discusses the African-American literary tradition as double-voiced, using Du Bois's notion of the double-consciousness of African Americans as both American and African. He discusses the ways in which black writers draw upon both the Western literary canon and a vernacular black tradition in their writings. Gates coins the concept of signifyin(g) as an example of the vernacular tradition's unique features. Related to Saussure's discussions of the **SIGNIFIER** and **SIGNIFIED**, signifyin(g) consists of a set of rhetorical devices used by black writers, including "testifying, calling out (of one's name), sounding, rapping, playing the dozens."[1] He connects this tradition to the trickster figures Esu Elegbara from the Yoruba tradition and the Signifying Monkey from the African-American tradition. Thus signifyin(g) appears in the African-American literary tradition as a theme and as a textual strategy: the texts depict characters signifyin(g) while enacting it themselves.

Recent African-American studies have broadened their focus beyond the United States to look at the larger **ATLANTIC WORLD** created by the slave trade. British scholar Paul Gilroy's book *The Black Atlantic* (1993), for example, promotes the study of Atlantic contact zones created by the slave trade. Harkening back to the pan-African movement of the early twentieth century, Gilroy suggests that work on the black experience should span Europe, Africa, and the Americas. Crucially important to African-American studies and to American studies more generally is the goal of integration and canon revision. While some courses focus exclusively on African-American writers, the desegregation of American literature anthologies and courses more generally is the result of the efforts of scholars like Gates and others to break down the barriers of a formerly all-white literary tradition.

The Diversity of Literary Traditions

Gates says that his goal is to integrate departments of English at all levels: the student body, the faculty, and the curriculum. This goal needs to include more than just black and white, however, to reflect the diversity of America. The first Ethnic Studies departments in the US came about because of student activism at the University of California, Berkeley, and at San Francisco State in 1969. Ethnic studies includes a variety of subfields, such as Native American studies, Chicano/a studies (studies of the Mexican American experience), Latino/a studies (which includes people from other parts of the Latin American world), and Asian American studies. MELUS, the Society for the Study of the Multi-Ethnic Literature of the United States, was founded in 1973 as an umbrella organization for these varied approaches, which also have their own individual conferences and organizations. Scholars of ethnic studies don't believe there is an essential difference between black, white, Latino/a, Asian-American, or Native American writing that is tied to biology or "race." Instead they focus on

---

1   Henry Louis Gates, Jr., *The Signifying Monkey: A Theory of Afro-American Literary Criticism* (New York: Oxford UP, 1988), 52.

the shared socio-cultural experiences, common histories, and common experiences of oppression, discrimination, and segregation of minorities within the US. (Race may be a fiction but racism and its effects are unfortunately real.)

The Latino/a literary tradition goes back to the first New World encounters between the Spanish conquerors and the peoples they conquered. Initially written in Spanish, Latino/a texts began appearing in English in the nineteenth century. Chicano/a activism in the US coalesced in 1965, when César Chávez (1927–1993) started to organize migrant farm workers in California. Chicano/a studies, which began at California schools, has continued to grow since the late 1960s. As the Latino/a population in the US increases in size, the field will only expand. Scholars of Latino/a literature often focus on issues of the borderlands, identity, canon formation, and the recovery of forgotten or excluded texts. A number of influential scholars in the field, such as the brothers Ramón and José David Saldívar and Héctor Calderón, were at one time associated with Yale University. Ramón Saldívar, for example, studied with deconstructive critics Paul de Man and J. Hillis Miller in the 1970s and only later turned to Chicano/a literature.

The work of poet Gloria Anzaldúa (1942–2004) showcases the intersections of gender, sexuality, and ethnicity. *This Bridge Called My Back* (1981), which she coedited with Cherríe Moraga, is a groundbreaking collection of essays and poems by women of color. Anzaldúa's *Borderlands/La Frontera: The New Mestiza* (1987) is another highly influential, experimental work. Her central trope is the *mestizo*, a Spanish word meaning "mixed" and referring to the mixed descent of Latino/as from the Spanish conquerors, the Aztecs they conquered, other North American Indians they intermarried with, and Africans brought to the New World to be slaves. The book mixes poetry and prose, Spanish and English, memoir and theory. In it she connects the borderlands in the US Southwest and the mixture of cultures and peoples there with her multiple identities as a feminist, lesbian, and woman of color.

In a similar vein, bell hooks [Gloria Watkins] (b. 1952) explores the intersections of racism and sexism in her works on black feminism. Her book *Ain't I a Woman* (1981) deals with the black female experience: "When black people are talked about the focus tends to be on black *men*; and when women are talked about the focus tends to be on *white* women."[1] hooks contends that for black women the experiences of racism and sexism can't be separated. Her study explores the experience of black women under slavery and after. Since the publication of this book, hooks has become a public intellectual and prolific author, one of the most visible academic figures today.

---

1   bell hooks, *Ain't I a Woman: Black Women and Feminism* (Boston: South End Press, 1981), 7.

Feminist Theory and Criticism

As the examples of hooks and Anzaldúa suggest, struggles for gender and racial equality are related to parts of the larger civil rights struggles of the twentieth century. Just as ethnic studies strives for diversity in terms of faculty, students, and curriculum, **FEMINIST** theorists promote women's voices at the levels of students, teachers, authors, and institutional power. Feminists often refer to first-wave, second-wave, and third-wave feminisms. First-wave feminists of the late nineteenth and early twentieth centuries fought for the right to vote, women's education, the right for women to enter the workplace, and other issues. The 1848 women's rights convention at Seneca Falls, New York, marked a starting point for these efforts, which intensified in the last decades of the nineteenth century and resulted in British women getting the right to vote in 1918 and America ratifying the Nineteenth Amendment to the Constitution allowing women's suffrage in 1920. Second-wave feminists of the 1960s and 1970s were part of the larger civil rights movement and advocated equal pay, abortion rights, and other matters. The stereotypical image of a "bra-burning" feminist stems from this era of organized protests (some feminist activists did literally burn bras as a symbolic gesture). Much like ethnic studies, women's studies and later gender studies courses and programs were established at universities at this time as a result of activists' efforts. In the US, feminist activism in the 1970s revolved around the Equal Rights Amendment, a proposed constitutional amendment granting equal rights to women under the law. The amendment, first proposed in the 1920s after women's suffrage, was revived in the 1970s and is still not yet ratified, though it is frequently brought before Congress. The so-called third wave of feminism can be traced to the early 1990s. While the 1980s was a period of greater conservatism in the US, activism revived in the 1990s around the time of the first Gulf War. Rather than feminism being divided into discrete waves, however, it's perhaps better seen as a continuous history from the nineteenth century to the present day.

Founding Figures

Christine de Pizan (see Chapter 3) and Mary Wollstonecraft (see Chapter 4) are often cited as pioneers of feminism. Turning to the twentieth century, British novelist Virginia Woolf's *A Room of One's Own* (1929) is a landmark text of feminist literary criticism. Originally lectures she gave to two women's colleges the previous year on the topic of women in fiction, the book tells a story, lightly fictionalized, of Woolf's own experiences. She describes visiting the dining halls of a men's college and a women's college, the men's lavish and the other poor. In another chapter she goes to the British Museum to research what men have written about women (much of it extremely sexist) over the years. A later chapter envisions what life would have been like for "Shakespeare's sister." If Shakespeare had a sister with the same talent as him, Woolf hypothesizes, she would not have been able to receive an education or to write for the theater. Woolf imagines she ends up committing suicide: "Any woman born with a great gift in the sixteenth century would certainly have gone crazed, shot herself, or ended her days in some lonely cottage outside the village, half witch, half wizard, feared and mocked at."[1] She traces the history of women writers from the seventeenth century onwards, praising Aphra Behn as the first professional woman writer. In her conclusion, she encourages her female audience to write, saying that a woman needs £500 and her own room to do so. (Keep in mind that one pound from 1928 is worth 40 times as much today, so that £500 is the equivalent of around £20,000.)

Another groundbreaking early-twentieth-century feminist thinker, French existentialist philosopher Simone de Beauvoir, was intellectually and romantically associated with Sartre (see above). She transformed his ideas into one of the most influential feminist texts of the twentieth century, *The Second Sex* (1949). Her book takes *woman* as its subject: her biology and history, various myths of woman, and the different social roles open to women. She begins with Sartre's existentialist premise that existence precedes essence, that humans are the sum total of what they do rather than possessing some predetermined essence: "One is not born, but rather becomes, woman. No biological, psychic, or economic destiny defines the figure that the human female takes on in society."[2] Even though there's no unchanging female essence that would limit women's possibilities, Beauvoir analyzes the impediments to women becoming the equals to men in society. She identifies a variety of myths of woman, including the saintly mother, the temptress, the muse, the angelic virgin, and above all the woman as mystery. These myths then become accepted as reality in a manner similar to Nietzsche's description of the process of concept-formation in "On Truth and Lying in a Non-Moral Sense" (see Chapter 5). Nietzsche talks about how humans form concepts by ignoring the individual differences among things (he uses the example of leaves), highlighting similarities to create the concept of a thing ("leafness" in the Platonic sense), and then forgetting that the concept is a human creation and believing it to be eternal and unchanging. Beauvoir contends that the same process creates the concept of the feminine.

1 Virginia Woolf, *A Room of One's Own* (Orlando: Harcourt Brace Jovanovich, 1957), 51.
2 Simone de Beauvoir, *The Second Sex*, trans. Constance Borde and Sheila Malovany-Chevallier (New York: Vintage, 2010), 283.

Rather than looking at each woman as an individual, the myth of the feminine projects an unchanging essence onto all women. If a woman doesn't match up because she chooses to work rather than get married or wear trousers rather than a skirt, the *woman* is judged to be defective and not feminine, rather than the myth being judged to be inadequate to define women's realities. She compares the experience of women to that of black people under racism and Jews under anti-Semitism, highlighting these shared struggles against oppression. All of these groups are *others* of the dominant group, in Sartre's terms. Just as Fanon would describe the black experience of seeing oneself in the eyes of the white other, so too do women internalize their own sense of inferiority by seeing themselves as the Other to man: "He is the Subject; he is the Absolute. She is the Other" (6). Beauvoir's text was extremely successful and translated into many languages. One of her American readers, Betty Friedan (1921–2006), went on to write *The Feminine Mystique* (1963), a book indebted to Beauvoir and sometimes credited with igniting the second wave of feminism in the US.

Later Feminist Theorists

Building upon the works of Woolf and Beauvoir, feminist scholars in the 1960s and 1970s studied women's writing and worked to bring more women's voices into the canon and the classroom. Even though women since Sappho had been contributing to the literary tradition, women writers often were not treated as seriously as male writers by male critics and were not included in academic literary studies. The New Critics hardly ever dealt with women writers, for example, and even more progressive thinkers like Jacques Derrida focused mostly on male writers. Feminist critics seek a coeducational canon that includes significant numbers of women writers, while also addressing the obstacles women writers faced in the past, such as exclusion from higher education.

In *A Literature of Their Own* (1977), a pioneering academic study of women novelists, Elaine Showalter parallels the experience of women writers with those of other "subcultures," such as black writers and Jewish writers, just as Beauvoir had done. She highlights the common experiences of oppression shared by women writers and celebrates some lesser-known writers, such as the first-wave feminist writers of the 1880s to 1910s who were involved with the suffrage movement. Only two years after Showalter, Sandra Gilbert and Susan Gubar produced another highly influential feminist study. At Indiana University, beginning in 1974, they co-taught a course on women writers that shares a name with the book they would publish as a result, *The Madwoman in the Attic* (1979), a reference to an imprisoned female character in Charlotte Brontë's novel *Jane Eyre* (1847). This massive, 700-page study of major women writers such as Jane Austen, George Eliot, and Emily Dickinson focuses on the shared experiences of these writers. Gilbert and Gubar do not believe that women write differently than men because of biology, but rather because of their common struggle against patriarchy. Women in the nineteenth century, denied the same education as men, were physically confined, could not travel on their own (unlike men), and had to struggle to make their way in a male-dominated literary world. Gilbert and Gubar went on to edit *The Norton Anthology of Literature by Women* (1985), helping to recover the voices of even more women writers.

Feminist theory is a varied, interdisciplinary field that brings together scholars from a range of backgrounds who are interested in issues of gender. In the 1970s in France, a group of scholars, including Julia Kristeva and Luce Irigaray (b. 1930), developed an influential combination of feminism and psychoanalytic theory (see Chapter 9). Anthropologist Gayle Rubin coins the phrase **THE SEX/ GENDER SYSTEM** in her essay "The Traffic in Women: Notes on the 'Political Economy' of Sex" (1975), which examines different cultures' kinship systems, particularly their practices of exchanging women through marriage. Based on her study of these practices, Rubin proposes that scholars make a distinction between biological *sex* and cultural *gender*, analogous to the Marxist base/superstructure distinction. Sexual difference, like the economic base, serves as a foundation upon which are built a range of gendered traits and practices that are culturally constructed and contingent. Gendered aspects of culture include the types of clothing men and women are expected to wear, the division of labor within a family, and the types of names given to girls versus boys. To cite just one very trivial example, in many cultures the color pink is associated with femininity and girls, whereas blue is a boy's color. At the beginning of the twentieth century, however, the gendered associations were exactly reversed: pink was the color for baby boys and light blue for baby girls. This simple reversal illustrates just how arbitrary some gender distinctions can be. Feminist scholars debate the extent of biology in determining gender differences: some feminists concentrate on the essential, biological differences between men and women relating to issues such as motherhood (while not using them as a justification for sexism), while others focus on the culturally constructed gendered differences.

Sexuality and Queer Theory

LGBT (lesbian, gay, bisexual, and transgender) studies grew out of feminist and gender studies but with a focus on issues related to sexuality. In 1980, poet Adrienne Rich (1929–2012) complained that the feminists of the 1970s had ignored the lesbian experience. Her essay "Compulsory Heterosexuality and Lesbian Existence" reviews a number of recent works of feminist scholarship that assume that the history of women's experience is heterosexual. Rich contends that compulsory heterosexuality is a tool of male domination that makes women sexually available to men. Feminists who ignore lesbian existence are unwittingly playing into the ideology of compulsory heterosexuality that sees lesbianism as deviant. Since that time, feminists and other scholars have developed a rich body of scholarship on lesbianism and on sexuality more broadly.

Many scholars working in this area embrace the term **QUEER THEORY** to describe their work, reclaiming a formerly derogatory term for gays and lesbians and echoing the gay activist slogan "We're here, we're queer, get used to it." Like the other movements discussed in this chapter, LGBT studies is tied to civil rights struggles, specifically the gay rights movement, which gained momentum in the 1970s after the 1969 Stonewall Riots, which arose after a police raid on a gay bar in the West Village in New York. At the time, raids on gay bars were a frequent occurrence, and laws existed prohibiting gay sex and cross-dressing. In fact, sodomy laws (which include prohibitions on certain sexual acts, even between married heterosexual couples) were only declared unconstitutional in the US in 2003 with the Supreme Court's ruling in *Lawrence v. Texas*. Since that time, gay activists have fought for funding for HIV/AIDS research and more recently for marriage equality.

Within literary studies, queer theory looks for inspiration to the late works of Michel Foucault (who was gay), discussed in the previous chapter. The completed volumes of his *History of Sexuality* (1976–84) open up new possibilities for the study of sexuality. His work traces the ways in which power shapes even something that seems completely natural: our ideas about sex and sexuality. He characterizes the modern age as a period when discourse about sex has flourished. While we think of the Victorian period as one of sexual repression, for example, he sees it as a time when there was an "incitement to discourse" about sex, with regulations about sexual practices and acts, psychoanalytic studies of sexual deviants, monitoring of children's sexuality, and so forth. The concept of the homosexual developed in nineteenth-century psychoanalytic thought as a way to characterize a type of person: "Homosexuality appeared as one of the forms of sexuality when it was transposed from the practice of sodomy onto a kind of interior androgyny, a hermaphrodism of the soul. The sodomite had been a temporary aberration; the homosexual was now a species."[1] In a later volume, Foucault explores alternative cultural arrangements for sexuality, such as the ancient Greeks' focus on the older man-adolescent relationship (something Plato frequently discusses). While Foucault's writings on discourse and power influenced the development of new historicism, his writings on sexuality inspired a range of investigations into sexuality and literature, studies of gay writers, studies of the history of sexuality in literature, and examinations of homoerotic aspects of texts.

Sedgwick and Butler

Eve Kosofsky Sedgwick, a pioneer of queer theory and an early adopter of Foucault's ideas in literary studies, published *Between Men* (1985) just as gay and lesbian studies was coalescing as an academic field. In it she looks at eighteenth- and nineteenth-century British writers and the concept of **HOMO-SOCIALITY**, meaning bonding or emotional relations between members of the same sex. Homosociality is distinct from homosexuality, same-sex sexual relations. Sedgwick contends that for women, homosociality and homosexuality exist along a spectrum, while for men homophobia interrupts that continuum. That is, in our culture women can be friends, compliment each other's appearance, and even share physical contact such as hand-holding or hugging, without insinuations of homosexuality or lesbianism. For men, however, homophobia is so strong in the culture that they often must make assertions of their straightness when engaging in homosocial bonding. The culture has changed greatly since Sedgwick wrote this, but differences persist in how popular culture depicts male (rather than female) bonding, often defusing the homosexual threat through a joke or an "I'm not gay" assertion. Sedgwick's study looks at how homosociality is defused in British novels through erotic "triangles." Placing a female love interest between two male characters defuses the threat of homosexuality, a pattern that can be seen from Lancelot/Arthur/Guinevere to Harry/Ron/Hermione.

In a later work, *Epistemology of the Closet* (1990), Sedgwick looks at the way the binary opposition homosexual/heterosexual became central to twentieth-century thought. As Foucault had discussed in *History of Sexuality*, the concept of a homosexual develops in nineteenth-century psychoanalysis as a "species" rather than being tied to previous understandings of sodomy as an act. As sexuality becomes an identity category (rather than merely a description of behavior) and homosexuality has to be kept "in the closet," it becomes a central secret.

---

1   Michel Foucault, *The History of Sexuality*, Vol. 1, trans. Robert Hurley (New York: Vintage, 1990), 43.

Judith Butler (b. 1956), a famously rigorous thinker, is often cited alongside Sedgwick as a founding figure in queer theory. Her training is in philosophy, not literary studies, having written a dissertation on twentieth-century Hegelian thought. In her book *Gender Trouble* (1990), Butler begins with Rubin's sex/gender distinction: sex is biological, gender is culturally constructed. Her interest in the body stems from Foucault's work, though Foucault has very little to say about women and women's bodies. Butler studies the ways in which gender is performative – how gender identity is created through a cultural performance that conceals its origins to make it seem natural. She mentions drag as a way to illustrate the idea of gender as performance. Drag artists such as RuPaul Charles brilliantly showcase the performance of gender through parody and in the process subvert established gender identities.

Disability and Environmental Studies

Other political approaches include disability studies and environmental studies, interdisciplinary fields that bring together scholars interested in a particular topic. Disability studies includes social and political theorists, medical scholars, and cultural and literary theorists interested in issues related to mental and physical disabilities, while environmental studies brings together writers, environmental scientists, ecologists, and a range of other scholars interested in the relationship between humans and the natural world.

The theoretical movement associated with environmental studies is sometimes called **ECOCRITICISM** and developed as a part of the increased concern for ecology in the 1960s and 1970s. Recent environmental catastrophes and climate change have spurred growth in this field. Ecocriticism, or the study of literature and the environment, came into its own in the 1990s with the publication of Jonathan Bate's *Romantic Ecology* (1991) and Lawrence Buell's *The Environmental Imagination* (1995) and the founding of the Association for the Study of Literature and the Environment (ASLE) in 1992. Ecocritics study how nature is depicted in writing, both in the works of canonical writers such as Wordsworth and Thoreau and in twentieth- and twenty-first-century ecological texts. More recently a subfield of **ANIMAL STUDIES** has explored the connections between humans and animals as represented in texts. Jacques Derrida's 1999 essay "The Animal That Therefore I Am" helped to inspire investigations of the human/animal relation in literary and philosophical texts and to deconstruct the hierarchical opposition between the animal and the human.

French historian of science Bruno Latour (b. 1947) has also turned to issues of climate change in his recent works. In a number of important essays, he worries that the relativism and anti-foundationalist ideas of "French theory" are now providing intellectual support to people who want to deny climate change. In *Reassembling the Social* (2005) and other writings starting in the late 1970s, Latour has studied the ways in which scientific phenomena are culturally constructed. Rather than merely saying they're culturally constructed, however, he takes concepts and objects and examines them not as givens but as assemblages, as networks constructed by various actors (including nonhumans). Latour's **ACTOR-NETWORK THEORY** bears some relation to Marx's idea of a commodity. A simple commodity such as a t-shirt contains complex, global relations among producers, manufacturers, distributors, and salespeople, and a similar disassembly can be performed on any object. Latour in particular studies scientific discoveries and their dependence upon laboratory space, technicians, equipment, funding, and other matters. Actor-network theory breaks apart complex abstractions such as *society* or *nation,* instead learning from the actors involved, using the anthropological tools of observation or Geertzian thick description. In his recent work Latour has examined the interactions of humans and nature in the Anthropocene, a term coined by ecologists to designate the geologic age when humans began to affect the planet in adverse ways. (It echoes parallel designations such as Pleistocene.)

Although it may not be a good idea to speculate about anything – the 1989 movie *Back to the Future Part II* imagined flying cars in the year 2015 – there is little doubt that political approaches will continue to play a major role in the future of literary studies. The profession of literary studies and the students who study literature no longer consist mostly of white males, society is becoming ever more global because of migration and technology, and environmental crises loom on the horizon. In this context, a future of literary theory that doesn't engage with sociopolitical issues seems unimaginable.

Suggestions for Further Reading

Calderón, Héctor, and José David Saldívar, eds. *Criticism in the Borderlands: Studies in Chicano Literature, Culture, and Ideology.* Durham, NC: Duke UP, 1991.

Steele, Tom. *The Emergence of Cultural Studies 1945–65: Cultural Politics, Adult Education, and the English Question.* London: Lawrence and Wishart, 1997.

Warhol, Robyn R., and Diane Price Herndl, eds. *Feminisms: An Anthology of Literary Theory and Criticism.* 2nd ed. New Brunswick, NJ: Rutgers UP, 1997.

Westling, Louise. *The Cambridge Companion to Literature and the Environment.* Cambridge: Cambridge UP, 2014.

Nine: Twentieth- and Twenty-First-Century Psychoanalytic Approaches

IN THE LAST THREE chapters I have discussed formalist approaches that concentrate on literary form and historical and political approaches that study texts in relation to their larger contexts. In this chapter, I turn to a set of approaches to literature that concentrate on *minds*. The theorists discussed in this chapter all are interested in various ways in what goes on inside people's heads: authors' psychology, the mental dimensions of the reading process, and even the psyches of fictional characters. Psychological approaches to literature begin with Sigmund Freud. Even though many of his ideas are no longer accepted within the discipline of psychology, his works raise new questions and create new avenues of study. From there I trace the psychoanalytic tradition in literary studies through French psychoanalysts such as Jacques Lacan and Julia Kristeva. Finally, I discuss phenomenology, hermeneutics, reader-response criticism, and more recent approaches that draw upon neuroscience and cognitive studies.

Freud and Freudian Criticism

With Freud we arrive at the last of the three major German-speaking theorists of alienation who shaped the direction of literary theory in the twentieth century. The first was Nietzsche (see Chapter 5), who theorizes about the human condition as one of alienation from the truth, focusing on the role of language and concept formation. For Marx (see Chapter 8), capitalism produces alienation. Workers are alienated from their labor, and we are all prisoners of ideology. Alienation for Freud, in contrast, has to do with the mind's alienation from itself. In Freud's influential **PSYCHOANALYTIC** theory, humans are necessarily alienated from our unconscious desires.

Reading Freud can be both enjoyable and frustrating. His writing is engaging and often funny, and he frequently illustrates his points with literary examples. Many of his broad overarching claims, though, sound rather far-fetched, such as his theory of penis envy. Although some of his claims have been discredited, his influence on twentieth-century intellectual history and literary theory in particular can't be overstated. Beginning with *The Interpretation of Dreams* (1900), Freud published a series of books and articles that gained him fame and disciples within psychoanalysis, the admiration of artists and writers, and even pop-culture notoriety. The Internet Movie Database (imdb.com) lists dozens of film and television credits for the character "Sigmund Freud." Montgomery Clift plays him in John Huston's film *Freud: The Secret Passion* (1962; see Figure 8), with a screenplay originally written by Jean-Paul Sartre (Huston rejected Sartre's script because it was too long). Freud travels through time with Socrates, Joan of Arc, and Billy the Kid in *Bill & Ted's Excellent Adventure* (1989). He also makes appearances in episodes of the TV shows *The Twilight Zone*, *Saturday Night Live*, *Sabrina, the Teenage Witch*, and *Frasier*.

As with Marx, key concepts for understanding Freud's thinking can be found scattered in many of his works. Here are some of the terms and concepts that have most influenced literary theory and criticism:

+ **Unconscious**: For Freud, beneath our conscious thoughts and feelings lie unconscious desires that often originate in early childhood. These unconscious desires can manifest themselves in dreams, neuroses, and slips of the tongue (popularly called Freudian slips). The unconscious is much larger than the conscious mind (Freud compares it to an iceberg where only a small portion is visible and a much larger portion is hidden beneath the surface), but the unconscious can't be accessed directly. Psychoanalysis can help patients understand and come to terms with their unconscious.

+ **Manifest vs. latent content**: In *Interpretation of Dreams*, Freud distinguishes between the manifest content of a dream – or the dream as a patient remembers it – and the latent content – or the unconscious desires that lie behind the dream and that an analyst can help bring to the surface. Freud interprets literary works in the same manner that he interprets dreams, divining the unconscious desires that motivate literary characters and their authors and that shape works of art.

Figure 8: Poster for John Huston's *Freud*.

+ **Condensation**: the process whereby dreams condense recent experiences, bodily sensations, childhood memories, and unconscious desires into a single dream. Freud calls dreams "brief, meagre and laconic in comparison with the range and wealth of the dream-thoughts."[1] In a dream, a single figure might condense aspects of more than one person – a figure in your dream could be both your old fourth-grade teacher and your current boss at the same time, a place could be both the house you grew up in and a palace in France.

+ **Displacement**: the process whereby dreams take an element with strong feelings attached to it and displace those feelings onto something that doesn't evoke intense emotion. Rather than dreaming directly about a source of anxiety, unconscious desire, or fear, that emotional content gets displaced onto something less significant to the dreamer. For example, a dreamer who is extremely anxious about an upcoming move to a new city might dream about going out and not having shoes on. The brain displaces the real-life anxiety onto something benign as a way to work through the feelings and thus to allow a person to sleep through the night.

+ **Overdetermination**: the third process of dream creation whereby dreams stem from multiple causes at once. In *Interpretation of Dreams* Freud analyzes dozens of his own dreams and those of his patients. In a surprising number of them, he uncovers a root cause that originates in early childhood complexes. A dream might be provoked by a more immediate occurrence but can also stem from an unconscious repressed wish at the same time. Freud famously finds sexual symbols everywhere in the dreams he interprets, seeing hats, buildings, and staircases, among other things, as phallic symbols. He also believes that literary works are **OVERDETERMINED**, an idea that becomes a founding principle of psychoanalytic literary criticism, saying that "all genuinely creative writings are the product of more than a single motive and more than a single impulse in the poet's mind, and are open to more than a single interpretation."[2] Just as a psychoanalyst can bring out things in a patient's unconscious not apparent to that individual, a psychoanalytic literary critic can find meanings within a text of which the author might not have been conscious of when writing it.

---

1   Sigmund Freud, *The Interpretation of Dreams*, *The Standard Edition of the Complete Psychological Works of Sigmund Freud*, trans. James Strachey (London: Hogarth P, 1966), 4:279.

2   Freud, *Interpretation of Dreams*, 4:266.

+ **Wish fulfillment**: At their root, dreams represent wish fulfillment for the dreamer. Freud analyzes dreams and works of literature to find the latent unconscious desires beneath their manifest content. Unconscious desires can be fulfilled within a dream or a work of literature rather than being acted upon in reality.

+ **Oedipus complex**: Freud terms the most common wish he finds the **OEDIPUS COMPLEX**, named after the Greek legend of Oedipus and Sophocles' play *Oedipus the King* (c. 429 BCE). Oedipus unwittingly murders his father and then marries his mother, and Freud suggests that all children go through a phase where they are in love with one parent and hate the other. He says that the story of Oedipus has had such resonance in Western culture because everyone shares this universal, unconscious desire: "It is the fate of all of us, perhaps, to direct our first sexual impulses towards our mother and our first hatred towards our father. Our dreams convince us that this is so."[1] Normally a child outgrows this "primeval" state and moves on, but those repressed childhood wishes find an outlet in dreams, works of literature, and elsewhere. In this same section of *Interpretation of Dreams*, Freud discusses Hamlet as an example of a character who doesn't act upon his Oedipal desires. Hamlet hesitates in killing his uncle because Claudius was living out Hamlet's Oedipal fantasy: he killed Hamlet's father and married his mother.

+ **Penis envy**: one of Freud's most notorious and discredited ideas. In *Three Essays on the Theory of Sexuality* (1905), Freud claims that when little girls discover that little boys have penises but they don't, they are overcome with jealousy, even wishing to have penises and (in extreme cases) wishing to become boys themselves. Naturally, feminist theorists have challenged this notion, just as scholars of sexuality have discredited Freud's ideas about homosexuality as an "aberration." (The American Psychiatric Association classified homosexuality as a mental disorder until 1973.)

+ **Ego, id, superego**: In later writings, Freud developed a theory of the psyche that superseded his earlier work on the unconscious and conscious. The ego, a Latin word meaning *I*, is the conscious mind, and the id, Latin for *it*, is the unconscious. In addition, the mind internalizes a sense of right and wrong or of the law and develops curbs to unconscious desires through a superego. The superego provides a check on people acting upon the erotic

---

1   Freud, *Interpretation of Dreams*, 4:262.

and violent urges that come from the id, a kind of conscience or a moral compass.

+ **The uncanny**: a complex concept in Freud's thought, which he defines as "that class of the frightening which leads back to what is known of old and long familiar."[1] UNCANNY effects result from a return of the repressed, from repressed or unconscious material coming to light to produce an unsettling effect. Often this repressed material consists of beliefs a culture has outgrown, such as the belief in magic and sorcery or in mind control, but it can also include infantile wishes, such as the desire to return to the mother's womb. Among the many things that produce a creepy, unsettling, but somehow eerily familiar (the German word, *unheimlich*, contains the root word for *home*) feeling, Freud lists dolls, automatons, doubles (when we say someone has an uncanny resemblance to someone else), telepathy, coincidences, ghosts, haunted houses, and being buried alive. He illustrates his ideas with another literary example, this time German Romantic writer E.T.A. Hoffmann's short story "The Sand-Man" (1816). The story concerns a character's fear of a sandman who comes and steals children's eyes, while also involving a beautiful automaton, and Freud analyzes the story's use of these uncanny elements, ultimately tracing the unconscious meaning of the tale back to a primal fear of castration. He says that not all stories that employ these types of elements are uncanny, however. Fairy tales with talking animals, magic fairies, and the like aren't uncanny because the uncanny must involve an element of uncertainty. In a clearly non-realistic context, such as a fairy tale or a children's cartoon, the uncanny just doesn't create the unsettling feeling that it does in a work of gothic horror, where the unrealistic intrudes on a more recognizably real world. Scholars of gothic literature have made much use of Freud's discussion of the uncanny in literature.

+ **Drives**: In *Civilization and Its Discontents* (1930) and elsewhere, Freud discusses the fundamental drives or instincts that guide human behavior and shape civilization. Naturally, the erotic drive or libido is central to all of Freud's thinking, but alongside it humans possess a death drive or instinct for violence, cruelty, and aggression. (In other words, people just want to have sex and fight.) Repression of these fundamental drives creates civilization, and Freud theorizes that Eros and death are in a constant struggle throughout human history. Writing in the aftermath of World War I, it

---

1   Freud, "The Uncanny," *Standard Edition*, 17:220.

is no wonder Freud saw the death drive as the greatest threat to human civilization.

Though a psychoanalyst by profession, Freud was also widely read in literature and makes use of Sophocles, Shakespeare, Hoffmann, and other writers to illustrate his ideas. He also directly influenced the modernist literary movement of the first decades of the twentieth century. His study of the nonlinear, associative way the mind works helped to shape the stream of consciousness technique of writers such as James Joyce (1882–1941) and Virginia Woolf. In fact, the Hogarth Press, started by Woolf and her husband Leonard, was the first to publish Freud's complete works in English. Freud also psychoanalyzed the poet H.D. (Hilda Doolittle, 1886–1961) in the 1930s, and her poetry shows the influence of Freudian thinking. In a broader sense, Freud's openness about discussing sexuality paved the way for a period of greater sexual liberation in the twentieth century.

Almost immediately after the publication of *Interpretation of Dreams* in 1900, Freud's students and other early psychoanalysts begin to publish works of psychoanalytic literary criticism. These books and articles often treat authors and even literary characters as patients, psychoanalyzing them and diagnosing their conditions. Freud's student Ernest Jones, for example, published a paper called "The Œdipus-Complex as an Explanation of Hamlet's Mystery: A Study in Motive" (1910). In it, he elaborates upon Freud's brief discussion of *Hamlet* (initially just a footnote) in *Interpretation of Dreams*, confirming Freud's initial diagnosis of Hamlet's unconscious desire to murder his father and sleep with his mother. Other early psychoanalysts diagnosed authors. Lucile Dooley, for example, concluded in 1920 that Charlotte Brontë was neurotic: "The secret of this tremendous power of passion in her fiction is emotional conflict in her own soul."[1] Favorite "patients" for early psychoanalytic literary critics included Jonathan Swift, Edgar Allan Poe, Lord Byron, and Percy Shelley, who were diagnosed as manic-depressive, neurotic, a narcissistic sadist, and a repressed homosexual, respectively.

Freud's students and followers also used his ideas to study mythology, just as Freud himself had done with the Oedipus myth. Otto Rank (1884–1939), a student of Freud, became one of the first to use Freud's ideas to discuss myth in *The Myth of the Birth of the Hero* (1909). In other works, such as *The Artist* (1907) and *Art and Artist* (1932), Rank studies the psychology of the artistic personality, trying to deduce the psychological basis for artistic creation.

---

1   Lucile Dooley, "Psychoanalysis of Charlotte Brontë, as a Type of the Woman of Genius," *American Journal of Psychology* 31 (July 1920): 223.

Freud (who died in 1939) continues to influence literary studies, often in combination with other critical approaches. Ideas and concepts from Freud – the unconscious, Oedipal conflict, repression, anxiety, and the uncanny – continue to be a part of the vocabulary of literary theory. Harold Bloom's *The Anxiety of Influence* (1973), for example, uses Freudian ideas about anxiety and Oedipal conflict to theorize about how writers influence each other. Another American academic, Peter Brooks, combines psychoanalysis and narratology. In *Reading for the Plot* (1984), Brooks discusses narrative plots in terms of desire in the psychoanalytic sense. He discusses the way plots are a form of desire that keeps the reader moving through the text, wanting to know what happens. Psychoanalytic theorist Shoshana Felman writes about madness and trauma in literature in numerous publications, while Norman Holland has psycho-analyzed the responses of individual readers in his book *Five Readers Reading* (1975).

Jungian Criticism

While Freud and later Jacques Lacan (discussed below) form two of the major touchstones for later psychoanalytic theory, Carl Jung, a younger contempo-rary of Freud in psychoanalysis, has influenced a separate but related tradition of Jungian archetypal theory. Jung struck up a friendship with Freud in 1906 but broke from him in 1913 and went on to develop his own very distinctive approach to the study of the mind. Rather than seeing the unconscious as a repository of dark desires that go back to early childhood, Jung posited the idea of a shared collective unconscious that stores deep archetypes. Freud analyzed the psychology of the individual while Jung aimed to analyze all of humanity. In 1927 Jung defined the collective unconscious as "the whole spiritual heritage of mankind's evolution, born anew in the brain structure of every individual."[1] As the human race evolved, he argues, primitive experiences produced archetypes in the brain that were originally responses to the environment. For example, primitive people experienced hunger and therefore developed archetypal gods of food as a response, while their experiences with danger produced the concept of dragons. These archetypes exist as mental structures that form the basis for all the world's mythologies and religions.

Though few psychoanalysts would identify as Jungians today, Jung's ideas influenced a number of scholars of literature, religion, and myth in the mid-twentieth century. Maud Bodkin's *Archetypal Patterns in Poetry* (1934) is

---

1   Carl Gustav Jung, *The Portable Jung*, ed. Joseph Campbell (New York: Penguin, 1976), 45.

one of the earliest important applications of Jung's ideas to literature. Joseph Campbell's *The Hero With a Thousand Faces* (1949), though, is probably the most famous of these works. In it, he uses Jungian archetypal theory to discuss heroes and heroism. Campbell's work became popular and has had a lasting impact on pop culture: George Lucas has said Campbell's ideas were a major influence on the creation of *Star Wars*.

Canadian critic Northrop Frye's version of archetypal criticism, outlined in his *Anatomy of Criticism* (1957), became highly influential in the years when New Criticism was waning. Frye uses Jung's concept of archetypes as a way to examine the underlying myths and symbols of different literary genres (romance, comedy, tragedy, and satire), and these genres' correspondence to the four seasons. Frye didn't believe in the collective unconscious, however, but instead used Jung's archetypes in a more literary or metaphoric way.

Jacques Lacan

French psychoanalyst Jacques Lacan is often grouped with Derrida and Foucault as one of the major poststructuralist thinkers of the twentieth century. Lacan's career began earlier than Derrida's and Foucault's, in the 1930s, though his influence on literary theory occurs around the same time as theirs. In the 1950s Lacan began a series of influential seminars on Freud and psychoanalysis that were later published in a collection called *Écrits* (1966). In his seminars, Lacan brings Ferdinand de Saussure's **STRUCTURALIST** linguistics (see Chapter 6) into dialogue with Freud. Fundamental to his theory is the idea that the unconscious is structured like a language: "What the psychoanalytic experience discovers in the unconscious is the whole structure of language."[1] The structure of language shapes our mental life and our unconscious.

Lacan's writings often use Saussure's distinction between **SIGNIFIER** and **SIGNIFIED**, with priority placed on the signifier. Saussure writes about the realm of signifiers as an endless chain, with one signifier leading to another (if you look a word up in the dictionary, you just find more words: you can never get "beyond" language). For Lacan, subjectivity is created through language, but because language is just an endless chain of signifiers we can never get beyond it to the real. Desire moves us from signifier to signifier, endlessly along this chain, creating a state of alienation. In his writings, Lacan distinguishes between the **IMAGINARY**, the **SYMBOLIC**, and the **REAL**. For Lacan, the imaginary is the realm of mental

---

1 Jacques Lacan, "The Agency of the Letter in the Unconscious, or Reason Since Freud," *Écrits*, trans. Alan Sheridan (New York: W.W. Norton, 1977), 147.

images, the pictures that run through our brain. The symbolic is the realm of language and signification. The real is a difficult concept: it's that which can't be captured in language, inaccessible to us because we're trapped in the imaginary and symbolic realms.

Another key concept for Lacan is the mirror stage, which he first describes in a 1949 essay "The Mirror Stage as Formative of the Function of the I as Revealed in Psychoanalytic Experience." In it, Lacan discusses the moment when infants recognize themselves in the mirror. For the first time they see themselves as beings separate from their mothers' bodies, usually when they are around six months old or later. Lacan says that this experience first forms a sense of self in the child and thus an entry into the realm of the imaginary. Soon thereafter, babies start acquiring language and thus enter the realm of the symbolic. Like other French thinkers of this generation, Lacan looked back to Hegel's master-slave dialectic (see Chapter 4) and the idea of recognition of the other as the way identity is formed. Lacan stresses the element of desire in this process. People desire to be recognized by the other, and they recognize their own desire through that desire for recognition. In Lacan's model the desire for recognition takes priority over other desires, such as Freud's erotic and death drives. This desire for recognition takes place in language and is deeply linguistic. In a talk called "The Signification of the Phallus" (1958), he discusses Freud's theory of penis envy, redefining the phallus as a "signifier of the Other's desire." We desire to be recognized and desire to be desired, and the phallus serves as that signifier of desire. Lacan's model of Freud's Oedipal complex is similarly linguistic: "If the mother's desire *is* for the phallus, the child wants to be the phallus in order to satisfy her desire," but the name of the father separates the child from the mother and thus from desire.[1]

Though often challenging to read (like other poststructuralist thinkers), Lacan's writings have influenced a range of different theoretical approaches. Because of his psychoanalytic training, Frantz Fanon refers to Lacan's work in *Black Skin, White Masks* (1952), while Louis Althusser uses Lacan extensively in his version of **MARXISM**. For the most part, though, Lacan's impact on literary theory didn't take place until the 1970s and can be seen most directly in the work of feminist thinkers such as Julia Kristeva, film scholars, and later Lacanians such as Slavoj Žižek.

---

1   Jacques Lacan, "The Signification of the Phallus," *Écrits: The First Complete Edition in English*, trans. Bruce Fink (New York: W.W. Norton, 2006), 583, 582.

Julia Kristeva

Bulgarian psychoanalytic literary critic Julia Kristeva (b. 1941) is a complex thinker with a long career. She studied linguistics in Bulgaria and then came to Paris in 1966, where she studied semiotics with Roland Barthes (see Chapter 6). Because she could read Russian, she was familiar with the works of Russian Formalists and with Mikhail Bakhtin's publications (see Chapters 6 and 8, respectively). Kristeva and fellow Bulgarian Tzvetan Todorov helped to popularize these Russian works in France and to introduce them to a non-Russian-speaking audience. In a 1969 essay on Bakhtin, Kristeva coined the term **INTERTEXTUALITY** to characterize his theory of **DIALOGISM**.

In the 1970s Kristeva trained as a psychoanalyst, and her many publications use psychoanalytic theory extensively, especially the ideas of Freud and Lacan. Kristeva's work, like Lacan's, fuses psychoanalysis and linguistics. Her 1973 dissertation, published in book form as *Revolution in Poetic Language* (1974), puts forward "a theory of signification based on the subject."[1] Saussure's model of structuralist linguistics focuses on *langue* rather than *parole*, that is, the structural system of language rather than the way individual speakers used that system. Kristeva instead looks at speaking subjects who have drives and desires that are structured by that language, as Lacan had done. From the Russian Formalists she takes the distinction between ordinary language and poetic language, and her book studies the emergence in the late nineteenth century of certain avant-garde ways of writing that recognize the ways in which language shapes subjectivity. She argues that writers such as James Joyce, Georges Bataille (1897–1962), and Stéphane Mallarmé (1842–98) create a form of poetic language that is akin to delirium.

In a later work, *Powers of Horror* (1980), Kristeva introduces the influential concept of **THE ABJECT:** something that is neither subject or object, something that can't be assimilated. She calls it "radically separate, loathsome. Not me. Not that. But not nothing, either. A 'something' that I do not recognize as a thing."[2] Thus the abject is something that is both a part of an individual and not part of the individual, and that consequently blurs the boundaries of self and other. She provides examples of what she's trying to define: waste, sewage, corpses, wounds, bodily fluids. All of these things tend to produce a kind of nauseous, gagging feeling in the subject because they remind us of our animal natures. They need to be cast off, excluded, or made taboo in order to preserve

---

1 Julia Kristeva, *Revolution in Poetic Language*, trans. Margaret Waller (New York: Columbia UP, 1984), 15.
2 Julia Kristeva, *Powers of Horror: An Essay on Abjection*, trans. Leon S. Roudiez (New York: Columbia UP, 1982), 2.

our identities. Her book goes on to discuss literary examples of the abject, using the works of Marcel Proust, Fyodor Dostoevsky (1821–81), and especially Louis-Ferdinand Céline (1894–1961).

Heirs to Lacan

Along with Kristeva, other French scholars developed a feminist version of psychoanalytic theory in the 1970s. Hélène Cixous (b. 1937), for example, wrote a dissertation on Joyce in 1968 and became director of the Centre d'Études Féminines (Center for Feminine Studies) in 1974. Her feminist critique of Freud and Lacan concentrates on the differences between female sexuality and male sexuality. Freud's and Lacan's psychoanalytic models both place men at the center, with women merely as subordinate or marginal. Freud's Oedipal complex refers to a male child's desire for his mother, for example, while the theory of penis envy suggests that girls are inferior to, and thus jealous of, boys. Similarly, Lacan's model of subjectivity uses this Freudian framework, even while redefining some of Freud's concepts like castration and the phallus in terms of language. In her famous essay "The Laugh of the Medusa" (1975), Cixous counters the phallocentrism of Freudian and Lacanian thinking, developing a concept of L'ÉCRITURE FÉMININE (feminine writing). The history of writing, she says, is male-dominated and phallocentric. Women must strive to write against this tradition, she argues, and develop a feminine practice of writing, based on female sexuality, which is non-phallic, decentralized, and nonlinear. Another French feminist psychoanalyst, Luce Irigaray, studied with Lacan but also critiques him in her publications. In her celebrated essay "This Sex Which Is Not One" (1977), Irigaray, like Cixous, critiques phallocentrism and characterizes female sexuality as multiple and decentered.

Lacan's ideas are taken up within film studies in the 1970s, particularly by British scholars associated with the journal *Screen*. Among these, the best known figure is Laura Mulvey (b. 1941), a psychoanalytic feminist film theorist. In her essay "Visual Pleasure and Narrative Cinema" (1975), Mulvey critiques the phallocentrism of most cinema. The pleasure that spectators get from going to movies, she suggests, is voyeuristic. In particular, the spectacle of watching the female body on screen produces pleasure. Using Lacan's ideas about desire for the other and identification, she discusses the way in which most films are designed with a male viewer in mind and a female as the object of his gaze. Women watching movies are thus placed in a position of having to identify with the male gaze and to objectify the female body. Mulvey calls for feminist filmmakers to undo the phallocentric male gaze of cinema and create a new style of filmmaking, akin to the French calls for a feminine writing.

Though decidedly not a feminist, the Slovenian theorist Slavoj Žižek (b. 1949) also uses Lacan's terminology to analyze film. Part of a circle of Slovenian academics interested in Lacan's thought, Žižek began writing in the 1980s. In the first of his books to be translated into English, *The Sublime Object of Ideology* (1989), Žižek announces his three aims: 1) to introduce some of the main concepts from Lacanian psychoanalysis; 2) to return philosophy to Hegel as read through Lacan; and 3) to use Lacanian concepts to study ideology. In numerous publications and public lectures, Žižek has continued these aims, cross-pollinating Lacanian psychoanalysis with Marxism to study politics, ideology, and totalitarianism. His writing often uses movies and pop-culture examples to illustrate theoretical points, and he has also written extensively on film and even appeared on film. In addition to starring in a documentary about himself, *Žižek!* (2005), he has written and appeared in the documentaries *The Pervert's Guide to Cinema* (2006) and *The Pervert's Guide to Ideology* (2012).

Phenomenology

I touch upon **PHENOMENOLOGY**, or the philosophical study of perception, briefly in Chapter 6 in the context of Derrida. Phenomenologists believe that all we can know are our perceptions of things, not the things themselves, so we must study perception in order to understand the world. German philosophers Edmund Husserl and Martin Heidegger developed phenomenological thought in the early twentieth century, and the French phenomenologist Maurice Merleau-Ponty (1908–61) continued in their tradition. In *The Phenomenology of Perception* (1945), Merleau-Ponty emphasizes the role of the body and the senses in perception. Phenomenologists want to understand perception, and in order to do so Merleau-Ponty suggests they need to look at the body in which an individual mind is enclosed, the eyes and ears the body sees and hears with, for example.

Phenomenology, like psychoanalysis, thus studies what goes on inside people's heads, though with a philosophical rather than a medical framework. In literary studies, phenomenology influences both studies of authors' consciousnesses and more reader-oriented approaches. Belgian phenomenologist Georges Poulet (1902–91) developed the author-oriented side of things. Poulet's *The Interior Distance* (1952) investigates the consciousnesses of a variety of French writers. By consciousness, Poulet doesn't mean a historical worldview in the history of ideas sense (see Chapter 7). Rather, he studies the writing of various authors in order to understand the shape of the author's thinking, the way they conceive of time and space, for instance.

Poulet taught at Johns Hopkins in the 1950s, and there he influenced the early works of his young colleague J. Hillis Miller. Miller's first book studies Charles Dickens's novels in order to reconstruct "the original unity of a creative mind," his obsessions, attitudes, and mental structures.[1] Miller contends that every sentence Dickens wrote, whether coming from the mouth of a character or in his own voice, emanated from a single consciousness, and he attempts to use those words to reconstruct the inner workings of the mind that created them. In a later book, *The Disappearance of God* (1963), Miller extends his phenomenological approach in order to study five nineteenth-century writers. In the later 1960s Miller moved on from phenomenology to deconstruction, just as Jacques Derrida had done, and phenomenological studies became infused with new theoretical approaches.

Hermeneutics

A close cousin of phenomenology, **HERMENEUTICS** is a distinctively German strain of thought that investigates interpretation. The word derives from a Greek word meaning "to interpret" and can refer both to processes of interpretation and to studies of those processes. Initially, biblical hermeneutics consisted of the methods developed to interpret the Bible (see Chapter 3), but nineteenth-century German thinkers developed a branch of hermeneutics interested in understanding the process of understanding in order to strive for more accurate interpretations of all kinds of texts. Twentieth-century phenomenologists Heidegger and Husserl were heirs to this tradition of trying to study perception and interpretation.

A key figure in twentieth-century hermeneutic literary theory is Hans-Georg Gadamer (1900–2002). In his book *Truth and Method* (1960) he asks how it is that we can understand anything. Two key concepts from this work are the hermeneutic circle and the concept of a horizon. The hermeneutic circle, a concept Gadamer adapts from Heidegger's work, refers to the fact that we can only understand a whole in relation to its parts and parts in relation to the whole. He discusses how a reader "projects before himself a meaning for the text as a whole as soon as some initial meaning emerges in the text. Again, the latter emerges only because he is reading the text with particular expectations in regard to a certain meaning."[2]

---

1   J. Hillis Miller, *Charles Dickens: The World of His Novels* (Bloomington: Indiana UP, 1958), ix.
2   Hans-Georg Gadamer, *Truth and Method*, trans. Garrett Borden and John Cumming (New York: Crossroad, 1985), 236.

To illustrate the concept of a hermeneutic circle, let's say you're given a book with no title page and no cover, and asked to read it. It begins "When I wake up, the other side of the bed is cold. My fingers stretch out, seeking Prim's warmth but finding only the rough canvas cover of the mattress." How does a reader make sense of this? Who is speaking? Is Prim a lover, a wife, a dog? The next three sentences answer some of these questions: "She must have had bad dreams and climbed in with our mother. Of course, she did. This is the day of the reaping."[1] We now know that Prim is the speaker's sister, and that they seem to be children who are anxious about a "reaping." Are they farmers? As you might know, and as the footnote below tells you, this is the first paragraph of Suzanne Collins's *The Hunger Games* (2008). As the reader progresses, it soon becomes clear that this book is an example of the dystopian young adult (YA) novel subgenre. As we learn a little bit about the characters and the setting, we project a meaning for the text as a whole and judge it against that meaning. We only know that it's a YA novel based on the parts we've read thus far (maybe the first chapter), but we can only understand those parts based on a preconceived notion of the whole, of what it means to be a YA novel of this type. So genres form a kind of hermeneutic circle. We come to know a genre by reading examples of works from that genre, but we can only understand those texts if we already have a conception of the genre. What if Suzanne Collins hadn't intended to write a YA novel at all, but meant this to be a poem or a biography?

To take another example, let's say you are given a second book, and read the first paragraph: "There is one mirror in my house. It is behind a sliding panel in the hallway upstairs. Our faction allows me to stand in front of it on the second day of every third month, the day my mother cuts my hair."[2] Without knowing anything else about the text, you can probably already detect some similarities to the opening of *The Hunger Games*. A first-person narrator speaks in the present tense. The sentences are fairly short. The speaker is young enough to still live with her mother. The world being described is not quite the real, present-day world, based on the details of the hidden mirror and "our faction." Interpreting Veronica Roth's *Divergent* (2011) becomes much easier because our prior knowledge of this subgenre helps to make sense of what we're reading. Based just on this small portion of the text, a reader might form a set of expectations about the work as a part of the dystopian YA subgenre. In fact, those expectations might lead a reader either to enjoy the work because it confirms expectations, or to find it too closely modeled upon previous works (like Collins's) and thus find it derivative.

---

1   Suzanne Collins, *The Hunger Games* (New York: Scholastic, 2008), 3.
2   Veronica Roth, *Divergent* (New York: HarperCollins, 2011), 1.

Gadamer also investigates how to break out of the hermeneutic circle. Key to breaking out of the circle is the concept of a horizon. A concept derived from Husserl, a horizon forms the limits of our understanding. The horizon moves as we move forward and can be expanded by exposure to new points of view. The more different types of writing you read, for example, the broader your horizons will be. Gadamer's student Hans Robert Jauss (1921–97) further developed the concept of horizon to discuss historical **HORIZONS OF EXPECTATION**. In an influential essay, "Literary History as a Challenge to Literary Theory" (1970), Jauss says that both formalist and Marxist critics ignore the audiences for works of literature, and he calls for an aesthetics of reception that tries to reconstruct the horizon of expectations for a work at the moment of its first reception. Critics should try to see how a work fits into its moment in time, determining what kinds of questions the text was originally trying to answer. Reception theorists look at book reviews, initial audience reactions to works, and other texts of the time in order to reconstruct the horizon of expectations for a work. In the example above, a reception theorist in a hundred years would be interested in how the horizon of expectations differed between *The Hunger Games* and *Divergent*. If, for some unlikely reason, *Divergent* became canonized and *The Hunger Games* faded into obscurity, a critic might be led to see it as an innovative, unusual work. Knowing that *The Hunger Games* was a big success, Roth's work can be seen as trying to cash in on that popularity. A reception theorist could study the reactions of readers who found the work derivative rather than innovative, looking at book reviews, comments on Goodreads and other websites, or other works within the subgenre to reconstruct the reception of the work.

Reader-Response Criticism

Gadamer, Jauss, and others study the phenomenology of reading and interpretation, trying to understand how readers make sense of works both in a general sense and historically. At the same time they were writing, American academic Stanley Fish (b. 1938) was developing his own version of a reader-centered approach in the 1960s and 1970s. Fish began his career as a historical scholar, writing a dissertation on the Renaissance poet John Skelton at Yale in 1962. He first introduced what would become known as **READER-RESPONSE THEORY** in his book *Surprised by Sin* (1967), a study of John Milton's *Paradise Lost* (1667).

Initially, he later explained, he was trying to solve a problem in Milton scholarship. Milton scholars fundamentally disagreed about how to read the "moral" of his epic. Some critics look to the end of the poem and read it as advocating the moral that, in Adam's words, "to obey is best" (12.561). Others, following the lead of Romantic writers Percy Shelley and William Blake, see Satan as the hero of the poem and Eve's act of disobedience as the result of her free will, an act that leads to all of human history. Fish reconciles the two approaches by arguing that the act of reading *Paradise Lost* leads readers to recognize their sinful natures and to attempt to correct them. The experience of reading the text itself mirrors Adam and Eve's experience of making an error and then striving to correct it.

Fish's influential method concentrates on the act of reading as it takes place over time. In this work, he argues that Milton was conscious of the fact that reading is a temporal process and that readers' eyes must move back and forth across the page, trying to make sense of what they're reading as they go along. He gives the example of these lines describing Satan's spear from Book 1:

> His spear, to equal which the tallest pine
> Hewn on Norwegian hills, to be the mast
> Of some great ammiral, were but a wand (1.292–94)

As we read the word "spear," we conjure up an image of a spear in our mind. Then we get to the phrase "the tallest pine," and immediately connect the two, creating a mental image of an extremely tall spear. We happily live with this image as we read line 293 and the start of 294, until we get to the end of the line and the words "but a wand." Suddenly the image we've been working with is denied us. The tall Norwegian pine we thought was the size of his spear is merely the size of a wand in comparison with the unimaginable height of Satan's spear. Through this process, which Milton repeats throughout the poem, Fish says that the reader "is confronted with evidence of his corruption and becomes aware of his inability to respond adequately to spiritual conceptions."[1] The process described above takes place over just a few seconds, but the experience of reading the poem as a whole is simply a larger version of this process of having to revise assumptions.

Fish developed his reader-centered approach specifically to deal with Milton's technique, but in later works he extends his method to discuss other authors, arguing that critics should analyze readers rather than texts. In so doing, he directly challenges William Wimsatt and Monroe Beardsley's affective fallacy (see Chapter 6), which states that critics should not confuse a work with its effect on readers. Fish says that, on the contrary, a work *is* its effect on readers. Later, Fish developed the idea of interpretive communities in order to explain

---

1   Stanley Eugene Fish, *Surprised by Sin: The Reader in* Paradise Lost (London: Macmillan, 1967), ix.

why reading isn't purely subjective and individual, and how it is that two readers ever agree on a text. Interpretive communities consist of people who have
learned to read in the same way. Thus literary scholars of the same generation
and cultural context agree because they have been trained in the same kind of
reading strategies – the New Critics find moments of ambiguity and paradox
wherever they look because that's what they're looking for, while deconstructionists find unstable binary oppositions and feminists find gender dynamics.
Throughout his later writings, Fish calls for critics to be more self-conscious of
their methods: "The moral is clear: the choice is never between objectivity and
interpretation but between an interpretation that is unacknowledged as such
and an interpretation that is at least aware of itself."[1]

Wolfgang Iser (1926–2007), Jauss's colleague at the University of Konstanz
in Germany, is another important reader-oriented theorist who takes a more
phenomenological approach to the reading process. His book *The Implied
Reader* (1972) studies a range of English novels and the involvement of readers
in creating meaning, using the phenomenological ideas of Poulet and Husserl
to study the minds of readers. He says that meaning is prestructured in the
text but only produced through reading. In this way his concept of an implied
reader parallels Wayne Booth's notion of an **IMPLIED AUTHOR** (see Chapter 6).
Booth contends that while we can never access the real flesh-and-blood author, authors create a second self in the text that stands behind their creations.
Similarly, Iser believes that authors create an implied, ideal reader within their
texts, one who must fill in gaps and make connections, anticipate the action
and revise his or her understanding as he or she reads. An implied reader is "a
textual structure anticipating the presence of a recipient."[2] He acknowledges
that reading experiences won't be the same for different readers, nor will they be
the same for the same readers as they reread – one's experience of a text changes
dramatically once you know how the book ends.

Cognitive Approaches

As our understanding of the brain has changed, literary approaches that focus
on the mind have assimilated new insights and new terms. Beginning in the
1950s, a cognitive revolution has produced new insights into the way the brain

---

1   Stanley Fish, *Is There a Text in This Class? The Authority of Interpretive Communities* (Cambridge:
    Harvard UP, 1980), 167.
2   Wolfgang Iser, *The Act of Reading: A Theory of Aesthetic Response* (Baltimore: Johns Hopkins UP,
    1978), 34.

works. Scholars in a variety of fields, including psychology, anthropology, and linguistics, developed the field of **COGNITIVE STUDIES**. One of the most famous of these figures is linguist Noam Chomsky (b. 1928), who put forward a theory that language isn't merely arbitrary, as Saussure had claimed, but that the deep grammatical structures of all languages emanate from grammatical structures in the brain. In recent years, new brain-mapping technologies have allowed scientists to better understand the workings of the brain.

Some literary scholars in the 1980s and 1990s began to draw upon the work of cognitive scientists in order to ask questions about literary topics. Mark Turner's *Death Is the Mother of Beauty* (1987), for example, uses the theory of metaphor in linguistics and cognitive science to study literary metaphors, starting from the premise that "Human language relies on common mental systems shared by members of a linguistic community."[1] Cognitive theorists see the structures of the brain as products of long evolutionary development (not in the sense of Jungian archetypes but in a more physiological sense of neurons and receptors) and use insights from cognitive studies to ask literary questions. Lisa Zunshine, for example, asks why we read fiction, while Blakey Vermeule wonders why we care about fictional characters. Central to the work of Zunshine and Vermeule is the concept of **THEORY OF MIND**, the human ability to recognize that other people have minds and to interpret their behavior based on deductions about their mental states. By allowing readers access to the interior states of characters, fiction engages theory of mind in a deeply satisfying way.

Like digital humanities, cognitive literary studies is an interdisciplinary field that integrates aspects of the sciences with the humanities. While digital humanists are more likely to collaborate with people from computer science, cognitive literary theorists work with scholars in psychology and neuroscience. Some projects in this area have employed brain-scanning technology, for example, to study the effects of literary texts on the brain. In this way, cognitive theorists are employing twenty-first-century technologies to explore some of the same issues that interested the earlier phenomenologists.

Suggestions for Further Reading

Homer, Sean. *Jacques Lacan*. London: Routledge, 2005.
Morrison, Claudia C. *Freud and the Critics: The Early Use of Depth Psychology in Literary Criticism*. Chapel Hill: U of North Carolina P, 1968.

1   Mark Turner, *Death Is the Mother of Beauty: Mind, Metaphor, Criticism* (Chicago: U of Chicago P, 1987), 133.

Porter, Stanley, and Jason C. Robinson. *Hermeneutics: An Introduction to Interpretive Theory*. Grand Rapids, MI: William B. Eerdmans, 2011.

Van Meurs, Jos, and John Kidd. *Jungian Literary Criticism, 1920–1980: An Annotated Critical Bibliography of Works in English (With a Selection of Titles After 1980)*. Methuen, NJ: Scarecrow Press, 1988.

Ten: From Theory to Practice

IN CHAPTERS 2 TO 9 I've sketched a brief history of literary theory and criticism from antiquity to the beginning of the twenty-first century. While it is impossible to do justice to the richness and variety of this history in such a short space, I hope I have at least given a sense of the broad outlines of some of the major theoretical approaches to literature and of their interconnections. Along the way I have from time to time illustrated ways to put these theoretical ideas into practice, either by providing examples from the theorists' and critics' own work or by inventing examples of my own. In this chapter, I work through a few more examples of ways to put theory into practice, drawn from the theoretical approaches discussed in the earlier chapters and using as my case studies William Shakespeare's tragedy *Hamlet* (1600–01) and Mary Shelley's novel *Frankenstein* (1818).

I have selected these texts for a number of reasons. First, both of these works are highly canonical today, frequently taught at both the high-school and college levels, and the basic outlines of their plots should be familiar to most readers. Second, these texts lend themselves well to a wide range of theoretical approaches and have been interpreted in different, often conflicting ways over centuries. Third, I have taught both of these texts many times and have seen first-hand that they can provoke lively disagreements in the classroom and offer inexhaustible material for new interpretations.

Before turning to the two texts, I should provide two notes of caution about this chapter. First, my aim in this chapter is to illustrate the directions that different theoretical approaches to *Frankenstein* and *Hamlet* could take. At times I will merely gesture toward certain ways of reading these texts (which have long critical histories behind them), such as Freudian discussions of *Hamlet* and feminist readings of *Frankenstein*. At other times, I point out possible directions for research that use particular theoretical concepts and methods. In these instances, I do not provide thorough and exhaustive readings of these texts but may focus only on a single passage, scene, or question that could provide a starting point for a more thorough study. In this way, I aim to show how to put theoretical perspectives to work rather than to come to a single, correct interpretation of a text; that is, in this chapter the primary texts by Shakespeare and Shelley serve as a means to illustrate different literary methodologies rather than be studied for their own sake. Using multiple theoretical perspectives on a single text, even when those perspectives contradict each other, can help you to become a better reader and critic, to get outside of your comfort zone as a reader.

My second note of caution is a simple *spoiler alert*. In my discussion of these texts, I assume that readers are at least familiar with their plots, perhaps through one of their many film adaptations or just through cultural osmosis. If you haven't yet read one or both of these works, however, I apologize in advance for the plot spoilers to follow. In order to illustrate how to apply different theoretical perspectives, it is necessary to discuss the fates of various characters and the shape of the plot of each work as a whole.

The Example of Hamlet

Shakespeare's poetic and dramatic works loom large in the history of English literature, and they also occupy a prominent place in the history of literary theory. Sigmund Freud used Shakespeare to illustrate his psychoanalytic principles on a number of occasions, while Karl Marx admired Shakespeare's works. NEW HISTORICISM (see Chapter 7) began with a group of Shakespeare and Renaissance scholars in the late 1970s. Today, Shakespeare continues to be taught and written about from POSTCOLONIAL, QUEER, FEMINIST, DIGITAL HUMANITIES, and many other perspectives.

Shakespeare's plays have a long and complicated textual history, which I will try to simplify here. Shakespeare composed *Hamlet* in 1600 or 1601. No manuscripts of any of his plays in his own handwriting have survived, so we don't know precisely which words Shakespeare initially wrote when he put quill to paper. Instead, scholars have had to reconstruct what they think the original texts said by using several editions of his works (referred to as *folios* or *quartos* depending on the size of the edition) printed in the seventeenth century. These editions sometimes vary quite drastically from each other. For example, Hamlet's most famous soliloquy begins "To be, or not to be, I there's the point" (rather than "that is the question") in the first quarto edition of 1603. Editors for centuries have tried to reconstruct the best version of the text by comparing the variants. In what follows I will be using the Riverside edition of Shakespeare's works, and will refer to the text using act, scene, and line numbers in parentheses.[1]

Hamlet's Organic Unity

One of the first ways to approach any text is through the study of its form, using the concept of **ORGANIC UNITY** as a way to anchor a **CLOSE READING** of a portion of the text. The notion of a work of literature as an organically unified whole goes back to Aristotle's *Poetics* (see Chapter 2). Aristotle contended that a good tragedy should contain nothing extraneous: no single piece could be removed without affecting the meaning of the whole. Samuel Taylor Coleridge, borrowing from the German Romantics, gave Aristotle's model of artistic unity a spiritual dimension with his focus on the esemplastic power of the imagination, while Edgar Allan Poe turned Coleridge's organic unity into a mathematical formula in his essay "The Philosophy of Composition" (see Chapter 5). In the twentieth century, the **NEW CRITICS** (see Chapter 6) used Coleridge's discussions of organic unity as one of the foundations of their influential method of close reading. Though the heyday of New Criticism has passed, texts like *Hamlet* are still taught using close reading strategies.

One way to conceptualize this model of artistic unity is to think of it as a Jenga tower. For those unfamiliar, Jenga is a game where players build a tall, narrow tower out of wooden blocks. Then each player takes turns removing a block at a time from within the tower. The person who removes the piece that topples the tower loses the game. In a work of drama, removing one tiny piece, such as a scene, a minor character, or a speech, might not make the entire work collapse immediately, but in some small way it will affect the work's structural integrity. Removing Hamlet, for example, would quite likely render the meaning of a play called *Hamlet* unrecognizable, but how much would the play be altered if you removed a more minor character such as Ophelia or Fortinbras? This type of thought experiment can help to illustrate just how integral each minor character or incident is to the unity of the whole, demonstrating that every aspect of a work is there for a reason.

With *Hamlet*, a **FORMALIST** critic could study how even the most minor characters contribute to the meaning of the work as a whole. When staging Shakespeare's plays, directors sometimes cut a minor character or two, or will trim scenes. A formalist approach to *Hamlet* might look at the ways even the most minor of characters function within the plot structure, develop themes

---

1   *The Riverside Shakespeare*, 2nd ed., ed. G. Blakemore Evans (Boston: Houghton Mifflin, 1997).

and motifs, and in other ways add to the meaning of the work as a whole. For example, the character of Osric the courtier appears only in Act 5, Scene 2, near the end of the play, in the capacity of delivering a message from the King to Hamlet. In a short conversation with Hamlet, Osric conveys some plot points the audience needs to anticipate and understand the duel that is about to take place (and that leads to the deaths of Laertes, Gertrude, Claudius, and Hamlet). In addition to his function in supplying bits of plot information, Osric provides Hamlet an opportunity to mock the inflated speech of courtiers. Osric speaks in a very pretentious, formal manner, and Hamlet mocks him in response: "Sir, his definement suffers no perdition in you, though I know to divide him inventorially would dozy th'arithmetic of memory, and yet but yaw neither in respect of his quick sail" (5.2.108–11). Hamlet's words parodying Osric are inflated to the point that they make almost no sense. And because the words sound nonsensical, this passage provides a brief moment of comic relief before the bloodbath to follow. They also allow Hamlet one last chance to display his contempt for flatterers and sycophants, previously seen in his interactions with Polonius and with Rosencrantz and Guildenstern. Finally, Hamlet's mockery of Osric showcases a moment where language breaks down, which underscores the theme of meaninglessness and absurdity that runs throughout the play. If a director were to remove this short scene with Osric, the whole Jenga tower that is *Hamlet* wouldn't topple, but it might be ever so slightly weakened.

Another type of close reading could examine a brief passage from the text rather than a minor character. To illustrate, I have chosen a few lines from early in the play, in Act 1, Scene 4. In this scene, Hamlet, his friend Horatio, and the officer Marcellus seek out Hamlet's father's ghost on the ramparts of the castle. They hear King Claudius and his guests in the midst of a rowdy night of heavy drinking in the rooms below them. Hamlet then comments to Horatio on the Danish reputation for revelry:

> This heavy-headed revel east and west
> Makes us traduc'd and tax'd of other nations.
> They clip us drunkards, and with swinish phrase
> Soil our addition, and indeed it takes
> From our achievements, though perform'd at height,
> The pith and marrow of our attribute. (1.4.17–22)

In the lines that follow, Hamlet makes a larger point about how people can't choose their birth and their fate. Those later lines obviously have profound significance in a tragedy that is all about birth and destiny. What about the earlier lines, though, about the Danish reputation for carousing?

A close reading could focus on Shakespeare's use of figurative language and metaphor in the passage. The phrases "heavy-headed revel," "swinish phrase," "soil our addition," and "marrow of our attribute" all employ figures of speech that compare human behavior either to parts of the body or to aspects of nature. A "heavy-headed" celebration evokes a range of associations. First, it metonymically associates the festivities Hamlet and Horatio overhear with the headache that will inevitably arrive with the hangover the next morning, suggesting that actions have consequences and thus, in some small way, tying into the central revenge plot. Just as wine takes its revenge on you the next day if you overindulge, if you murder your brother his ghost will haunt your castle seeking vengeance. "Heavy-headed" also could mean stupid or blockheaded, or could conjure up an image of partiers so intoxicated that they can't hold their heads up any more. These different meanings all have to do with the effects of revelry on the body: it gives you a headache, makes you stupid, and makes you pass out. (Perhaps there's also a sense of hanging one's head in shame at work here? Once you begin free-associating in a close reading you can unlock all sorts of possibilities.) "Swinish phrase" and "soil our addition" suggest a new set of associations. A textual note explains that "addition" means titles, so Hamlet is saying that other nations, by calling the Danes drunkards, sully the Danish titles of honor such as *Prince* and *King*. "Swinish" refers to the phrase these other nations use to talk about the Danes, but it can also serve well as a description of the Danes themselves. Swine or pigs wallow in mud to keep cool, and a "swinish phrase" dirties both the person uttering it and the people they're describing. There's also possibly the suggestion that men give in to their animal natures through overindulgence in both alcohol and trash-talking. The use of an animal metaphor links this passage to a motif of animals that runs throughout the play: "springes to catch woodcocks" (1.3.114), "hardy as the Nemean lion's nerve" (1.4.83), "if, like a crab, you could go backwards" (2.2.203), "I am pigeon-livered" (2.2.516), "of the chameleon's dish" (3.2.92), "special providence in the fall of a sparrow" (5.2.198), and many others. This repeated comparison of animals to humans connects to a larger pattern within the text of subverting hierarchies or blurring boundaries, such as the distinctions between sane and insane and human and animal. Finally, the metaphor of "marrow of our attribute" compares attribute or reputation to bone marrow. Bone marrow is at the very center of the skeleton and provides sustenance to the body, so the metaphor suggests the centrality of reputation to Hamlet. Part of his reason for seeking revenge on Claudius has to do with issues of reputation: he doesn't want a murderer to get away with being king; he wants his true character exposed. The marrow metaphor links back to the "heavy-headed revel" of the start of the passage, and the two bodily metaphors contrast each other: the wilting effects of drunkenness weakening the strength of the marrow of reputation. The pig metaphor furthers this sense of drunkenness as destructive and dirtying, and all three metaphors rely on living things, animal and human.

In his book *S/Z* (see Chapter 5), Roland Barthes dissects a Balzac short story sentence by sentence, looking at the different codes in play in the text. *Hamlet* is much too long and complex a play to be given the same line-by-line treatment, but a miniature version of Barthes's model could work to discuss the different codes at work in the passage above. Aside from the play of metaphors in the passage, the lines also serve to illustrate Hamlet's character early in the text by showing his sobriety at this moment of celebration. Everyone else is having a good time while he is out in the cold, philosophizing and ghost-hunting. Simultaneously, the passage foreshadows Hamlet's later "antic disposition" or pretended madness, since drunkenness can be seen as a kind of temporary madness. Perhaps the scene also foreshadows the end of the play where Gertrude drinks poisoned wine intended for Hamlet. Hamlet's sobriety on the ramparts of the castle contrasts with Claudius's drunkenness below him and forces the audience not only to compare the two and to hold Hamlet in higher regard for his sobriety and wisdom, but also to see Hamlet as literally placed above Claudius. Finally, the passage fills in some of the political background of the play. At the end of the play, Fortinbras of Norway becomes the new King of Denmark. (Partly this is because there's hardly anyone else alive by the end.) Additionally, however, "other nations" like Norway do not respect the Danes and thus have been maneuvering to conquer them from the outset. Obviously Fortinbras is avenging his father's death rather than lashing out at Danish drunkenness, but these lines remind us of the larger political context of Denmark and its neighbors "east and west." Removing these six lines won't destroy the structure of the play, but through close reading you can see the multiple functions they serve in the text, and thus they enrich one's reading experience of the whole.

This operation of close reading can be applied to any aspect of the text by any reader, and each time it will produce slightly different results. There's no one right answer when it comes to close reading. Instead, close scrutiny of the language and structure of a text can help you to think about the work in new ways, showcase your critical prowess, and highlight the richness of the text.

Hamlet's Theatricality

Another formalist approach to reading *Hamlet* could focus on issues of performance and theatricality. Motifs of trapping and deception are woven throughout the text, from Hamlet's feigned madness to Claudius's smiling villainy. Issues of performance and the theater connect to these motifs, since acting can be viewed as a form of deception: Hamlet puts on an act of insanity, while Claudius performs his lies before the court. In fact, Hamlet ultimately confirms Claudius's guilt by staging a play within the play, called, significantly, "The Mouse-Trap." At the end of the play, Fortinbras has just reached Denmark, and sees the bodies of Hamlet, Gertrude, Laertes, and Claudius. He asks what has happened, and Horatio (one of the only characters left alive at the end, since Ophelia, Polonius, Rosencrantz, and Guildenstern have all met their ends) orders "these bodies / High on a stage be placed to the view" (5.2.359–60). Horatio orders the bodies of all those killed to be placed on a stage (and they already are on a stage if the play is being performed on one) and says he is going to narrate to all those who have arrived an explanation of what happened. In essence, the play ends with the beginning of another play, this one reenacting the same play the audience has just seen.

This sort of circularity and use of metafiction (devices that call attention to the fictionality or artificiality of a work) can provide a basis for a **DECONSTRUCTIVE** reading of the text. The plays within plays within plays in *Hamlet* create an effect of *mise-en-abîme*, a French term meaning "placed in an abyss." *Mise-en-abîme* is often compared to the effect you get if you stand between two mirrors that face each other, that sense of infinite regression or endless reflections of the same thing. Founder of deconstructive criticism Jacques Derrida (see Chapter 6) likens this effect to the endless deferral of **SIGNIFIERS** in language. You can never get beyond language, because one signifier leads to the next signifier endlessly down the chain, without ever getting to a truth or presence beyond language. Similarly, in *Hamlet* you can never get beyond performance and play (another favorite Derrida term). You can't even get beyond the text, since the play ends by restarting the beginning again.

A deconstructive reading focusing on play and performance naturally would look closely at the scenes where Hamlet interacts with a traveling troop of actors that comes to Elsinore. Hamlet and the leader of the troop have a number of lengthy conversations about acting and performance, including a moment where the First Player reenacts a scene from another play about the Trojan War at Hamlet's request. In another conversation with Hamlet and the players, Polonius mentions that he played Julius Caesar while at the university (3.2.97). Taking a metatheatrical approach, you could consider the multiple dimensions of this utterance: here an actor, performing a role in a play by Shakespeare, speaks about his performance as a character (and Shakespeare even wrote his own play about Julius Caesar). In the scene where the players put on "The Mouse-Trap," real-life actors are playing actors performing a play to an audience on stage, and that audience is itself performing to the audience in the theater. This chain of reflections and deferrals can create a dizzying sense of groundlessness, a feeling that nothing is real, thus placing the audience in a situation much like Hamlet's madness.

Moving beyond the play itself to its influence in literary history and popular culture, some adaptors of *Hamlet* have chosen to foreground these sorts of issues of theatricality and performance. A 2000 film adaptation set in modern-day New York features Hamlet (played by Ethan Hawke) delivering his "To be, or not to be" soliloquy in the Action section of a Blockbuster Video store, for example. Playwright Tom Stoppard explores the metafictional and existential aspects of *Hamlet* in his rewriting of the play from the perspective of two minor characters in *Rosencrantz and Guildenstern Are Dead* (1966), an example of the genre of theater of the absurd. (As a side note, Disney's *The Lion King* [1994] and *The Lion King 1½* [2004] pay homage to *Hamlet* and *Rosencrantz and Guildenstern Are Dead*, with the first movie telling a happier version of *Hamlet*'s plot of a murderous uncle and his disenfranchised nephew and the second retelling the story from a pair of minor characters, here Timon the meerkat and Pumbaa the warthog.)

Hamlet in Literary History

Turning to historical approaches, *Hamlet* provides endless material for a historically minded critic. One approach, for example, would be to examine the play's place in literary history, particularly its relation to the subgenre of the revenge tragedy, a particularly violent dramatic form – featuring plots revolving around characters seeking vengeance for past crimes – that became very popular in the late sixteenth century. The authors of these plays were inspired by the Roman tragedies of Seneca, which often featured revenge plots, and by more recent Italian novellas and tales of revenge. The first Elizabethan revenge tragedy, Thomas Kyd's *The Spanish Tragedy* (1587–89), was highly successful and was followed by many other similar plays, such as Thomas Hughes's *The Misfortunes of Arthur* (1588) and John Marston's *Antonio's Revenge* (1599). Literary historian Fredson Bowers describes the formula of the revenge tragedy: "a murder is committed secretly, the name of the murderer is given to the revenger by a medium which he distrusts; delay results until additional facts corroborate the ascription, but then the revenger is hampered by the counterdesigns of his enemy and all perish in the catastrophe."[1] Sounds a lot like *Hamlet*, doesn't it? A critic interested in theater history and the history of popular genres could look at

---

1   Fredson Thayer Bowers, *Elizabethan Revenge Tragedy 1587–1642* (Princeton, NJ: Princeton UP, 1940), 104.

the ways Shakespeare was working from this established template, even as he made it his own and influenced later revenge tragedies. By seeing the play in this generic context, some of its peculiarities, such as the appearance of the ghost at the beginning of the play and Hamlet's repeated hesitation in seeking revenge, make a lot more sense. These features are aspects of the genre Shakespeare is working with rather than just elements unique to *Hamlet*.

Shakespeare, like most Elizabethan dramatists, borrows his stories from history, novellas, and mythology. So a historical critic might also examine the sources for *Hamlet* beyond the influence of Kyd and the revenge tragedy. In the case of *Hamlet*, Shakespeare bases his play on an episode in a twelfth-century history of Denmark, Saxo Grammaticus's *Historiae Danicae*. Historian Hayden White (see Chapter 7) studies the way in which historians take the raw materials of history, the chronicle of events, and give them narrative form as tragedy, comedy, satire, or romance. In order to study the way Shakespeare shapes his source material, you could adapt White's model for talking about historians' use of source material to talk about a more literary context. Shakespeare takes the raw material from the Danish chronicle of Saxo Grammaticus and shapes it into his great tragedy by foregrounding certain events, leaving others out, and adding new details. Shakespeare takes many of his key plot points from Saxo's story of Amleth, which originated as oral legend. Two brothers, Ørvendil and Fengi, jointly rule Jutland in Denmark. Fengi murders his brother and marries his brother's wife Geruth. Ørvendil's son Amleth fears his uncle/new stepfather and thus pretends to be mad. Fengi suspects that Amleth is only pretending to be mad, so he tests Amleth's madness three times: first by using a young woman as bait, then by spying on Amleth and Geruth in her chamber, and finally by sending him to England with two companions to be killed. Amleth manages to escape through his wiles (though his companions aren't so lucky) and returns to Denmark.

Though some of the names are changed, the above summary of Saxo's Amleth story corresponds very closely to the plot of *Hamlet*. Shakespeare leaves out or modifies key aspects of his sources as well. To cite just one major difference, Amleth's story isn't a tragedy: when he returns from England he exacts revenge on Fengi and becomes the new king. So Shakespeare takes a story of successful vengeance and turns it into one where no one comes out a winner, where "purposes mistook / Fall'n on the inventors' heads" (5.2.366–67). Amleth's story also takes place over a longer span of time and includes a great many more episodes than does the adaptation. As White discusses in relation to historians, here Shakespeare shapes his material into a central narrative arc, foregrounding the incidents and elements that will tell the most compelling tragic story rather than trying to follow his source particularly closely.

Shakespeare's shaping of historical material also highlights how permeable the boundaries between history and fiction are in the Renaissance. Shakespeare can take an episode from history, keep some names almost the same (Geruth to Gertrude) and change others entirely (Fengi to Claudius), and alter the destinies of some individuals (King Amleth to dead Hamlet). The historical setting of the play is also ambiguous. Saxo's story, culled from folk traditions, takes place in pre-Christian medieval Denmark. Shakespeare moves the setting forward to a Christian context, as evidenced by the frequent references in the play to Christianity, prayer, angels, penance, and the afterlife. The play also includes some very topical references to Shakespeare's own historical moment, such as the ongoing rivalries among London theatrical troops. Thus the play brings together medieval Danish legend and seventeenth-century London, fact and fiction, pagan revenge and Christian salvation. No wonder it has provided endless material for historicist scholars.

Hamlet and Class

You can also use concepts from the political approaches discussed in Chapter 8 to analyze *Hamlet*. The medieval Danish setting is perhaps a little too white, monocultural, and pre-colonial to apply many concepts from postcolonial, race, and ethnicity studies to the text itself. The closest the play gets to depicting any kind of cultural or geographic diversity is restricted to northern Europe: Fortinbras invading from Norway, Rosencrantz and Guildenstern meeting their fate in England, and Laertes going away to France. A study that surveys the history of performances of *Hamlet*, however, could examine recent color-blind castings of the play, such as Peter Brook's 2002 BBC adaptation starring black British actor Adrian Lester as Hamlet.

Within the text itself rather than its performances, one way to approach the play in terms of politics would be to use a **MARXIST** lens to look at issues of class and power. Most of the characters in *Hamlet* belong to the ruling classes, but a few characters represent the **SUBALTERN**, the working classes, the ruled rather than the ruling. These characters often exist at the margins of the text and play only minor roles, such as the sentinels Barnardo and Francisco who deliver the play's first lines. A great place to begin a class-based reading of the text might be Act 5, Scene 1, the scene featuring the gravediggers. The two gravediggers are identified in the text just as "clowns," meaning lower-class individuals. That fact alone suggests the subordinate status of the working classes, who aren't even allowed names within the play.

Within their scene, however, these "clowns" are given the opportunity to question the social hierarchy of their culture, giving voice to some fairly radical sentiments. The scene opens with the two men digging a grave for Ophelia while they discuss her suicide. They raise the issue of whether she should be allowed a Christian burial (not permitted to suicides) and the role of the coroner in determining the case. They discuss the case using a comic subversion of legal language: "It must be *se offendendo*, it cannot be else. For here lies the point: if I drown myself wittingly, it argues an act, and an act hath three branches – it is to act, to do, to perform; argal, she drown'd herself wittingly" (5.1.9–12). Here you could bring in Homi Bhabha's concept of colonial mimicry (see Chapter 8) to talk about the ways these working-class characters mimic, and thus subvert, the language of learning and the legal system. Alternatively, you could use Mikhail Bakhtin's concept of heteroglossia (see Chapter 8) to discuss the meeting of different voices representing different social strata in the text, from king to actor to gravedigger.

This same character goes on to jokingly question the logic of social hierarchies, saying "there is no ancient gentlemen but gard'ners, ditchers, and grave-makers; they hold up Adam's profession" (5.1.28–30). Though used to introduce a joke, this questioning of the established social order creates a fissure in the text through which a Marxist critic could read a larger radical critique of society. By saying there are no "ancient gentlemen" and mentioning Adam, the gravedigger calls attention to the common descent of all humanity and the fact that social classes and inherited titles are a later invention and thus not inherent. Shakespeare portrays these gravediggers in a comic yet sympathetic way, and when Hamlet and Horatio encounter them a few lines later, Hamlet seems to admire them. His admiration for these humble workers stands in contrast to his contempt for nearly all the upper-class characters, from his scorn for his mother and uncle to his scenes with courtiers Polonius, Rosencrantz and Guildenstern, and Osric, where he mocks and manipulates them. If you combine the gravediggers' comic questioning of the social order with the larger theme that "something is rotten in the State of Denmark" (1.4.90), that the state is corrupt and needs to be reformed, you can see the outline of a Marxist analysis beginning to take shape.

Hamlet and Gender

Just as a Marxist reading can take a marginal voice in the text like that of the working classes and use it as the starting point for a larger political exploration, so too a feminist critic might focus on the marginal status of women in the play. In Shakespeare's time, and until the restoration of the British monarchy in 1660, women were not allowed to act on the English stage. Instead, young men or boys would play women's roles. Thus many sixteenth- and early-seventeenth-century dramas contain very few female characters, especially when compared to the plays of the Restoration, when actresses appeared on the stage for the first time and were accordingly featured very prominently. The lack of female roles in itself provides fodder for a feminist study of the text. In the case of *Hamlet*, though, the two central women in the play, Hamlet's mother Gertrude and his love interest Ophelia, are intriguing characters who have long been of interest to feminist scholars.

These scholars have investigated how gender relations and women's experiences are depicted in the text in a variety of ways. The first woman we meet is Gertrude, with whom Hamlet has some serious psychological issues (which **PSYCHOANALYTIC** critics have long been obsessed with). In his first soliloquy Hamlet utters the famous line "Frailty, thy name is woman!" in reference to his mother. Later on he is misogynistic with Ophelia, admonishing her with the words "get thee to a nunnery." In the scene following the one where we first see Gertrude, Ophelia makes her first appearance listening to a lecture from her brother Laertes. When their father Polonius enters, he lectures both his children. The scene highlights Ophelia's lack of agency and even lack of voice. She has no free will but must take orders from the various men around her. Polonius later uses his daughter as bait to try to determine the cause and scope of Hamlet's madness. When she reports back to her father on Hamlet's condition, her function in the play is to shed light on Hamlet's character.

Simone de Beauvoir's discussion of the myths of woman (see Chapter 8) works well here in elucidating the depiction of Ophelia and Gertrude in the text. These female characters are myths more than they are individuals: Ophelia the tragic waif, Gertrude the bad, weak-willed mother. Ophelia and Gertrude are the only two women in the text, and they appear alone together only briefly for a few lines in Act 4, Scene 5. In the end, both women are dead because of the men around them. Ophelia is driven mad by Hamlet's murder of her father, and Gertrude inadvertently drinks poisoned wine that her husband had intended for her son. Feminist critics have seen the marginal status of women in this play, and in Shakespeare's plays more generally, as both a product and a critique of patriarchal society. Either way, the female characters shed light on the limited roles available to women at this time.

Hamlet's Melancholy

In the early twentieth century, Freud and his follower Ernest Jones developed a very influential reading of *Hamlet* as a story about the **OEDIPUS COMPLEX** (see Chapter 9). Claudius murders Hamlet's father and marries his mother and is thus living out the primal Oedipal fantasy all children share. In their reading,

Hamlet hesitates in his revenge because he sees Claudius living out his unconscious desires. Productions of *Hamlet* sometimes play up this Oedipal dimension of the text by adding an element of sexual tension to the scenes between Hamlet and his mother, particularly Act 3, Scene 4, which takes place in the Queen's chamber. When making his 1947 film version, Laurence Olivier even consulted Jones about the Freudian interpretation of the play.

Even if you're not convinced of the validity of that particular reading of the play, clearly family issues are significant to the text and have provided abundant material for psychoanalytic criticism. The plot revolves around a father (in ghost form) asking his son to avenge his murder by his brother. The character of Fortinbras provides a double of this parental dynamic. On the day Hamlet was born, Hamlet's father (also named Hamlet) killed Fortinbras's father (also named Fortinbras), and Fortinbras Jr. wants revenge for his father's death. The first words out of Hamlet's mouth in the play are even puns on *kin* and *kind*, *sun* and *son*, suggesting that father/son relationships and kinship dynamics are on his mind and central to the story.

Hamlet's soliloquies provide ample material for investigating other aspects of character psychology. After his pun-filled exchanges with Gertrude and Claudius at the beginning of the play, Hamlet launches into his first soliloquy, a kind of interior monologue spoken out loud directly to the audience. In his speech, he expresses suicidal wishes:

> O, that this too too sallied flesh would melt,
> Thaw, and resolve itself into a dew!
> Or that the Everlasting had not fix'd
> His canon 'gainst self-slaughter! O God, God,
> How weary, stale, flat, and unprofitable
> Seem to me all the uses of this world! (1.2.129–34)

Treating Hamlet as though he were a real person and using his soliloquy as if spoken by Hamlet the patient in a psychiatrist's office, a psychoanalytic critic would perhaps diagnose him as suffering from depression. His suicidal thoughts and lack of interest in "all the uses of this world" are telltale symptoms of depression, perhaps even Seasonal Affective Disorder brought on by the long winter nights in Elsinore. Throughout the play, Hamlet describes his emotional life in ways that suggest he is suffering from a form of depression. In dialogue with Rosencrantz and Guildenstern, for example, Hamlet famously describes his symptoms: he has "lost all [his] mirth, foregone all custom of exercises," the world appears to him to be a "foul and pestilent congregation of vapors," and he takes no pleasure from other people (2.2.291–96).

Another type of approach could combine a psychological perspective and a historical one to examine Hamlet's condition in the context of seventeenth-century medicine. Renaissance medical experts would have said that Hamlet suffers from melancholy as a result of having his bodily humors out of balance. At that time, medical science believed that the body contained four essential humors: blood, phlegm, yellow bile, and black bile. If one of the four humors was out of balance and predominated, it produced a certain personality type: blood corresponded to a sanguine personality (good-humored), phlegm to phlegmatic (cold and unemotional), yellow bile to choleric (angry), and black bile to melancholic (mournful). In the late sixteenth century, melancholy became the subject of much discussion, with medical treatises written about it (it was considered a form of madness) and melancholy characters such as Hamlet appearing frequently on stage. Countless interpretations of *Hamlet* are possible by looking at the text itself, individual performances and adaptations of it, its place in popular culture, its influence on other writers, and so on.

The Example of Frankenstein

In the preceding discussion, I have barely scratched the surface of ways to discuss *Hamlet* using literary theory. For the sake of variety, though, I now turn to Mary Shelley's novel *Frankenstein; or, the Modern Prometheus* to discuss a few other critical perspectives. Shelley's most famous novel has become part of our cultural landscape, familiar to most people, even those who haven't read it. The text itself is complicated and a good place to try out different theoretical approaches, as critics have been doing for almost two centuries.

Mary Wollstonecraft Godwin Shelley came from a radical literary family. Her parents were the English radical writers Mary Wollstonecraft (see Chapter 4), who died because of complications related to her daughter's birth, and William Godwin (1756–1836). When she was still a teenager, Mary eloped from her father's house with the poet Percy Shelley (see Chapter 5), who was already married. The following year, in 1815, Mary lost a baby. Even though she was only 18 years old when she began writing *Frankenstein*, her literary pedigree and life experiences helped to shape the text into something original and memorable. The novel was immediately successful and was even adapted for the stage several times during Shelley's lifetime. Today it is considered one of the greatest of all gothic horror stories, a forerunner of science fiction, and a literary classic.

In 1831, Shelley published a revised edition of the text, which contains many significant differences from the 1818 original: she modified the language and even changed some plot details. Textual critics have studied the differences between the two. Unlike Shakespeare's folios and quartos, where critics try to reconstruct the best version of the text, speculating on what Shakespeare's original version would have been, Shelley's versions are treated by critics as two separate texts. In my discussion below I will be using the 1818 text.[1] When discussing the text, remember that the scientist's name is Victor Frankenstein, who I call alternately *Victor* and *Frankenstein*. The being he creates, often thought of in popular culture as "Frankenstein," doesn't have a name. Victor calls his creation *monster, creature, fiend, devil*, and many other derogatory names. Critics usually call him the monster or the creature, and I use both below.

Frankenstein and Narratology

One of the first things that readers often notice about the text is its unusual mode of narration or way of telling the story. The book opens with a heading: "Letter I. To Mrs. Saville, *England*. St. Petersburgh, Dec. 11th, 17— " (49). For its original British readers, a Russian setting would have been exotic, but the device of having a story told in the form of letters (called an epistolary novel) would have been very familiar, as epistolary novels had been popular in Britain since the seventeenth century. As you read on, though, you discover that the letters merely provide a frame story for two embedded narratives. The letter writer, Robert Walton, embarks on a polar expedition, and while heading for the North Pole his ship encounters a man on the ice who turns out to be Victor Frankenstein. The ship takes Victor on board, and he later tells his story to Walton. That story makes up the bulk of the novel, with Walton's voice returning in the last pages of the book. Within the embedded story, Victor recounts the creature's narration of the events immediately after his creation, so that the creature's story is contained within Victor's story, which is contained within Walton's letter.

Using terms from **NARRATOLOGY** or the study of narrative (see Chapter 6), one can map out the structure of this complexly organized novel. Narratologist Gérard Genette distinguishes between fable (**FABULA**), the raw materials of the story or the events as they take place chronologically, and subject (**SYUZHET**), the way the events are conveyed to the reader. Table 3 compares the events of the story as they occur versus the way they're arranged within the novel.

Comparing the fable to the subject, you can see how much chronological

---

1   Mary Shelley, *Frankenstein: The Original 1818 Text*, ed. D.L. MacDonald and Kathleen Scherf, 2nd ed. (Peterborough, ON: Broadview P, 2000). References will be cited by page number in parentheses within the text.

Frankenstein's fable	*Frankenstein*'s subject
1. Victor Frankenstein's birth and childhood	14. Robert Walton embarks for the North Pole
2. Victor creates a creature who comes to life	15. Walton's ship encounters Victor
3. The De Lacey family encounters difficulties	16. Victor tells Walton his story
4. The creature leaves Victor, observes the De Laceys	1. Victor Frankenstein's birth and childhood
5. The creature kills William Frankenstein	2. Victor creates a creature who comes to life
6. Victor returns home, Justine executed for William's murder	6. Victor returns home, Justine executed for William's murder
7. Victor meets the creature in the Alps	7. Victor meets the creature in the Alps
8. The creature tells his story to Victor	8. The creature tells his story to Victor
9. The creature asks for a mate	4. The creature leaves Victor, observes the De Laceys
10. Victor creates, then destroys mate	3. The De Lacey family encounters difficulties
11. The creature kills Henry Clerval	5. The creature kills William Frankenstein
12. The creature kills Elizabeth	9. The creature asks for a mate
13. Victor pursues the creature	10. Victor creates, then destroys mate
14. Robert Walton embarks for the North Pole	11. The creature kills Henry Clerval
15. Walton's ship encounters Victor	12. The creature kills Elizabeth
16. Victor tells Walton his story	13. Victor pursues the creature
17. Victor dies	17. Victor dies
18. The creature encounters Walton, heads off to die	18. The creature encounters Walton, heads off to die

Table 3: Fable and Subject in *Frankenstein*

restructuring Shelley employs. Readers begin close to the end of the chronology, then jump back in time to near the beginning and then return to the frame
story at the end. Within this basic flashback structure other chronological
shifts occur, such as the jump back in time when Victor hears the creature's account of what happens when he leaves Victor and observes the De Lacey family.
Within the creature's account (which is embedded within Victor's account,
which is in turn embedded within Walton's letter), we hear the story of the
troubles of the De Lacey family.

This nested set of stories within stories within stories could lend itself to another deconstructive reading of the type I discuss above in relation to *Hamlet's*
play within a play. Another option, however, that provides insight into the
book's dynamics, would be to employ a **RHETORICAL** framework using Wayne
Booth's concept of an **UNRELIABLE NARRATOR** (see Chapter 6), a narrator whose
values or account of events differs from that of the **IMPLIED AUTHOR**. Textual
clues can lead readers to question the reliability of certain narrators, perhaps
because their ethical norms are so far beyond the pale of conventional morality
or because they leave out crucial information or contradict themselves in the
text, or because their perspective is inherently flawed (as in the case of child
narrators, for example). Walton's letters to his sister don't immediately seem
questionable, but Victor's version of events raises some serious questions about
his sanity and his judgment. Victor says himself that "sometimes a kind of
insanity possessed me" (173). When he introduces Victor's text, Walton even
includes a disclaimer for his transcription of Victor's tale, saying that he tried
"to record, as nearly as possible in his own words, what he has related during
the day" (62).

Shelley has chosen to frame her story in this way, as a transcription of an oral
account included within a letter. She could simply have presented a first-person
or even a third-person novel without the frames. The multiple frames force the
reader to think about the transmission of the story and thus to think about its
status *as a story*, to question its reliability, like listening to a ghost story around
a campfire. Readers are provoked to question Victor's reliability, for example,
in the portion of the story regarding creating a mate for the creature. After
Victor and the creature reunite in the Alps, the creature asks Victor to create
him a mate who can be his companion, since every human he has encountered
so far has shunned him. After this, Victor embarks on a journey to the farthest
reaches of Scotland in order to satisfy this request. He describes his travels to
a tiny, remote Scottish island, but doesn't explain where he procures the raw
materials for making this second creature. After he has completed his work,
only then does he think about the possibility that "a race of devils would be
propagated upon the earth" if the two creatures had children (190). It seems

difficult to believe that Victor had been toiling away constructing a mate for his creature for months, and that the possibility of the two creatures procreating never occurred to him. This seems like revisionist history, at best, on Victor's part, and leads readers to question his version of events, or at least his judgment. Similarly, Victor's narrative casts the creature as the villain, a monstrous killing machine who must be destroyed. However, in the creature's own account of his actions, readers often find him sympathetic. He is alone, having to make his way in a world that shuns the very sight of him. Victor's condemnation of the creature is undercut by the creature's own words, which Victor recounts.

Frankenstein and History

Just as with *Hamlet*, historical approaches to *Frankenstein* can go in a number of directions. Because *Frankenstein* was an immediate success and has been adapted countless times, a **CULTURAL STUDIES** perspective (see Chapter 8) could look at the afterlife of the text in popular culture. In addition to the many theatrical, film, and television adaptations of *Frankenstein*, the monster has had a long life beyond literature in everything from children's cartoons to breakfast cereal (Franken-Berry was introduced in 1971). **BOOK HISTORIANS** (see Chapter 7), similarly, could study different printings of the text or illustrated editions to see how the creature is depicted.

Another type of historical approach focusing on the novel itself rather than adaptations or printed books could build upon Michel Foucault's model of **DISCOURSES** (see Chapter 7). In *Archaeology of Knowledge*, Foucault theorizes about the history of ideas, stating that intellectual history should not study particular disciplines or authors but should instead look at the larger discourses of a historical period. These discourses, shaped by power relations, regulate what's possible to say and even to think at any given moment. Foucault uses the example of madness as a way to illustrate his model. In order to understand discourses of madness in a particular era, as Foucault had done, you would need to look at medical texts, laws regarding insanity, fictional works, memoirs, and so forth. In that way, you could understand how ideas of sanity and insanity were shaped by their moment in time, were contingent and thus not universal.

Because *Frankenstein* is a novel about a scientist and depicts his scientific research, a historical critic might want to investigate the text in relation to the scientific discourses of the early nineteenth century. *Frankenstein* is also a novel that is deeply concerned with issues of education. Among the many novelistic subgenres it belongs to, one of the most important is the *Bildungsroman* (or novel of education). Walton recounts his education in the opening letters of the novel, describing how his early reading of travel stories made him become an explorer, and later both Victor and the creature describe their early education. The creature's outlook on the world is shaped by only a few books: C.F. Volney's *Ruins of Empires* (1791), John Milton's *Paradise Lost* (1667), Johann Wolfgang von Goethe's *Sorrows of Young Werther* (1774), and a volume of Plutarch's *Lives* (75 CE). In contrast, Victor receives a scientific education. He says that the turning point that decided his fate happened when he discovered works of alchemy by Paracelsus, Albertus Magnus, and Cornelius Agrippa at age 13. Later he studies more modern scientific texts about "the wonderful effects of steam," "experiments on an air-pump" (69), and electricity.

One way to situate the novel in a larger **INTERTEXTUAL** framework would be to look specifically at the texts mentioned within the novel – not only the books the characters read, but other texts alluded to, such as Samuel Taylor Coleridge's "Rime of the Ancient Mariner" and William Wordsworth's "Tintern Abbey" (both 1798). In terms of scientific discourses, you would then look specifically at the books that form Victor's scientific education. In a broader sense, though, Frankenstein's experiments can be studied in relation to larger discourses about vitalism, or the relation between matter and life, in the late eighteenth and early nineteenth centuries, not just the books Victor mentions. Vitalism was a contentious issue at the moment Shelley began writing her novel. Scientists such as John Abernethy (1764–1831) contended that a substance exists that produces life. This was not a soul or any kind of supernatural entity but a material substance that he and others believed could be located.[1] In fact, the first sentence of the 1818 preface to the novel grounds it in its scientific context: "The event on which this fiction is founded has been supposed, by Dr. [Erasmus] Darwin, and some of the physiological writers of Germany, as not of impossible occurrence" (47). In the 1831 preface to the revised edition Shelley elaborates upon the scientific inspiration behind her story: "Perhaps a corpse would be re-animated; galvanism had given token of such things: perhaps the component parts of a creature might be manufactured, brought together, and endued with vital warmth" (357).

Within the text itself, however, Victor refuses to say precisely what this vital principle that brings the creature to life consists of. He merely tells Walton, "I became capable of bestowing animation upon lifeless matter" (80) but refuses to go into any more detail because he doesn't want his experiment to be repeated. Film adaptations, such as James Whale's *Frankenstein* (1931) and *Bride of Frankenstein* (1935), and even Mel Brooks's parody *Young Frankenstein* (1974), have solidified the image of a mad scientist Frankenstein in his gloomy

---

1   For a good discussion of Romantic-era vitalism, see L.S. Jacyna, "Immanence or Transcendence: Theories of Life and Organization in Britain, 1790–1835," *Isis* 74 (September 1983): 310–29.

laboratory (aided by a creepy assistant) using electricity to bring the creature to life, usually on the proverbial dark and stormy night. In part this is because the vitalist controversy of the early nineteenth century had ended. Because scientists no longer seriously sought out a fluid or substance that could give life to inert matter, the intellectual background of the story shifts from current scientific controversy to Gothic fantasy. That is, because by the twentieth century the scientific discourses had shifted away from the vitalist search for a particular substance that produces life, the scientific background of *Frankenstein* becomes lost. Reconstructing the scientific discourses of the early nineteenth century (or reconstructing the **HORIZON OF EXPECTATIONS** for its original readers, in Hans Robert Jauss's term, discussed in Chapter 9) can help us to see the text in a new light. Because people thought the science of *Frankenstein* was possible at the time, the novel would have been more frightening to its initial readers, or frightening in a more realistic way, than a mere monster story would be. In this light, the novel can be seen as a forerunner of books, comics, and movies that play on our contemporary scientific anxieties about contagious diseases (as in zombie stories) or genetic engineering (as in clone stories).

Frankenstein and Orientalism

Just as with *Hamlet*, using political perspectives can illuminate certain aspects of *Frankenstein*. Feminist critics have naturally gravitated to this novel, written by a woman who is herself the daughter of one of the founding figures of feminism. One line of feminist inquiry into the text concerns issues of motherhood. Turning to author biography, a feminist critic could study the text in light of the information that Shelley's mother died as a result of complications surrounding childbirth and Shelley herself had lost a baby the year before the novel was published. The novel's exploration of a horrible, motherless act of life-giving can be seen as an outgrowth of Shelley's complex anxieties about giving birth – she in essence could think of herself as causing her mother's death by being born and then also feel guilty for having survived while her baby died the previous year. Frankenstein is sometimes likened to a godlike creator, at other times to a parent. He calls the creature, for example, "the wretch ... to whom I had given life" (103). Both parent and child survive the act of creation in the text, at least for a time, but that act of creation brings nothing but misery to both parties and to everyone Victor loves (his brother, his best friend, and his new wife, among others).

You can also use postcolonial theory a bit more easily with this text than with *Hamlet*. The story takes place in Western Europe, in Switzerland, Germany, France, England, Scotland, and Ireland. A postcolonial critic such as

Edward Said (see Chapter 8), however, might be most interested in the Eastern "others" at the edges of the text. Specifically, in the De Lacey episode within the creature's tale, the creature observes an unhappy family in a cottage and learns language from them. While he is observing them, a young woman named Safie comes to stay with them and is learning French. Felix De Lacey reads from Volney's *Ruins of Empires* to her, describing the "slothful Asiatics" (144), among other things. Safie's first education in French is thus to learn negative cultural stereotypes about "Asiatic" people. Safie herself is the daughter of a "Christian Arab, seized and made a slave by the Turks" (149). Her father is a Turkish merchant, repeatedly called "the Turk" rather than given a name. "The Turk" is a stock Orientalist villain, his Muslim religion repeatedly brought up in a negative way in the text. He is described as greedy, vindictive, and oppressive to his daughter. In the midst of a novel where even a serial-killing humanoid is given complex motivations and treated sympathetically, the cartoonish villainy of "the Turk" stands out as an example of Orientalism.

Frankenstein and Homosociality

Marxist theorist Louis Althusser developed a model of **SYMPTOMATIC READING** (see Chapter 8) as a way to diagnose what's being left out of a text, on the model of a psychoanalyst studying a patient's gaps and omissions – what they *aren't* saying just as much as what they *are*. A symptomatic reading of *Frankenstein* might focus on the very minor role of women in the text. While for Shakespeare the lack of women stems both from the fact that all female roles on the Elizabethan stage would have been performed by young male actors and from the lack of women in his source material, something different is at work in Shelley's text. The early-nineteenth-century novel is a female-dominated genre. Because the novel was not considered a prestigious genre, it was associated with female and lower-class readers – aristocratic men, though they did consume novels, were supposed to be reading more "manly" genres, such as history and divinity. Women writers produced a large proportion of novels at this time, and even novels by men often centered on female protagonists. The fact that this novel by a woman at times seems so deeply uninterested in women could help to ground a queer reading of the text (see Chapter 8). The lack of women and of romantic love in part stems from the fact that the book seems to be much more focused on male-male relationships.

Victor does have a love interest, Elizabeth Lavenza, his first cousin, who was raised as his sister, but the creature kills her on her wedding night. Victor, however, never expresses strong passion for her, and their love plot seems secondary to all the other events in the text. (His father suggests the marriage as a way for Victor to get out of his funk following his creation of the monster.) In place of strong romantic feelings, the text emphasizes same-sex bonds between men. Eve Sedgwick's concept of **HOMOSOCIALITY**, the non-sexual bonds between members of the same sex, can help to foreground this dimension of the text.

In place of a compelling love story we have multiple stories of male friendship and attraction, particularly between Walton and Frankenstein and between Clerval and Frankenstein. Right at the outset, Walton writes to his sister, "I have no friend, Margaret" (53), just as a heroine of a nineteenth-century novel might begin a courtship story alone and looking for love. Walton expresses no interest in finding a woman but instead seems dejected by his lack of male friendship. He expresses his loneliness to his sister in a way that echoes the language of sentimentality and romantic courtship: "I desire the company of a man who could sympathize with me; whose eyes would reply to mine" (53). After Walton's crew rescues Frankenstein, Walton is immediately attracted to him: "I never saw a more interesting creature" (58). Walton describes his love for Frankenstein, calling him "attractive and amiable" (60). Shelley uses the language of the courtship novel to characterize the bonds between these two men. Victor also has strong affective bonds with Henry Clerval, of whom he says, "Excellent friend! how sincerely did you love me" (97) and "your form so divinely wrought, and beaming with beauty" (182). Furthermore, Victor is at times feminized, especially in his habit of fainting at moments of crisis, similar to the heroine of a gothic novel.

A queer reading of the novel might see this homosocial dimension as concealing a repressed homoeroticism. Same-sex attraction could also help to explain Victor's odd behavior regarding his marriage. After his father proposes that Victor marry Elizabeth, Victor agrees, but says he must first go on a two-year trip with Henry. Ostensibly this trip gives him the opportunity to create the mate the creature had requested, but he did not need to travel for so long and in the company of Henry to perform his task. Was he trying to forestall his marriage and spend some quality time with his "divinely wrought" friend? Further adding to this queer reading of the text, you could consider the moment after Frankenstein destroys the creature's mate and the creature's vow to be "with you on your wedding-night" (193). Victor goes ahead with the wedding and as a consequence the creature murders Elizabeth. Again we are led to question Victor's lack of foresight (and, indeed, his reliability). He says to Elizabeth immediately before she is murdered, "I have one secret, Elizabeth, a dreadful one" (212). The specter of Victor's same-sex desire is raised by this need to confess a dark secret to one's bride before consummating the marriage.

The Sublime, the Abject, the Uncanny

Critics have used a number of other terms discussed in previous chapters to analyze various aspects of *Frankenstein*. First, the concept of the **SUBLIME**, a type of aesthetic sensation that produces wonder and fear, developed by Longinus (see Chapter 2) and elaborated upon by Burke and Kant (see Chapter 4), is mentioned in the text. Within the novel Victor describes Alpine landscapes and powerful storms as sublime, often using Burke's distinction between the sublime and the beautiful: "This valley is more wonderful and sublime, but not so beautiful and picturesque as that of Servox" (121). In a larger sense, the descriptions of the creature and the experience of reading the novel can be thought of as sublime, producing terror and awe for **AESTHETIC** effect.

Another concept that works well in relation to the text is Julia Kristeva's definition of the **ABJECT** (see Chapter 9) as something that is neither subject nor object, neither self nor other, neither dead nor alive, but which must be excluded. The abject helps to explain both the creature and Victor's reaction to him. Victor fashions the creature out of materials from "the dissecting room and the slaughter-house" (82), out of body parts and tissue, both human and animal. So the creature is made up of many of the things that produce disgust in Kristeva's account: corpses, bodily fluids, waste. Here's how Victor describes his creature at the moment he comes to life: "His yellow skin scarcely covered the work of muscles and arteries beneath; his hair was of a lustrous black, and flowing; his teeth of a pearly whiteness; but these luxuriances only formed a more horrid contrast with his watery eyes, that seemed almost of the same colour as the dun white sockets in which they were set, his shriveled complexion, and straight black lips" (85). This passage focuses on tissues and fluids (muscles and arteries, watery eyes, sockets), describing the physical body of the creature in great detail. (You can also possibly detect a racialized dimension to add to the creature's otherness with his "yellow skin" and "black lips.") Frankenstein, instantly disgusted by the creature, rushes out of the room. In Kristeva's account, the abject has to be expelled in order to maintain a sense of the self, to keep boundaries stable. The creature is alive and not alive, human and animal, transgressing all the boundaries of what it means to be human and what it means to be alive. Thus Victor must expel him in order to keep his own sense of identity intact.

Alternatively that uncertainty about the creature's status can also be seen in relation to Freud's notion of the **UNCANNY** (see Chapter 9), that uneasy feeling produced by ghosts, automata, coincidences, and other phenomena. The creation scene takes place on a "dreary night in November" (84), and Victor calls the creature a "dreaded spectre" (89), so there is an element of ghost story at play in the text. The text also employs a number of doubles, another phenomenon

Freud categorizes as uncanny. Walton, with his pursuit of scientific knowledge, serves as a double for Victor. Likewise, the creature forms a double with both Walton and Victor. Throughout the novel, episodes and incidents are uncannily repeated, from the creature's pursuit of Victor mirroring Victor's pursuit of the creature to the repeated stories of education to the two trial scenes involving Justine and the De Laceys. The amount and tone of doubling give the book uncanny associations. Kristeva distinguished the abject from the uncanny in her discussion, but perhaps you could uncover aspects of each at work at various points in the text.

Moving Forward

Frankenstein and *Hamlet*, as we have seen, both work well for a variety of theoretical approaches. They're rich, multifaceted texts, so you can always find something to talk about. In developing your own framework for interpreting texts, here are a few further suggestions for how to put theory into practice:

1. **Decide which questions you're most interested in**. As you read a text for the first time, make note of the places where the text intrigues, confuses, or angers you. You can then turn those emotional responses into theoretical gold. Angry when a heroine is too passive? Do a feminist critique! Haunted by a sociopath? Psychoanalyze him! Find a place where you just can't get the gist of what the narrator is saying? Perfect opportunity for a close reading.

2. **Determine what kind of information you need to answer your questions**. Some approaches, as I discuss above, require outside research, while others can make do with only the text. Outside research could include looking into the historical or biographical context, exploring other critics' interpretations of a text, or applying terms and concepts from theoretical texts. When using concepts from literary theory, always make sure to define your terms. Many of the central concepts introduced in this book — the unconscious, ideology, allegory, gender, colonialism, and on and on — have long histories and meanings that change over time and in the hands of different theorists.

3. **Remember that in answering one question, you're leaving out others**. No single reading of a text will ever be definitive, and that's not the point. Rather, critics seek to create interesting, compelling studies of texts that

will shed new light on some aspect or other of them. As you think about the question you're choosing to answer, don't focus so exclusively on your question that you neglect everything else. Keep your mind open to other questions that may in fact relate to yours. If you're studying the biographical aspects of a text, for example, the historical context unrelated to the author's biography will obviously shape both author and text. In a similar way, formal aspects of the text can be shaped by historical and biographical forces, including political dimensions.

4. **Consider whether certain approaches will work better or worse for your particular text.** Though almost any text can yield almost any type of theoretical approach, certain approaches provide more natural pairings for certain texts. As we have seen in Chapters 2 to 9, theorists often develop their approaches in response to particular authors, genres, and literary movements. The New Critics' close reading method works especially well for difficult, modernist poetry because that's what it was designed for. Stanley Fish's version of **READER-RESPONSE CRITICISM** arose as a response to a problem in Milton studies. Aristotle's *Poetics* describes the dramatic structure of Greek tragedies, though it can be applied to other types of texts. Elaine Showalter, Sandra Gilbert, and Susan Gubar developed feminist criticism in order to study women authors. Henry Louis Gates, Jr.'s concept of *signifyin(g)* adapted **POSTSTRUCTURALIST** theory to accommodate the African-American literary tradition. Postcolonial studies blossomed as a field because of the growth of writings from ex-colonies across the globe. None of this means you can't use reader-response criticism to discuss *Invisible Man* or a postcolonial framework to analyze *Paradise Lost*; but you should consider the histories of different theoretical approaches as you choose to adopt them and consider the adjustments you might need to make in order to employ an approach outside the context it was developed for.

5. **Synthesize different approaches.** Like Victor Frankenstein assembling a living creature from various parts, good literary critics can blend theoretical approaches. If you follow one approach too closely you risk seeming too one-dimensional, particularly if you employ a lot of terminology from a single, distinctive theorist. Today, scholars tend to appropriate terms and concepts from a variety of critical approaches, including those outside of the central tradition of literary studies. As you develop as a scholar, you might find certain key theorists that you keep going back to; that is the first step towards becoming a literary theorist yourself.

6. **Develop your own voice**. Finally, don't be afraid to take risks and to develop your own unique perspective. If you support your interpretation with evidence and build a compelling argument, you will likely convince others of your point of view. People still read Shakespeare's plays and Shelley's novels because there's always a new insight waiting to be discovered.

Suggestions for Further Reading

Babb, Lawrence. *The Elizabethan Malady: A Study of Melancholia in English Literature from 1580 to 1642*. East Lansing: Michigan State College P, 1951.

Gowland, Angus. *The Worlds of Renaissance Melancholy: Robert Burton in Context*. Cambridge: Cambridge UP, 2006.

Hansen, William F. *Saxo Grammaticus and the Life of Hamlet*. Lincoln: U of Nebraska P, 1983.

Glossary

THE ABJECT. Julia Kristeva's term for something that blurs the boundaries of self and other or of animal and human, such as waste, corpses, and bodily fluids. The experience of the abject produces disgust and unease because it reminds people of their animal nature and mortality.

ACTOR-NETWORK THEORY. A critical approach developed by scholars in science studies that breaks apart complex abstractions, looking at individual human and non-human actors involved in a phenomenon and at the networks they create.

AESTHETICS. The branch of philosophy that explores questions of art and beauty.

ALLEGORY. A story that uses symbolism to conceal a hidden meaning, as in a parable.

ANIMAL STUDIES. A critical approach interested in the connections between humans and animals in texts.

APORIA. A term from deconstructive theory meaning an unresolvable contradiction or moment of undecidability in a text that reveals its underlying structure.

ART FOR ART'S SAKE. The idea that art and literature should not try to convey messages but instead should exist for their own sake and to provide beauty and pleasure.

ATHEISM. The rejection of the belief in any sort of gods or higher powers.

ATLANTIC WORLD. A geographic descriptor used by historians and literary critics to talk about the networks created by the slave trade in the Americas, the Caribbean, Africa, and Europe.

BOOK HISTORY. The study of texts as material objects, including matters such as the history of printing and the book trade.

CANON. A set of generally agreed-upon classic works.

CATHARSIS. Aristotle's term for the cleansing or purgation audience members experience when watching a tragedy and experiencing pity and fear for the fate of a tragic hero.

CLOSE READING. An approach to literary texts that pays careful attention to language, including word choices, tone, ambiguity, irony, rhetoric, structure, allusion, and a range of other matters.

COGNITIVE STUDIES. An interdisciplinary field interested in the way the brain works.

CRITICAL THEORY. A term for theoretical writings, often with a strong philosophical dimension, including but not limited to those that deal with literary and cultural concerns.

CULTURAL CAPITAL. Pierre Bourdieu's term to describe the way in which people's tastes can serve as a mark of distinction. An individual's taste in food, books, and other items is socially determined, and in turn it helps to determine one's social status.

CULTURAL CONSTRUCTION. The idea that concepts and values are not universal but are instead products of particular historical and cultural circumstances.

CULTURAL MATERIALISM. A British term for approaches to literature and culture that look at their historical, political, and material contexts.

CULTURAL STUDIES. An interdisciplinary field originally developed by British Marxist thinkers in the 1930s to 1960s that studied working-class and popular culture. Today the field includes a broader array of topics and approaches related to the study of culture.

CULTURAL THEORY. Theoretical works that study culture in a broad sense, including popular culture.

DECADENCE. A late-nineteenth-century literary and artistic movement characterized by its interest in art for art's sake and its celebration of beauty, transgression, and excess.

DECONSTRUCTION. A critical approach developed by Jacques Derrida and others that seeks to reveal the "constructedness" of literary texts, philosophical concepts, and other matters.

DEFAMILIARIZATION. A Russian Formalist term for the way that works of art and literature can make familiar things seem strange and unfamiliar.

DEISM. The belief in a higher power who created the world but rejection of any accepted religion or belief in that power's interference in the workings of the world.

DIALECTIC. Broadly speaking, dialectic means debate or disagreement, as in the example of Plato's dialogues. G.W.F. Hegel uses the term to describe the way history progresses through the clash of opposing forces that come together to create new syntheses. Karl Marx modifies Hegel's model into a model of history moving forward through class conflict.

DIALOGISM. Mikhail Bakhtin's idea that multiple voices intersect and can come into dialogue in the novel.

DIGITAL HUMANITIES. The use of digital technologies to aid in literary studies and other areas of the humanities.

DISCOURSE. Michel Foucault's term for his object of study. Rather than studying specific disciplines or authors Foucault says scholars should look at the larger discourses of a historical period. These discourses, shaped by power relations, regulate what's possible to say and even to think at any given moment.

ECOCRITICISM. The study of literature and the environment.

L'ÉCRITURE FÉMININE. A French phrase meaning feminine writing. French feminists like Hélène Cixous and Luce Irigaray believe that the history of writing is phallocentric or male dominated. They contend that women must strive to develop a non-phallic, decentralized, and nonlinear form of writing.

EKPHRASIS. The technique of describing a work of art within a literary work.

EMPIRICISM. A philosophical movement which contends that there are no innate categories in the human mind but that individuals learn about the world through observation and experience.

EPISTEMOLOGY. The branch of philosophy that studies questions of knowledge.

ETHICS. The branch of philosophy that explores questions of morality.

ETHNIC STUDIES. An umbrella term for a variety of subfields, including African-American studies, Native American studies, Chicano/a studies, Latino/a studies, and Asian-American studies.

FABULA/SYUZHET. A distinction developed by the Russian Formalists: fabula or fable is the raw material of the story, the events of the story chronologically arranged, and syuzhet or subject is the way in which the writer shapes and presents those materials.

FEMINISM. The political movement dedicated to advancing women's rights.

FIELDS. Pierre Bourdieu's term for the space of competition that structures the literary and artistic worlds, among other things. Individual players enter the literary field, for example, by taking a position in relation to the other players.

FORMALISM. A range of critical approaches to literature that look at literary form and literary language.

FREUDIANISM. A critical approach that applies Sigmund Freud's psychoanalytic concepts to literary works.

GENDER AND SEXUALITY STUDIES. An interdisciplinary field that studies issues related to gender and sexuality.

HABITUS. Pierre Bourdieu's term for the underlying mental structure that determines how people act, what they like, and how they perceive the world. It develops in childhood and is socially and culturally determined rather than innate.

HEGEMONY. Antonio Gramsci's term for the intellectual and moral control (as opposed to the direct domination) a dominant group has over subaltern groups who don't hold power.

HERMENEUTICS. A branch of thought that explores issues related to interpretation.

HISTORICISM. A range of critical approaches that investigate literary works as products of their historical moment.

HOMOSOCIALITY. A term characterizing non-sexual but emotional relationships between members of the same sex.

HORIZONS OF EXPECTATION. A term for the set of expectations and beliefs that would have been in place for an audience when a work was first released. Hans Robert Jauss studies how horizons of expectations shape the original reception of a work.

HUMANISM. A movement to revive the study of ancient Greek and Roman classics that began in Italy in the fourteenth century and later spread throughout Europe to Germany, France, Britain, and elsewhere.

IDEALISM. A range of philosophical approaches that posits the existence of universal ideals.

IDEOLOGICAL STATE APPARATUSES (ISAs). Louis Althusser's term for institutions that help maintain state power, including religion, the educational system, the family structure, political parties, and the media.

IMAGINARY, SYMBOLIC, REAL. Jacques Lacan's terms for the three realms of experience. The imaginary is the realm of mental images, the pictures that run through our brain. The symbolic is the realm of language and signification. The real is that which can't be captured in language, inaccessible to us because we're trapped in the imaginary and symbolic realms.

IMPLIED AUTHOR. Wayne Booth's term for the version of the author's self that stands behind a work of literature. Although readers can never access the "true" self behind a piece of writing, they can discern the presence of an implied author or "second self" as distinct from the characters and narrator the author creates.

IMPRESSIONISM. A term associated with Walter Pater's criticism. Pater believes that the purpose of art is to produce an impression in the mind of the spectator or reader, and the role of the critic is to describe that impression.

INTERDISCIPLINARY. Work that draws from multiple academic disciplines.

INTERTEXTUALITY. A term coined by Julia Kristeva to describe the ways texts are interrelated and part of larger linguistic and cultural structures beyond the control of a single author.

JUNGIANISM. A critical approach that applies Carl Jung's ideas about the collective unconscious and archetypes to literary works.

LACANIANISM. A critical approach that applies Jacques Lacan's psychoanalytic concepts to literary works.

LITERARY CRITICISM. The study of literary works, including studies of individual authors, genres, literary movements, and the like.

LITERARY THEORY. A broad range of theoretical writings that touch upon issues relevant to literary criticism, including issues of interpretation, language, reading, and culture.

MARXISM. A critical tradition that grows out of the work of Karl Marx and applies his ideas to literature and culture.

METAPHYSICS. The branch of philosophy that studies the nature of reality and of being.

MIMESIS. Representation or imitation.

NARRATOLOGY. A set of critical approaches interested in narrative, including issues related to point of view, plot construction, and the ways in which writers play with time and chronology.

NATIONALISM. The promotion of a particular nation or nationality.

NEO-ARISTOTELIAN. A critical approach that developed at the University of Chicago beginning in the 1930s, neo-Aristotelianism attempted to revive Aristotle's interest in genre and rhetoric.

NEOCLASSICAL. Literary and artistic movements that look back to ancient Greece and Rome for inspiration.

NEOLIBERALISM. A doctrine that came to prominence in the late 1970s and early 1980s promoting free markets, deregulation, and privatization.

NEW CRITICISM. A critical approach developed by a group of mostly Southern critics in the early twentieth century. New Critics developed the practice of close reading and avoided historical or psychological studies of literature.

NEW HISTORICISM. A term coined by Stephen Greenblatt to characterize the more political, theoretical, and self-conscious historicist criticism of the late 1970s and after.

NIHILISM. The philosophy of nothingness, which asserts that life has no inherent meaning.

OEDIPUS COMPLEX. Sigmund Freud believed that all boys experience a stage of development where they have feelings of attraction for their mothers and murderous impulses toward their fathers, like the mythical king Oedipus. Normally children outgrow this stage, but these primal desires can manifest themselves in dreams, slips of the tongue, and neuroses.

ORGANIC UNITY. An idea that can be traced back to Aristotle and that approaches literary texts as though they are complete wholes. No single piece of an organically unified work can be removed without affecting the whole.

OVERDETERMINATION. Sigmund Freud's term for the way in which dreams and literary works can stem from multiple sources, even sources unconscious to the dreamer or artist. Psychoanalytic critics can reveal these sources.

PANOPTICON. Jeremy Bentham's architectural model structured around a central watchtower. In a panoptic prison, prisoners' cells all face the tower, but the prisoners can't see whether a guard is in the tower at any given time. Michel Foucault uses Bentham's panopticon as an emblem of how power operates in the modern state: it's everywhere and nowhere.

PARATEXTS. Gérard Genette's term for elements of a text that stand outside of the story itself, including prefaces, titles, chapter epigraphs, and indexes.

PHENOMENOLOGY. The philosophical study of consciousness and perception.

PHILOLOGY. The historical study of languages.

POETICS. The study of the technical side of poetry, including rhyme and meter.

POSTCOLONIALISM. A term for approaches to literature that examine issues related to colonialism and its aftermath.

POSTMODERNISM. A complex term that can refer to either the historical period beginning after World War II and characterized by globalization and consumerism or to a specific artistic movement characterized by pastiche, self-consciousness, and fragmentation.

POSTSTRUCTURALISM. A group of critical approaches that build upon and modify structuralism. The key difference between structuralists and poststructuralists is that poststructuralists deny any universal truths and instead celebrate the "play" of language.

PRACTICAL CRITICISM. A critical approach developed by I.A. Richards and other British critics. Practical critics pay close attention to language and ignore issues of history and psychology, much like the American New Critics.

PRINT CULTURE. A term used to characterize the monumental shifts that took place after the introduction of the technology of printing, as distinguished from oral and manuscript culture.

PSYCHOANALYTIC CRITICISM. A broad term for approaches to literature that draw upon psychoanalysis.

QUEER THEORY. The theoretical study of sexuality, gay and lesbian literature, transgender issues, and related matters.

READER-RESPONSE THEORY. Approaches to literature that concentrate on readers rather than authors or texts.

REIFICATION. The way in which relations between people begin to look like relations between things in commodity capitalism. Reification produces, in Georg Lukács's account, the fragmentation of knowledge into individual disciplines, the division of labor and specialization of the workforce, and the destruction of images of society as a whole or totality.

RELATIVISM. The idea that values and beliefs are relative rather than universal.

RHETORIC. The study of language as a means of persuasion.

SCHOLASTICISM. A medieval Christian intellectual movement that uses rigorous philosophical methods to study the Bible, theological issues, and other matters.

SEMIOLOGY. The study of signs in culture. Semiologists attempt to discern the signified content behind cultural signifiers.

SEX AND GENDER. Feminists distinguish biological sex, the fact of being born male or female, from cultural gender, the set of culturally constructed traits we associate with a particular sex including names, clothing, social roles, and even colors.

SIGNIFIED, SIGNIFIER, SIGN. In Ferdinand de Saussure's linguistic theory, a signifier is a word and signified is the meaning of the word, what the word represents. Signifier and signified taken together make up the sign.

SKEPTICISM. In philosophy, skepticism is an approach that questions truth-claims.

STRUCTURALISM. An intellectual movement interested in the structures underlying language, culture, mythology, and literature.

STRUCTURALIST ANTHROPOLOGY. Claude Lévi-Strauss's method, modeled on Ferdinand de Saussure's structuralist linguistics, of breaking aspects of culture, such as myth and kinship structures, into their smallest possible structural elements.

STYLISTICS. A theoretical approach inspired by Roman Jakobson and Russian Formalism that uses elements of linguistics to study literary language.

SUBALTERN. Non-dominant groups within a society.

SUBLIME. A literary effect that produces a feeling of wonder or astonishment.

SYMPTOMATIC READING. Louis Althusser's method of reading the gaps and omissions within a text, analogous to the way an analyst studies what a patient omits.

THEORY OF MIND. The human ability to recognize that other people have minds and to interpret their behavior based on deductions about their mental states.

TOTALITY. A concept in Hegelian and Marxist thought referring to the whole. For G.W.F. Hegel this is the essence that produces the underlying unity of an age, and for Karl Marx it is the relations of production that determine a historical era.

TYPOLOGY. A strategy of reading an Old Testament story as an allegory for a New Testament one, developed by Christian theologians as a way to reconcile apparent contradictions in scripture.

UNCANNY. Sigmund Freud's term for an uneasy sensation created by something strange yet familiar.

UNRELIABLE NARRATOR. Wayne Booth's term for a narrator whose facts or values are at odds with the implied author's.

UTILITARIANISM. A philosophical movement that contends that the best actions are those that result in the greatest good for the greatest number of people.

Index

a priori and *a posteriori*, 108
Abernethy, John, 249
the abject, 221–22, 253
abolitionist movement, 100, 102–03, 114
abolitionist novel, 121
abortion rights, 203
Abrams, M.H., *A Glossary of Literary Terms*, 41
L'Académie française, 98
Achebe, Chinua, "An Image of Africa," 198
actor-network theory, 210
Adams, Hazard, *Critical Theory Since Plato*, 43
Addison, Joseph, 96–97
Adorno, Theodor, 188–89, 193
    Dialectic of Enlightenment, 189
The Adventures of Huckleberry Finn (Twain),
    35, 120
The Aeneid (Virgil), 54
Aestheticism, 120, 127–31. *See also* art for art's
    sake
aesthetics of reception, 226
affective fallacy, 146, 227
African-American studies, 42, 181, 194, 199–201
    double-consciousness, 200
    goal of integration and canon revision, 201
African diaspora, 196–97
Against Nature (Huysmans), 131
AIDS, 172, 207
Ain't I a Woman (hooks), 202
Alexander the Great, 54, 65
alienation, 184–85, 187, 211–12, 219
All for Love (Dryden), 89
allegory, 51, 74–76, 78–80
allegory of the cave, 51–53
Althusser, Louis, 149, 198
    "Contradiction and Overdetermination," 191
    "Ideology and Ideological State
        Apparatuses," 191
    references to Lacan, 220

successor to Sartre, 190
Altick, Richard, *The English Common Reader*,
    166
American Anthropological Association (AAA),
    21
American Declaration of Independence, 102
American Founding Fathers, 101–02, 162
American Historical Association (AHA), 21
American imperialism, 196
American New Critics. *See* New Criticism
American Psychological Association (APA), 21
American Revolution, 95, 101, 114, 195
American Sociological Association (ASA), 21
American Studies, 173–74
anagnorisis, 57–58
anagogical interpretation, 75
analytic philosophy, 107, 143
Anatomy of Criticism (Frye), 219
ancient Greece, 20, 100
ancient Greek and Roman writers, 46–67, 70, 77.
    See also names of individual writers
    allegorical interpretations of, 79
    loss of texts, 46–47
Anderson, Benedict, 121
Animal Farm (Orwell), 51
animal studies, 209
"The Animal That Therefore I Am" (Derrida),
    209
Anthropocene, 210
anthropology, 13, 18, 20, 24, 149–50, 168, 172
anti-theory backlash, 26
antiquarianism, 161–64, 176
    female scholars, 162
    Notes and Queries, 163
Antonio's Revenge (Marston), 238
Antony and Cleopatra (Shakespeare), 89
anxiety, 214, 218
The Anxiety of Influence (Bloom), 34, 218

267

Anzaldúa, Gloria
 Borderlands/La Frontera, 202
 This Bridge Called My Back, 202
Apollo, 132
Apollonian and Dionysiac tendencies in Greek
 art, 132
aporia, 155–56
Aquinas. *See* Thomas Aquinas, Saint
Arabic-speaking scholars, 77
arbitrary nature of the sign, 139
The Archaeology of Knowledge (Foucault), 170, 248
Archetypal Patterns in Poetry (Bodkin), 218–19
Aristotle, 20, 46, 54–62, 77, 88, 129
 art makes the world a better place, 60
 belief in the unity of a dramatic work, 59
 narrative form, 57–58
 Poetics, 47, 54–60, 88–89, 117, 120, 147, 233
 Rhetoric, 60–62
Arnold, Matthew, 143
 criticism should *not* respect national
  boundaries, 126
 critics should transcend partisanship, 125
 "The Function of Criticism at the Present
  Time," 125–26
Ars Poetica (Horace), 34, 62–63
"Ars Poetica" (MacLeish), 63
Art and Artist (Rank), 217
art for art's sake, 35, 128, 130–31, 133, 175, 190
The Artist (Rank), 217
Asian-American studies, 194, 201
Association for the Study of Literature and the
 Environment (ASLE), 209
Astell, Mary, *A Serious Proposal for the Ladies*,
 103
Astrophil and Stella (Sidney), 89
atheism, 81, 101
Atlantic Monthly, 36
Atlantic world, 201
Auerbach, Erich, *Mimesis*, 51
Augustine, Saint, Bishop of Hippo, 71
 On Christian Doctrine, 71–72
"Auld Lang Syne" (Burns), 104
Austen, Jane, 120, 123, 206
 Emma, 29
 Mansfield Park, 198
 Pride and Prejudice, 57–58
author biography, 13, 32–33, 38, 44, 146, 164, 250
author-function, 32–33
authors' consciousnesses, 223
author's intentions, 33, 146
author's work should speak for itself, 32, 146

authorship, 145. *See also* writers
 conventions of, 33
 eighteenth century, 33
 historically constructed, 32
 implied author, 148, 228, 247
 Middle Ages, 32
 writing as a profession, 95
avant-garde, 189, 221
Averroes, 77

Bachelard, Gaston, 170
Back to the Future Part II (1989), 210
Bacon, Francis, 88
Badiou, Alain, 155
Baker, Houston, 200
Bakhtin, Mikhail, 186–87, 241
 concept of dialogism, 169, 187, 221
 popularized in France by Kristeva and
  Todorov, 221
 The Problems of Dostoevsky's Poetics, 186–87
 Rabelais and His World, 187
Bal, Mieke, *Narratology*, 153
Baldwin, James, 199
Balzac, Honoré de, 182, 188
 "Avant Propos," 123
 La Comédie humaine, 122–23
 history of everyday life, 123
 Le Père Goriot, 122–23
 "Sarrasine," 151
Baraka, Amiri, 200
Barthes, Roland, 150–51
 "The Death of the Author," 151, 170
 Mythologies, 150
 S/Z, 151–52, 236
 structuralist element in his work, 150
 theory of intertextuality, 170, 178
 Writing Degree Zero, 150
base and superstructure, 183, 191, 206
Bataille, Georges, 221
Bate, Jonathan, *Romantic Ecology*, 209
The Battle of the Books (Swift), 95
Baudelaire, Charles, 128
 "The Painter of Modern Life," 130
Baudrillard, Jean, 194
Beardsley, Monroe, 146, 227
beauty, 52, 109, 129–30
Beauvoir, Simone de, 49, 111, 132, 204–05
 feminist existentialism, 190
 on myths of woman, 204, 242
 The Second Sex, 204–05
Behn, Aphra, 204

Oroonoko, 102
Being and Nothingness (Sartre), 155, 190, 197
Being and Time (Heidegger), 154
Bender, John, *Imagining the Penitentiary*, 173
Benjamin, Walter, 188–89
    "The Storyteller," 189
    "The Work of Art in the Age of Mechanical
        Reproduction," 189
Bentham, Jeremy, 120, 170–71
Beowulf, 31
Berkeley, George, 106–07
Bersani, Leo, 169
Between Men (Sedgwick), 17, 208
Bhabha, Homi, 241
    "Signs Taken for Wonders," 199
Bible, 73–75
    biblical canon, 71
    biblical interpretation, 72–77, 224
    Book of Kells, 83
    Genesis, 74
    Gutenberg Bible, 81
    Hebrew Bible, 74, 76
    New Testament, 54, 71, 74
    role of printing press in disseminating, 82, 84
Bibliographical Society, 176
bibliography, 176–77
Bildungsroman, 120, 248
Bill & Ted's Excellent Adventure (1989), 212
binary oppositions, 150, 156–57, 169, 175
Biographia Literaria (Coleridge), 117–18
biographical studies. *See* author biography
biology and gender, 206
Birmingham Centre for Contemporary Cultural
    Studies, 193
The Birth of Tragedy (Nietzsche), 132
Black Arts movement, 197, 200
The Black Atlantic (Gilroy), 201
black feminism, 202
Black Power movement, 197, 200
Black Skin, White Masks (Fanon), 197, 199, 220
Black Studies, 200. *See also* African-American
    studies
Blake, William, 116, 119, 227
Blindness and Insight (De Man), 157
Bloom, Allan, 36
    The Closing of the American Mind, 26–27
Bloom, Harold, 34–35, 156
    The Anxiety of Influence, 34, 218
Boccaccio, Giovanni, 78–79, 152
    Decameron, 79
    Genealogy of the Pagan Gods, 79

Bodkin, Maud, *Archetypal Patterns in Poetry*, 218
Bolt, Usain, 61
book history, 176–77, 248
Book of Common Prayer, 85
Book of Kells, 83
The Book of the City of Ladies (Christine de
    Pizan), 79–80
Book-of-the-Month Club, 176
book reviews, 36, 96–97, 125–26
Booth, Wayne, 147–48
    implied author, 148, 228, 247
    The Rhetoric of Fiction, 147
    unreliable narrator, 148, 247–48
Borderlands/La Frontera (Anzaldúa), 202
The Boston Globe, 34
Boswell, James, *The Life of Samuel Johnson*, 97,
    106–07
Bourdieu, Pierre, 174–76
    Distinction, 174, 176
bourgeoisie and proletariat, 184
Bowers, Fredson, 238
Bowie, David, 128
Bradley, A.C., *Shakespearean Tragedy*, 30
brain-mapping technologies, 229
"breaking the fourth wall," 148
"The Briar Patch" (Warren), 146
bricolage/bricoleur, 149
Bride of Frankenstein (1935), 249
British cultural studies. *See* cultural studies
British imperialism, 195, 197
Broadview Editions, 44
Brontë, Charlotte, 36, 217
    Jane Eyre, 120, 205
    Shirley, 121
Brook, Peter, 240
Brooks, Cleanth
    Understanding Fiction, 145
    Understanding Poetry, 145
    The Well-Wrought Urn, 145, 160–61
Brooks, Mel, 249
Brooks, Peter, *Reading for the Plot*, 218
Brown University, 178
Buell, Lawrence, *The Environmental Imagination*,
    209
Bunyan, John, *The Pilgrim's Progress*, 85
Burke, Edmund, 253
    *Philosophical Enquiry into the Origin ... Ideas
        of the Sublime and Beautiful*, 109
Burke, Kenneth
    A Grammar of Motives, 147
    A Rhetoric of Motives, 147

Burns, Robert, "Auld Lang Syne," 104
Butler, Judith, *Gender Trouble*, 209
Byron, George Gordon, Baron, 116, 217
Byzantine Empire, 69

Calderón, Héctor, 202
Calvin, John, 84, 100
Calvinism, 84, 100
Cambridge University, 21, 73, 192
Camões, Luis de, *Lusiads*, 87
Campbell, Joseph, *The Hero With a Thousand Faces*, 219
"Can the Subaltern Speak?" (Spivak), 199
Candide (Voltaire), 101
Canguilhem, George, *The Normal and the Pathological*, 169
canon, 26–27, 41, 71, 126, 176, 201
    attempt to establish during Enlightenment, 95
    expansion of, 35–36, 181, 201, 205
    men dominated before 20th century, 36, 205
canon wars. *See* culture wars
The Canterbury Tales (Chaucer), 42, 82
Capital (Marx), 181, 185
capitalism, 106, 185
    capitalist mode of production, 182, 184
    consumer capitalism, 128
    global capitalism, 194
capitalization, 32
Carby, Hazel, 200
carnivalesque, 187
catachresis, 64
The Catcher in the Rye (Salinger), 35
categorical imperative, 108–09
categories of poetry (Aristotle), 55
Catholic Church, 70, 84, 87, 101
Caxton, William, 84
Céline, Louis-Ferdinand, 222
Celtic languages, 86
censorship, 35, 49, 101
Cervantes Saavedra, Miguel de, *Don Quixote*, 30
Césaire, Aimé, 196
    Discourse on Colonialism, 197
Chakrabarty, Dipesh, 199
Charlemagne, 69
Charles, RuPaul, 209
Chartier, Roger, 177
Chaucer, Geoffrey, 126
    The Canterbury Tales, 42, 82
    source for philologists, 137
Chávez, César, 202

Chavis, John, 199
Chicago School, 147. *See also* neo-Aristotelian critics
Chicano/a activism, 24, 202
Chicano/a studies, 201
Chicano Movement, 24
China, 81, 186
Chomsky, Noam, 229
Christianity, conversion to, 70
Christianity Not Mysterious (Toland), 101
Christine de Pizan, 203
    The Book of the City of Ladies, 79–80
Church of England, 84–85, 92
Cicero, 61, 63
Civil Rights Act (1965), 200
civil rights movement, 24, 180, 195, 197, 200
Civilization and Its Discontents (Freud), 216
Cixous, Hélène, 152
    feminist critique of Freud and Lacan, 222
    "The Laugh of the Medusa," 222
clarity of style, 26, 63, 97
Clarkson, Kelly, "Stronger [What Doesn't Kill You]," 131
class struggle, 184
classical curriculum, 20–21
Classical era of Greek history, 46
classics reproduced by printing press, 82
classification, 55–56, 61, 147
Clift, Montgomery, 212
close reading, 18–19, 22, 31, 38, 44, 144–45, 151, 157–58, 233–36
    centrality to literary studies, 19
    organic unity as a foundation of, 233
    residue of New Criticism, 27
The Closing of the American Mind (Bloom), 26–27
Cloud Atlas (2012), 52, 132
Cloud Atlas (Mitchell), 131
cognitive literary studies, 228–29
cognitive studies, 22, 27, 229
Coleridge, Samuel Taylor, 59, 108, 116, 128–29, 140, 233
    Biographia Literaria, 117–18
    on imagination, 117, 233
    "Kubla Khan," 117, 165
    "The Rime of the Ancient Mariner," 117, 165
collective unconscious, 218
Collier, Mary, 104
Collingwood, R.G., *The Idea of History*, 167
Collins, Suzanne, *The Hunger Games*, 225–26
Collins, Wilkie, 120

colonialism, 114, 127, 195–97
colonies in the Americas, 92
    haven for religious refugees, 85
La Comédie humaine (Balzac), 122–23
comedy, 55, 87, 167
commodification of art, 194
commodity fetishism, 185, 187, 210
The Communist Manifesto (Marx), 181–82
Communist Party, 190
Communist utopia, 112
comparative ethnic studies, 194
composition and rhetoric, 17
"Compulsory Heterosexuality and Lesbian
    Existence" (Rich), 207
condensation, 214
"Condition of England" novels, 121
The Condition of Postmodernity (Harvey), 194
Conrad, Joseph, *Heart of Darkness*, 198
Constantine the Great, 70
consumerism, 128, 183–85, 194
containment, 173
continental philosophy, 107, 143. *See also*
    individual philosophers
"Contradiction and Overdetermination"
    (Althusser), 191
A Contribution to the Critique of Political Economy
    (Marx), 183
conventions of authorship, 33
conventions or rules for writing, 28
copyright, 32, 95
Corneille, Pierre, "Of the Three Unities of
    Action, Time, and Place," 88–89
countercultural figures (1960s and 1970s), 128
Course in General Linguistics (Saussure), 138–40,
    149
Cousin, Victor, 130
Crane, R.S., 147
creative writing, 17
Crime and Punishment (Dostoevsky), 187
criminality, 170
The Critical Difference (Johnson), 157, 161
Critical Inquiry, 199
critical race theory, 194
Critical Review, 97
critical theory, 13, 188
Critical Theory Since Plato (Adams), 43
Criticism and Ideology (Eagleton), 193
"Criticism Inc." (Ransom), 145
Critique of Judgment (Kant), 109
Cuddon, J.A., *The Penguin Dictionary of Literary
    Terms and Literary Theory*, 41

Culler, Jonathan, *Literary Theory*, 43–44
cultural anthropology, 172
cultural capital, 175
Cultural Capital (Guillory), 176
cultural construction, 14, 16, 24, 32, 206, 210
Cultural Literacy (Hirsch), 27
cultural materialism, 168
cultural studies, 174, 177, 181, 192–93
cultural theory, 13
Culture and Imperialism (Said), 198
Culture and Society (Williams), 193
culture industry, 189
culture wars, 27, 36. *See also* canon
cybernetics, 178
"A Cyborg Manifesto" (Haraway), 178

D'Alembert, Jean-Baptiste le Rond, 99
Dante Alighieri, 77–78
    The Divine Comedy, 77–78, 119
    On Eloquence in the Vernacular, 86
    "Letter to Can Grande," 75, 77
Dark Ages. *See* medieval era
Darwin, Charles
    evolutionary theory, 114
    Origin of Species, 124
Darwin, Erasmus, *The Loves of the Plants*, 105
David Copperfield (Dickens), 29
Davis, Natalie Zemon, *The Return of Martin
    Guerre*, 168
De Man, Paul, 156–57, 173, 199, 202
    Blindness and Insight, 157
    wartime journalism, 157, 176
Death Is the Mother of Beauty (Turner), 229
Death of a Salesman, 56
"The Death of the Author" (Barthes), 151, 170
decadence, 115, 127–28, 130–31
Decameron (Boccaccio), 79
decolonization, 196
deconstruction, 23–24, 26, 151, 154–57, 173, 199,
    237
    De Man revelations and, 176
    New Criticism and, 154
    New Historicism and, 167
    public backlash against, 157
    Russian Formalism and, 154
defamiliarization, 141
A Defence of Poetry (Shelley), 119
A Defence of Poetry (Sidney), 89, 119
*The Defense and Enrichment of the French
    Language* (du Bellay), 86
Defoe, Daniel, 96

deism, 81, 101
Deleuze, Gilles, 194
dénouement, 58
depersonalization, 144, 146
Derrida, Jacques, 23–24, 26, 132, 151, 154–57, 167,
    219, 237
    "The Animal That Therefore I Am," 209
    ethical turn, 154
    existentialism and, 155, 190
    Foucault and, 169
    influences, 154
    model of language, 156
    Of Grammatology, 155–56, 199
    phenomenology and, 155
    "Structure, Sign, and Play in the Discourse
        of the Human Sciences," 23–24, 50, 149,
        155
    Writing and Difference, 155
desire, 208, 212, 215–17, 220, 222, 252
Destruktion, 155
detective fiction, 128, 134, 153
determinism, 124–25, 183, 190
dialectic, 111–12, 182–83
Dialectic of Enlightenment (Adorno and
    Horkheimer), 189
dialogism, 169, 187, 221
dialogues, 47–48, 53
dianoia, 55–56
Dibdin, Thomas, 176
Dickens, Charles, 17
    admired by Marx, 182
    David Copperfield, 29
    Great Expectations, 120
    Hard Times, 121
    Miller's study of, 224
Dickinson, Emily, 206
A Dictionary of Narratology (Prince), 154
Dictionary of National Biography, 115
Dictionary of the English Language (Johnson),
    97–98
Diderot, Denis, 99
digital humanities, 22, 27, 177–79, 232
Dionysius, 132
disability studies, 209
The Disappearance of God (Miller), 224
disciplinary boundaries, 17–18, 20–21, 170
Discipline and Punish (Foucault), 170–71
discontinuity, theme of, 169–70
Discourse Networks 1800/1900 (Kittler), 178
Discourse on Colonialism (Césaire), 197
discourses, 102, 155, 160, 170, 173, 186, 248–50

disinterestedness, 125–26
Disney cartoons, 189
displacement, 214
distant reading, 179
Distinction (Bourdieu), 174, 176
Divergent (Roth), 225–26
diversity, 35–36, 201–02
The Divine Comedy (Dante), 77–78, 119
divine inspiration, 53–54, 117–18
divine right of kings, 102
Dollimore, Jonathan, 168
dominant, emergent, residual, 27
Don Quixote (Cervantes), 30
Dooley, Lucile, 217
Doolittle, Hilda [H.D.], 217
Dostoevsky, Fyodor, 222
    Crime and Punishment, 187
double-consciousness, 200
Douglass, Frederick, The Narrative of the Life of
    Frederick Douglass, 36, 121
Doyle, Arthur Conan, 134
Dracula (Stoker), 133
drag artists, 209
drama, 17, 55–60, 87
    comedy, 55, 87
    tragedy, 28, 55–56, 87, 167, 238–40
drives, 216–17
Druidism, 70
Dryden, John, All for Love, 89
Du Bellay, Joachim, The Defense and Enrichment
    of the French Language, 86
Du Bois, W.E.B., 194–96, 199–200
Duck, Stephen, 104
The Dunciad (Pope), 96
duration, 152
Dutch language, 86

Eagleton, Terry
    Criticism and Ideology, 193
    Literary Theory, 43
    Marxism and Literary Criticism, 193
Early American Imprints, 32
Early English Books Online, 31–32
early modern era. See Renaissance
Eco, Umberto, 150
ecocriticism, 209
economic determinism, 183, 190
The Economy of Prestige (English), 176
Écrits (Lacan), 219
l'écriture féminine, 222
Edinburgh Review, 97

editorial detachment, 96, 125
education, 52, 91, 193, 248
    female education, 103–04
    free public education, 184
    gentlemanly education, 20, 22, 46
    integration of higher education, 199–200
    liberal education, 73, 126
    opportunities expanded in 19th century,
        21, 114
    Plato on, 48–49
    printing press and, 82
ego, 215
Eichenbaum, Boris, 140
The Eighteenth Brumaire of Louis Bonaparte
    (Marx), 184
Eliot, George, 33, 206
    Middlemarch, 120
Eliot, T.S., 143
    concept of depersonalization, 144, 146
    "Tradition and the Individual Talent," 144
The Elizabethan World Picture (Tillyard), 165, 172
Ellison, Ralph, *Invisible Man*, 35, 42
Elstob, Elizabeth, 162
Emerson, Ralph Waldo, 129
Emma (Austen), 29
empiricism, 99, 106
Empson, William, *Seven Types of Ambiguity*, 144
Encyclopedia Britannica, 99
Encyclopédie, 99
end of history, 112, 182
Engels, Friedrich, 181, 186
"England in 1819" (Shelley), 119
English, James, *The Economy of Prestige*, 176
The English Common Reader (Altick), 166
English language, 69, 86, 93
Enlightenment, 68, 91–112
Enlightenment as extension of the Renaissance
    (table), 93
Enlightenment skepticism. *See* skepticism
The Environmental Imagination (Buell), 209
environmental studies, 209
epic poetry, 28–29, 54–55, 87
episteme, 169
epistemology, 107
Epistemology of the Closet (Sedgwick), 208
Equal Rights Amendment, 203
Equiano, Olaudah, 103, 116
Erasmus, Desiderius, 80
essay form, 28, 87–88
An Essay on Criticism (Pope), 63
Essays (Montaigne), 85

Esu Elegbara, 201
ethics, 35, 107–08, 119, 154
ethnic cleansing, 121
ethnic studies, 24, 27, 174, 180, 201
ethos, 55–56, 61
European voyages of discovery, 68, 85
Everyman, 87
evolution, 124–25
existentialism, 132, 154–55, 190, 197, 204–05
"The Experimental Novel" (Zola), 124
experimental science. *See* science
experimental writing, 104–06, 133, 141, 221

Fable of the Bees (Mandeville), 105
fabula and syuzhet, 153, 245
fabula and syuzhet (table), 246
facsimile texts, 31–32
The Faerie Queene (Spenser), 32
fairy tales, 116, 152
Falling Into Theory (Richter), 43
false consciousness, 183
fan fiction, 30
Fanon, Frantz, 111, 190, 205
    Black Skin, White Masks, 197, 199, 220
    The Wretched of the Earth, 197
Fascism, 114, 121, 186
fashion, 96, 128, 130, 183
A Feeling for Books (Radway), 176
Felman, Shoshana, 218
The Feminine Mystique (Friedan), 205
feminism, 24, 38, 40, 100, 114, 177–78, 180,
    202–06
    deconstruction and, 157
    early feminism, 103–04
    existentialism and, 190, 204
    Frankenstein and, 250
    Hamlet and, 232, 241–42
    new historicism and, 169
    psychoanalysis and, 220–22
    seeking coeducational canon, 205
Fichte, Johann Gottlieb, 117
fiction, 17, 133–34, 229. *See also* novel
Field, Michael, 33
Fielding, Henry, *Tom Jones*, 148
fields (Bourdieu), 175–76
Fifty Shades of Grey (James), 30
film, 17, 52–53, 58–59, 134
    concept of the male gaze, 222
    film studies, 20
    Lacanian criticism and, 222
Fish, Stanley, 131, 226–28, 255

idea of interpretive communities, 227–28
Surprised by Sin, 226–27
Fishburne, Laurence, 52
Five Readers Reading (Holland), 218
flâneur, 130
flashback, 152, 247
Flaubert, Gustave, 124, 148
Madame Bovary, 123
focalization, 153
folklore, 116, 152
foreshadowing, 152
form and content distinction, 28–29, 31
formalism, 23, 38, 60, 135–58
Anglo-American, 142–48
Hamlet and, 233–36
turn away from in 1960s, 146
"The Forms of Power and the Power of Forms in the Renaissance" (Greenblatt), 166
Foucault, Michel, 26, 132, 149, 160, 167, 169–72, 174, 198, 219
advocated prison reform, 172
The Archaeology of Knowledge, 170, 248
on author-function, 33
compares schools, factories, and military barracks to prisons, 171
concept of panopticon, 170–71
Discipline and Punish, 170
emphasis on discontinuity in the history of thought, 169
The History of Sexuality, 16, 170, 207–08
influence on new historicism, 167, 169, 173
influenced by Sartre, 190
model of discourses, 169–70, 173, 248
new terms, 170
The Order of Things, 169–70
power, 171, 173, 191
theory of intertextuality, 170, 178
"What Is an Author?," 32–33, 186
four-level interpretive method, 73–75, 78
Foxe's Book of Martyrs, 85
France
Enlightenment in, 91, 99
French Communist Party, 190
French language, 85, 93
French Revolution, 95, 101–03, 114–15
literary salons, 103
Middle Ages, 69
Frankenstein (1931), 249
Frankenstein (Shelley), 37, 231, 244–54
book historians and, 248
cultural studies and, 248

film adaptations, 249
flashback structure, 247
historical approach, 248
homosociality and, 251–52
intertextuality and, 249
narratology and, 245–48
Orientalism and, 250–51
political perspectives, 250–51
queer reading, 251–52
science of, 250
Frankfurt School, 169, 174, 188–89, 192
critical theory of, 188
influence on cultural studies, 192
Franklin, Benjamin, 162
Frasier, 212
free indirect style, 123–24, 153
free trade, 194
"French theory" in America, 23
Freud, Sigmund, 14, 22, 40, 190–91, 211–18, 253–54
alienation, 185, 211–12
Civilization and Its Discontents, 216
feminist uses of, 221–22
followers used his ideas to study mythology, 217
founder of new discourse, 186
Freudian slips, 212
The Interpretation of Dreams, 212, 214–15, 217
key concepts, 212–16, 218
openness about discussing sexuality, 217
as pop cultural figure, 212
reading of *Hamlet*, 215, 242–43
stream of consciousness technique and, 217
Three Essays on the Theory of Sexuality, 215
use of Shakespeare, 232
Freud: The Secret Passion (1962), 212
Freytag, Gustav, 58
Freytag's pyramid, 58–59
Friedan, Betty, *The Feminine Mystique*, 205
Frye, Northrop, 167
Anatomy of Criticism, 219
version of archetypal criticism, 219
"The Function of Criticism at the Present Time" (Arnold), 125–26

Gadamer, Hans-Georg
hermeneutic circle, 225–26
Truth and Method, 224
Game of Thrones (TV series), 70
Gargantua and Pantagruel (Rabelais), 187
Gaskell, Elizabeth, *North and South*, 121

Gates, Henry Louis, 199–201, 255
  The Signifying Monkey, 200
Gautier, Théophile, 121
  Mademoiselle de Maupin, 130
gay rights movement, 172, 207
Geertz, Clifford, 172
  The Interpretation of Cultures, 168
  thick description, 168, 210
Geist, 110–11
gender and sexuality, 14, 27, 35, 42, 180, 202–09
Gender Trouble (Butler), 209
genealogy, 171
Genealogy of the Pagan Gods (Boccaccio), 79
Genette, Gérard, 153
  fabula and syuzhet, 153, 245–46
  Narrative Discourse, 152, 161
genocide, 121
Genre (journal), 166
genre, 28–29, 55, 86–88, 147, 179, 225, 238–39
Gentleman's Magazine, 94
geometry, 73
George III, King of England, 101
georgic, 105
German unification, 114, 121
German idealism, 106, 108, 110
German language, 86
German Romanticism, 117
Germanic languages, 86
Gibbon, Edward, 161
Gilbert, Sandra, 205–06, 255
  The Madwoman in the Attic, 205
  The Norton Anthology of Literature by
    Women, 206
Gilroy, Paul, The Black Atlantic, 201
Ginsberg, Allan, 128
Ginzburg, Carlo, 167
global capitalism, 194
global literary tradition (or world literature),
  126
A Glossary of Literary Terms (Abrams), 41
God, 50, 71–72, 74, 102, 106–07, 118–19, 132
"God is dead," 132
God's Not Dead (2014), 132
Godwin, William, 244
Goethe, Johann Wolfgang von, 117
  call for a world literature, 126
  Sorrows of Young Werther, 249
Goodreads site, 34, 226
Google Books, 95
gothic, 110, 116, 128, 133, 216, 244, 250
Graffigny, Françoise de, 103

Grahame-Smith, Seth, Pride and Prejudice and
  Zombies, 30
grammar, 73, 152
A Grammar of Motives (Burke), 147
Gramophone Film Typewriter (Kittler), 178
Gramsci, Antonio, 186, 198
  concept of hegemony, 169, 186, 191
  concept of the subaltern, 186, 199
Graves, Robert, A Survey of Modernist Poetry, 144
The Great Chain of Being (Lovejoy), 165
Great Expectations (Dickens), 120
Greek culture, 46, 54
Greek language, 46, 54, 65
Greenblatt, Stephen, 172–73
  "The Forms of Power and the Power of
    Forms in the Renaissance," 166
  Renaissance Self-Fashioning, 172
  Shakespearean Negotiations, 172
Greg, Sir Walter Wilson, 176
Grimm brothers, 137
  collecting of folklore and fairy tales, 115–17
Grimm's Law, 137
grotesque, 187
Grub Street writers, 95–96
Guattari, Félix, 194
Gubar, Susan, 205–06, 255
  The Madwoman in the Attic, 205
  The Norton Anthology of Literature by
    Women, 206
Guha, Ranajit, 199
Guide of the Perplexed (Maimonides), 76
Guillaume de Lorris, Roman de la Rose, 78
Guillory, John, Cultural Capital, 176
Gulliver's Travels (Swift), 51
Gutenberg, Johannes, 81, 83
Gutenberg Bible, 81

habitus, 174
Haitian revolution, 103, 198
Hall, Stuart, 192
  Marxist version of media studies, 193
  The Popular Arts, 193
Hamlet (Shakespeare), 37, 56, 231–44
  adaptations of, 238
  as case study, 232–44
  and class, 240–41
  and close reading, 233–36
  and deconstruction, 237
  and gender, 241–42
  Hamlet's melancholy, 242–44
  in literary history, 231, 238–40

metafictional and existential aspects, 238
and psychoanalysis, 242–43
sources for, 239
theatricality, 236–38
undecidable questions, 37
Haraway, Donna
"A Cyborg Manifesto," 178
Simians, Cyborgs, and Women, 178
Hard Times (Dickens), 121
Harlem Renaissance, 196, 200
Harry Potter series (Rowling), 34–35, 208
Hartman, Geoffrey, 156
Harvard University, 173
Harvey, David, The Condition of Postmodernity, 194
Hawthorne, Nathaniel, The Scarlet Letter, 120
Hayles, N. Katherine, How We Became Posthuman, 178
Haywood, Eliza, 96
Love in Excess, 123
Heart of Darkness (Conrad), 198
Hebrew Bible, 74, 76
Hegel, G.W.F., 106–07, 117, 181
Dialectic, 111–12, 181
ideas of history, 110–12
master-slave dialectic, 197, 220
Phenomenology of Mind, 111
philosophical idealism, 110
philosophical version of God, 110–11
hegemony, 169, 186, 191
Heidegger, Martin, 154–55, 190, 223–24
Being and Time, 154
membership in the Nazi party, 157
Hellenistic world, 54, 65
hemispheric studies, 174
Henry VIII, King of England, 84
heresy of paraphrase, 145
hermeneutic circle, 224–25
hermeneutics, 224–26. See also interpretation
The Hero With a Thousand Faces (Campbell), 219
heteroglossia, 187
Hirsch, E.D., Cultural Literacy, 27
Historiae Danicae (Saxo Grammaticus), 239
historical context, 31–32, 42
historical determinism, 184
historical novels, 120, 122
historically black colleges and universities (HBCUs), 200
historicism, 22–23, 38–39, 44–45, 111, 127, 160–79
in 18th and 19th century, 160–63
looking for connections, 161

"old historicist" studies, 165–66
resurgence of, 26
history, 20, 24, 106, 161
History of England (Macaulay), 103
History of English Literature (Taine), 126
History of English Poetry (Warton), 162
history of ideas, 165, 169
The History of Sexuality (Foucault), 16, 170, 207–08
Hitler, Adolf, 192. See also Nazism
HIV/AIDS research, 207
Hoffmann, E.T.A., 117, 217
"The Sand-Man," 216
Hogarth Press, 217
Hoggart, Richard, 192–93
The Uses of Literacy, 192
Holland, Norman, Five Readers Reading, 218
Hollywood, 58, 189
Holmes, Sherlock, 134
Holy Roman Empire, 69
Homer, 46, 49, 66, 87, 92, 105, 118
The Iliad, 48, 54
The Odyssey, 48, 54
homophobia, 208
homosexuality
as an "aberration" (Freud's ideas), 207–08, 215
in 19th-century psychoanalytic thought, 207–08
homosocial relations, 17
homosociality, 17, 208, 251–52
defused through erotic triangles, 208
hooks, bell, Ain't I a Woman, 202
Horace, 47, 88, 97
Ars Poetica, 34, 62–63
contrast with Longinus, 67
good poetry should delight and instruct, 34, 63
on clarity and simplicity, 63, 97
horizon, concept of, 224, 226, 250
Horkheimer, Max, 188, 193
Dialectic of Enlightenment, 189
horror genre. See gothic
"How Many Children Had Lady Macbeth?" (Knights), 30
How We Became Posthuman (Hayles), 178
Howard University, 200
Hughes, Langston, 196, 199
Hughes, Thomas, The Misfortunes of Arthur, 238
humanism, 80–81
humanities computing. See digital humanities

Hume, David, 100–01, 106, 132, 161
"Of the Standard of Taste," 105
The Hunger Games (Collins), 225–26
Husserl, Edmund, 223–24, 226, 228
The Origin of Geometry, 154
phenomenology of, 154
Huston, John, 212
Huysmans, J.-K., *Against Nature*, 131
hybridity, 105, 199
hyperbaton, 64
hypertext projects, 178

id, 215
The Idea of History (Collingwood), 167
Ideal (Plato), 50, 52, 55
idealism, 49, 91, 106–12
identity
Hegel's discussion of, 111
Lacan's views, 220
ideological state apparatuses (ISAs), 191
ideology, 183, 186, 192
"Ideology and Ideological State Apparatuses"
(Althusser), 191
Ideology and Utopia (Mannheim), 192
The Idler (Johnson), 97
The Iliad (Homer), 48, 54
I'll Take My Stand ("Twelve Southerners"), 146
illuminated manuscripts, 82–83
"An Image of Africa" (Achebe), 198
imaginary (Lacan), 219
imagination, 97, 116–17, 119, 127–28, 233
"imagined communities," 121
Imagining the Penitentiary (Bender), 173
implied author, 148, 228, 247
The Implied Reader (Iser), 228
impressionism, 131, 144, 146
Incidents in the Life of a Slave Girl (Jacobs), 121
Industrial Revolution, 114, 116, 193
Inferno (Dante), 77
Inquisition, 101
Institute for Social Research, 188
Institutio Oratoria (Quintilian), 63
intentional fallacy, 146, 148
interdisciplinarity, 20, 170, 179, 206, 229
The Interior Distance (Poulet), 223
Internet, 178
Internet Archive, 95
Internet memes, 28
Internet Movie Database, 212
interpellation, 191
interpretation, 39, 145. *See also* hermeneutics

biblical, 68, 70–77
secularization of, 77–79
The Interpretation of Cultures (Geertz), 168
The Interpretation of Dreams (Freud), 212, 214–15,
217
interpretive communities, 227–28
intersectionality, 202
intertextuality, 151, 170, 173, 178, 221, 249
An Introduction to Bibliography (McKerrow), 177
Invisible Man (Ellison), 35, 42
Ion (Plato), 47, 53
Irigaray, Luce, 206
"This Sex Which Is Not One," 222
irony, 64
Iser, Wolfgang, *The Implied Reader*, 228
Islam, 69, 73, 77, 84
Italian language, 85, 93
Italian unification, 114, 121
Ivanhoe (Scott), 188

Jacobs, Harriet, *Incidents in the Life of a Slave
Girl*, 121
Jagger, Mick, 26
Jakobson, Roman, 142, 149
James, E.L., *Fifty Shades of Grey*, 30
James, Henry, 124, 148
Jameson, Fredric, 193–94
Marxism and Form, 193
"Postmodernism, or the Cultural Logic of
Late Capitalism," 193
Jane Eyre (Brontë), 120, 205
Jauss, Hans Robert, "Literary History as a
Challenge to Literary Theory," 226
Jean de Meun, *Roman de la Rose*, 78
Jefferson, Thomas, 102
Johns Hopkins Guide to Literary Theory and
Criticism, 43
Johns Hopkins University, 21, 156, 165, 224
Johnson, Barbara, *The Critical Difference*, 157, 161
Johnson, Samuel, 97–99, 119, 147
Dictionary of the English Language, 97–98
The Idler, 97
The Lives of the Poets, 97
The Rambler, 97
Jones, Ernest, 242
"The Œdipus-Complex as an Explanation of
Hamlet's Mystery," 217
Jonson, Ben, 87
Joyce, James, 217, 221
Jung, Carl, 40, 218
archetypal theory, 219

influence on criticism, 218–19
Juvenal, 62

Kant, Immanuel, 49, 106–10, 117, 129–30, 253
  a priori and *a posteriori*, 108
  categorical imperative, 108
  Critique of Judgment, 109
  noumena and *phenomena*, 108, 154
  on the sublime, 109, 253
  "What Is Enlightenment?," 100, 115
Keats, John, 116, 118
keywords as key to determining critical approach, 40–42
Keywords (Williams), 193
King Lear (Shakespeare), 172
Kittler, Friedrich
  Discourse Networks 1800/1900, 178
  Gramophone Film Typewriter, 178
Knights, L.C., "How Many Children Had Lady Macbeth?," 30
Koyré, Alexandre, 170
Kristeva, Julia, 142, 150–51, 220–22, 253–54
  the abject, 221–22, 253–54
  combination of psychoanalysis and linguistics, 221
  feminism and psychoanalytic theory combination, 206
  Powers of Horror, 221
  Revolution in Poetic Language, 221
"Kubla Khan" (Coleridge), 117, 165
Kyd, Thomas, *The Spanish Tragedy*, 238

labor movement, 114, 181
  declining power of unions, 194
  trade unionism of early 20th century, 40, 184
Lacan, Jacques, 40, 149, 191, 193, 219–20
  Écrits, 219
  impact on feminist thinkers, 220–21
  influence, 222–23
  "The Mirror Stage as Formative of the Function of the I," 220
  model of Freud's Oedipal complex, 220
  seminars on Freud and psychoanalysis, 219
  "The Signification of the Phallus," 220
Lady's Magazine, 94
Lafayette, Mme de, *La Princesse de Clèves*, 123
Landow, George, 178
language, philosophy of, 143
language vs. speech (Saussure), 138
Latin, 46, 77, 85, 93
Latino/a studies, 194, 201–02

Latour, Bruno, 209–10
  actor-network theory, 210
  and the Anthropocene, 210
  Reassembling the Social, 210
"The Laugh of the Medusa" (Cixous), 222
Lawrence v. Texas, 207
The League of Extraordinary Gentlemen (Moore), 30
Leavis, F.R., 144
Leavis, Q.D., 144
Lecture on the Philosophy of Art (Schelling), 117
Leitch, Vincent, *The Norton Anthology of Theory and Criticism*, 43
lending libraries, 94, 120
Lenin, V.I., 40, 186
Leonardo da Vinci, 80
Leopold II of Belgium, 196
Lester, Adrian, 240
"Letter to Can Grande" (Dante), 75, 77
Lévi-Strauss, Claude, 24, 149–50, 152, 168
  binary oppositions, 150, 169
  Derrida's discussion of, 140–50, 155–56
  The Savage Mind, 150
  Structural Anthropology, 149
  "The Structural Study of Myth," 149
Lewis, C.S., *The Lion, the Witch, and the Wardrobe*, 51
Lewis, Matthew, 110
lexis, 56
LGBT (lesbian, gay, bisexual, and transgender) studies, 207. *See also* queer theory
Library of Alexandria, 46
The Life of Samuel Johnson (Boswell), 97, 106–07
linguistics, 17, 41, 140, 221
The Lion, the Witch, and the Wardrobe (Lewis), 51
The Lion King (1994), 238
literacy, 34, 116, 166, 193
  women and working-class, 82, 93
"Literary History as a Challenge to Literary Theory" (Jauss), 226
literary studies, 21
  as an academic discipline, 21, 114, 125, 135, 144, 181
  expansion of, 146
  interdisciplinarity, 20
  Marxist ideas influenced (latter part of 20th century), 193
  in modern research university, 22, 126
  object and method of study, 17–18
  organized around period specialties, 164
  professional associations, 21

specialized vocabulary of, 22, 41
literary theory and criticism, 13–14, 16, 42, 78, 107
   borrowings from philosophical debates, 107
   connection with political activism, 24
   literary theory vs. literary criticism, 16
   questioning underlying assumptions, 100
Literary Theory (Culler), 43–44
Literary Theory (Eagleton), 43
A Literature of Their Own (Showalter), 205, 255
lithography, 189
Liu, Alan, 178
The Lives of the Poets (Johnson), 97
Lives (Plutarch), 249
Locke, John, 101, 106
logic, 73, 107
logos, 61–62
Loki, 70
Lolita (Nabokov), 148
Lollards, 84
London Magazine, 94
London Review of Books, 36
long eighteenth century. *See* Enlightenment
Longinus, 47, 62, 147, 253
   On the Sublime, 65–67, 109
Lord, Albert B., *The Singer of Tales*, 92
Lord of The Rings (Tolkien), 70
Louis XVI, King of France, 101
Louisiana State University, 145
L'Ouverture, Toussaint, 103
Love in Excess (Haywood), 123
Lovejoy, Arthur, *The Great Chain of Being*, 165
The Loves of the Plants (Darwin), 105
Lowes, John Livingston, *The Road to Xanadu*, 165, 172
Lucas, George, 219
Lukács, Georg, 188
   "Reification and the Consciousness of the Proletariat," 187
Lusiads (Camoes), 87
Luther, Martin, 68, 92, 100
   Lutheranism, 84, 100
   Ninety-Five Theses, 84
Lyotard, Jean-François, 194
Lyrical Ballads, preface (Wordsworth), 118

Macaulay, Catharine, *History of England*, 103
Macherey, Pierre, *A Theory of Literary Production*, 191
Machiavelli, Niccoló, 80
MacKay, Claude, 196
MacLeish, Archibald, "Ars Poetica," 63

Mad Men (TV series), 24
Madame Bovary (Flaubert), 123–24
Mademoiselle de Maupin (Gautier), 130
The Madwoman in the Attic (Gilbert and Gubar), 205
magazines, 36, 94, 96, 120
Maimonides, Moses, 77
   Guide of the Perplexed, 76
Making a Social Body (Poovey), 173
The Making of the English Working Class (Thompson), 193
Mallarmé, Stéphane, 221
"The Man of the Crowd" (Poe), 130
Mandel, Ernest, 193
Mandeville, Bernard, *Fable of the Bees*, 105
Mannheim, Karl, *Ideology and Utopia*, 192
Mansfield Park (Austen), 198
Marcuse, Herbert, 188
Marie Antoinette, 101
Marlowe, Christopher, 87, 137
Marston, John, *Antonio's Revenge*, 238
Martin, George R.R., *A Song of Ice and Fire*, 70
Marx, Karl, 14, 40, 110, 141, 160, 174, 181–85, 192
   admired Shakespeare, 232
   alienation, 211–12
   Capital, 181, 185
   The Communist Manifesto, 181–82
   A Contribution to the Critique of Political Economy, 183
   Early Marxist theory and criticism, 186–93
   The Eighteenth Brumaire of Louis Bonaparte, 184
   founder of new discourse, 186
   political manifestations of his ideas, 40
   theory of history, 112, 126
   "Theses on Feuerbach," 180
   version of Hegel's dialectic, 112, 181–82, 184
Marxism, 22, 27, 40, 177, 181–94, 220
   influence on New Historicism, 168, 193
   later Marxist theory and criticism, 193–94
   and media studies, 193
   Russian Formalism and, 141–42
Marxism and Form (Jameson), 193
Marxism and Literary Criticism (Eagleton), 193
master-slave dialectic, 111, 197, 220
The Matrix (1999), 52–53
May 1968 in Paris, 24, 26
McGann, Jerome, 178
McKenzie, D.F., 176
McKeon, Richard, 147

McKerrow, R.B., 176
    An Introduction to Bibliography, 177
McLuhan, Marshall, 92, 177–78
The Meaning of Meaning (Richards and Ogden), 143
media theory, 92, 178, 193
medieval era, 68–80
    allegory and symbolism, 78
    authorship, idea of, 32
    carnival, 187
    curriculum, 73
    drama, 87
    growth of cities, 68
    inspiration for fantasy writers, 70
    manuscripts, 70, 82–83
    religion, 77
    rhetoric, 147
    romances, 78
    theology, 54
melos, 56
MELUS (Society for the Study of the Multi-Ethnic Literature of the US), 201
Melville, Herman, *Moby-Dick*, 120
Meno (Plato), 48
Merleau-Ponty, Maurice, *The Phenomenology of Perception*, 223
mestizo, 202
metafiction, 237
Metahistory (White), 167
metalepsis, 64
Metamorphoses (Ovid), 79
metaphor, 64
metaphysics, 107
meter and rhyme, 38, 42
method and object of academic disciplines (table), 18
metonymy, 64
microhistory, 167–68
Middle Ages. *See* medieval era
Middlemarch (Eliot), 120
Mill, John Stuart, 120
Miller, D.A., *The Novel and the Police*, 173
Miller, J. Hillis, 156, 166, 176, 202, 224
    The Disappearance of God, 224
Miller, Perry, 173
Milton, John, 95, 126, 255
    Paradise Lost, 54, 87, 119, 226–27, 249
mimesis, 51, 59–60, 120
Mimesis (Auerbach), 51
mimicry, 199
minstrels, 86

"The Mirror Stage as Formative of the Function of the I" (Lacan), 220
Les Misérables, 26
The Misfortunes of Arthur (Hughes), 238
Mitchell, David, *Cloud Atlas*, 131
Moby-Dick (Melville), 120
mode of production, 182
Modern Language Association (MLA), 21, 41
"A Modest Proposal" (Swift), 148
Montaigne, Michel de, 87
    Essays, 85
Monthly Review, 97
Montrose, Louis, 167, 172
mood, 152
Moore, Alan, *The League of Extraordinary Gentlemen*, 30
Moore, Marianne, "Poetry," 63
Moraga, Cherríe, *This Bridge Called My Back*, 202
morality, 35, 52, 97, 119
morality plays, 87
More, Thomas, 172
    Utopia, 85
Moretti, Franco, 165, 178–79
The Morphology of the Folktale (Propp), 152
Moscow Linguistic Circle, 140, 142
Muhammad, Prophet, 69
Mulvey, Laura, "Visual Pleasure and Narrative Cinema," 222
muse, 54, 118, 204
music, 54, 73, 140
    highest form of art, 131–32
Muslims. *See* Islam
Mussolini, Benito, 186
The Myth of the Birth of the Hero (Rank), 217
Mythologies (Barthes), 150
mythology, 149–50
    Greek, 49, 54, 79
    myths of woman, 204–05, 242
    Norse, 70
    Yoruba, 201
mythos, 55–56

Nabokov, Vladimir, *Lolita*, 148
naïve art, 104
Napoleon I, Emperor of the French, 102, 122
narration, 29
    flashback, 152, 247
    focalization, 153
    free indirect style, 123–24, 153
    self-conscious, 148

stream of consciousness, 217
unreliable, 148, 247
Narrative Discourse (Genette), 152, 161
Narrative of the Life of Frederick Douglass
(Douglass), 36, 121
narratology, 38, 60, 142, 152–54, 218
Frankenstein (Shelley), 245–48
terminology, 152–53
Narratology (Bal), 153
nationalism, 114–15, 121–22, 126, 129
Native American studies, 194, 201
Native Son (Wright), 190
natural selection, 124
naturalism, 124–25, 188
nature, 116, 118–19, 209
Nazism, 35, 114, 121, 132, 157, 192
Neal, Larry, 200
Négritude, 196
neo-Aristotelian critics, 22, 40, 147–48, 175
criticism of New Critics, 147
interest in genre and classification, 147
interest in rhetoric, 147
neoclassicism, 88, 104, 116
neoliberalism, 194
New Criticism, 22, 27, 59, 142–46, 148, 154, 233
associated with Southern Agrarianism, 146
associated with universities in the US South,
144
close reading, 18, 144, 177
depersonalization (use of), 144
emphasis on white male canon, 145–46, 205
key ideas, 145–46
neo-Aristotelian critics on, 147, 175
opposition to historicism, 164, 167, 175
The New Criticism (Ransom), 143
new historicism, 166–74, 176, 193
alternative to formalism, 167
debt to Marxism, 168
paired with cultural materialism, 168
Shakespeare and, 232
New Testament, 54, 71, 74
New World, 80, 85, 195
New York Review of Books, 36
newspapers, 94, 120
Nietzsche, Friedrich, 49, 131–33, 154
alienation, 185, 211
anti-foundationalist ideas, 132
arbitrary nature of language, 156
The Birth of Tragedy, 132
The Genealogy of Morals, 172
Nazis' embrace of, 132, 157

notion of eternal recurrence, 131
"On Truth and Lies in a Non-Moral Sense,"
43, 132, 204
skepticism, 132
nihilism, 132
nineteenth century, 114–34
novel, 120–25
realism, 133
Ninety-Five Theses (Luther), 84
Nobel Prize, 176
The Normal and the Pathological (Canguilhem),
169
Norman invasion of England, 69
Norse mythology, 70
North and South (Gaskell), 121
Northrup, Solomon, *Twelve Years a Slave*, 121
Norton Anthology of African American Literature,
200
Norton Anthology of Literature by Women
(Gilbert and Gubar), 206
Norton Anthology of Theory and Criticism
(Leitch), 43
Norton Critical Editions, 44
Notes and Queries, 163
noumena and *phenomena*, 108, 154
novel, 88, 115, 120–21, 123, 188
abolitionist novel, 121
Bildungsroman, 120, 248
detective fiction, 128, 134, 153
eighteenth-century, 93–94
historical novel, 120, 122, 188
nineteenth-century, 120–25
published anonymously, 33
role in shaping national identities, 121
science fiction, 128, 133, 178, 244
young adult, 225
The Novel and the Police (Miller), 173
Nutting, Alissa, *Tampa*, 148

O'Brien, Tim, *The Things They Carried*, 32
Occupy Wall Street movement, 26, 184
O'Connor, Flannery, 28
The Odyssey (Homer), 48, 54
Oedipus complex, 215, 218, 220, 222, 242
"The Œdipus-Complex as an Explanation of
Hamlet's Mystery" (Jones), 217
Oedipus the King (Sophocles), 55, 57–58, 215
Of Grammatology (Derrida), 155–56, 199
"Of the Standard of Taste" (Hume), 105
"Of the Three Unities of Action, Time, and
Place" (Corneille), 88–89

Ogden, C.K., *The Meaning of Meaning*, 143
Old Testament. *See* Hebrew bible
Olivier, Laurence, 243
Olson, Elder, 147
On Christian Doctrine (Augustine), 71–72
On Eloquence in the Vernacular (Dante), 86
On the Sublime (Longinus), 65–67, 109
"On Truth and Lies in a Non-Moral Sense"
    (Nietzsche), 43, 132, 204
opsis, 56
optimism, 91
oral tradition, 53, 86, 116, 177
The Order of Things (Foucault), 169–70
organic unity, 59, 127–29, 140, 233–36
Orgel, Stephen, 172
Orientalism, 197–99
Orientalism (Said), 198
The Origin of Geometry (Husserl), 154
Origin of Species (Darwin), 124
Oroonoko (Behn), 102
Orthodox Church, 84
Orwell, George, *Animal Farm*, 51
the other, 111, 197, 205, 220
Ottoman Empire, 196
outsider artists, 104
overdetermination, 191, 214
Ovid, *Metamorphoses*, 79
Oxford University, 21, 73, 192
Oxford English Dictionary, 115

paganism, 70
Paine, Thomas, *The Rights of Man*, 103
"The Painter of Modern Life" (Baudelaire), 130
Pamela (Richardson), 93–94
    working-class heroine, 94
pamphlets, 95
Pan-African movement, 196, 201
panopticon, 170–71
papacy, 69–70
Paradise Lost (Milton), 54, 87, 119, 226–27, 249
Paradiso (Dante), 77
paradox, 145
paraphrase, heresy of, 145
paratext, 153
pastoral, 88
Pater, Walter, 140
    impressionism, 131, 144, 146
pathos, 62
*The Penguin Dictionary of Literary Terms and
    Literary Theory* (Cuddon), 41
penis envy, 212, 215, 220

Percy, Thomas, *Reliques of Ancient Poetry*, 162
Le Père Goriot (Balzac), 122–23
performativity, 209
peripeteia, 57
The Pervert's Guide to Cinema (2006), 223
The Pervert's Guide to Ideology (2012), 223
Petrarch, 68, 80, 87
Phaedrus (Plato), 47, 53
phallocentrism, 222
phenomenology, 41–42, 154, 157, 172, 223–24, 228
Phenomenology of Mind (Hegel), 111
The Phenomenology of Perception (Merleau-
    Ponty), 223
philology, 22–23, 132, 137–38, 164, 176, 186
philosopher king, 48–49
*Philosophical Enquiry into the Origin … Ideas of
    the Sublime and the Beautiful* (Burke), 109
Philosophical Transactions, 94
philosophy, 13, 16, 20, 24, 52, 106. *See also*
    individual philosophers
    ancient quarrel between poetry and, 49, 51
"The Philosophy of Composition" (Poe), 129, 233
The Picture of Dorian Gray (Wilde), 131
The Pilgrim's Progress (Bunyan), 85
Plato, 35, 46–54, 63, 77, 119
    dialogues, 47
    idealism, 49–50, 55
    Ion, 47, 53
    Meno, 48
    Phaedrus, 47, 53
    The Republic, 47–53, 67, 120
    sublimity in his writing, 66
    theory of forms, 49–51, 132, 154
play of language, 155, 169
Plutarch, *Lives*, 249
Poe, Edgar Allan, 128–29, 144
    ideas draw on Aristotle, Kant, Coleridge, 129
    international audience, 129
    "The Man of the Crowd," 130
    "The Philosophy of Composition," 129, 233
    psychoanalytic diagnoses, 217
    "The Raven," 129
poetics, 39, 89, 140
Poetics (Aristotle), 54–60, 88–89, 117, 120, 147, 233
    influential work in history of literary
        criticism, 54
    lost section, 47
poetics of culture, 172
Poétique, 152
poetry, 17, 20, 54, 89, 115–19, 140
    Aristotle's classification of, 55

Boccaccio's discussions of, 79
epic, 28–29, 54–55, 87
georgic, 105
Plato's mistrust of, 49
poetic form, 13, 38–39, 42, 89, 118, 129, 221
poets as "unacknowledged legislators of the world," 119
sonnet form, 28–29, 87
"spontaneous overflow of powerful feelings," 118
true poetry comes from the gods, 53
"Poetry" (Moore), 63
point of view. *See* narration
political approaches to literature, 39, 42, 45, 180–210
political economy, 182
political revolutions, 91, 100–02, 114, 116, 119, 122, 180–81, 196. *See also* names for specific revolutions
political theory, 13, 20
Pollard, A.W., 176
polysemous text, 75, 77
Poovey, Mary, *Making a Social Body*, 173
Pope, Alexander, 95
    The Dunciad, 96
    An Essay on Criticism, 63
The Popular Arts (Hall and Whannell), 193
popular culture, 17, 26, 96, 131–32, 188, 192–93, 212, 248
The Popular Novel in England, 1770–1800 (Tompkins), 165
Portuguese language, 85
postcolonial theory, 41, 157, 168, 180, 190, 194–99
    drew upon Marxist ideas, 193
    and *Frankenstein*, 250–51
postmodernism, 104, 193–94
"Postmodernism, or the Cultural Logic of Late Capitalism" (Jameson), 193
poststructuralism, 23–24, 27, 138, 169
    transition from structuralism, 150–51
Poulet, George, 172, 224, 228
    The Interior Distance, 223
power, 170–71, 173, 186, 191
Powers of Horror (Kristeva), 221
practical criticism, 18, 143–46
Practical Criticism (Richards), 144
Prague Linguistic Circle, 142
Presbyterianism, 84
Pride and Prejudice (Austen), 57–58
Pride and Prejudice and Zombies (Grahame-Smith), 30

Prince, Gerald, *A Dictionary of Narratology*, 154
La Princesse de Clèves (Lafayette), 123
Princeton University, 199
The Principles of Literary Criticism (Richards), 143
print culture, 92–96, 177
printing, invention of, 68, 80–84, 177
The Problems of Dostoevsky's Poetics (Bakhtin), 186–87
progress, 91, 110, 116
The Progress of Romance (Reeve), 162
Project Gutenberg, 95
proletariat, 184
Propp, Vladimir, *The Morphology of the Folktale*, 152
Protestant Reformation, 68, 70, 75, 80, 84–85, 92, 100
Protestantism, 84–85
    dissenting forms of, 85, 103
Proust, Marcel, 124, 161, 222
    Remembrance of Things Past, 152
pseudonyms, 33
psychoanalytic theory, 30, 39, 42, 191, 211–23
    feminist versions of, 221–22
psychological realism, 123
psychology, 13, 20, 40
public libraries, 114, 120
Publications of the Modern Language Association (PMLA), 41–42
publishing industry, 36, 95–96
Purdue Online Writing Lab, 44
Purgatorio (Dante), 77
Puritanism, 92, 173

quadrivium, 73
Quakerism, 103
queer theory, 16–17, 180, 207–09, 232, 251–52
Quintilian, 47, 61–64, 97
    Institutio Oratoria, 63

Rabelais, François, *Gargantua and Pantagruel*, 187
Rabelais and His World (Bakhtin), 187
race and racism, 126–27, 195, 200–01, 253
    intersections of racism and sexism, 202
    as a pseudo-science, 127, 183–84
    theories of racial inferiority, 102
Radcliffe, Ann, 110
Radway, Janice
    A Feeling for Books, 176
    Reading the Romance, 176
Ralph Roister Doister (Udall), 87

The Rambler (Johnson), 97
Rank, Otto
    Art and Artist, 217
    The Artist, 217
    The Myth of the Birth of the Hero, 217
Ransom, John Crowe, 146
    "Criticism Inc.," 145
    The New Criticism, 143
"The Raven" (Poe), 129
reader-response criticism, 223, 226–28
reading, 85, 145. *See also* literacy
    growth during Enlightenment, 95
    instruction vs. entertainment, 34–35
    reader, role of, 33–35, 40, 151
Reading Experience Database, 33–34
Reading for the Plot (Brooks), 218
Reading the Romance (Radway), 176
Reagan, Ronald, 194
real (Lacan), 219–20
realism, 93, 115, 120–25, 188
Reassembling the Social (Latour), 210
reception studies, 45, 226
Reeve, Clara, *The Progress of Romance*, 162
Reeves, Keanu, 52–53
reference books, 94
reification, 187
"Reification and the Consciousness of the
    Proletariat" (Lukács), 187
Reign of Terror (1793), 101
relativism, 26
religion, 70. *See also* names of specific religions
    critiques of, 81
    false consciousness for Marx, 183
    questioning value of, 100–01
    wars of, 84, 92, 101
Reliques of Ancient Poetry (Percy), 162
Remembrance of Things Past (Proust), 152
Renaissance, 32, 54, 80–89, 91
    literary criticism in, 88
    new genres in, 86–88
    rediscovery of classical learning, 68, 79–80,
        161
    Renaissance men, 80
    secularization during, 77
    transition from Middle Ages, 80
Renaissance Self-Fashioning (Greenblatt), 172
Representations, 172
The Republic (Plato), 47–53, 67, 120
The Return of Martin Guerre (Davis), 168
revenge tragedies, 238–39
Revolution in Poetic Language (Kristeva), 221

rhapsode, 53
rhetoric, 17, 19–20, 60–65, 73, 147–48
Rhetoric (Aristotle), 60–62
The Rhetoric of Fiction (Booth), 147–48
A Rhetoric of Motives (Burke), 147
Rich, Adrienne, "Compulsory Heterosexuality
    and Lesbian Existence," 207
Richards, I.A., 131
    founder of practical criticism, 143
    The Meaning of Meaning, 143
    Practical Criticism, 144
    The Principles of Literary Criticism, 143
Richardson, Samuel, *Pamela*, 93–94
Richter, David, *Falling Into Theory*, 43
Riding, Laura, *A Survey of Modernist Poetry*, 144
The Rights of Man (Paine), 103
"The Rime of the Ancient Mariner" (Coleridge),
    117, 165
The Road to Xanadu (Lowes), 165, 172
Robespierre, Maximilien, 102
Roman de la Rose (Guillaume de Lorris and Jean
    de Meun), 78
Roman Empire, 46, 62, 68–69, 85
romance, 39, 115, 167, 176
Romance languages, 85
Romanian language, 85
Romantic Ecology (Bate), 209
Romantic era. *See* Romanticism
Romanticism, 109–10, 115–17, 173
A Room of One's Own (Woolf), 203–04
Rosencrantz and Guildenstern Are Dead
    (Stoppard), 238
Rossetti, Dante Gabriel, 178
Roth, Veronica, *Divergent*, 225–26
Rousseau, Jean-Jacques, 101–02
    The Social Contract, 101
Rowlandson, Thomas, "Veneration," 162
Rowling, J.K., 34–35
Royal Society of London, 94, 162
Rubin, Gayle, 209
    "The Traffic in Women," 206
Ruins of Empires (Volney), 249, 251
Russell, Bertrand, 107, 143
Russian Formalism, 138, 140–42, 152–54
    and Anglo-American formalisms, 142–43
    defamiliarization, 141
    popularized in France by Kristeva and
        Todorov, 221
    scientific manner, 141, 143
    used Saussure's ideas about linguistic
        structure, 140

Russian Revolution, 141, 181, 186

S/Z (Barthes), 151–52, 236
Sabrina, the Teenage Witch, 212
Said, Edward, 197–98, 251
    Culture and Imperialism, 198
    Orientalism, 198
Saldívar, José David, 202
Saldívar, Ramon, 202
Salinger, J.D., The Catcher in the Rye, 35
salonnières, 103
San Francisco State University, 200–01
Sand, George, 33
"The Sand-Man" (Hoffmann), 216
Sappho, 47, 66
"Sarrasine" (Balzac), 151
Sartre, Jean-Paul, 111, 132, 212
    Being and Nothingness, 155, 190, 197
    existentialism, 190, 197
    Marxism, 190
    What Is Literature?, 190
satire, 62, 95, 162, 187
Saturday Night Live, 212
Saussure, Ferdinand de, 24, 72, 133, 137–40, 150
    arbitrary nature of language, 139, 156
    Course in General Linguistics, 138–40, 149
    language vs. speech, 138
    signified, signifier, sign, 138, 150–51, 201, 219, 237
    syntagms, 139–40
The Savage Mind (Lévi-Strauss), 150
Saxo Grammaticus, Historiae Danicae, 239–40
Scandinavia, 70
Scandinavian languages, 86
The Scarlet Letter (Hawthorne), 120
Schelling, Friedrich, Lecture on the Philosophy of Art, 117
Schiller, Friedrich, 117
Schlegel, August, 117
Schlegel, Friedrich, 117
scholarly editing, 32, 44
scholasticism, 72–73
science, 91, 100, 107, 114, 123, 210
    authorship, 32–33
    Frankenstein and, 248–50
    Royal Society of London, 94, 162
    scientific method, 18, 124, 141
science fiction, 128, 133, 178, 244
Scott, Sir Walter
    Ivanhoe, 188
    Waverley novels, 122

Scottish Enlightenment, 105–06
Screen, 222
Scrutiny, 144
Scudéry, Madeleine de, 103
The Second Sex (Beauvoir), 204–05
second-wave feminism, 203, 205
Sedgwick, Eve Kosofsky, 16, 252
    Epistemology of the Closet, 208
    Between Men, 17, 208
self-conscious narration, 148
self-consciousness, 14, 111, 167, 197
self-fashioning, 172
semiotics, 150
Seneca, 46
Seneca Falls Convention (1848), 114, 203
serialization, 120
A Serious Proposal for the Ladies (Astell), 103
Seven Types of Ambiguity (Empson), 144
sex/gender distinction, 209
sex/gender system, 206, 209
sexuality, 202, 207–08
    culturally constructed, 16, 170
Shakespeare, William, 17, 87, 95, 126, 172
    Antony and Cleopatra, 89
    Freud's use of, 217
    Hamlet, 37, 56, 231–44
    King Lear, 172
    scholarly editions, 177
    The Tempest, 85
    textual history, 232
    Twelfth Night, 16, 172
Shakespearean Negotiations (Greenblatt), 172
Shakespearean Tragedy (Bradley), 30
"Shakespeare's sister," 204
Shelley, Mary, 120
    Frankenstein, 37, 231, 244–54
Shelley, Percy, 110, 116, 118, 217, 227, 244
    A Defence of Poetry, 119
    "England in 1819," 119
Shirley (Brontë), 121
Shklovsky, Victor, 105, 141
short story form, 28
Showalter, Elaine, A Literature of Their Own, 205, 255
Sidney, Sir Philip, 79
    Astrophil and Stella, 89
    A Defence of Poetry, 89, 119
"The Signification of the Phallus" (Lacan), 220
signified, signifier, sign, 138, 150–51, 201, 219, 237
signifyin(g), 201
The Signifying Monkey (Gates), 200

"Signs Taken for Wonders" (Bhabha), 199
Simians, Cyborgs, and Women (Haraway), 178
simile, 64
Sinfield, Alan, 168
The Singer of Tales (Lord), 92
Sir Gawain and the Green Knight, 78
Skelton, John, 226
skepticism, 81, 91, 93, 100–01, 106, 132
slave narrative, 36, 121
slave trade, 92, 102–03, 195–98, 201
Slavic languages, 86
Smith, Adam, *Wealth of Nations*, 106
social construction. *See* cultural construction
The Social Contract (Rousseau), 101–02
social history, 40
Society for the History of Authorship, Reading, and Publishing (SHARP), 177
Society of Antiquaries, 162
sociology, 13, 18, 20, 24, 106, 176
    of culture, 174–77
    of knowledge, 192
Socrates, 47–54, 100
    death, 52
    poetry can corrupt the minds of youth, 49
    speech is superior to writing, 53
Socratic method, 48
sodomy laws, 207
A Song of Ice and Fire (Martin), 70
sonnet form, 28–29, 87
Sophocles, 46, 217
    Oedipus the King, 55, 57–58, 215
Sorrows of Young Werther (Goethe), 249
sound recording, 188
source studies, 45, 165
Southern Agrarianism, 146, 200
Soviet Union, 40, 140–41, 184, 186–87
Soyinka, Wole, 200
Spain, 69, 76
Spanish language, 85
Spanish/Portuguese colonialism, 195–96
The Spanish Tragedy (Kyd), 238
Spectator (Addison and Steele), 96
speech-act theory, 157
speech vs. writing, 53
Spenser, Edmund, *The Faerie Queene*, 32
Spirit (Hegel), 112
spirit of the age, 111
spirituality, 119
Spivak, Gayatri Chakravorti, 157
    "Can the Subaltern Speak?," 199
Springarn, J.E., 143

Stalin, Joseph, 40, 142, 187
Stanford Literary Lab, 178
Stanford University, 35
Star Wars, 219
Steele, Richard, 96
Sterne, Laurence, *Tristram Shandy*, 104–05, 141, 148
Stoic philosophers, 49
Stoker, Bram, *Dracula*, 133
Stonewall Riots (1969), 207
Stoppard, Tom, *Rosencrantz and Guildenstern Are Dead*, 238
"The Storyteller" (Benjamin), 189
Stowe, Harriet Beecher, *Uncle Tom's Cabin*, 121
stream of consciousness, 217
"Stronger" (West), 131
"Stronger [What Doesn't Kill You]" (Clarkson), 131
structural anthropology, 24, 140, 168–69
Structural Anthropology (Lévi-Strauss), 149
structural linguistics, 137–40, 219, 221
"The Structural Study of Myth" (Lévi-Strauss), 149
structuralism, 23–24, 138, 149–52, 169–70
"Structure, Sign, and Play in the Discourse of the Human Sciences" (Derrida), 23–24, 50, 149, 155
stylistics, 142
subaltern, 186, 199, 240
Subaltern Studies collective, 199
sublation, 111
sublime, 65–67, 109–10, 116, 253
The Sublime Object of Ideology (Žižek), 223
subversion, 173
Summa Theologica (Aquinas), 73
superego, 215
Superman, 132
surplus value, 185
Surprised by Sin (Fish), 226–27
Surrey, Henry Howard, Earl of, 87
surveillance, 170–71
A Survey of Modernist Poetry (Riding and Graves), 144
Swift, Jonathan, 95
    The Battle of the Books, 95
    Gulliver's Travels, 51
    "A Modest Proposal," 148
    psychoanalytic diagnoses, 217
Swift, Taylor, 61
symbol, 78
symbolic (Lacan), 219–20

symbolists, 144
symptomatic reading, 191, 251
synchronic linguistics, 139
synecdoche, 64
syntagms, 139–40

tabula rasa, 106
Taine, Hippolyte, 200
    History of English Literature, 126–27
    racialized literary history, 127, 160
Tampa (Nutting), 148
Tarantino, Quentin, 59
taste, 105, 174, 176
Tate, Allen, 146
Tatler (Addison and Steele), 96
technical communication, 61
The Tempest (Shakespeare), 85
    "the text itself," 142
Thatcher, Margaret, 194
theatre of the absurd, 238
theology, 20, 54, 70–77
A Theory of Literary Production (Macherey), 191
Theory of Literature (Wellek and Warren), 142, 164
theory of mind, 229
"Theses on Feuerbach" (Marx), 180
thick description, 168, 210
The Things They Carried (O'Brien), 32
third-wave feminism, 203
Third World writers, 35, 197–99
This Bridge Called My Back (Anzaldúa and Moraga), 202
"This Sex Which Is Not One" (Irigaray), 222
Thomas Aquinas, Saint, 75
    four levels of interpretation, 73–75
    Summa Theologica, 73
Thompson, E.P., 192
    The Making of the English Working Class, 193
Thor, 70
Thoreau, Henry David, 209
Three Essays on the Theory of Sexuality (Freud), 215
Tieck, Ludwig, 117
Tillyard, E.M.W., The Elizabethan World Picture, 165, 172
Times Literary Supplement, 36
Todorov, Tzvetan, 142, 152–53, 221
Toland, John, Christianity Not Mysterious, 101
Tolkien, J.R.R., Lord of the Rings, 70
Tolstoy, Leo, 123
    War and Peace, 122

Tom Jones (Fielding), 148
Tompkins, J.M.S., The Popular Novel in England, 1770–1800, 165
totality, 111, 187
trade unionism, 40, 184
"Tradition and the Individual Talent" (Eliot), 144
"The Traffic in Women" (Rubin), 206
tragedy, 28, 55–56, 87, 167, 238–40
    catharsis, 60
trickster figure, 201
Tristram Shandy (Sterne), 104–05, 141, 148
trivium, 73
tropological interpretation, 74
Trotsky, Leon, 142
troubadours, 86
True Detective (2014), 132
Truth and Method (Gadamer), 224
Turner, Mark, Death Is the Mother of Beauty, 229
Twain, Mark, The Adventures of Huckleberry Finn, 35, 120
Twelfth Night (Shakespeare), 16, 172
"Twelve Southerners," I'll Take My Stand, 146
Twelve Years a Slave (Northrup), 121
Twilight fan fiction, 30
The Twilight Zone, 212
typicality, 188
typological interpretation, 73, 75

Udall, Nicholas, Ralph Roister Doister, 87
uncanny, 40, 216, 218, 253–54
Uncle Tom's Cabin (Stowe), 121
unconscious, 212, 218
    structured like a language, 219
Understanding Fiction (Brooks and Warren), 145
Understanding Poetry (Brooks and Warren), 145
unities, dramatic, 88
universal suffrage, 184
universities. See also names of individual universities
    growth in 19th century, 114
    historically black colleges and universities (HBCUs), 200
    modern research university, German origins of, 137
    organized around academic departments, 20–21
University of California, Berkeley, 172, 201
University of Chicago, 147
University of Konstanz, 228
University of London, 21

University of Paris, 73
unreliable narrator, 148, 247
urbanization, 116
use-value and exchange-value, 185
The Uses of Literacy (Hoggart), 192
USSR. *See* Soviet Union
utilitarianism, 120–21
Utopia (More), 85

Vanderbilt University, 144
"Veneration" (Rowlandson), 162
Vermeule, Blakey, 229
vernacular, 85–86, 89, 93
Verne, Jules, 133
VIDA: Women in Literary Arts, 36
Vietnam War, protests against, 24
A Vindication of the Rights of Woman
    (Wollstonecraft), 103–04
Virgil, 46, 77, 87
    The Aeneid, 54
virtual reality, 178
"Visual Pleasure and Narrative Cinema"
    (Mulvey), 222
visual rhetoric, 61
vitalism, 249–50
Voice of the Shuttle website, 178
Volney, C.F., *Ruins of Empires*, 249, 251
Voltaire, 100–01
    Candide, 101
voyages of exploration, 85, 87

Wachowski, Andy, 52
Wachowski, Lana, 52
Waldensians, 84
Walker, Joseph Cooper, 162
Walpole, Horace, 162
War and Peace (Tolstoy), 122
Warren, Austin, *Theory of Literature*, 142, 164
Warren, Robert Penn
    "The Briar Patch," 146
    Understanding Fiction, 145
    Understanding Poetry, 145
Warton, Thomas, *History of English Poetry*, 162
Washington, Booker T., 200
Waverley novels (Scott), 122
Wealth of Nations (Smith), 106
Webster, Noah, 99
The Well Wrought Urn (Brooks), 145, 160–61
Wellek, René, *Theory of Literature*, 142, 164
Wells, H.G., 133
West, Cornel, 200

West, Kanye, "Stronger," 131
Whale, James, 249
Whannell, Paddy, 193
"What Is an Author?" (Foucault), 32–33, 186
"What Is Enlightenment?" (Kant), 100
What Is Literature? (Sartre), 190
Wheatley, Phillis, 103
White, Hayden, 239
    Metahistory, 167
white supremacy, 35, 41, 127, 145–46, 181. *See also*
    race and racism
Wikipedia, 44, 99
Wilde, Oscar, 35, 121, 128
    The Picture of Dorian Gray, 131
William the Conqueror, 69
Williams, Raymond, 27, 168, 192, 198
    Culture and Society, 193
    Keywords, 193
Wimsatt, W.K., 146, 227
wish fulfillment, 215
Wittgenstein, Ludwig, 107, 143
Wollstonecraft, Mary, 116, 203, 244
    A Vindication of the Rights of Woman,
        103–04
women
    female-led literary salons, 96
    men's writing about, 80, 204
    myths of woman, 204–05, 242
    women readers, 96
    women's education, 21, 103, 203
    women's movement, 24, 114, 180. *See also*
        feminism
women's suffrage, 203
women writers, 35–36, 96, 251
    bringing in to canon, 35
    male pseudonyms, 33
women's studies, 181, 203. *See also* feminism,
    gender and sexuality
Woods, Tiger, 61
Woolf, Virginia, 124, 204, 217
    A Room of One's Own, 203–04
Wordsworth, William, 110, 116, 128, 209
    interest in nature, 118
    Preface to *Lyrical Ballads*, 118
"The Work of Art in the Age of Mechanical
    Reproduction" (Benjamin), 189
working-class culture, 192
The Wretched of the Earth (Fanon), 197
Wright, Richard, 199
    Native Son, 190
writers. *See also* authorship; women writers

professionalization, 93
should work to make the world a better
    place, 35
Writing and Difference (Derrida), 155
Writing Degree Zero (Barthes), 150
Wyatt, Thomas, 87, 172

Yale Critics, 156–57
Yale University, 145, 202, 226
Yearsley, Ann, 104
Young Frankenstein (1974), 249

zeitgeist, III, 192
Žižek! (2005), 223
Žižek, Slavoj, 193, 220
    The Sublime Object of Ideology, 223
Zola, Émile, 124–25
    "The Experimental Novel," 124
    naturalism, 188
Zunshine, Lisa, 229

From the Publisher

A name never says it all, but the word "Broadview" expresses a good deal of the philosophy behind our company. We are open to a broad range of academic approaches and political viewpoints. We pay attention to the broad impact book publishing and book printing has in the wider world; for some years now we have used 100% recycled paper for most titles. Our publishing program is internationally oriented and broad-ranging. Our individual titles often appeal to a broad readership too; many are of interest as much to general readers as to academics and students.

Founded in 1985, Broadview remains a fully independent company owned by its shareholders—not an imprint or subsidiary of a larger multinational.

For the most accurate information on our books (including information on pricing, editions, and formats) please visit our website at www.broadviewpress.com. Our print books and ebooks are also available for sale on our site.

broadview press
www.broadviewpress.com

The interior of this book is printed on 100% recycled paper.